The Continuing Struggle for Democracy in Latin America

Other Titles in This Series

Brazil: Foreign Policy of a Future World Power, Ronald M. Schneider

Mexico's Economy: A Policy Analysis with Forecasts to 1990, Robert E. Looney

The Future of Brazil, edited by William H. Overholt

The Politics of Chile: A Sociogeographical Assessment, César Caviedes

Technological Progress in Latin America: The Prospects for Overcoming Dependency, edited by James H. Street and Dilmus D. James

Westview Special Studies on Latin America and the Caribbean

The Continuing Struggle for Democracy in Latin America
edited by Howard J. Wiarda

This integrated collection of original essays evaluates and assesses whether democracy is viable in Latin America and, if so, how and in what form. The authors examine the significance, for both Latin America and the United States, of the dominance of authoritarian political systems in most Latin American countries; explore the implications of assessing Latin America through our own liberal-democratic and often ethnocentric biases; and discuss whether it is possible to derive a theory of democracy from the Latin American experience, rather than our own. In the process, they survey Latin America's historic quest for democracy, focusing on the various groups and elites involved in the struggle and assessing the policy failures and potentials of the 1960s, 1970s, 1980s, and beyond.

Howard J. Wiarda is professor of political science, adjunct professor of labor relations, and chairman of the Program in Latin American Studies at the University of Massachusetts.

The Continuing Struggle for Democracy in Latin America
edited by Howard J. Wiarda

Coauthored by:
Lee C. Fennell
William L. Furlong
Lawrence S. Graham
Jack W. Hopkins
Michael J. Kryzanek
Paul H. Lewis
Anthony P. Maingot
Ronald C. Newton
Neale J. Pearson
Iêda Siqueira Wiarda
Howard J. Wiarda

Westview Press / Boulder, Colorado

Westview Special Studies on Latin America and the Caribbean

All rights reserved. No part of this publication may be reproduced or transmitted in any form or by any means, electronic or mechanical, including photocopy, recording, or any information storage and retrieval system, without permission in writing from the publisher.

Copyright © 1980 by Westview Press, Inc.

Published in 1980 in the United States of America by
  Westview Press, Inc.
  5500 Central Avenue
  Boulder, Colorado 80301
  Frederick A. Praeger, Publisher

Library of Congress Cataloging in Publication Data
Main entry under title:
The Continuing struggle for democracy in Latin America.
  (Westview special studies on Latin America and the Caribbean)
  Essays in honor of Harry Kantor.
  Bibliography: p.
  1. Latin America—Politics and government—1948- —Addresses, essays, lectures. 2. Democracy—Addresses, essays, lectures. 3. Kantor, Harry. I. Wiarda, Howard J., 1939- II. Fennell, Lee C. III. Kantor, Harry.
F1414.2.C623   320.9'8'003   79-13551
ISBN 0-89158-663-6

Printed and bound in the United States of America

To Harry Kantor

Mentor, Inspiration, Colleague, and Friend

From his former students

Contents

List of Figures and Tables xi

Preface xiii

Part 1
Introduction: A Perspective and Framework

1. Is Latin America Democratic and Does It Want To Be?
   The Crisis and Quest of Democracy in the Hemisphere,
   Howard J. Wiarda 3

Part 2
**Long-Range Perspectives on the Quest
for Democracy in Latin America**

2. Critical Elections and Critical Coups: The Processes
   of Sociopolitical Realignment in Latin American
   Development, *Howard J. Wiarda* 27

3. Latin American Populism: Some Notes on Periodization,
   Ronald C. Newton 71

Part 3
**Group Politics and Democratic Pluralism
in Latin America: Prospects and Weaknesses**

4. Peasant and Worker *Sindicatos* and Democracy in
   Latin America, *Neale J. Pearson* 79

5. Women, Population Policy, and Democracy in
   Latin America, *Iêda Siqueira Wiarda* 107
6. Political Parties, Opposition Politics, and Democracy
   in Latin America, *Michael J. Kryzanek* 127
7. Democracy and Elites in Latin America, *Jack W. Hopkins* .. 147

Part 4
Has Democracy Failed?

8. Democratic Political Development and the Alliance for
   Progress, *William L. Furlong* 167
9. Development Strategies and the Decline of the Democratic
   Left in Latin America, *Paul H. Lewis* 185
10. Leadership and the Failure of Democracy, *Lee C. Fennell* ... 201

Part 5
Is Democracy Still Viable?

11. Ideological Dependency and the Origins of Socialism
    in the Caribbean, *Anthony P. Maingot* 217
12. The Struggle for Democracy and Human Rights in
    Latin America: Toward a New Conceptualization,
    Howard J. Wiarda 231
13. Democracy and the Bureaucratic State in Latin America,
    Lawrence S. Graham 255

Part 6
Conclusion: The Continuing Struggle
for Democracy in Latin America

14. Latin American Democracy: The Historic Model and
    the New Openings, *Howard J. Wiarda* 275

A Selected Bibliography 295

About the Contributors 299

Index 303

Figures and Tables

Figures

2.1 The Changing Structure of Society and Power in Iberian and Latin American Development 33
2.2 Coups in Latin America: Five Year Moving Average, 1823-1966 40
2.3 The Incidence of Coups and Latin American Imports from the United States and Great Britain, 1854-1910 42
2.4 Dominican Republic: Electoral Participation, 1844-1970 45
2.5 Dominican Republic: Total Vote as Percentage of Total Population 46
2.6 Critical Realignments in Latin America: Five Year Moving Average 51

Tables

2.1 Percentage of Voting-Age Population Voting in National Elections Nearest to the Year 1960 44
2.2 Critical Realignments in Latin America, 1795-1974 50
2.3 Realigning Periods in Latin American Development 56
4.1 Population and Per Capita Income of the Americas in the Mid-1970s 81
4.2 Economically Active Population and Membership in National and Hemispheric Organizations by Ideological Orientation, 1975 88
4.3 Representational and Brokerage Activities of Local Peasant Leaders, Venezuela, 1961-1965 90
4.4 Numbers and Wages of Employees By Size of Firm, Brazilian Industries of Transformation, 1966 95
4.5 Population, Municipios, Federations and Sindicatos of Urban and Rural Workers in Selected Brazilian Regions, 1969 96

4.6 Population Density, Literacy, and Social Group Infrastructure in Selected Brazilian States, 1959-1960 97
4.7 Comparative Education of Peasants and Leaders in Venezuela and Honduras 98
4.8 Relationship of Municipios with ANACH Groups Sending Delegates to Seventh Intermediate Congress, September 28-30, 1977, and Land Distributed in Amounts and Families, Honduras 101
11.1 Parliamentary Elections, 1966 223
11.2 On the Positive Effects of Western Imperialism 227
14.1 Measuring Democracy in Latin America 287
14.2 Composite Scores and Democratic Rank-Ordering of Latin American Regimes 288

Preface

Democracy in Latin America seems everywhere to be threatened, not only by the recent rash of military coups and widespread violations of human rights but also by a whole new body of literature that questions whether "democracy" is the goal toward which Latin America aspires or whether the presumed "struggle" for it is the best and most appropriate way to approach the area. And yet, throughout the hemisphere, the democratic mythos remains very much alive, the struggle for democratic participation and freer societies still goes on, and the aspiration for democratic development continues to constitute a major societal goal. Democracy is under attack, but it is certainly too early to sound its death knell; and a group of younger scholars has recently sought to revive the democratic dream by arguing that while democracy as North Americans conceive it may be fading throughout Latin America, the efforts by Latin Americans to devise democratic structures more in keeping with their own history and cultures constitute both a hopeful and a progressive sign.

Harry Kantor has been one of this country's foremost champions of democracy in Latin America, but as a scholar and teacher he was consistently wise and foresighted enough to see that democracy would have to come on Latin America's own terms rather than on the institutional bases of U.S.-style democracy. Harry Kantor was a remarkable scholar and teacher in the area of Latin American politics and society who, prior to his recent retirement as professor of political science and of Latin American studies at Marquette University, had a long and distinguished career at the University of Florida and in its Center for Latin American Studies. Professor Kantor was a close personal friend and student of Haya de la Torre and the Peruvian Apristas, of José Figueres and *Liberación Nacional,* of Rómulo Betancourt and *Acción Democrática,* of Juan Bosch and the Dominican Revolutionary Party, and of Luis Muñoz Marín, Galo Plaza, Arturo Frondizi, Jesús de Galíndez, and a host of other democratic leaders.

Harry Kantor helped discover and make known the ideas of the Latin American democratic-Left long before they became fashionable and was one of the area's strongest spokesmen for a social-democratic reformism. Professor Kantor was an advisor and intimate friend of a dozen Latin American presidents and scores of party heads and labor leaders, and his research on Latin American politics made him one of the foremost scholars of his generation. In addition, Harry was an inspiring, colorful, dynamic, outspoken, and controversial mentor and teacher who spent more time and dedication on his students than anyone most of us have ever encountered. He produced, particularly during that period of the 1960s when Latin American studies at the University of Florida and elsewhere were at their height, a remarkable number of young Ph.D.s who have by now risen to prominence as leading scholars, teachers, and policy makers in the Latin America area.

A number of these younger scholars and former students determined to collaborate on a volume of substantive research and writing in his honor. Our intention from the first, it should be emphasized, was to create a *substantive* volume organized around a single dominant theme. We wanted to produce a solid and provocative book and not merely a loose collection of "puff," as many *festschrift* are. The theme, "the continuing struggle for democracy in Latin America," was chosen both because it is of critical concern and importance and because it was the primary subject of Harry Kantor's work. Not all of us, it should be said, are convinced that "the continuing struggle for democracy in Latin America," at least as conceived from a North American perspective, is the correct way to approach Latin American politics and social change; but it does provide us with a unifying theme and an issue to which to react, both for and against. It makes for a lively, provocative, and I hope controversial, discussion.

The introductory chapter raises the fundamental issue of whether Latin America is or wants to be democratic, argues that most of our intepretations of the area have been posited on a North American understanding of that term, and asks whether it is possible to fashion a Latin American conception of democracy. Some historical considerations of democracy and militarism in Latin America are put forth provocatively in the second chapter, which deals with critical coups and critical elections, and in the third chapter, Ronald C. Newton depressingly yet colorfully argues that the era of Latin American democratic populism may have already passed.

In Part 3 we deal with some of the major groups and forces in Latin America: their strengths, their weaknesses, and their prospects. Neale J. Pearson traces the rise—and limitations—of peasant and worker *sindicatos* and their place within a more democratic system. Iêda Siqueira Wiarda, writing on population policy, questions how successfully programs of family planning can be implemented without a greater involvement of the major client group affected—the women— and suggests that population officials stop thinking of women merely as "targets" and more as participants in the entire policy process. Michael J. Kryzanek, an undergraduate student of Harry Kantor at Marquette and then a graduate student of the editor at the University of Massachusetts (and therefore a Kantor "grandchild"?), focuses on political parties and the difficulties of opposition politics and democracy in Latin America. Jack W. Hopkins concludes this section with a chapter covering a variety of elites and their relations to democratic development in Latin America.

William L. Furlong leads off Part 4—"Has Democracy Failed?"— with a discussion of the myopic efforts of the United States to bring U.S.-style democratic development to Latin America through the Alliance for Progress. The decline of the Latin American democratic-Left is the subject of the intriguing chapter by Paul H. Lewis. Lee C. Fennell argues that, in addition to the usual factors cited, the failure of Latin America's own democratic leaders to govern more effectively also helps explain democracy's uncertain tenure throughout the area.

In Part 5 some more hopeful prospects are raised and the questions of whether democracy remains viable and in what forms are explored. Anthony P. Maingot discusses ideological dependency and the struggle for democracy and socialism in the Caribbean. Howard J. Wiarda, focusing on the human-rights issue, strongly critiques the North America-derived indices of the progress of democracy in Latin America, but puts forth an alternative democratic model based on Latin America's own traditions and experiences. Lawrence S. Graham, who has written some of the best analyses of the bureaucratic state in Latin America, discusses that theme here as well, but within that context he also sees the possibilities for democratic growth. In the Conclusion we return to that same theme, providing a statement and critique of the historic models of Latin American politics and change and showing how both within and without that model new democratic openings may occur.

The essays collected here, with one exception, are published for the first time. They draw upon the considerable research experience of all the contributors and their measured judgments and assessments after some years of observing and writing about Latin America. Not all topics and subject matters are dealt with here, of course, and the book does not seek comprehensive coverage of all the Latin American countries. But it certainly raises the key issues and provides for some lively, interesting discussion. The theme of *The Continuing Struggle for Democracy in Latin America* is too important to be long ignored or shunted aside. Hence if this book serves to prod and provoke our thinking on the subject, it will have fulfilled a useful purpose.

Howard J. Wiarda

Part 1
Introduction: A Perspective and Framework

1
Is Latin America Democratic and Does It Want To Be? The Crisis and Quest of Democracy in the Hemisphere

Howard J. Wiarda

The United States seems destined by Providence to plague America with misery in the name of liberty.
—Simón Bolívar

Everywhere in Latin America democracy seems to be dead, dying, or under siege. Twelve of the twenty republics (and the vast majority of the Latin American population) are presently (spring 1978) governed by military regimes,[1] and in five of the remaining countries the military is so close to the surface of power as to make the civil/military distinction nearly meaningless.[2] It has now become commonplace to point to the decline of civilian democracy throughout the continent, the rash of military coups since the 1960s, the rise of corporate-authoritarian regimes in such formerly democratic nations as Chile and Uruguay, the use of torture and repression in Argentina and Brazil, and widespread violations of human rights. Meanwhile, the number of genuinely democratic regimes has shrunk to a mere handful: Colombia, Costa Rica, Venezuela. And even these are often perceived to be elite-directed democracies (Colombia and Costa Rica) or else the product of such fortuitous circumstances (the vast quantities of oil in Venezuela) that their experiences are unlikely to be imitated elsewhere.

The problem is not just the rising tide of military-authoritarian-corporatist rule, however, but a growing body of literature and interpretation that sees authoritarianism, corporatism, and elitism as essential, almost "natural" aspects of the Latin American tradition.[3] Democracy and its usual accompanying paraphernalia (checks and balances, elections, separation of powers, free press, and the like) are often viewed in the newer interpretations as foreign, and inappropriate, Anglo-American imports artificially imposed on a culture and society where they do not fit, ill suited to Latin America needs. In some of the overly deterministic expressions of this argument, democratic reformism is hence viewed as futile, since, if Latin America is *inherently* elitist and authoritarian, no amount of democratic reform-mongering is likely to suceeed. Democracy is in trouble in Latin America, therefore, not just because of spreading militarism but because a whole new school and generation of Latin American historians and social scientists have pronounced it as irrelevant to or outside the main currents of the Latin American tradition. Sometimes these interpretations, by rationalizing it, have also provided—most often inadvertently—justification and legitimacy for military-authoritarian rule.

This book wrestles with these themes. It traces the preoccupation in Latin American studies with the issue of democratic development, the biases that perspective has given our understanding of Latin America, and the possibilities for a Latin American democracy based on its own rather than North America's conception of the term. It analyzes the causes and manifestations of democracy's decline, as well as the possibility that the present wave of authoritarian-military regimes may, like others in the past, be a passing wave, ephemeral and not permanent.

The essays collected in this volume seek also to clarify the meaning of the recent corporatist and bureaucratic-state interpretations of Latin America and whether these approaches militate against the possibilities for Latin American democracy or may be compatible with it. We shall be examining the blends and fusions that may exist, for while corporatism and authoritarianism represent one, heretofore largely neglected, aspect of the Latin American tradition, it is not the only one. There are stong liberal, democratic, and social-democratic currents as well, which should not be ignored or swept aside in our new preoccupation with these other themes. The fact is that Latin America remains a mix; an amalgam of a corporatist-authoritarian tradition, a liberal-democratic one, and a newer socialist one. Much of politics centers on the conflict between these contrasting traditions and the various compromises and accommodations used to reconcile them. Among these are various democratic possibilities, though as we shall see in the Conclusion, the form democracy takes will likely be closer to a Latin American understanding of that word than the North American. The struggle for democracy in Latin America will, therefore, continue, and it behooves us to know both the older and now largely outdated meanings of that term and the newer conceptions, as well as the elements in the struggle itself.

Latin American Studies and the Quest for Democracy

Latin American studies in the United States have long been

preoccupied with the presumed quest of the Latin American nations (whether real, imagined, or wishful) for democracy. From the early Puritan preoccupation with the "black legend" of Spanish—and Catholic!—atrocities, to the famous (or infamous) doctrine that bears the name of President Monroe, to Henry Clay's and John Quincy Adams's efforts to assist in separating Spain from her colonies, to the advocates of "manifest destiny" who, in the name of democracy and progress, deprived Mexico of half her national territory, to Teddy Roosevelt's and Woodrow Wilson's undoubtedly sincere efforts to bring, missionary-style, the "benefits" of democracy to "our little brown brothers," using a "big stick" or the marines if necessary, to John Kennedy's Alliance for Progress and President Carter's concern for human rights, the United States has consistently sought to export and impose its own democratic political institutions on an area that it has seen as mystifyingly authoritarian, chaotic, nondemocratic, Catholic-inquisitorial, "oligarchic," "feudal," or "underdeveloped."[4] Latin American studies in the United States, unhappily, have historically not only served as the handmaiden of this design and effort but have frequently provided the rationalization and intellectual justification as well.[5]

It is clear that the attempt to bring U.S.-style democracy to Latin America is not just a recent or ephemeral preoccupation, but stems more basically from the historic drives, ambitions, and presuppositions of the North American nation. It reflects our Protestant and Lockean heritage and, conversely, what Richard M. Morse called our "insensitivity and vague hostility" toward the oftentimes nondemocratic and non-egalitarian assumptions of historic Catholic political culture.[6] It reflects the great power ambitions of the United States and it clearly also serves our foreign-policy designs for hegemony in the Western Hemisphere.

Perhaps most important, it mirrors our sense of superiority, the notion that we are the most modern and developed of nations, the Churchillian idea that Anglo-American democracy is the "worst form of government except for all others," and the parallel presumption of the social sciences that the nations of the "North" (Europe and America) represent the leading edge of "advanced" sociopolitical change, whose experience can only be repeated and palely imitated—generally much later—by the nations of the "South." Marx's dictum that "The more developed nations only show to the less developed the mirror of their own future" is perhaps the most well-known expression of this latter sentiment, although the belief is widespread in the social sciences among Marxists and non-Marxists alike. Hegel provided an early, not atypical, and particularly devastating comment that relegated the entire

New World to prehistory, or nonhistory: "What has taken place in the New World up to the present time is only an echo of the Old World—the expression of a foreign life—and as a Land of the Future, it has no interest for us here, for as regards History our concern must be with that which has been and that which is."[7] Hegel (and many European and North American thinkers since that time) left Latin America, as Jean Franco shows, with only two possible alternatives: becoming an echo of the old world, placing hope in the continent's future realization and "developing" toward and perhaps one day catching up with the model and example of the advanced nations; or working for the assimilation of advanced "civilization" into Latin American life. But note that nowhere in either alternative does Latin America or its civilization have any value or worth of their own, let alone something they could teach to the rest of the world; Latin America is only derivative. In short, both as northerners (North Americans and North Europeans) and as social scientists we *believe* the myth of our superiority and Latin American inferiority. Our social science and our policy initiatives all reflect this fundamental ethnocentrism.[8]

Despite the historic European and North American efforts—and sometimes because of them—the quest for democracy in Latin America seems not to have proved very successful. For as the quote from Bolívar with which we began this chapter implies, in the name of liberty and democratic development we have as often plagued Latin America with misery as with good deeds. Democracy, as North Americans understand it, is in retreat, under attack from both the Right and the Left. A host of authoritarian-military regimes have substituted themselves for civilian representative rule. Elsewhere, Left-authoritarians have taken power and effectively subverted the middle way of social democracy. Human rights are frequently violated, coups occur with the same regularity as before, and the optimism for democracy that accompanied Kennedy's original Peace Corps and Alliance for Progress conceptions is now dead. Across the board, democracy appears to be faring badly; some would go so far as to pronounce Latin America's quest for the same—and by extension all of Latin American history—a "failure."[9]

It is difficult to think of history as a "success" or "failure," however. History is, rather, a neutral process, and unless one imposes a set of preconceived moral standards on it, it can hardly be branded a "success" or "failure." But perhaps that is part of the trouble with Latin American studies and helps explain why we so often think of Latin American history or development as "failed," "dysfunctional," or in terms of other euphemisms. Perhaps we have applied the wrong or inappropriate standards. Perhaps we have judged Latin America by U.S. standards and expectations rather than by its own. Using U.S. standards or criteria of development and democracy, one would almost necessarily conclude that Latin America's history has been a "failure," for it has not developed the separate and coequal parliament or courts, the system of local government, the traditions of party politics, loyal opposition, regular elections, and so forth that we deem to be necessary for democratic growth. But are there other criteria that might be used, criteria that reflect Latin America's own expectations instead of North America's, measures by which Latin American history may be judged a "success" and not a "failure"?

Our authors are of several minds on this issue, reflecting a debate that rages widely in the humanities and social sciences and with important policy implications, as to whether and to what degree there exist universal principles of "right" moral behavior (or developmental criteria) or whether these must be determined on a national, regional, or culture-area level. Some of the essays here are cast within "the struggle for democracy" universal or U.S.-style tradition. Others are skeptical whether "the struggle for democracy" theme is the proper and correct way to interpret Latin American history and politics and are frankly hostile to an approach they see as derived from the United States and with little relevance to the Latin American culture area. They would agree that it is impossible to label any history a "failure" and argue that our doing so reflects merely our own ethnocentric biases and not the realities of Latin American development.

Still others, while recognizing the biases and ethnocentrism that pervade a "struggle for democracy" focus that derives its chief assumptions from the U.S. experience, have sought nonetheless to analyze what is, after all, a still genuine and deep-rooted *Latin American* desire for democracy. But these writers have tried to discover an indigenous Latin American sense and meaning of democracy, different from and perhaps not altogether inferior to the North American one. It is a critical and important debate, with major implications for Latin America, for our understanding of the area, and for policy. Building upon this discussion, a number of our contributors seek to reformulate and reconceptualize the "struggle for democracy" issue as it relates to Latin America.

Latin America and Its "Struggle for Democracy"

To what extent is Latin America democratic? To what extent does it wish or aspire to be? To what extent can Latin America be interpreted through a liberal and democratic model of development? These questions have from the beginning preoccupied both Latin Americans and outside students of the area. They continue to concern us today.

It is probably to be expected that the United States should seek to interpret—and remake—Latin America in terms of its own democratic ethos and institutions. We like to think of ourselves as "the greatest democracy on earth," and the tendency is probably natural to interpret the political struggle of others in the light of our own behavior and expectations. Nor is the tendency to view the rest of the world through its own ethnocentric biases entirely confined to the United States.

So long as the United States remained a minor power, our fervor for democratic rule was largely confined to moral suasion and righteous injunctions. We sympathized with the struggles of Latin America for independence from Spain and the efforts of these early "new nations" to write democratic constitutions and to fashion representative governments. But beyond that we seldom went, and our trade and contacts with the area in the early nineteenth century remained limited. The era of "manifest destiny" was probably the first large-scale effort to bring the "benefits" of democracy to territories that once belonged to Spain, to blend our desires to expand democracy with our self-interest and power ambitions, and to use force if necessary to implement those goals. The Spanish-American War of 1898—in which, under the guise of freeing Cuba, Puerto Rico, and the Philippines from the yoke of some supposed Spanish cruelty and oppression, we annexed them as colonies or dependencies—represents another clear-cut effort on our part to export our brand of democracy while simultaneously acquiring a series of client states and territories to serve our ambitions for major-power status.

Although it would be easy to dismiss the speeches of our leaders regarding our concern to export democracy as mere rationalizations for baser motives, such a view would be too simple. There can be little doubt that William Jennings Bryan, Teddy Roosevelt, and Woodrow Wilson were sincere in their desires to bring the "blessings" of democratic rule to Panama, Haiti, Nicaragua, Cuba, Mexico, the Dominican Republic, and other lands that we annexed or on whose shores we landed the marines. To dismiss our moral fervor for democracy as a mere smokescreen for imperial designs and colonialism is to fail to understand the American tradition and its, admittedly self-righteous and ethnocentric, democratic ethos. Even Lyndon Johnson, when he sent twenty thousand troops into Santo Domingo and then even greater numbers into Vietnam in the two major interventions of the 1960s, was operating, by his own lights, from the same liberal-democratic premises.[10] And who could doubt the sincerity of Jimmy Carter's concern for human rights, or the indignation of members of the Latin American Studies Association in passing resolutions condemnatory of authoritarian regimes?

The issue would be simple if it only involved the attempt of the United States to impose, by example or force, its particular democratic conception on Latin America. The matter is complicated, however, by the fact that in their laws and constitutions the Latin American nations have apparently also adopted the democratic model. "Checks and balances," "federalism," "bills of rights," and the like were incorporated into the basic law of every Latin American nation. Moreover, among Latin American intellectuals, particularly during the nineteenth century but continuing to exist as a strong strain today, liberalism and republicanism seemed to lie also at the heart of Latin American aspirations.[11]

The apparent quest of the Latin American nations for democratic representative rule—and the constant thwarting and frustration of those goals—produced several important results. Among Latin American intellectuals, and often the general public, it gave rise to what may be termed the "myth of democratic incapacity," a certain national inferiority complex, the belief that because of some character or culture flaw Latin America was incapable of democratic rule, and, hence, the search for villains and scapegoats.[12] In some of the classic writings of Latin American sociology the villains included the Catholic Church, caudilloism, the Spanish past, the "hybrid" racial mix of the population, the Indian subculture, independence from Spain, "feudalism," "capitalism," and the United States.[13] The myth of democratic incapacity and the national inferiority complex also inspired a frenetic search for other holistic solutions also imported from the outside: positivism, socialism, communism, even fascism. Implied in the search for outside solutions was the widespread belief in Latin America, bolstered by the North American sense of superiority and corresponding disdain for things or peoples Latin American, that there was nothing of value in their own society, culture, and institutions. Only in relatively recent times, with the rise of the Apristas in Peru and other movements, do we begin to see developing new and progressive efforts to take, critically and selectively rather than with the blind enthusiasm of the past, what is useful from the outside and blend and fuse it with indigenous Latin American institutions and practices.[14]

North Americans too looked at Latin America in terms of its presumed quest for democracy. The early scholars often took at face value the articles in the Latin American constitutions providing for democratic rule.[15] Naturally, since few of the Latin American states lived up to constitutional expectations, their histories were usually written in terms of their "frustrated" or "thwarted" march toward representative democracy. Latin America was pictured as "struggling" for democracy but it was clearly a slow, pained, uphill, frequently reversible process. In perhaps the classic statement of this point of view, in a 1950 special edition of the *American Political Science Review*, the "pathology of democracy in Latin America" served as *the* focus. Only one of the contributors seemed troubled by that focus, pointing out that of the words in the title only "of" and "in" were neutral, while "Latin America" was itself a misnomer and "pathology" and "democracy" can get us into water as hot and deep, in his words, "as any that lies under the thin ice over which the social sciences skate."[16]

The "pathology of democracy" view shaped an entire generation— and more—of serious students of Latin America, perhaps the first to study the area in a scholarly way.[17] Their interpretation, based strongly on the North American experience, was that Latin America represented a "flawed," "imperfect," "incomplete," yet "evolving" or "progressing" area for democratic growth. Few in the social sciences questioned whether U.S.-style democracy was desired, let alone appropriate or functional for Latin America; that was simply assumed, not entirely unexpectedly in the light of the U.S. position as the world's leading power and influence in the post–World War II period. Even those who pointed out that Latin America was "different" still continued to hold out hope that one day it would develop more democratic institutions. The criteria used to evaluate Latin America remained strictly U.S.-based.

However, the "pathology of democracy" approach is interesting not just as a historical relic but also because it helped determine the questions asked and conclusions reached. To a large degree this legacy still remains powerful. Thus, if democracy à la the United States is an ethical "good" to which Latin America also aspires, then military coups and interventions in civilian affairs are necessarily "bad" and to be condemned.[18] If separation of powers is a superior moral principle, then the centralized organic systems of Latin America cannot possibly function well or democratically. If separating church from state is similarly a sine qua non for democracy, then the church's influence has to be curbed and pervasive Catholic culture eliminated.[19] Along with the army and the church, the oligarchy, hierarchy, and elitist rule were viewed as the "enemies" of democracy that had to be overcome. Personalism, *continuismo*, caudilloism, and executive predominance also had to be exorcised.

If some institutions were vilified by ostensibly unbiased historians and social scientists and condemned to obsolescence or irrelevance, others necessarily had to be praised and elevated to a position of importance out of proportion to their real influence in Latin America. Thus, if personalism and a national patron-client system were "bad," political parties were "good"; and Russell Fitzgibbon admonished an entire generation of political scientists to study them. If caudilloism and all-powerful executives were "bad," then a stronger parliament, court system, and local government were all "good"—even though these institutions had seldom played much of a role in the Latin American tradition or were specifically assigned a weaker position than was true of North American constitutionalism. Based in large part on indices such as these (strong parliaments, courts, parties, local government, etc.), Fitzgibbon published a series of articles purporting to measure the "progress of democracy" in Latin America every five years.[20]

The point of these comments is not to disparage democratic values or institutions. Indeed, these values are strongly held by probably all the contributors to this volume. The difficulty comes, however, when scholars apply their personal or particular values to Latin America. First, this emphasis has given rise to a great deal of what we may term "wishful sociology"—that is, analysis based more on *our* North American hopes for the area rather than on the actual experience of Latin America. Second, it reveals the pervasive ethnocentrism of our usual approach to Latin America, one based on liberal-Lockean and Anglo-American conceptions rather than one derived from Latin America's own experience. And third, the "pathology" focus has biased the questions raised and answers given in our study of Latin America, literally painting some institutions in the blackest of terms, glorifying others undeservedly, and meanwhile, because of these blind spots, ignoring the dynamics and realities of how politics and change in Latin America do in fact occur.

The most recent expression of the democratic bias in our approach to Latin America is in the development literature, particularly that of the 1960s. Beginning with Almond and Coleman's enormously influential volume, *The Politics of the Developing Areas*,[21] and finding expression also in the writings of the recent giants of the social sciences—Seymour M. Lipset, Karl Deutsch, Talcott Parsons, Reinhard Bendix, W. W. Rostow, Edward Shils, and Samuel P. Huntington—the mobilization of the democratic bias took a new and more sophisticated turn. Whereas the emphasis of the "older school" had been placed chiefly on institutions (congress, elections, courts, etc.), the newer approach heavily stressed political-sociological factors (the "input" functions). But interestingly, the "inputs" stressed as critical for a "modern" nation (political parties, a pluralist interest group structure, an informed citizenry participating in regular elections, and so forth) once again posited a political system that looked "just like us" and toward which other nations presumably inevitably "developed." The development literature emphasized "social mobilization" and such "prerequisites of democracy" as "middle class societies" and broad (electoral) participation.

Again, few of us would quarrel with these ideals and certainly the development literature offered some new perspectives. But what bears emphasis is the familiar biases built into the approach. The "developed" society posited in the literature consistently bore a striking resemblance to the United States: democratic, pluralist, secular, achievement-oriented, and so on. "Traditional" institutions in Latin America and elsewhere, such as the church, personalism, militarism, ascriptive behavior, familism, particularism and the like, were condemned to disappear in the wake of "modernization." Although the terms are different and the biases somewhat less manifest, the dichotomies of the development literature bore a striking similarity to the older idea that U.S.-style democracy was "good" and everything else "bad."

The model of political society envisioned also derived largely from the U.S. experience, based on pluralist and democratic theory and assumptions.[22] Not only were the major Latin American institutions dismissed as "backward" and "underdeveloped," but no thought whatsoever was given to the possibility that "democracy" and "participation" might mean different things in different cultural contexts or be organized through distinct institutional mechanisms. And so an entire generation of graduate students, armed with this conceptual baggage, descended upon Latin America looking for a form of "development" that could not possibly exist. They studied political parties and "interest aggregation," political groups and "interest articulation," the emergence of "pluralism," elections, etc.—almost always from a U.S. perspective. Of course few found these institutions and patterns functioning or even existent in most Latin American countries. It is no wonder that many of them wrote dissertations and learned articles pronouncing Latin America "underdeveloped" or "dysfunctional," for in the absence of institutions conforming to their preconceived notions of what a "developed" society looked like, they were bound to reach that conclusion. The same concepts and presumptions dominated our Agency for International Development (AID) and foreign assistance programs during the 1960s, and there the results were even more nefarious. For not only did AID seek to create institutions that had no solid grounding in Latin American realities (for example, community development programs based on the U.S.

conception of strong, active, local government) but it also served to undermine those Latin American institutions that did work by consigning them to the category of "traditional" and, hence, to the dustbins of history.

Although some more experienced Latin Americanists were skeptical of the new approach from the beginning,[23] it was not until later that the biases of the development model were examined. Then, in a remarkably revealing autobiographical note published in 1970 that has not received the attention it deserved, Gabriel A. Almond, probably the most influential advocate of the developmentalist approach, stated explicitly the values and assumptions that had undergirded his earlier formulation.[24] He writes that his first field experience in a developing nation came in 1962, several years *after* his basic theories had been advanced in *The Politics of the Developing Areas*, apparently a priori. And instead of the supposedly "neutral" and "scientific" variables used for analyzing the transition from "traditional" to "modern," we receive confirmation from Almond that the development concept also involved his personal "search for grace and redemption," that his concern was as much with promoting democratic development as analyzing it, that his model and the policy recommendations following from it were based more on a *faith* in democracy than on empirical research, and that he and the other members of the Social Science Research Council's Committee on Comparative Politics, whose concepts dominated the field during the 1960s, were caught up in what Almond calls the Kennedy-esque "Peace Corps mood" of the times—the effort to *bring* democracy and social justice to the less developed nations.

From the foregoing it is clear that what Almond and his colleagues were advocating was not just "development" as a neutral process amenable to scholarly analysis but development as an ethical "good." Furthermore, development as they conceived it was tied intimately to the North American, or perhaps Northwest Europe–North American, experience and practice of democracy. Now, none of us could be against "development," just as we would not be against "democracy." Our point is not to question these values as values. But it is to show the origin of that approach, its grounding in a particular (U.S. and European) political tradition rather than on more universal principles, its biases and its fundamental ethnocentrism. For the terms are not "value free" and social-scientific but heavily charged and prejudicial; they have elevated our own political experience into a reified model for others to emulate, meanwhile dismissing the existing institutional arrangements of Latin America as outdated and irrelevant.

But other scholars have become convinced Latin American institutions cannot so easily be dismissed, and at the least the question of the universality of North American or northwest European democratic norms and their applicability to Latin America should remain open instead of closed. One is tempted indeed to rephrase Bolívar to say that it is no longer in the name of liberty that the United States is destined to plague Latin America but in the name of "development." The questioning and assessment of just how relevant the democratic-developmentalist model is to Latin America lie at the heart of this book.

Implications of the Democratic Bias: A Critique

Viewing Latin America through the democratic prism of U.S. values and social-science assumptions offers numerous advantages. It is a simple approach and easy to understand, and does not involve the complexities of mastering a foreign language and coming to grips with a foreign culture on its own terms rather than our own. It helps make us feel superior and "modern" by positing the United States as a moral and democratic society to which all other nations aspire and into which they inevitably develop. It is also a useful device for getting students interested in the area and, for a time, for prying foreign assistance funds from an often reluctant Congress. Moreover, on the surface, it seems to correspond to the goals of the Latin American nations, as expressed in their laws and constitutions.

While the approach that sees Latin American development in democratic or would-be democratic terms, based on the U.S understanding of that term—the historic, hallowed, and still venerated one— sentiment is now growing that it is a wrong and misleading focus. Among younger scholars especially, an attitude of severe questioning of the moral "superiority" of U.S. institutions has emerged, and a corresponding new appreciation of Latin American culture, civilization, and the special nature of its development processes. The sense is now widespread that the U.S.-inspired democratic focus has not only perpetuated our misunderstandings of Latin America but, in serving frequently as a smokescreen for other U.S. purposes, has wreaked downright harm on the area. Some of the criticisms and ramifications of the "democratic" bias may be summarized as follows:

1. The approach is ethnocentric, patronizing, preachy. The U.S. model is no longer widely admired abroad, nor is U.S. society any longer viewed as the ideal end-product of the development process. Any approach that sees the rest of the world exclusively through North American eyes is bound to be biased and false. Such moral superiority may have been appropriate when the United States was the world's

greatest power, widely admired and emulated, but those times have passed. A large dose of cultural relativism is now required, a new *verstehen* approach, an ability to deal with other societies on their terms and in their own language.[25] That obviously does not mean that we stop making moral judgments or that cultural relativism be carried to the point of accepting a Hitler. But it does imply that we avoid knee-jerk judgments, that we hold our moral righteousness in abeyance until we fully understand the phenomena we would otherwise be quick to condemn. We may even want to empathize with the policies of a Fidel Castro or an Omar Torrijos, for example, instead of condemning them as "Caribbean despots" or "tin horn dictators." Missionary and Peace-Corps-style efforts to bring the "benefits" of "democracy" to our little brown or black brothers" à la Teddy Roosevelt, Wilson, Kennedy, or Carter will no longer do; in fact, such efforts in the present context not only won't work but may well prove counterproductive. President Carter's efforts to impose a U.S.-centered concept of human rights on Latin America provides a major case in point: not only will such pressures not change the attitudes of Latin America's governing elites but, as the ruptures with Argentina, Brazil, Chile, El Salvador, and Uruguay indicate, they may produce a harmful backlash. In short, the U.S. model will no longer wash, and efforts to impose it are almost certain to produce harmful and unanticipated consequences.

2. The view that sees Latin America as struggling toward democracy, or pictures its political evolution as a constant conflict between "democracy" and "dictatorship," or "enlightenment" versus "reaction," is far too simple and one-dimensional. Thinking in such terms is too confining. It not only glosses over the realities of Latin American politics and change but it ignores the various alternative positions and types of regimes spaced out between these polar extremes, where, in fact, *all* the Latin American nations are situated. The "dictatorship"/ "democracy" framework restricts the range of developmental alternatives and ignores other possibilities. Forcing Latin America to choose between the one and the other imposes a constrictive straitjacket on the area and implies a series of false choices instead of realistic ones. Latin America has historically demonstrated a genius for improvisation and compromise between its stated abstract goals and the actualities of its social, political, and economic life. The time has come when we may begin to appreciate the genius and functionality of such half-way houses, rather than belittling or condemning the area out of hand or forcing it to choose artificially among unrealistic alternatives. Even the terms in which we discuss Latin America, in short, and attempt to impose our preferred solution on it, are a form of cultural imperialism.[26]

3. Viewing Latin American history as a "struggle for democracy," one must almost necessarily brand that history as "unsuccessful," since few if any countries of the area have fully lived up to the goals their constitutions proclaim. But history, we have already said, cannot be "successful" or "unsuccessful" unless we impose some "higher" criteria on it—in this case the biased, ethnocentric criteria of U.S.-style democracy. By these criteria Latin American history may indeed be a "failure," but by others—to be advanced below—it may be considered about as "successful" as that of other nations. The moral conclusions reached depend obviously on the measures used and the values underlying them.

The "history-as-failure" theme also finds recent manifestation in the development literature, where the word "dysfunction" is used instead. Thus, if political parties in Latin America fail to develop or perform the functions ascribed to U.S. political parties, they must be "dysfunctional." If the trade unions fail to adopt a nonpolitical, collective-bargaining orientation, they must be "dysfunctional." If a "middle class society" fails to develop on the U.S. model, several things may be "dysfunctional." If the armed forces refuse to remain subservient to civilians, they must be "dysfunctional." The same goes for AID programs, based similarly on the U.S. model. If agrarian reform, administrative "modernization," family planning, and other programs introduced largely through U.S. initiative fail or produce unintended consequences, it is not the programs or their assumptions that are at fault but the Latin American systems, which are again "dysfunctional." But note the "dysfunctional" label in all these areas is always used with regard to North American criteria. Furthermore, what North American social science has pronounced "dysfunctional"—personalism, nepotism, coups, political trade unions, military intervention and the like—may be quite functional, albeit not necessarily attractive, in Latin American political society. We need obviously to examine the functionality of numerous Latin American institutions, but the criteria to be used must be theirs, not ours.[27]

4. Looking at Latin America not through its own eyes but through our culture-bound perspectives serves not only to perpetuate myths about the area but also to retard our understanding of how Latin American institutions actually do function. Instead of simply lamenting or condemning the irregularity of democratic elections, it may be suggested we should instead examine the dynamics and regularities of coups and the coup process.[28] Instead of our usual knee-jerk condemnations of the "oligarchy," we might more appropriately examine the realities of elite circulation and renewal.[29] Instead of

expressing wishful thinking about the future pluralist-participatory role of peasants and workers in the political process, we might, perhaps more importantly, concentrate on the corporative control mechanisms used to structure their participation, as well as the structured violence these same groups in turn use to make their influence felt.[30]

Hence, instead of speaking about the "pathology of democracy" in Latin America, let us look carefully at the actual functions of elections, parliaments, parties, and the like. And rather than condemning the military out of hand as a "predatory force," let us examine realistically the overlaps and dynamic cross currents of military-civilian politics. Instead of dismissing as "false consciousness" the conservative attitudes peasants and workers frequently hold, let us consider why such values remain so strong and often quite rational. A host of such exciting questions and research areas exist for which answers will not be found if we continue to study Latin America in the light of the U.S. experience. But we can begin to deal with these issues if we start to treat Latin American institutions and political practices realistically, without condescension, in terms of how these institutions function within the Latin American context and not by some presumed "universal model" that upon close examination derives directly from the United States.[31]

5. The use of a "democratic model" of development derived from the United States would not be so dangerous if it involved merely ethnocentrism. The trouble is, the "democratic smokescreen" has been used as a cover for far more dangerous acts. Under the banner of "democracy" we have invaded, occupied, and sometimes pillaged various Latin American countries. Using the same "democratic" cover, we have helped overthrow governments in Brazil, Chile, Ecuador, the Dominican Republic, Guatemala, Honduras, and other nations. Our Central Intelligence Agency (CIA) has subverted and helped ruin the Latin American labor movement, our military missions have myopically strengthened the one institution in Latin America that hardly needs strengthening, we have assassinated heads of state and numerous others, and we have inflicted violence by hired street thugs, strafed and napalmed rural villages, and taught modern torture techniques. Under the guise of reform and democratization we have reorganized the land title systems of several Latin American nations chiefly to the advantage of U.S. investors; those same rationalizations have facilitated the economic penetration and machinations throughout the continent of the big corporations and multinationals. Whether we approve of any or all of these actions or not, and though many of our policies have produced positive as well as negative results, there can be no doubt that "democracy" and "development" have frequently been useful hand-

maidens of U.S. imperialism in Latin America. They give "democratic" legitimacy to actions that would otherwise be seen as nefarious and self-serving.[32]

6. The use of the "democratic" label implies not just political and economic imperialism but cultural imperialism as well. Is it not the ultimate in arrogance that we should presume to judge Latin America not by its values but by our own? How presumptuous of us to force our criteria of the just society on a culture area where the beliefs and traditions are quite different! Is it not a form of cultural imperialism to impose the norms and formulae derived from European and North American social science on an area where they fit imperfectly at best? Why should we expect Latin America to imitate our institutions or to live up to our criteria when its history and background are distinct? Do we really know what's best for the rest of the world, and is it not terribly conceited of us to think that our form of government is the best for all times and places? The assumption that we do have all the answers and that it is our right and duty to export them seems to constitute a form of imperialism as much as the economic sense of that word. What perhaps is the ultimate in such cultural imperialism is the fact that so many Latin Americans themselves "bought" these same myths of the natural "superiority" of the United States and the inferiority, incapacity, and lack of worth of their own culture and institutions. But that is another story that deserves full-length treatment of its own.[33]

The "Struggle for Democracy" Theme: A Reexamination and a Look Ahead

Up to this point we have been rather harsh both on the "struggle for democracy" literature as it is applied to Latin America, and on those who have advanced such views. Let us look at some more complex dimensions of the issue.

The fact is that those who look on Latin America exclusively through the ethnocentric perspective of the U.S. experience, or those who use "democracy" as a smokescreen to disguise less glorious pursuits, deserve all the lumps and condemnation here given. And it is true that for a long time the "pathology of democracy" approach dominated much academic thinking on Latin America. But the situation is not so simple. For there is a tradition of genuine struggle for democracy in Latin America, and it should not simply be set up as a straw man, all that much easier to knock it down.

In the first place there is a powerful current of Latin American thought and action—although probably not a majority current anywhere in the area—that remains committed to democratic, representative government in the liberal-Lockean sense. This element takes seriously the principles of separation of power, checks and balances, an apolitical military, etc., as articulated in the laws and constitutions. It believes in political parties, regular elections, limited government, the classic human rights, and representative government in the Anglo-American sense. Like the older generation of U.S. political scientists concerned with Latin America, it sees the struggle for democracy there as a long, uphill process. But it remains committed to the struggle while also recognizing that democratic theory and actual political practice in Latin America may never be fully reconciled.[34] Except in a mere handful of countries, this concept of democracy is limited to a generation that is now fading from the scene.

A second, newer current in Latin America remains committed to social and economic democracy, but political democracy has been largely abandoned. This posture is strong among intellectuals and university students, where the admiration for the U.S. political system has waned or disappeared but where the demand for redistribution of national resources is powerful. The assumptions of this group tend to be Marxian rather than Lockean; it usually dismisses or denigrates the political variables and institutions about which North American political scientists write and concentrates on the themes of dependency, class structure, colonialism, and imperialism. "Democracy" has not been entirely abandoned as a national goal but it has been redefined in socioeconomic terms instead of political.[35]

A third group, both within Latin America and with its counterparts in North American academe, has abandoned democracy as a goal all across the board. It tends to emphasize Latin America's authoritarian tradition and dismiss its democratic one as mere concessions to the foreign fads. Beneath the democratic facades of those laws and constitutions, this argument runs, are a host of provisions that provide for authoritarianism and special privilege. The extensive powers of the president, the weakness of courts, congress, and local government, the special privileges given the army and the church, and the restrictions on the franchise and popular participation all point to the conclusion that Latin America's founding fathers intended from the beginning not to enshrine democratic principles but authoritarian, elitist rule. The principles of separation of powers and so on were merely *para ingles ver* ("for the English—or Americans—to see") but were not meant to correspond to actual reality. In this view the Latin American tradition has never been, or aspired to be, democratic but rather authoritarian and, in Glen Dealy's words, "monistic" to its core.[36] This frankly authoritarian tradition finds present-day expression in the authoritarian-technocratic regimes of Argentina, Brazil, Chile, Mexico, Nicaragua, Peru, Uruguay—regimes that are not just authoritarian but often take pride in same and laud it as an integral, "natural" part of the Latin American tradition.

Still a fourth position—and one that may well now represent the dominant one, although with ample room for variation within this category—tries to blend and reconcile the democratic with the more authoritarian traditions. This view sees both currents operating simultaneously in Latin America and seeks to analyze the blends and overlaps, as well as the conflicts, that may exist between them. It rejects the simplicities of the "pathology of democracy" approach, based as it is on North American perspectives, but it also recognizes the democratic tradition in Latin America—in *its* sense of the word rather than ours. It seeks to understand what Latin America means by such terms as "rights," "participation," "pluralism," "representation," even "democracy" itself, and to relate that to the broader Latin American political tradition, rather than imposing a U.S. understanding on the area.

At the same time this approach seeks to understand coups, military intervention, patron-client relations, and the like in the light of Latin American expectations and political behavior, not just condemn these features out of hand. It may favor "pluralism" and "social justice" but it does so on Latin American terms, not North American. It seeks to comprehend what elections or the voting act means in the Latin American context and how and why these are different from the U.S. conception. It comes to grips with civil-military relations not from the point of view of a more "advanced" political culture where coups do not occur but in the light of a Latin American political culture where these and other forms of violence are a normal, regular part of the political process. This approach, in short, shows how the democratic and the authoritarian traditions, both strongly present in Latin America, may be combined and reconciled, or may fragment and diverge, with both dynamic tendencies being perpetually present. Probably the majority of the authors in this study, although they assume different positions, could be characterized as within this tradition of more realistic interpretation, of reconciling or seeking to show the crazy-quilt patterns of a democratic tradition mingled with the authoritarian, elitist, and corporatist one.[37]

Seen in this light it may yet be possible to reconcile a concern for democracy in Latin America with the sophisticated and realistic scholar's recognition of the strength of outer currents, or the special meaning democracy carries in Latin America, or the ingenious overlaps that exist. Let us see how our various authors approach these issues. We shall return to the themes of the viability of democracy in Latin America, the appropriateness of the democratic focus, and the special meaning the term carries in that culture area, in the Conclusion.

Notes

1. Argentina, Bolivia, Brazil, Chile, Ecuador, El Salvador, Guatemala, Honduras, Panama, Paraguay, Peru, Uruguay.
2. Cuba, the Dominican Republic, Haiti, Mexico, Nicaragua. Cuba and Mexico may be special cases.
3. See Frederick Pike and Thomas Stritch (eds.), *The New Corporatism: Social and Political Structures in the Iberian World* (Notre Dame, Ind.: Notre Dame University Press, 1974); James Malloy (ed.), *Authoritarianism and Corporatism in Latin America* (Pittsburgh: University of Pittsburgh Press, 1977); and Howard J. Wiarda (ed.), *Politics and Social Change in Latin America: The Distinct Tradition* (Amherst: University of Massachusetts Press, 1974).
4. Important surveys include Samuel Flagg Bemis, *The Latin American Policy of the United States* (New York: Norton, 1967); J. Lloyd Mechan, *A Survey of United States–Latin American Relations* (Boston: Houghton-Mifflin, 1965); and Charles Gibson (ed.), *The Black Legend: Anti-Spanish Attitudes in the Old World and the New* (New York: Knopf, 1971).
5. Charles Wagley (ed.), *Social Science Research on Latin America* (New York: Columbia University Press, 1964); Richard M. Morse, "The Strange Career of Latin American Studies," *Annals of the American Academy of Political and Social Science*, No. 356 (November 1964); and Kalman H. Silvert, "Politics and the Study of Latin America," paper presented at the 1973 Annual Meeting of the American Political Science Association, New Orleans, September 4-8.
6. Richard Morse, "The Strange Career of Latin American Studies," 11.
7. G.W.E. Hegel, *The Philosophy of History*, trans. J. Sibree (New York: 1956), 87; quoted in Jean Franco, "The Specter of Anachronism and the Latin American Writer," Paper presented at the Seventh National Meeting of the Latin American Studies Association, Houston, November 2-5, 1977.
8. Critiques of the ethnocentrism of the development literature are now widespread and too numerous to cite; see the discussion that follows, as well as, by the present author, *Dictatorship, Development, and Disintegration: Politics and Social Change in the Dominical Republic* (Ann Arbor: Xerox Monographs, 1975), 57-68.
9. The "history as failure" theme dominates much popular, official, and journalistic thinking on Latin America, as well as the more scholarly works with titles such as "One Minute to Midnight in Latin America," "Latin America:

Evolution or Revolution," "One Spark from Holocaust: The Crisis in Latin America," or "Latin America: The Eleventh Hour."

10. See Doris Kearns, *Lyndon Johnson and the American Dream* (New York: Harper and Row, 1976).

11. Although the democratic ideas were widely diffused through Latin America during the nineteenth century, incorporated in the basic laws and constitutions, and seemed everywhere triumphant, the precise meaning of that term remained unclear. Writers such as Bolívar, Sarmiento, Alberdi, and Herrera remained skeptical of the suitability of democratic, representative government in Latin America, and as early as the 1830s the democratic ideas had been redefined in terms of a more conservative, elitist, and authoritarian vision. Beginning in midcentury with the influence of positivism, the conservative and elitist revision of the earlier democratic idea was further reinforced. On this see especially Glen Dealy, "Prolegomena on the Spanish American Political Tradition," *Hispanic American Historical Review*, 48 (1968), 37-58.

12. Howard J. Wiarda, "Latin American Intellectuals and the 'Myth' of Underdevelopment," paper presented at the Seventh National Meeting of the Latin American Studies Association, Houston, November 2-5, 1977; also the paper presented at the same panel by Richard M. Nuccio, "Spain, Latin America and the Myth of Democratic Incapacity."

13. Some of the classic statements include Tibor Mende, *America Latina Entra en Escena*; Francisco García Calderon, *Latin America*; Manuel Ugarte, *Destiny of a Continent*; Alcides Arguedas, *Puebla Enferma*; Julio Ycaza Tigerino, *Sociología de la Política Hispanoamericana;* José E. Rodo, *Ariel*; German Arciniegas, *The State of Latin Amrica*; Antenor Orrego, *Pueblo Continente*; and Luis Alberto Sánchez, *Examen Espectral de América Latina*.

14. The Apristas sought to borrow from democratic and Marxist theory but to adapt it to the realities of Latin America; see Harry Kantor, *The Ideology and Program of the Peruvian Aprista Movement* (Berkeley: University of California Press, 1953). Other interesting efforts during this period to blend outside ideologies with indigenous realities include Vargas' Brazil, Perón's Argentina, Mexico and the PRI.

15. See Mary Wilhelmine Williams, *The People and Politics of Latin America* (Boston: Ginn, 1930); also James (Lord) Bryce, *South America* (New York: MacMillan, 1914).

16. W. Rex Crawford, "The Pathology of Democracy in Latin America: A Sociologists's Point of View," *American Political Science Review*, 44 (March 1950). Crawford went on to say, "The term 'pathological' suggests too strongly a complacent superior attitude on our own part that may fit the propagandist or the naive and uninformed man on the street, but not the social scientist. The world does not fall into the patterns of perfect democracy and the outer darkness as Mr. Churchill has supposed. Can we not accept a certain relativity in these matters and remember the large-sized mote in our own eye?"

17. In the 1940s and 1950s one thinks particularly of the general works by Asher Christensen, Russell H. Fitzgibbon, Austin MacDonald, J. Lloyd Mecham, William S. Stokes, Harold W. Davis, Rosendo Gomez, Miguel Jorrín,

and William Pierson and Federico G. Gil.

18. Edwin Lieuwen, *Arms and Politics in Latin America* (New York: Praeger, 1960).

19. J. Lloyd Mecham, *Church and State in Latin America* (Chapel Hill: University of North Carolina Press, 1934).

20. See Fitzgibbon's "Measurement of Latin American Political Phenomena: A Statistical Experiment," *American Political Science Review*, 45 (June 1951), 517-23; "A Statistical Evaluation of Latin American Democracy," *Western Political Quarterly*, 9 (September 1956), 607-19; (with Kenneth F. Johnson) "Measurement of Latin American Political Change," *APSR*, 54 (September 1961), 515-26; and "Measuring Democratic Change in Latin America," *Journal of Politics*, 29 (February 1967), 129-55. A more extensive critique of the Fitzgibbon measures may be found in Chapter 12.

21. (Princeton: Princeton University Press, 1960).

22. See Robert A. Packenham, *Liberal America and the Third World: Political Development Ideas in Foreign Aid and Social Science* (Princeton: Princeton University Press, 1973).

23. Harry Kantor, although himself a social-democrat, was too solidly gounded in the realities of Latin America to accept as valid the asumptions of either the Alliance for Progress or the developmentalist literature. He was strongly critical of George Blanksten's Latin America chapter in *The Politics of the Developing Areas*, although it must be said that at the time some of his students, the present editor included, found it more attractive.

24. *Political Development: Essays in Heuristic Theory* (Boston: Little, Brown, 1970), Introduction.

25. *Verstehen* is discussed in Talcott Parsons, *The Structure of Social Action* (New York: Free Press, 1968), Chapter 16; for an application see Jean Duvignaud, *Change at Shebika: Report from a North African Village* (New York: Pantheon, 1970).

26. Some other implications are discussed in Howard J. Wiarda, "Corporatism and Development in the Iberic-Latin World: Persistent Strains and New Variations," *Review of Politics*, 36 (January 1974), 3-33; reprinted in Pike and Stritch (eds.), *op. cit.*

27. As L. N. McAlister argues, military intervention in politics in Latin America may be neither "pathological," "aberrant," nor "dysfunctional" but a normal, regular, quite functional part of the political process. See his *The Military in Latin American Socio-Political Evolution* (Washington: Center for Research in Social Systems, 1970).

28. See Chapter 2.

29. The classic formulations of Mosca and Pareto are still the best source; see also Howard J. Wiarda, "Toward a Framework for the Study of Political Change in the Iberic-Latin Tradition," *World Politics*, 25 (January 1973), 206-35.

30. James L. Payne, *Labor and Politics in Peru: The System of Political Bargaining* (New Haven: Yale University Press, 1965).

31. Kalman H. Silvert provides a neat cataloguing of the divergent foci of

North American political science as compared with what we must study if we are to understand Latin America, in *op. cit.*

32. See Chang Do Hah and Jeanne Schneider, "A Critique of Current Studies of Political Development and Modernization," *Social Research*, 35 (Spring 1968), 130-58; also Teresa Hayter, *Aid as Imperialism* (Baltimore: Penguin, 1971); and Susanne J. Bodenhumer, *The Ideology of Developmentalism: The American Paradigm Surrogate for Latin American Studies* (Beverly Hills, Cal.: Sage, 1971).

33. See especially the papers by John Martz, "Latin American Intellectuals and Latin American Studies: The Structuring and Sociology of Research," and by Jean Franco, "The Specter of Anachronism," presented at the Latin American Studies Association panel on "Latin American Intellectuals and the 'Myth' of Underdevelopment," and *supra*, n. 12.

34. Based on my own research experience in the Dominican Republic, I am consistently surprised to find how strong the liberal-democratic tradition is there, despite the unhappy history of dictatorship and American intervention and the spreading popularity of other, more radical solutions. It should perhaps be noted that, as a student of Russell Fitzgibbon, as well as a friend of so many Latin Americans of the democratic-Left, Harry Kantor is strongly influenced and encouraged by the democratic-socialist thread of this current.

35. Many of the "dependencia" writers fall within this school, such as Fernando Henrique Cardoso, Pablo González Casanova, Aníbal Quijano, Julio Cotler, Octavio Ianni, Theotonio dos Santos.

36. See Glen Dealy, "The Tradition of Monistic Democracy in Latin America," in Wiarda (ed.), *Politics and Social Change in Latin America, op. cit.*, 71-104; also John Mander, *The Unrevolutionary Society: The Power of Latin American Conservatism in a Changing World* (New York: Knopf, 1969).

37. These themes also lie at the heart of both the general analysis and the country-by-country treatments in Howard J. Wiarda and Harvey F. Kline (eds.), *Latin American Politics and Development* (Boston: Houghton-Mifflin, 1979).

Part 2

Long-Range Perspectives on the Quest for Democracy in Latin America

2
Critical Elections and Critical Coups: The Processes of Sociopolitical Realignment in Latin American Development

Howard J. Wiarda

Analysts of (North, *sic*) American politics have long been in substantial agreement that the elections of 1800, 1828, 1860, 1896, and 1932 marked critical turning points in the nation's development. In a seminal article published in 1955, entitled "A Theory of Critical Elections," V.O. Key sought to give this idea greater rigor and precision by focusing empirically on voter realignments in the 1890s and the 1928-36 period, and by suggesting some important directions for future research.[1] In 1960 MacRae and Meldrum examined critical elections in Illinois;[2] that same year E. E. Schattschneider focused generally and theoretically on the institutional and policy changes brought on by major electoral shifts,[3] and *The American Voter* included "realigning elections" within its elections typology.[4] More recent studies have expanded our factual knowledge of electoral realignments,[5] and there are by now at least two full-length books, the one dealing with elections and the other more with the party system, focusing on the theme.[6] The "critical elections" concept has by now crept into the popular literature,[7] and its notoriety is sufficiently established that in such books as *The Emerging Republican Majority* and *The Real Majority* it has been twisted and coopted by both major parties for partisan purposes.[8]

Although Key entitled his pathbreaking study "A *Theory* of Critical Elections" and called upon scholars to test his concept comparatively, there has in fact been little theorizing on the subject and almost no comparative research. Few efforts have been made to link the "critical elections" concept to the broader and conceptual issues of change and development in the American polity,[9] for instance, and the comparative research has been largely limited to Britain and Western Europe.[10] It is

The author wishes to thank Harvey F. Kline and Iêda Siqueira Wiarda for their comments on an earlier draft of this chapter. A more detailed version, in which the military is looked at in the light of Latin American state society relations, is forthcoming in monograph form from the Center for International Studies, Ohio University.

the purpose of this chapter to try to fill some of these gaps, both by joining the "critical elections" and "critical realignment" concepts with broader theories of socio-economic and systemic changes and by providing a comparative perspective thus far lacking that seeks to challenge some of the biases and ethnocentrism that pervade the literature. For, by focusing on Latin America and its distinct processes of social and political change, it is clear that the "realignment" concept must be expanded to encompass both "critical elections" *and* "critical coups" (as distinct from "everyday" barracks uprisings, *pronunciamientos*, and palace revolts) as dynamic, functional, and perhaps predictable aspects of the political process. The first part of this discussion expands on that theme, the second part advances some preliminary ideas for testing it empirically and suggests additional areas of study that emerge from the research.

Several important hypotheses and assumptions, elaborated in more detail later in the discussion, are involved: (1) that Latin American coups, and the coup process, are in some sense analogous to, or the functional equivalent of, elections and the electoral process in the Anglo-American tradition; (2) that some coups are more important than others, i.e., that there are "critical" and "realigning" coups as well as "critical elections"; (3) that clear and discernible "systemic" political patterns exist in a continent that to North Americans often seems to be characterized by chaos and anarchy; (4) that such patterns are more or less regular and hence empirically measureable and predictable; and (5) that these patterns tell us a great deal about the Latin American change process, about the periodicity and stages of Latin American development, and about class and structural shifts and fundamental sociopolitical realignments. Although the analysis offered is preliminary and based upon still incomplete data, it carries important theoretical and comparative implications. It may even carry implications for the country where the "critical elections"/"critical realignment" concepts were devised and where many are now talking of the need, even the imperative, of expanding the range of political choices and providing for a broader range of electoral, or systemic, alternatives.

Critical Elections and Critical Coups:
Some Orienting Concepts and Theories

Much of the early literature on critical elections in the United States was atheoretical. In his original formulation,[11] Key was concerned primarily with positing the "critical elections" concept and suggesting measures to test it. He defined "critical elections" as those in which "there occurs a sharp and durable electoral realignment between parties," and he focused specifically on Massachusetts (actually only two communities) in testing his hypotheses regarding electoral shifts in the 1890s and the 1928-36 period. Although he identified critical elections as those "in which the depth and intensity of electoral involvement are high" and "in which more or less profound readjustments occur in the relations of power within the community," he was not so much concerned with exploring the dynamics of and reasons for these changes. Even in his later article, where he presented the broader concept of "secular realignment," a process that operates "inexorably, and almost imperceptibly, election after election, to form new party alignments and to build new party groupings," Key was concerned more with measuring these phenomena than with relating them to broader, systemic changes in the American polity, or to our theoretical understanding of them.[12]

A significant theoretical insight came from MacRae's and Meldrum's conclusion, based upon factor analysis, that showed both realigning cycles and short-term deviations, that critical realignments should be conceptualized not so much in terms of single electoral contests and their outcomes as the result of a massive, long-term series of adjustments in the nation's mass base.[13] Schattschneider's essay, although not empirically based, suggests some parallel phenomena, namely that realigning elections are part of a broader pattern of change and action, that electoral realignments implied not just altered voting behavior but also substantial changes in the institutional functioning and policy outputs of the entire system.[14]

Although also caught up in the U.S. liberal, Lockean, party, politics-as-usual syndrome, the studies of Burnham and Sundquist represent a significant theoretical advance in the "critical elections"/"critical realignment" literature. Burnham states that his concern is to assess the *implications* of critical, realigning elections for the U.S. political process.[15] He wants not only to identify these phenomena and place them in historical context but also to integrate them into a larger "theory of movement" in U.S. politics. He reminds us that "politics as usual" in the United States is not politics as always, that there are discrete types of voting behavior, that critical elections often imply major shifts in the socioeconomic base of the polity. He goes on to specify the ways in which critical realignments differ from eras of stable alignments or even deviating elections: they imply "intense disruptions" of traditional voting patterns, they are usually characterized by abnormally high political involvement, they have shown a remarkably uniform periodicity in their appearance, and they are normally associated with major constitutional readjustments and policy shifts.

Sundquist has added further to the theoretical discussion. He uses the following variables as measures of critical party and electoral realignments: the breadth and depth of underlying grievances, the capacity to provoke resistance, leadership challenges, the division of polar forces between parties, and the strength of existing party attachments. He spells out the various scenarios as regards the outcomes of different kinds of party realignments, or nonrealignments.[16] In the body of his book Sundquist goes in depth into the history of the critical periods in U.S. electoral politics: the realignment of the 1850s, the agrarian revolt and the rise of populism, the realignment of the 1890s, the potential realignment that was averted during the progressive era, the minor realignments of the 1920s, and the major one of the 1930s.

Both Burnham and Sundquist add significantly to our understanding of critical electoral realignments in U.S. political history and to our broader theoretical comprehension of the implication of this for the national polity. But both Burnham and Sundquist are mainstream U.S. political analysts and their studies, while provocative in some regards, leave out other important factors. They do not place much focus on the dynamics and processes of change or on the underlying causes of the alignments they have analyzed. They do not discuss how in some respects electoral mechanisms themselves serve to limit change or to frustrate genuine realignment. They do not examine critically the assumptions or biases of U.S. liberal democracy, nor is their work enriched through comparative data and insights. Perhaps such a view, up until recently, typified U.S. political science. What is needed, therefore, is both a broader comparative perspective and an emphasis on the whys of change and critical realignments, an analysis of the great motor forces such as class and sociopolitical changes that force such alignments to take place. These are the critical variables that both Burnham and Sundquist have neglected but that are necessary if we are to come to grips with the structural transformations that electoral and party realignments imply. This report has as one of its key purposes the reincorporation of the broad class, structural, and sociopolitical variables into our understanding of critical realignments and why they take place.[17]

When we turn to the political systems of Latin America, it is necessary first to make some general statements about the political process as a way of partially overcoming the prejudices with which North Americans view the area. The purpose of the following paragraphs is to set out a number of orienting terms and concepts, primarily for a North American reading audience, having to do with politics and the change process in Latin America. North Americans may find these materials challenging and perhaps disturbing; Latin Americanists will find some of this material familiar, but they too may want to peruse it so as to maintain the logic and thrust of the argument.

Charles W. Anderson has presented perhaps the single most sophisticated and widely accepted interpretation of the *system* of Latin American politics.[18] Anderson views Latin America in terms of a variety of corporate units or "power contenders" (army, church, organized labor, oligarchy, university, bureaucracy, etc.), whose power capabilities are neither exactly comparable (in the North American sense of counting all votes equally) nor compatible. Politics in Latin America may be described as the pattern by which various political claimants attempt to grasp and cope with the *variety* of political resources at their disposal, and the way the holders of diverse power capabilities characteristically interact.

Implied in Anderson's argument is the idea that there are carefully defined parameters and rules of the game in Latin American politics. These rules do not always correspond to North American conceptions of constitutional or electoral regularities, but they exist nonetheless. What to North Americans, whose knowledge of Latin America is usually limited to *New York Times* headlines and, worse, *New Yorker* cartoons, seems to be a dreary, comic-opera succession of coups and revolts, dictators, and men-on-horseback, may in fact be a quite regular and even predictable process. It is not, as Anderson reminds us, that the term "political system" is inappropriate for Latin America, implying a regularity and patterns that do not exist, but rather that those on the outside do not often comprehend how the Latin American *sistema* works. As Kalman H. Silvert puts it:

> "Unpredictable" and "unstable" are the two adjectives most often applied to Latin American politics. The implications of both pejoratives are equally erroneous. First, to be "unstable" is not necessarily to be "unpredictable." As a matter of fact, one of the easiest things to predict is instability itself. And second, some types of revolutionary disturbances do not indicate instability. If the normal way of rotating executives in a given country is by revolution, and there have been a hundred such changes in a century, then it is not facetious to remark that revolutions are a sign of stability—that events are marching along as they always have.[19]

Historically, the Latin American social and political systems may be pictured in terms of a pyramidal structure with one dominant figure or the central state apparatus at the apex and a large, undifferentiated mass at the bottom. Society at the upper levels of the pyramid consisted originally of three major estates or corporate groups: church, army, nobility. As Latin America developed, new "power contenders" were more or less continuously added on: first the creole elites who replaced the Spanish-born administrators; then the emerging liberals of the nineteenth century, the rising new men of wealth, commerce, and power; slowly, the middle sectors; later, organized labor; and eventually peasant elements and domestics. These changes (and they imply real changes; Latin America has never been so static as we imagine) have generally taken place within a controlled hierarchical, authoritarian, patrimonialist, elitist, and corporatist framework, as distinct from a liberal one.[20] The conditions of absorption of these new forces into the prevailing sociopolitical system are two: they must demonstrate a strength sufficient that they have to be taken seriously as a power contender (hence, labor's absorption into the system beginning in the 1930s and peasants only partially by the 1960s), and they must be willing to abide by the agreed-upon rules of the game.[21] The basic structure of the Latin American systems, the constant features, as well as the changes that have occurred, are summarized in Figure 2.1.

While new elements have thus, as indicated, been periodically added to the prevailing structure, old power contenders have seldom been totally eliminated. Only in Mexico, Cuba, and perhaps Bolivia, Peru, and Portugal (employing thus a political-culture area approach rather than one based simply on geography) have there been cases where an entire class and social order were eliminated. This implies that Latin American politics during long periods has been far more stable and far less "revolutionary" (involving a genuine class change) than is usually imagined. There may be numerous palace coups, *pronunciamientos*, barracks revolts, strikes, protest marches, and the like (themselves, as we shall see, subject to quite specific regularities), but few true revolutions.

Politics in Latin America, therefore, again following Anderson, is tentative in a way it has not been historically in North America. That is to say, the delicate, life-or-death (not literally, but in governmental terms) juggling of the balance among rival, ambitious power contenders is an everyday preoccupation. Elections do not carry the definitive legitimacy they do in North America, nor are political parties necessarily the chief or only vehicle of competitive politics, nor is the term of office fixed firmly by electoral mandate. The position of the national leadership is always exceedingly precarious. The president or ruling party (including often the army as the strongest "party") must be a tightrope walker who is simultaneously juggling a variety of balls in the air. Not only must the balance be maintained and very diverse and fragmented interests or corporate bodies be kept satisfied, but it is highly

FIGURE 2.1

The Changing Structure of Society and Power in Iberian and Latin American Development*

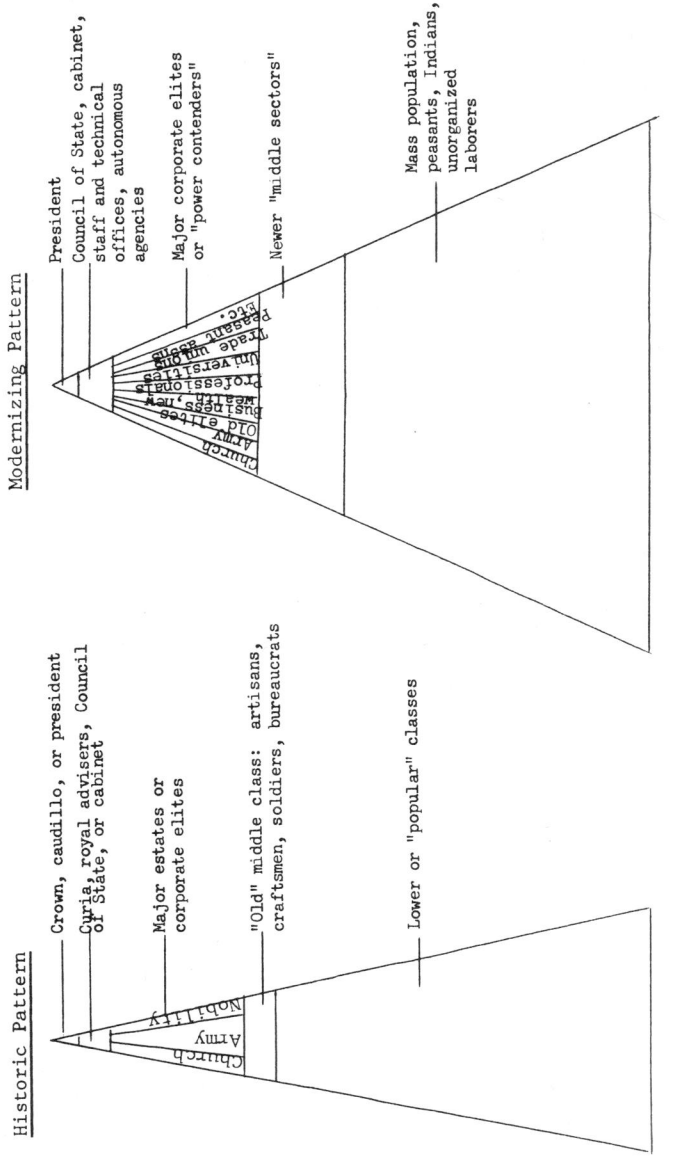

*Although the changing pyramids of power in Iberia and Latin America need to be analyzed in greater detail than is possible here, a project in which the author is presently engaged, it should be noted that the change process as here graphically described takes place at two distinct levels: (1) the gradual addition, accommodation, and absorption vertically of new corporate groups or "power contenders" into the prevailing system, and (2) the gradual absorption horizontally of newer elements into the elite and the middle sectors. But with these changes, note also that the historic pyramid of power remains in place, the system of heirarchy and of rigid class lines is retained, and the traditional corporatist and vertical structure continues.

33

likely that one of the balls being juggled may get out of hand, be dropped, or hit the juggler on the head, thus precipitating his own fall— an eventuality threatened not just at periodical electoral intervals but literally at any time. Again, there are carefully defined rules that spell out both the nature of permissible challenges to the leadership and its appropriate responses to such challenges.[22]

Many of these challenges are violent and extraconstitutional, yet the various forms of structured and usually carefully orchestrated violence are both widely accepted and constitute an important power factor in Latin American politics. Violence and revolutionary acts are not considered aberrant and exceptional in Latin America, as they are in the United States. Rather, violent upheaval is recurrent, chronic, regular, rule-conforming, and generally accepted as a "given." It is as much a part of the Latin American political culture as are electoral and constitutional politics in the United States.[23]

Elections in Latin America not only fail to carry the definitive legitimacy they do in North America but there are also other legitimized routes to power. The Latin American tradition has long included an admiration for, and afforded a certain legitimacy to, the grand heroic act, the successful definance of the system, the charismatic person (Perón, Castro) who goes outside the system and overcomes it. Such challenges may obviously come from the Left, Right, or Center. They may take the form of a heroic guerrilla struggle, a flawlessly planned and executed coup, a labor-sponsored general strike that topples an unpopular minister or president, carefully carried out street demonstrations, and the like. These events are as much a part of the normal political process as are elections; they proceed according to certain understood rules (the rights of asylum, exile, etc.); and they may be no more *opéra-bouffe* than North American elections. There are thus several legitimized routes to power in Latin America and not just one.

As regular elections and party politics are the manifest aspects of political culture in the Anglo-American democracies, revolutions and violence are a part of the Latin American political culture. These two forms of behavior in these two culture areas, respectively, are related to distinct political values and styles, demands and expectations, distinctive ways of recruiting political elites, alternative definitions of political skills within different political systems, and divergent strategies to pursue power and to produce diverse policy outcomes.[24] Further, in the Latin American context there is a pattern and regularity to such eruptions and perhaps a periodicity and progression in terms of stages of development, levels of participation, and class change. Implicit in these comments is the need, for comparative purposes, to expand the "critical elections" concept to encompass "critical coups" and other such nonelectoral changes as well. At the heart of this study is the idea that in Latin America what has been termed "critical realignments" can be either by elections *or* by coups, or some combination of the two, depending on the country, the time period, and the circumstances.

The coup d'état itself (broadly defined here to include all successful challenges to "the system") is a complex undertaking that merits further attention.[25] A coup is not a simple overnight occurrence. A great deal of planning and politics are involved. Public opinion must be prepared. Coalitions must be organized, not only among rival military factions but overlapping with various civilian groups. A coup is, thus, by no means an exclusively military undertaking but ordinarily a product of diverse political forces and much bargaining. A leader must be found, usually a centrist who is acceptable to all factions. There are gradations of support for the coup and, hence, various thresholds of participation in it. The old regime must be discredited. Preparations and execution must be perfect. Correct timing is essential.

The coup ordinarily will succeed only if it is in harmony with and supported by the major political actors, domestic and foreign. The coup thus is generally a part of the broader workings of the national political system, not extraneous to it. New coalitions must be arranged after the takeover. Usually some subtle cabinet or policy shift is involved; occasionally a coup may reflect a profounder transformation in the locus of political power. A class shift may occur. One must distinguish, therefore, between a coup that involves merely the substitution of one clique by another; a coup that implies the limited but still significant goals of changing government personnel, revolving elites in power, or shifting somewhat the foci of decision making or the thrust of public policy; and a profounder coup or revolution that leads to the addition of a new power contender and thus implies a class and/or structural **change (e.g., Peru in 1968, Portugal in 1974). Various gradations and mixed types may also exist.** And, finally, one must recognize the regular, normal, and profoundly political and system-conforming nature of the entire coup process.

The coup is so persistent in Latin America, so ubiquitous and intimately a part of the political culture, that it has produced its own nomenclature.[26] We indiscriminately use "revolutions" or "coups" to describe the repeated changeovers of Latin American governments, but Latin America's own language treats the phenomenon more subtly. The word *revolución* (as in Mexico or Cuba) signifies a profound change; the typical "barracks revolt," in contrast, is termed the *cuartelazo*; *machetismo* refers to hand-to-hand struggle; and *golpe de estado* means specifically to replace the existing government. The various stages of these processes also have their appropriate terms and provide hints of the kind of preparations and coalition-building required. The *trabajos* are the tentative soundings out of the political climate, the *compromisos* refer to the various deals and understandings of the participants, the uprising itself is called the *grito* or *pronunciamiento*. Then comes the usually elaborate, stylized march on the centers of power, the seizure of communications facilities, the exile of the old government, the establishment of the new *junta*, the parceling out of government posts, the reordering of the political equilibrium, and so on.

There is a civilian equivalent for almost all the actions given above. First, civilians may also use the threat of violence either to help topple an existing government or as a counterbalance to a military faction's threatening violence. Then there may be "manifestations": parades, rallies, strikes, demonstrations. Armed workers or students may take to the streets; peasants may begin seizing private landholdings or converging on the capital city. These may be accompanied or followed by isolated acts of violence: buses burned, windows broken, cars overturned, stores looted. Then may come a mass march on the national palace or an offending ministry that is purposely designed to produce counterviolence, martyrs, large headlines, and sympathy. This may be followed by a general strike designed to broaden the base of support for the movement and demonstrate a power capability by closing down the government. Terrorism, kidnappings, and assassinations usually represent an advanced state of political disintegration. Finally there may be full-scale guerrilla struggle or even civil war. These options, and the progression implied, form the civilian counterpart to military rumblings. Usually, however, civilian and military factions are intertwined in a variety of ways, implying that the hyphenated civil-military relations of which North Americans speak represent a false dichotomy in Latin America.

Although space limitations prevent our describing these processes in greater detail, enough has been said to provide a preliminary idea of the complexities and subtleties involved, the overlapping of civil and military politics, and the role of both elections and coups in the normal Latin American political process. In concluding this section, hence, it is appropriate to raise some more general questions for speculation, ignored thus far in the "critical elections" literature, that both Americanists and comparativists may wish to consider.

First, what of the range of options open to the two sets of systems, the North American and the Latin American? Merle Kling has presented an elegant argument that the acceptance of the regularity, discipline, and restraint of elections only as the route to power, as in the United States, contracts the range of program alternatives.[27] Since political violence of the sort described above for Latin America represents a deviant means of achieving power by the standards of North American political culture, the ends that it seeks are often considered deviant, or viewed with suspicion as well. A group that acquiesces in the prevailing electoral norms of a nonviolent political culture must also be prepared to limit the goals it seeks. The sequel to elections in a nonviolent political culture thus also implies limited changes in public policy and is unlikely to be marked by a radical rearrangement of the political system or drastic changes in policy.

In contrast, the range of possible outcomes accompanying a coup or successful revolt, in a culture of accustomed and accepted political violence, is far broader. It *may* imply merely a rotation of governing personnel, as in a nonviolent electoral political culture, and mean limited changes in public policy. In the terms used here, these would be nonrealigning coups. But, unlike an election, a revolt and the whole coup process may open the political system to more drastic or realigning changes, shifting personnel, eliminating classes or power contenders, and radically transforming the administrators and/or the beneficiaries of public policy. The range of changes engendered by elections in a culture of political nonviolence is a small one, but a much wider spectrum is often required to accommodate the range of changes generated by a successful revolution in a culture of political violence. Revolutionary means, Kling reminds us, are compatible with highly diverse ends.

Most of the nonrealigning coups in Latin America substitute one civil-military faction for another, thus leaving the essentials of the political order intact and public policy little affected. Such coups imply a rotation and elite circulation not unlike the usual American electoral turnover. Other coups involve subtle though limited shifts in the orientation of government, its personnel, and its programs. These are gradual and accommodative changes. Still others (Mexico, Cuba) reorder the political structure, eliminate old and/or add on new power contenders, and drastically redirect policy. Usually such changes, we have seen, are presaged or accompanied by accelerating violence and by new pressures for expanded participation. The potential scope of change encompassed by elections on the one hand and violence and coups on the other is, thus, quite different. For a culture of political violence legitimizes means that may yield widely divergent ends, whereas a culture of political nonviolence restricts the scope of change. As students of North American electoral politics are now forced also to consider the wider crisis of the North American system, the decline of the traditional parties, and the widespread desire for a broader political choice, the Latin American experience, with its more open-ended politics, including the ever-present possibility for both profound structural change as well as national breakdown, may offer lessons from which North Americans can learn.

Seen in the light presented here, the coup in Latin America becomes something of the functional equivalent of elections in North America. Leaders are recruited and selected, alternative programs weighed, coalitions built, public opinion consulted, new governments formed, etc. The differences between the two processes, the different problems faced, and the distinct levels of development in the two areas must also be borne in mind, however; and in the Latin American context it should be recalled that both the electoral and nonelectoral routes to power carry some (but not total) legitimacy. Further, if some of the hypotheses considered here have validity, one might begin to sort out periods of more-or-less politics-as-usual (where frequent barracks revolts and coups, as well as elections, may occur) from those periods when critical class and/or political realignments take place. The parallels with the "critical elections" literature is apparent; so too are the possibilities for fruitful comparative analysis of the differences.

These issues raise some intriguing questions. Is it possible to measure Latin American political change not through the usual indices used to gauge "democratization" (regular elections, party politics, loyal opposition, etc.), all based on a North American model, but in Latin America's own terms and context? Can we get away from our usual bias in favor of electoral politics as the only legitimate route to power to encompass other means used in other culture areas? Can we shed our ethnocentrism sufficiently to define change, development, and democratization on Latin America's own terms, not ours—that is, through the progressive incorporation (as defined and under the conditions described on pp. 31-32) of new power contenders into the political process by what may be either electoral or nonelectoral means, or both? This research seeks to suggest and illuminate, if not fully answer, questions such as these.

The section that follows explores these issues and hypotheses in greater depth. It traces the pattern and incidence of Latin American coups. It seeks to determine if there are regularities in these events. Are there periods in Latin American history of critical realignment? What are these periods and what is characteristic of each? Are there class changes as one proceeds from one period to the next, are there changes in the level of participation, are structural transformations implied? What are the implications of this in terms of Latin American development and what does this imply for our understanding of the area? What parallels and differences exist as regards the North American polity? Are the patterns in Latin American development predictable and, if so, what predictions can be ventured as concerning future political behavior? Finally, are there other questions regarding comparative systemic changes raised by an exploration such as this and what suggestions can be made for future comparative inquiry? The questions, and the issues, are both intriguing and challenging.

Critical Elections, Critical Coups, and Critical Realignments: Data, Indices, and Discussion

In this section some preliminary "tests" and indices are offered for the hypotheses presented earlier. No claim is made that a scientific "proof" has been provided. Rather, these are preliminary measures, in need of much additional refinement and precision, hopefully serving to stimulate the more detailed research on these subjects that is required.

The Incidence of Coups

There have been numerous statistical studies of the incidence of Latin American coups,[28] but the utility of these for our purposes has been limited by the fact that all coups are treated the same and the data are usually taken only from the 1930s on, a period that is too brief and too unrepresentative to measure broad systematic changes of a class or critical kind.

Edwin Lieuwen informs us that there were 115 successful coups in Latin America between independence and World War I, and many times that number of abortive revolts.[29] The best and most systematic data, however, derive from a study by Warren Dean that measured the incidence of Latin American *golpes* from 1823 until 1966.[30] The data are presented in Figure 2.2.

There are several interesting aspects to this figure, but for our purposes two seem especially notable: first, that the incidence of Latin American coups has been so constant over such a long period of time and thus could be considered, as the earlier Silvert quotation implied, a "normal," "regular" part of the political process. Contrary to some of the shorter-term studies, there appears to be no diminution in the numbers of coups over time; indeed the strong presence of the military in national political life seems to be constant, ongoing, and ubiquitous. Second, there appears to be a definite periodicity to the peaks and troughs. The eras of relatively high incidence of coups in Latin America are the 1820s, 1840s and 1850s, 1870s, the 1910-15 period, the early 1930s,

FIGURE 2.2

Coups in Latin America: Five Year Moving Average, 1823-1966

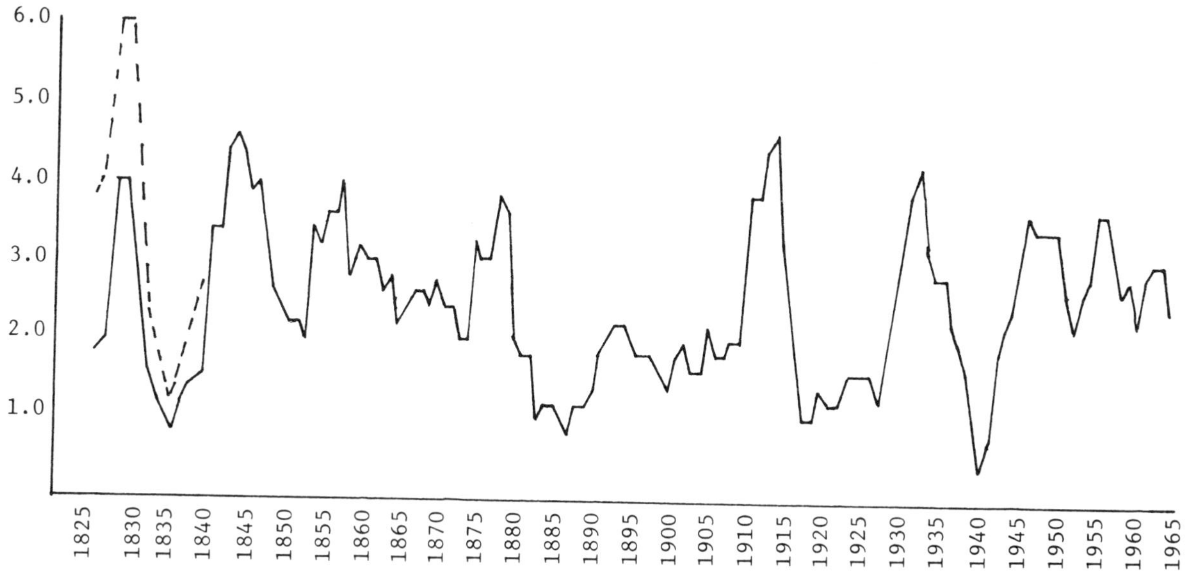

Source: Warren Dean, "Latin American Golpes and Economic Fluctuations, 1823-1966," Social Science Quarterly, LI (June, 1970), 70-80. The trend line for the first fourteen years has been revised somewhat to reflect the existence of fewer independent polities before 1840.

and then sporadically in the late 1940s and on into the 1960s.

Dean had another purpose in mind, however, and that involved an explanation of why these peaks and valleys occurred when they did. His hypothesis centered on economic factors and the relations between numbers of coups and world market fluctuations. He determined to plot his coup line against an index gauging prevailing economic conditions throughout the area, using as his measure figures on national imports. Although, as indicated in Figure 2.3, he was able to collect accurate economic data only as far back as 1854, Dean found that during the time period covered the two curves roughly corresponded. He then turned to the literature on business cycles and found that depressions occurred in 1828-30, 1839-42, 1855, 1885, and 1907-09. Although the same measure used by Dean could not be employed after 1910, there could be no doubt of the high correlation between the epidemic of fifteen coups occurring in the early 1930s and the world depression of that time. Arguing that the Latin American economies have always been dependent on the vagaries of economic forces beyond their borders, Dean concluded that world trade cycles, and hence the ups and downs of the Latin American economies, showed an interesting correspondence with fluctuations in the stability of the area's governments.

Although Dean's study raises numerous provocative points for future discussion and begins to speak to some of the themes of the present analysis, its purpose is different from that here undertaken. It takes us only part of the way toward the explanations we have suggested, and his data must, therefore, be supplemented with data derived from other sources. For there are other indicators besides business cycles to which one may turn to try to identify and measure the eras of critical change in Latin American political evolution. One such is electoral participation, a key variable that, as it turns out, complements nicely the discussion of the incidence of Latin American coups.

*Changing Electoral Participation and the
"Critical Realignment" Phenomenon in Latin America*

Unfortunately, we lack data on electoral participation for many countries going back as early as the 1820s, and what data are available are often noncomparable between countries. We do, however, have some hard data for some countries, as well as some useful informed impressions.

Historians Stanley J. and Barbara H. Stein have written that "a generous estimate of political participation of the male population in all the Latin American nations would probably approach 2 to 4 percent during most of the nineteenth century."[31] Although this statement is

FIGURE 2.3

The Incidence of Coups and Latin American Imports
from the United States and Great Britain, 1854-1910

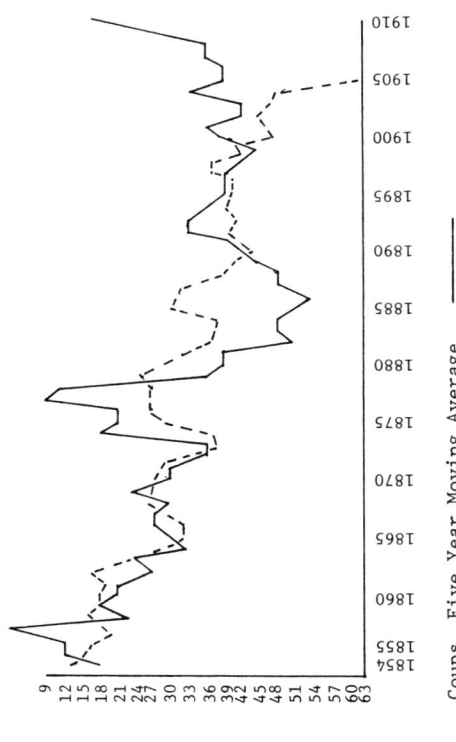

——— Coups, Five Year Moving Average

- - - - Imports to Latin America from
U.S. and Britain, ₤ millions

Source: Dean, "Latin American Golpes." It should be noted that the curve of imports has been drawn inversely; hence, as imports diminish, the line rises, showing the correspondence with the incidence of coups. The table begins in 1854 because that is the first year for which data are available; it ends in 1910 because after that the capacity to import loses its significance as a single measure of economic activity.

Critical Elections and Critical Coups 43

more or less valid, it does not tell the full story. For we know that suffrage was gradually extended throughout Latin America during the nineteenth century as modernization proceeded, that property and other restrictions on voting were slowly eroded, that several new elites were incorporated into the effective society, and that levels of participation gradually increased. The increases, furthermore, corresponded to several distinct periods: during roughly the first thirty years of national independent life, creole conservatives and *caudillos* dominated Latin American politics, suffrage was sharply limited, elections were often indirect, and the voting population was generally less than 1 percent. By the 1850s various liberal parties were challenging conservative rule, a new commercial class had begun to emerge, direct elections were instituted in many countries, and two parties began to compete for votes—in the process helping to expand participation.[32] During the rest of the nineteenth century and early twentieth, participation increased gradually until by the 1920s and 1930s the property and sex qualifications for voting were generally removed (although the literacy requirement was often kept) and the middle class was given the right to vote. By the 1950s and 1960s the literacy requirement was also generally removed and universal suffrage became the rule. As shown in Table 2.1, the percentage of those voting was in the range of 40 and 50 percent, roughly comparable to the United States.

Harder data are available from some individual countries; the electoral statistics used here for illustrative purposes are taken from the Dominican Republic because they are readily available and in convenient form.[33] Although no claim is made here that the Dominican data are necessarily representative for all Latin America, they are probably not altogether unrepresentative either; and preliminary indications are that, if comparable data were available for all the countries, the patterns would likely be remarkably parallel.[34] Figure 2.4 shows the Dominican Republic's increase in absolute voting population, 1844-1970; Figure 2.5 shows the increase in terms of the percentage of the voting population to the whole population.

The data in Figures 2.4 and 2.5 seem to indicate five distinct periods in terms of popular participation; hence, a periodization has been superimposed upon the data in Figure 2.5 and appropriate labels assigned to each. These periods for the Dominican Republic correspond rather closely to the hypothesized general periodization for all of Latin America given above, and to Dean's data on the incidence of Latin American coups and the correspondence of this to fluctuations in world market prices given in Figures 2.2 and 2.3. They also show when periods of major realignment took place.

TABLE 2.1

Percentage of Voting-Age Population Voting in National Elections Nearest to the Year 1960

Country	Percent	Country	Percent
Argentina	50.9	Paraguay	39.4
Bolivia	46.9	Peru	42.8
Brazil	41.1	Portugal	35.7
Chile	51.6	El Salvador	39.4
Colombia	51.2	Spain	29.6
Costa Rica	51.9	Uruguay	49.2
Cuba	52.9	Venezuela	58.0
Dominican Republic	51.2		
Ecuador	39.1		
Guatemala	38.8		
Haiti	54.6		
Honduras	41.8		
Mexico	41.5		
Nicaragua	61.0		
Panama	48.5		

Source: Philip Coulter, Social Mobilization and Liberal Democracy (Lexington, Mass.: Lexington Books, 1975), Table 1.1.

The first period, dating from the time of independence in 1844 through the mid-1860s, shows a participation level of less than 0.5 percent. The period was one of traditionalist, conservative, *caudillo* rule, of indirect elections, and of severe restrictions on the franchise. The second period, from the mid-1860s through the early 1880s, was one of broadened competition between the so-called *rojos* and *azules* (conservative and liberal elites), of increasing economic activity, of the slow emergence of a new commercial and import-export-oriented upper bourgeoisie, and of expanded (though still limited—5 to 12 percent of the population) participation through the use for the first time of direct popular elections. The third period, the 1880s to 1920s, was characterized by the establishment of a new breed of positivist "order-and-progress" authoritarian rule and of a new consolidating oligarchy

45

FIGURE 2.4

Dominican Republic: Electoral Participation, 1844-1970

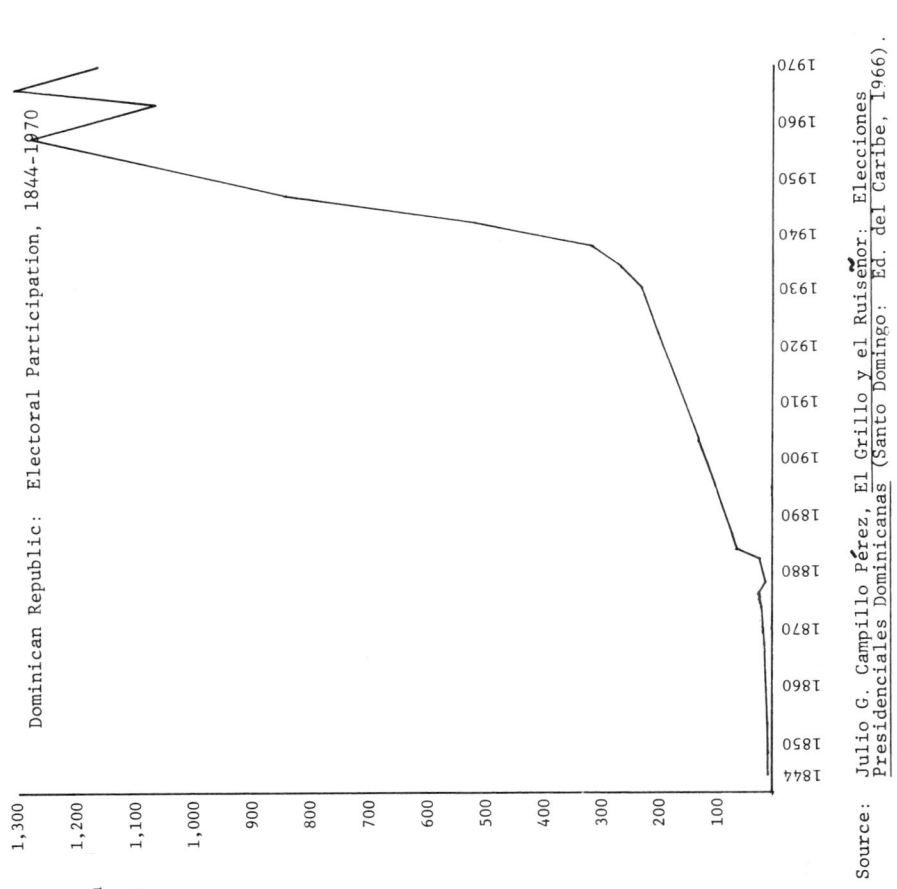

Source: Julio G. Campillo Pérez, El Grillo y el Ruiseñor: Elecciones Presidenciales Dominicanas (Santo Domingo: Ed. del Caribe, 1966).

FIGURE 2.5

Dominican Republic: Total Vote as Percentage of Total Population (with periodicity)

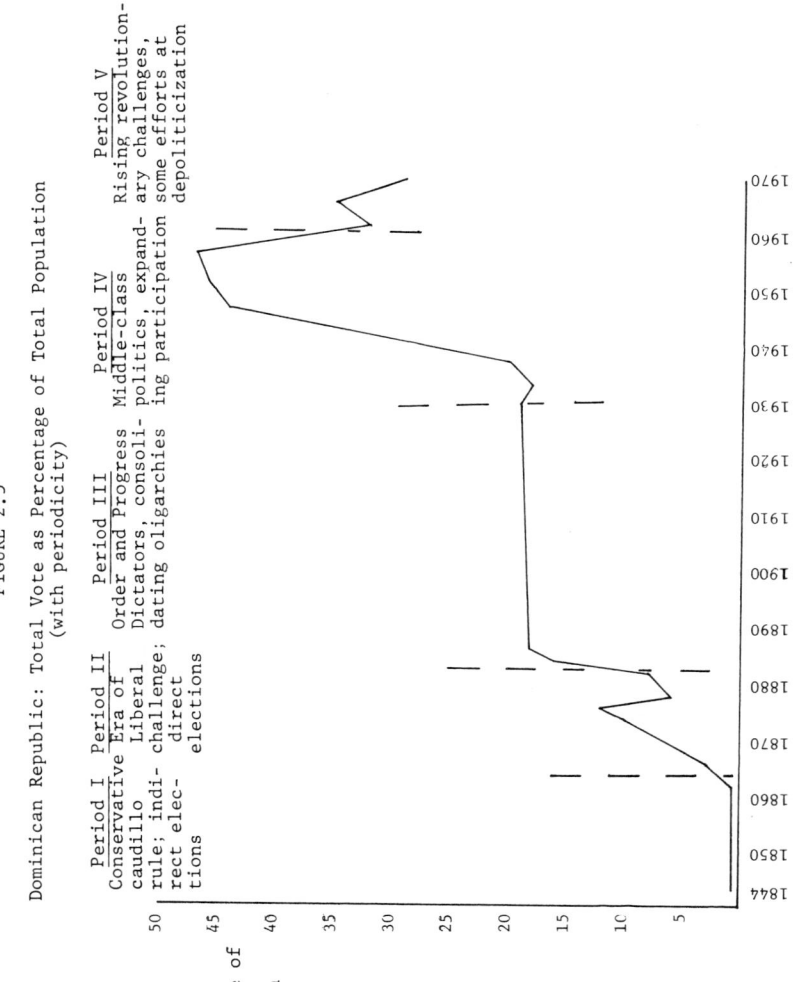

Source: Campillo Perez, El Grillo.

tying together old and new wealth. It was a period of economic take-off, gradually expanded suffrage (interruted by a period of indirect elections and U.S. military occupation), of an emerging capitalist and industrial element, and of an expanded and more secure economic oligarchy, stable in terms of class rule, though political instability remained.

The fourth period, beginning in the 1930s, was marked by the increasing participation of the emerging middle sectors into politics (including the army officer corps) for the first time. The sharp rise in the participation curve beginning in the 1940s stems not just from the absorption of this new "power contender" but also from the extension of suffrage to (middle class) women for the first time and, in addition, to Rafael Trujillo's decree making voting compulsory for all those eligible. Of course it must be remembered that Trujillo was a dictator and the elections during his rule manipulated, but still there can be no doubt that during his thirty-one years in power the percentage of the participatory population rose significantly. The fifth period, which may be set beginning in the early 1960s (although a case could be made for the 1950s), and continuing to the present, was a period of intense politicization, growing pressures from below, rising revolutionary fervor, and the expansion of participation to include (partially, at least) both urban and rural lower-class elements, or mass politics.[35]

The data raise important points for discussion. First, despite the Dominican Republic's reputation as one of the most unstable countries in Latin America, the tables used here show remarkable stability and continuity *within* periods. Second, they show some major quantum changes from one period to the next in an area and time period that we think of as locked into a stable, unchanging, immutable, "semi-feudal" social and political order. Third, the data indicate a steady, long-term progression and development, in class, issue, structural-institutional, and political participatory terms, from the early nineteenth century to the present. And fourth, there is a remarkably consistent periodicity to this data, in terms of the time span within each period of Dominican history *and* between each quantum change, roughly corresponding to a generation, and not altogether different from the periodicity of North American "critical" or "realigning" elections. It appears that the two nations, in not altogether nonparallel fashion but through sometimes distinctive means, have, however inadvertently, both more-or-less heeded the Jeffersonian dictum of requiring a revolution (defined as a major social and political restructuring) every twenty to thirty years. In this sense also, countries like the Dominican Republic can be shown to be neither so "static" nor so prone to "revolutions" as much popular lore would have them.

Critical Realignments and the Periodization of Latin American History

Data such as that above raise important issues and hypotheses and suggest that the same data from the other Latin American countries may yield important parallel, or at least comparable, findings. Unfortunately, the hard data available for the Dominican Republic, in terms of electoral participation, are not consistently or uniformly available for all the twenty Latin American republics, plus Spain and Portugal. Moreover, given our major hypothesis that critical realignments in this culture context may come through either the electoral route or the route of coup and revolution, with both these paths afforded some legitimacy, it is clear that, in any case, we would need a set of indices to measure such changes that is broader, and more encompassing, and that measures other aspects besides electoral participation.

To supplement the suggestive data already given on the incidence of Latin American coups, their correspondence with world market economic cycles, and changing levels of electoral participation, we have had to turn to other, sometimes "softer," data, such as national histories and interpretations. Where possible and feasible we have sought in the following discussion to rely on the statistical information that is available; in other instances we use a combination of empirical and more interpretive data. That approach involves some obvious limitations in our methodology and results. Nonetheless, the implications of the research results are sufficiently provocative that the undertaking seems eminently worthwhile. Until more precise measures are employed, however, the ideas presented here must be treated still as working, and not final, hypotheses, and the conclusions as tentative rather than definitive.[36]

"Critical realigments" in Latin America and Iberia, we have said, may occur through both electoral and nonelectoral means. Critical realignments are here defined, in keeping both with the theoretical discussion on "critical elections" (**Key, Burnham, Sundquist, Anderson**) included earlier and the empirical data on "critical coups" we have begun to develop, in terms of the following variables and hypotheses:

1. Critical realignments seem to occur at times of greatly expanded national participation and of abnormally high political involvement.
2. Critical realignments seem to occur at times of broad and deep popular grievances, in periods of increasing societal violence, tensions, coups; hence, the correspondence of the periodicity here

proposed with Dean's measure of the incidence of *golpes*. Such realignments are accompanied ordinarily by intense disruptions of social and political life and often by a polarization of sociopolitical forces.
3. Critical realignments tend to occur at times of major world economic crises, particularly during periods of declining world prices for the products Latin America exports.
4. Critical realignments involve a new political reordering, usually taking the form of a restructuring of the relative power of the various corporate groups that make up national society, and generally involving the adding onto, or incorporation of a new "power contender, in Anderson's terms, into the political arena.
5. Critical realignments generally involve a shift in the class basis of power. They are also normally associated with major policy shifts.

Table 2.2 and Figure 2.6, based upon both the indices already developed and the "softer" interpretations derived from the general histories,[37] seek to measure and map such critical alignments in modern Iberian and Latin American development in terms of the above criteria. Table 2.2 represents simply a counting of the number of such critical alignments, according to the criteria developed here, for each five-year time period, 1795-1974; Figure 2.6 shows that same data in graph form based upon the five-year moving average, and with a periodization superimposed upon the data.

The first such critical realignment recorded is the Haitian slave revolt and upheaval beginning in 1795, an event that led in its course to an independent Haiti but remained for a time an isolated event in terms of the broader Latin American panorama. The first *wave* of critical realignments occurred in the early 1820s, when the majority of the Latin American areas declared their independence from Spain (or from Portugal, in the case of Brazil).[38] However, this was a period not just of "separation" from the mother countries but, in keeping with the criteria developed earlier, of greatly increased pressures from creole elements for a broader say in politics and administration; of accelerating violence, revolt, and warfare; of major economic crisis; of a power and legitimacy vacuum occasioned by the withdrawal of the Crown and hence of the need for a fundamental political reordering; and finally of a power shift from an older peninsular elite to a new *criollo* aristocracy. In these terms, a "critical realignment" took place in a large number of the countries affected, and the period itself, the early 1820s, may be considered a "realigning period."[39]

TABLE 2.2

Critical Realignments in Latin America, 1795-1974

Period	Number of Critical Realignments	Period	Number of Critical Realignments
1795 - 1799	0	1885 - 1889	6
1800 - 1804	1	1890 - 1894	2
1805 - 1809	0	1895 - 1899	2
1810 - 1814	1	1900 - 1904	1
1815 - 1819	3	1905 - 1909	0
1820 - 1824	9	1910 - 1914	1
1825 - 1829	2	1915 - 1919	1
1830 - 1834	2	1920 - 1924	1
1835 - 1839	0	1925 - 1929	0
1840 - 1844	1	1930 - 1934	13
1845 - 1849	5	1935 - 1939	1
1850 - 1854	4	1940 - 1944	1
1855 - 1859	1	1945 - 1949	2
1860 - 1864	3	1950 - 1954	1
1865 - 1869	1	1955 - 1959	1
1870 - 1874	2	1960 - 1964	2
1875 - 1879	1	1965 - 1969	2
1880 - 1884	2	1970 - 1974	3

Source: See note 37.

The realigning period of the 1820s was followed by a period of quiescence, in which conservative *criollo*-oligarchic or *caudillo* politics predominated, that lasted until the late 1840s.[40] Then, in the aftermath of a new world economic crisis coupled with the powerful shock waves of the European revolutions of 1848, a series of new "realignments" began that lasted until the early 1860s. The restructurings of the midcentury reflected the rise of new liberal forces to challenge the prevailing conservatives, a new economic stimulus, gradually expanded participation, and the emergence of a new class of business and commercial elements (and, in some cases, a growing urban middle class of artisans, craftsmen, traders, and smaller merchants). This realigning period was a

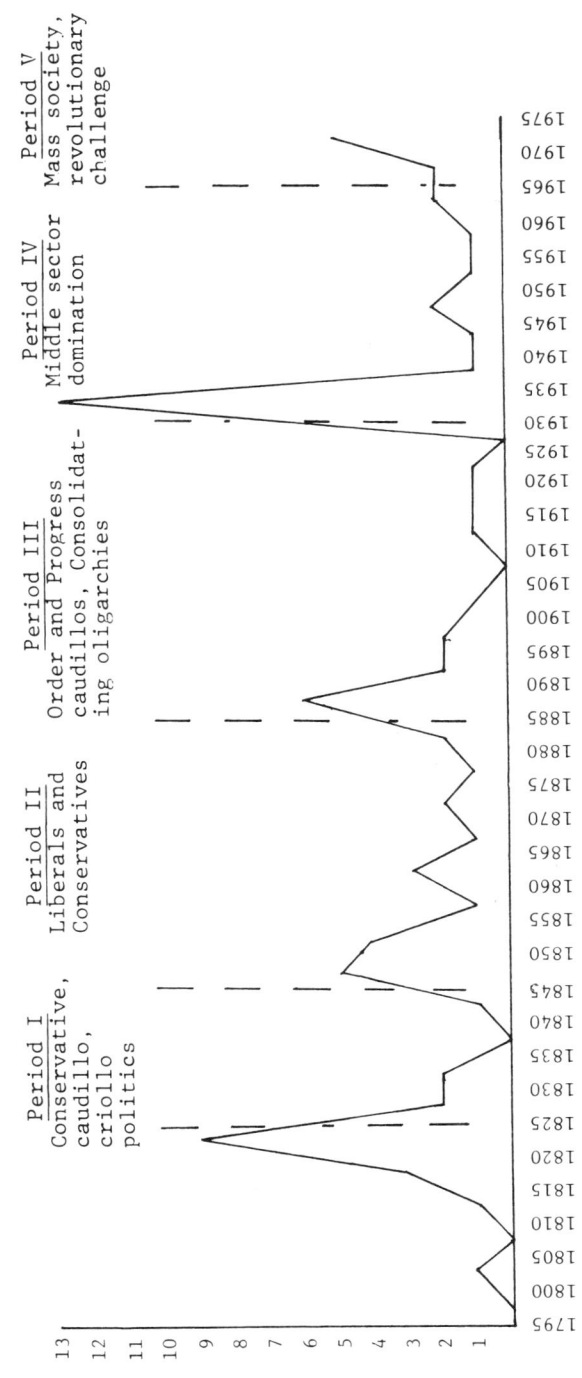

FIGURE 2.6

Critical Realignments in Latin America: Five Year Moving Average

Source: See note 37.

rather long one, reflecting both the uneven levels of development of the various nations of the area and the fact that the liberal "triumph" was nowhere near complete. In some cases new liberal regimes actually secured power, in others they alternated with *caudillos* and conservatives, in still others they failed to emerge at all. But of the fact that for the majority of the countries this was a critical, realigning period, there can be no doubt.[41]

Although in the following twenty-five to thirty years there were again numerous coups, *pronunciamientos*, and comings and goings of various liberal and conservative regimes, there were few critical realignments. The next peak period in terms of such realignments came in the late 1880s. This peak was neither so high as that of the 1820s nor so prolonged as the realigning period of the late 1840s to early 1860s. It marked a significant turning point, however, and paved the way for a period of unprecedented prosperity, population increase, commercialization, capitalization and economic development, the development of national institutional infrastructure (armies and bureaucracies), and, in Rostow's terms, industrial and national "take off."

There were two distinct but clearly related patterns for ushering in such a restructuring during this period. In Mexico, Venezuela, the Dominican Republic, and some other nations, development took place under the auspices of a new breed of positivist, "order-and-progress" *caudillos* who imposed order by authoritarian means and presided over and encouraged the building projects (docks, highways, railroads), immigration policies, and capital investment (usually foreign) that helped stimulate modernization. The other pattern, in Argentina, Brazil, Chile, Paraguay, and elsewhere, was that of the coming to power of new, consolidating oligarchies that also succeeded in imposing order and provided considerable economic stimulus through the expansion of production and trade and the reorganization of their societies for the development of producing export economies. This period was also marked by escalating violence and coups and was ushered in by still another major crisis and shakedown in the world market system. The realignments of the period were characterized by both a major political restructuring (the absorption of some new entrepreneurial elites into the prevailing systems) and by a shift in the class basis of power away from the older, traditional, stand-pat *hacendados* of the past to a newer **business–commercial-banking–import-export element. Frequently, the** older (land) and newer (capital) bases of wealth became intertwined.[42] During this period the United States came to replace Great Britain as the leading imperial and economic power within the area, and especially in the Caribbean–Central American region, where U.S. Marines were sent to preserve peace and protect American investments and often served to consolidate in power Latin America's own order-and-progress *caudillos* and oligarchies.

The period from the 1890s through the 1920s, although marked by frequent coups, was generally free of major upheavals. In Mexico in 1910 a violent revolution ushered in a fundamental restructuring of the sociopolitical order, and in some of the more advanced countries, Argentina in 1916 and Chile beginning in the early 1920s, the economic prosperity of the period and the growth for the first time of a sizable middle class helped usher in some early critical realignments that presaged what would occur, albeit often in quite different forms, in other countries a decade later. However, for approximately forty years the majority of the Latin American countries flourished under their new positivist, order-and-progress elites and oligarchies; and in many respects the period could be called the heyday of oligarchic rule. The indices show steady though not spectacular economic growth, agriculture was greatly expanded, new lands were opened up and colonized, production increased, industrialization began. Meanwhile, the seeds of the prevailing systems' own destruction had already been sown.

The next peak in Figure 2.6, the steepest and highest of all, occurred in the early 1930s. The immediate cause of the upheavals of the time was the world depression and the precipitous drop in the world market demand for Latin America's export products; however, longer-term social and political dissatisfactions were important as well. There were thirteen critical coups and changeovers in the 1930-34 period. These were not the usual palace revolts, however, but signalled the collapse of the older, now discredited pre-1930 oligarchic order, and the rise, stimulated by the economic prosperity of the previous period, of a new challenging middle class, sometimes populist and even with labor support, sometimes conservative or reactionary, but consistently eager to inherit the mantle of the old elites and to achieve the political power to go with its new economic importance. The period of the early 1930s is undoubtedly the most clear-cut break and period of realignment we have, and it led generally to both a major political restructuring and a growing middle-sector dominance of such institutions as the bureaucracy, universities, church, military officer corps, political party executive committees, and the like.

The period that followed was often turbulent in terms of numbers of coups and the circulation of these newer (and sometimes older) elites,[43] but there were few major realignments. However, the social pressures began to mount in the 1940s (Argentina, Guatemala, Costa Rica) and early 1950s (Bolivia) and accelerate in the late 1950s (Cuba) and early 1960s (Brazil, the Dominican Republic). With these countries in a sense "leading the way," as Mexico, Argentina, and Chile had in the earlier period, a new and more revolutionary (in the profounder societal sense) era, again roughly a generation distant from the previous, seemed to be beginning in the late 1960s (Peru, Panama) and carried on into the 1970s with the radical restructuring that began in Chile, Ecuador, Honduras, Portugal, and perhaps Spain. This is a period of accelerating popular pressure, of rising lower-class demands, of expanding electoral participation, and, of equal importance, of the extension of the labor laws of the 1930s to greater numbers of both urban and rural workers, of economic discontinuities, and even of the effort on the part of at least some groups to throw off or transcend the older pattern of accommodative, rival power-contenders politics (in the Anderson mold) and strike off in some genuinely socialist and/or syndicalist directions. This "massification" has also produced its counterrevolutionary responses, as in Argentina, Brazil, Chile, and Uruguay. Hence, at this point we do not know whether in this latest period the incidence of critical realignments will continue to rise, level off, begin to decline, or be turned in a counterrevolutionary direction. Up to now both the vestiges of the older order and the harbingers of the new, as well as various blends and fusions of both, continue, however uncomfortably, to coexist within the same political societies.

Table 2.3 presents, in terms of specific dates and nations, the raw data from which Table 2.2 and Figure 2.6 were derived. It does more than that, however; it also begins to map out and define the chronological periods ("generations," in Latin American terms) that emerge from the data and the development patterns (or lack thereof) of each individual nation. There are, of course, numerous problems of interpretation, ambiguity, and absence of clear-cut dividing lines, in certain cases, evidenced in the table, and clearly the indicators used here for measuring such "realigning" or "regenerating" periods need to be made more precise. An effort has been made to deal with some of the exceptions and ambiguities, in part at least, in the notes that accompany the table. A full explanation, however, would require book-length treatment and that, after all, is the concern of the numerous histories of the individual nations of Latin America. Individual country histories are of course absolutely necessary, but our purpose here has been to try to identify both the differences between countries and the common patterns that exist. That purpose, also valid, requires that we sacrifice some sense of historical uniqueness for the sake of gaining comparative insight.

Despite these difficulties, therefore, it is our conclusion that the comparative patterns, suggestive hypotheses, and ideas for further research that emerge from the data are sufficiently significant to make this exercise in comparative history and developmentalism worthwhile.

Ideas and Hypotheses

Among the major ideas and hypotheses suggested by the data, the first of which seems commonplace and not very startling but may bear repeating here, are the following:

1. Latin America would seem to provide a particularly fruitful area for comparative research. Given the common colonial background, culture, language, and institutions, the parallel patterns of historical development, and the striking similarities as well as differences between the nations of Iberia and Latin America, this culture area provides a particularly rich "living laboratory" for comparative social and political investigation and the testing of hypotheses.

2. There appears to be a definite periodicity in the independent histories of these nations that the usual history texts, organized on a country-by-country basis, fail to grasp.[44] The number of periods is five, with roughly a twenty-five to forty-year (or "generational") interval between each. These periods may be delineated as follows:

I. *1810s-1840s.* National independence achieved. Period of rule by *caudillos*, independence armies, and *criollo* elites. Patriarchal, patrimonialist society perpetuated but new issues (federalism, confederation, church and state) arise. Political and legitimacy vacuum begins to be filled, new elites rise to power. Participation: 0.5 to 2 percent of the population.

II. *Late 1840s-1880s.* National consolidation secured. Economic stimulus. First stages of modernization. Liberals challenge conservatives and sometimes gain, or alternate in, power. Upper bourgeoisie and small middle-class press for inclusion in "the system." Participation rises to encompass 2 to 10 percent of the population.

III. *Late 1880s-1929.* Period of order-and-progress *caudillos* and consolidating oligarchies. Economic take-off. Centralization. National infrastructure-building. Foreign finance capital enters on a larger scale. Trade and commerce increase, agriculture and mining expand. Heavy immigration, general population growth. Landed and business elites wedded. Participation rises, though still limited, to 10 to 20 percent of the population.

IV. *1930s-1960s.* Period of middle-class-elitist reorganization and consolidation, sometimes under populist leadership, sometimes

TABLE 2.3

Realigning Periods in Latin American Development

Country	I Conservative, Caudillo, and Creole Elites	II Liberal and Conservatives, Early Moderni- zation	III Order & Progress Caudillos, Consolidating Oligarchies	IV Middle-Class Hegemony "Systemic" Politics	V Massification and Revolutionary Challenges
Argentina	1816-52	1852-80	1880-1916	1916-45[1]	1945-
Bolivia	1825-80[2]		1880-1930		1952-
Brazil	1822-48	1848-89[3]	1889-1930	1930-63[4]	1964-
Chile	1818-60	1860-91	1891-1920	1920-70	1970-
Colombia	1819-49	1849-80	1880-1930	1930-[5]	
Costa Rica	1821[6], 1838-48	1848-89[7]	1889-1948[8]		1948-[9]
Cuba	(Spanish colonial rule)	1902-1933		1933-59	1959-
Dominican Republic	1821, 1844-61	1861-81[10]	1881-1930	1930-65	1965-[11]
Ecuador	1830-95[2]		1895-1930	1930-72	1972-[12]
Guatemala	1821[6], 1838-65	1865-85	1885-1931	1931-44	1944-[13]
Haiti	1804-43	1843-1915[14]	1915-34[15]	1934-[16]	
Honduras	1821[6], 1838	1891	1891-1932[17]	1932-1972	1972-[18]
Mexico	1821-55	1855-76	1876-1910	1910-[19]	
Nicaragua	1821[6], 1838-52	1852-89	1839-1933[20]	1931-68	1933-[23]
Panama	(Part of Colombia)		1903-31		1968-[21]

Country						
Paraguay		1811-70[2]	1874-1932[22]	1932-[23]		
Peru	1822-45	1845-86[24]	1886-1930	1930-68[25]	1968-[26]	
El Salvador	1821[6], 1838-63	1863-85	1885-1931	1931-[27]		
Uruguay		1825-72[28]	1872-1903[29]	1903-[30]		
Venezuela	1830-48	1848-1899[31]	1899-1935	1935-[32]		
Portugal	1822-51	1851-78[34]	1878-1910	1910-74[33]	1974-	
Spain	1814-33	1833-68	1875-1929	1929-74[35]	1975-	

Sources: See note 37.

[1] The revolutionary and middle-sector periods are fused in Argentina, as they are in Mexico from 1910 on, although with Perón a new equilibrium was introduced, along with considerable argument as to what precisely these changes meant.

[2] In Bolivia, as in Ecuador and Paraguay, no sharp break occurred during this early period; Liberal and consolidating oligarchical rule came later. The line between middle-class-dominated and revolutionary Bolivia is similarly blurred.

[3] After 1848 Pedro II consolidated his power, expanded liberal reforms, and checked various separatist movements.

[4] Rising revolutionary pressures in Brazil during this period, followed by a throwback to conservative and more narrowly based military rule. There are parallels in Argentina, Chile, and Uruguay.

[5] The modern period in Colombia is accompanied by gradually increasing participation, violence, populism, discord. The Colombia case may be parallel to those of El Salvador, Venezuela.

[6] Costa Rica, Guatemala, Honduras, Nicaragua, and El Salvador were part of the United Provinces of Central America, 1821-38.

[7] These two first periods overlapped a great deal in Costa Rica and were more stable and orderly than was the case elsewhere.

[8] This period and the previous one also overlap: consolidating oligarchy but middle class also brought in.

[9] The Costa Rican revolution of 1948 was a restructuring, though limited, revolution.

[10] In the Dominican Republic as in some other nations, the break between these first two periods was fuzzy, although present.

TABLE 2.3 (Cont.)

[11] Revolutionary upheaval put down by U.S. intervention, parallels with Guatemala and, in part, Chile.

[12] The precise nature of this realignment remains unclear.

[13] An incompleted and frustrated revolution, as in the Dominican Republic.

[14] Years of chaos and disorder; liberalism fails to develop.

[15] Years of U.S. Marine occupation.

[16] Still backward, little development, sporadic enlargements and contractions in participation. As a former French slave colony, Haiti's history is distinct from that of the other Latin American nations and should perhaps be omitted from comparative consideration here.

[17] Periods II and III fused in the Honduran case.

[18] As in Ecuador, the nature of this realignment remains unclear.

[19] The Mexican revolution included middle-class and mass aspects.

[20] Includes a lengthy period, 1912-33, of on-again, off-again U.S. occupation.

[21] Ingredients of middle-class, populist, and mass politics.

[22] Liberalism and era of consolidating oligarchy fused.

[23] In Nicaragua and Paraguay middle-class oligarchic rule is consolidated, some revolutionary pressures are felt, but authoritarian-conservative government remains in power.

[24] Anemic liberal consolidation.

[25] Increasing threat of mass revolution, in form of Aprista movement.

[26] Limited revolution under military/middle class auspices.

[27] "Controlled revolution" but gradually expanding participation.

[28] Fusion of these two periods; case similar to Costa Rica.

[29] Fusion of these two periods; political instability coupled with economic take-off.

[30] Middle-class but advanced social programs and enlarged participation; reversed, in steps, by the military beginning in late 1960s.

[31] Includes the Liberal period of Guzmán Blanco, 1870-88, and Cipriano Castro, 1888-99, the first of the Andean dictators.

[32] Greatly expanded participation and pluralism; only feeble revolutionary challenges.

[33] Portugal and Spain, since they are "old" nations rather than "new" ones, merit distinct treatment from that of their colonies in America (and are not, thus, included in Table 2.2 or Figure 2.6. Nonetheless, their histories from 1820 to the present are in many ways parallel to the Latin American nations.

[34] Period of "Rotativism."

[35] Includes both middle-sector-dominated Republic and middle-sector/conservative reaction to it.

with labor support. Industrialization and import substitution. New "power contenders" (middle sectors, organized labor) admitted to political arena. Accelerated social change, modernization, and economic development. Participation expands to encompass 20 to 30 percent of the populations.

V. *1960s-   .* Period of rising revolutionary pressures, new mass politics. Emergence of lower or "popular" classes into political arena for first time. Pressures not only for accommodation of new groups into the system but increasing challenges to "the system" itself. Some elites overcome by these pressures, others seek to lead the new changes. Participation rises to encompass (in varying degrees) 30 to 50 percent of the population. Such participation not limited to electoral participation but may include also general strikes, guerrilla challenges, peasant land takeovers, and the like. The rising pressures for change, expanded participation, etc., produced reactionary throwbacks in some countries.

3. There is a distinct "progression" and series of "stages" as between each of these periods. The results are remarkably parallel if one measures this periodicity in Marxian terms (class changes), liberal terms (increasing electoral participation), or from Latin America's own perspective (the expanding "power contenders" or "corporative" framework). Such periodicity provides us with a measure of the stages of Latin American development that is in contrast to our popular notions regarding the historic lack thereof in that context. Further, because it derives from the actual Latin American experience and data, it provides a far more interesting and accurate historical framework, and certainly less ethnocentric, than those purportedly "universal" unilinear models or "stages" of Almond, Black, Lipset, Rostow, Deutsch, Cutright, or Russett et al.[45] However, Table 2.3 does not provide adequately for regressions, throwbacks, fusions, or reactions. Although these aspects clearly require additional research, the suggestion should also be considered that, once a certain threshold of mobilization and change is passed in Latin America, it becomes virtually impossible to turn the clock back unless, as in Chile, the regime is willing to employ repressive measures on a major scale. Hence, even conservative regimes (Brazil is a prime example) have usually seen fit to ratify social change that has already occurred, meanwhile seeking to channel it in preferred directions.

4. The "realigning" transitions between each of these more-or-less stable periods represent some sharp turning points. They are usually brief (five to ten years) and imply some major realignments and

reorderings. They are generally signaled by political crises, economic downturns, and rising levels of violence and challenge to the prevailing systems. They imply usually a genuine class shift and the absorption of a new "power contender" in the "the system." They tend to come at a time of rising demands for a new reorganization or slicing of the national pie, and they are frequently accompanied by a sharp upward turn in participation levels. Such "breaks" or "realignments" may come about through electoral or nonelectoral means.

5. Although this research has concentrated on the major realigning periods and the realignments themselves, a further differentiation is required. One might thus distinguish between major realignments (such as those of the 1820s and 1930s) and somewhat more limited realignments (such as those of the 1850s and 1880s), and also between short-term and long-term realignments, between successful and frustrated or failed realignments. Realignments may take place gradually and relatively peacefully through the absorption of a new class of "power contender" into the system, or through the more violent elimination of an older one (as in Mexico in 1910, Bolivia in 1952, Cuba in 1959, Peru in 1968, and Portugal in 1974). Similarly, realignments may come through the reorganization and adjustment of an existing "power contender's" equilibrium from within or through overthrow from without, or with both indigenous and exogenous forces playing a role. The types and gradations as regards critical alignments and realigning periods need to be further elaborated.

6. The causes of these periodic realignments also need to be further studied. Is it socioeconomic factors that are critical, or political ones, or some combination of them varying over time? Are changing structural conditions the cause or are they cultural factors or perhaps generational ones? Are the triggering forces internal (the demands of a new "power contender" to be admitted to the system) or external (the European upheavals of 1848, changing world terms of trade, various American interventions and/or the responses to them)? In the footnoted explanations following Table 2.3 some patterns can be discerned that help provide answers to these questions, and clearly those explanations need to be considered in greater detail.

7. There may be some interesting hypotheses that can be generated from analyzing the cases in Table 2.3 that do not follow the general patterns. In some countries the division between each succeeding period is sharp, in others it is not so clear-cut, in still others there seems to be no "realignment" at all. Why or why not? And what about the exceptions themselves? Are there a series of hypotheses that might be tested as regards the exceptional cases, as follows:

A. It seems to be the case that those countries that experienced no break between Periods I and II, i.e., where traditional *caudilloism* was especially strong and where liberalism failed to emerge or was postponed, were doomed to longer periods of disorderly *caudilloism*, backwardness, chaos, and lack of socioeconomic differentiation (e.g., Bolivia, Dominican Republic, Ecuador, Honduras, Paraguay).

B. It seems to be the case that those nations that experienced no sharp break between Periods II and III failed to develop commercially, or were slowed in that development, and hence failed to make the transition from traditional agriculture to modern business capitalism and industrialization (e.g., Paraguay).

C. It seems to be the case that those countries that experienced no sharp break between Periods III and IV, that is, that failed to overthrow or set aside the older oligarchic order, were exceedingly violent and conflict-prone in the later 1930s, 1940s, and 1950s (e.g., Colombia, Peru, perhaps Guatemala).

D. It seems to be the case that those nations that experienced no sharp break between Periods IV and V, that is, where rising revolutionary pressures were repeatedly thwarted and repressed, have become stalemated, increasingly torn apart by violent, disintegrative social and political forces that have proved irreconcilable (e.g., Argentina, Chile, Uruguay, perhaps Mexico). A special subcategory is provided by those nations that experienced revolutions, but whose revolutions were aborted and frustrated from the outside (e.g., the Dominican Republic, Guatemala, Chile) and whose politics have also become immobilist and conflict- or breakdown-prone.

Other issues, patterns, and hypotheses may also be suggested from Table 2.3.

Conclusions and Implications

In his original article on "critical elections" Key had called for students of comparative politics to test his hypotheses in non-American field situations. Presumably Key meant the comparative study of *electoral* behavior, and over time a number of follow-up studies appeared, focusing chiefly on the Anglo-American democracies and, to a lesser extent, on the nations of northwest Europe. The present study argues that comparative studies dealing with the processes of realignment that are limited to electoral data alone are bound to be narrow, ethnocentric, and confined to a particular political culture area, that what is needed is a genuinely comparative and theoretical approach and perspective that considers such realignments more broadly as implying a fundamental social and political restructuring that may be brought about by either electoral or nonelectoral means. In this study we have focused on "critical coups" as being roughly the functional equivalent of "critical elections" in the Anglo-American nations, though it is clear that in the Latin American context *both* electoral *and* nonelectoral paths to power may be followed, with both of these enjoying, in law, political theory, and practice, varying claims to legitimacy.

The data presented here suggest a fruitful set of hypotheses for Latin Americanists and political scientists more generally. It forces us to reconsider the degrees and kinds of changes of the nineteenth century (perhaps the least understood period in Latin American history, usually dismissed as the "twilight of the middle ages"), the periodicity we ordinarily imply, the regularities, stages, and progressions in the Latin American development process, the parallel changes in so many countries of the area. We need far more research on each of these realigning periods as well as on the precise nature of the realignments themselves, on the stabler periods between each realignment and the factors leading subsequently to the reorganization of the existing equilibriums, the patterns that exist as well as the exceptions to them. Although there is ample room for disagreement on various of these aspects, it is hoped that some of the ideas offered may prove suggestive and stimulate the further research that is surely needed.

The ideas and research presented here challenge some familiar, often ethnocentric, presuppositions. They challenge the belief that elections provide, or should provide, the only legitimate route to power, that coups and revolutions are somehow illegitimate. By extension they challenge the long-standing American and Churchillian notion that democracy, Anglo-American style, is the best form of government. They challenge also the widespread social science notion of declining violence and military intervention as development goes forward, as argued in the Deutsch, Lipset, and Needler studies, by positing that coups and the coup process are normal, regular, recurring aspects of the political process.[46] At the same time they serve to alert us to the possibilities of a less ethnocentric, more eclectic, perhaps even Iberian and Latin American social science, by taking the distinct forms and processes of political change characteristic of that culture area, and the contributions Iberia and Latin America offer to our theory and understanding more generally of the change/development process, on their own terms and through their institutional arrangements, rather than through the biased view of North American hopes and wishes.[47] For this reason it is necessary to place the study of "critical coups" within the tradition of Latin American military behavior and to look at coups as a normal, often even functional aspect of the political process and "system." For this reason too we have sought to understand the dynamics of the development and realignment process within the Latin American context, and to view these comparatively.

The data suggest some provocative issues for Americanists as well as for comparativists and Latin Americanists. If it is argued that the coup process in Latin America is the functional equivalent of U.S.-style elections, that the former is perhaps no more comic opera than the latter, and that in both elaborate coalition-building is necessary that is in accord with democratic, pluralist principles, what implications does this have for our usual understanding of democratic theory and procedures? Consideration must also be given, in this time of demand for national change and wider political choice, to the argument presented earlier that coups and revolutions in the violent political culture of Iberia and Latin America open up a far broader range of possible outcomes than do elections in the nonviolent political culture of the United States—and we must weight the costs as well as the benefits of these alternative routes. And what of the periodicity that emerges from the data, which seems to be remarkably parallel to that given for the United States in the "critical elections" literature? Are there perhaps some common features heretofore neglected in the New World histories of these two areas, and are there perhaps parallel causes for these commonalities that stem from similar, broad-scale political and socioeconomic stimuli?[48] At the least, questions such as these may serve to challenge the common ethnocentric notions not only of most North Americans but also those of most members of the (North, *sic*) American Political Science Association; they may also stimulate a reexamination of these data and hypotheses from a genuinely comparative perspective.

There may, finally, be predictive implications in this research. If we know something comparatively about the stages and periodicity of Iberian and Latin American development and the realignment process there, then we can offer some possible predictions as well. Had American policy makers who dealt with the 1974 Portuguese upheaval any notion of the periodic realignments in Portuguese politics and history, implying *renovação* rather than full-scale *revolução*, it is likely the Communist threat would not have been perceived as so serious and the CIA machinations and NATO threats would not have been deemed appropriate responses. There would have been no question that the United States would have allowed the Portuguese revolution to run its course, relying on Portuguese solutions to Portuguese problems.

Or, let us take the case of Spain. Clearly Spain went through a realigning process from 1929-1939 that resulted in, among other things, the superimposition of a new middle-class order and system, however rightist in the end, onto the historic and elitist one. The rising level of tension, violence, and new pressures in Spain in the late 1960s to early 1970s would seem to indicate that a new realignment may well take place (is, in fact, taking place) in the mid-to-late 1970s. Although, as we have seen, the process of realignment in Iberia and Latin America tends to be far more open-ended than is the case of realigning elections in the United States, the broad contours of the Spanish realignment are probably predictable, implying a broadening of the elite, greater freedoms for middle-class elements, a restructuring of "the system" to bring in some of the newer power groups (such as labor and farm workers), broadened participation, and a reorganized formula for representation. Much the same kind of necessary realignment seems presently to be about to begin in Nicaragua, and perhaps shortly in Paraguay.

Changes such as these will probably not involve much development toward liberal democracy on the Anglo-American model (which seems to be the only one North American journalists have any conception of), but it will mean almost certainly a time of adjustment, rearrangement, and perhaps even unraveling of the sociopolitical fabric during the realigning period and then its likely reconsolidation (as in Portugal), under new arrangements and accommodations, in accord with the Iberic-Latin tradition of "renovations" or "regeneration." No, these changes will not likely be in accord with electoral and parliamentary forms imported from Britain or North America. But we should not dismiss the possibility that they will be any less significant for having taken this indigenous, Hispanic, or Luso-Hispanic form, or that on their own terms they may be just as "representative" or "participatory," maybe even "democratic," as if they had followed the liberal Anglo-American route.

Notes

1. V. O. Key, "A Theory of Critical Elections," *Journal of Politics*, 17 (February 1955), 3-18.

2. Duncan MacRae, Jr., and James A. Meldrum, "Critical Elections in Illinois, 1888-1958," *American Political Science Review*, 54 (September 1960), 669-83.

3. Schattschneider, *The Semisovereign People* (New York: Holt, Rinehart & Winston, 1960).

4. Angus Cambell et al. *The American Voter* (New York: Wiley, 1960), pp. 531-38.

5. For instance, Michael Rogin, "California Populism and the 'System of 1896,'" *Western Political Quarterly*, 22 (March 1969), 179-96.

6. Walter Dean Burnham, *Critical Elections and the Mainsprings of American Politics* (New York: Norton, 1970); and James L. Sundquist, *Dynamics of the Party System: Alignment and Realignment of Political Parties in the United States* (Washington, D.C.: Brookings, 1973).

7. *The Reporter*, November 7, 1963, pp. 23-6; and December 5, 1963, p. 8.

8. Kevin Phillips, *The Emerging Republican Majority* (New Rochelle, N.Y.: Arlington House, 1969); and Richard M. Scammon and Ben J. Wattenburg, *The Real Majority* (New York: Coward-McCann, 1970).

9. Burhnam and Sundquist do this to some extent for the American polity; see also William N. Chambers and Burnham (eds.), *The American Party System: Stages of Political Development* (New York: Oxford University Press, 1967).

10. David Butler and Donald E. Stokes, *Political Change in Britain: The Evolution of Electoral Choice* (London: Macmillan & Co., 1974); and Seymour M. Lipset and Stein Rokkan (eds.), *Party Systems and Voter Realignments: Cross-National Perspectives* (New York: Free Press, 1967).

11. Key, *op. cit.*, pp. 4, 16.

12. Key, "Secular Realignment and the Party System," *Journal of Politics*, 21 (May 1959), 198-210.

13. MacRae and Meldrum, *op. cit.*

14. Schattschneider, *op. cit.*, esp. pp. 78-96.

15. Burnham, *op. cit.*, p. 3ff.

16. Sundquist, *op. cit.*, chs. 2-3.

17. The Survey Research Center at the University of Michigan has used measures of Socio-Economic Status (SES) in its analysis of voting patterns, but its focus remains issues and, in keeping with the general cultural milieu, it has shied away from explicit attention to the class variable; see, for instance, Campbell *et al., op. cit.*

18. Anderson, "Toward a Theory of Latin American Politics," Graduate Center for Latin American Studies, Vanderbilt University, Occasional Paper no. 2 (Nashville, Tenn., February 1964), reprinted in Howard J. Wiarda (ed.), *Politics and Social Change in Latin America: The Distinct Tradition* (Amherst: University of Massachusetts Press, 1974), pp. 249-65. Anderson's was the most widely accepted of all the studies used in Latin American politics courses; see Henry C. Kenski, "Teaching Latin American Politics at American Universities: A Survey," *Latin American Research Review*, 10 (Spring 1975), 89-104.

19. Silvert, *The Conflict Society: Reaction and Revolution in Latin America* (New Orleans: Hauser, 1961), p. 20. The term "system" is emphasized here to counter the widespread misconception that Latin America is so chaotic and unstable as to best be characterized by the absence of any systemic politics. Such a conception is not only false but it also tells us something about the prejudices

many North Americans have regarding Latin America.

20. For the pattern see Howard J. Wiarda, "Toward a Framework for the Study of Political Change in the Iberic-Latin Tradition: The Corporative Model," *World Politics*, 25 (January 1973), 206-35. The static "sleepy" image of Latin America is the other sterotype we hold, seemingly in contradiction to the one of frequent revolts and "revolutions." The analysis presented here implies the area is neither so "sleepy" nor so "revolutionary" as the popular stereotypes would have it; indeed, it shows how these two images are really a part of the same phenomena, the two sides of the same coin, with both essential to an understanding of the Iberic-Latin change process.

21. Anderson, *op. cit.* For an examination of how the *sistema* worked for one such aspiring power contender, see Howard J. Wiarda, *The Corporative Origins of the Iberian and Latin American Labor Relations Systems* (Amherst: Labor Relations and Research Center, University of Massachusetts, 1976).

22. See, for instance, James L. Payne, "Peru: The Politics of Structured Violence," *Journal of Politics*, 27 (May 1965), 362-74; and his *Labor and Politics in Peru* (New Haven: Yale University Press, 1965).

23. Our usual models do not help much in explaining the pervasiveness and functionality of violence, broadly defined, in Latin American politics. On the one hand, we have the modal studies of France or the USSR, which specify the causes of these profounder revolutions, the rhythms of revolutionary movements, and the results of revolutionary overthrows, and which have been marked by their relative absence, up until recently, in Latin America's "unrevolutionary society." On the other, we have the constant, comic-opera coups of *New Yorker* cartoons. There is little literature, however, on how other, intermediate varieties of violence, such as seem generally characteristic of Latin America, produce subtle changes, cabinet reorganizations, elite circulations, reorganizations of the power contenders, and policy shifts. These are not always full-scale social revolutions in the Crane Brinton sense, but they are not mere palace revolts either. They are intermediate to both these polar models, and they lie at the heart of the Latin American change process. Two pioneering studies are William S. Stokes, **"Violence as a Power Factor in Latin American Politics,"** *Western Political Quarterly,* **5 (September 1952), 445-68;** and Merle Kling, "Violence and Politics in Latin America," in Paul Halmos (ed.), *The Sociological Review*, "Latin American Sociological Studies," Monograph 11 (Keele, Straffordshire: University of Keele, 1967), pp. 119-32.

24. Kling, *op. cit.*

25. The discussion here follows that of Martin C. Needler, "Political Development and Military Intervention in Latin America," *American Political Science Review*, 60 (September 1966), 616-26; and Kurt Conrad Arnade, "The Technique of the *Coup d'Etat* in Latin America," *United Nations World*, 4 (February 1950), 21-5.

26. Arnade, *op. cit.*, and S. E. Finer, "Military and Society in Latin America," in Halmos (ed.), *op. cit.*, pp. 133-52.

27. Kling, *op. cit.*

28. Needler, *op. cit.*, Robert D. Putnam, "Toward Explaining Military Inter-

vention in Latin American Politics," *World Politics*, 20 (October 1967), 83-110, which also contains interesting data on the earlier 1906-15 period; and Philippe C. Schmitter, "Military Intervention, Political Competitiveness and Public Policy in Latin America: 1950-1967," unpublished paper, Center for International Affairs, Harvard University, n.d.

29. Lieuwen, *Arms and Politics in Latin America* (New York: Praeger, 1961), p. 21.

30. Dean, "Latin American Golpes and Economic Fluctuations, 1823-1966," *Social Science Quarterly*, 51 (June 1970), 70-80.

31. Stein and Stein, *The Colonial Heritage of Latin America* (New York: Oxford, 1970).

32. The best study is by Tulio Halperin-Donghi, *The Aftermath of Revolution in Latin America* (New York: Harper & Row, 1973).

33. Julio G. Campillo Pérez, *El Grillo y el Ruiseñor: Elecciones Presidenciales Dominicanas* (Santo Domingo: Ed. del Caribe, 1966).

34. Some of the difficulties of collecting comparable data are illustrated by the case of Colombia. Colombia has been one of the most consistently "democratic" countries in Latin America in terms of its two-party system, regular elections, etc. In 1969-70 a group of political scientists at the Universidad de los Andes in Bogotá received a grant from an agency of the Colombian government to collect and compile electoral statistics. They found, however, that statistics having to do with elections prior to 1930 were collected sporadically, when at all, using different criteria for different elections, and by *departamentos* rather than nationally. After four years of work they were able to publish electoral statistics since 1930, but the task of collecting the earlier data proved impossible. These are some of the practical problems of research posed by this study.

35. For further discussion see Howard J. Wiarda, *Dictatorship, Development, and Disintegration: Politics and Social Change in the Dominican Republic* **(Ann Arbor: Xerox University Microfilms Monograph Series, for the Program** in Latin American Studies of the University of Massachusetts, 1975).

36. It may be recalled in this connection that Key's provocative and pathbreaking study was based upon the electoral returns in only two Massachusetts towns, Ashfield and Somerville. Key hence couched his conclusions in fittingly modest terms; the present analysis is offered in the same light.

37. There are various histories of Latin America during the independence period that provide useful comparative data. I have employed A. Curtis Wilgus and Raul D'Eca, *Latin American History* (New York: Barnes & Noble, 1963); Hubert Herring, *A History of Latin America* (New York: Knopf, 1968), E. Bradford Burns, *Latin America: A Concise Interpretive History* (Englewood Cliffs, N.J.: Prentice-Hall, 1972); Donald E. Worcester and Wendell G. Schaeffer, *The Growth and Culture of Latin America* (New York: Oxford University Press, 1971); Helen Miller Bailey and Abraham P. Nasatir, *Latin America: The Development of Its Civilization* (Englewood Cliffs, N.J.: Prentice-Hall, 1973). Political science texts that include useful comparative materials for each country include Harry Kantor, *Patterns of Politics and Political Systems in Latin America* (Chicago: Rand McNally, 1969); Russell H.

Fitzgibbon, *Latin America: A Panorama of Contemporary Politics* (New York): Apleton-Century-Crofts, 1971); Claudio Veliz (ed.), *Latin America and the Caribbean: A Handbook* (New York: Praeger, 1968); Martin C. Needler (ed.), Political Systems of Latin America (New York: Van Nostrand, 1970); and Ben B. Burnett and Kenneth F. Johnson (eds.), *Political Forces in Latin America* (Belmont, Cal.: Wadsworth, 1970).

38. It should, of course, be noted that not all of the Latin American countries became independent states at this time. Cuba remained a Spanish colony until 1898; the Dominican Republic, following a brief episode of independence in 1821, remained under Haitian occupation until 1844; Panama was still a part of Colombia; the several countries of Central America were federated in the United Provinces of Central America to 1838; Venezuela, Ecuador, and Colombia were unstably unified as Gran Colombia until 1830; Uruguay emerged as a buffer state between Argentina and Brazil only in 1828; Paraguay was long thought of as an Argentine province; and Bolivia's independence (in historian Hubert Herring's words) "was a vague afterthought of the wars of liberation." The figures used here, therefore, are based upon the number of entities (nations or federations) establishing their independence during this period and does not include the various subunits within these larger units that would later achieve independence. That considerably reduces the number of cases for this period and hence makes the number of critical realignments look even more impressive.

39. The best brief statement is Halperin-Donghi, *op. cit.*

40. We are here distinguishing between the periodic coups that are a normal part of the political process during this and other periods, and the more thorough restructurings and revolutions that imply major societal and political realignments. In the first sense, the period was hardly "quiescent"; in the second and stronger sense, it was.

41. Halperin-Donghi, *op. cit.*; and Roberto Cortes Conde, *The First Stages of Modernization in Spanish America* (New York: Harper, 1974).

42. H. Hoetink, *El Pueblo Dominicano, 1850-1900: Apuntes para su sociológia histórica* (Santiago, Dominican Republic: Universidad Católica Madre y Maestra, 1971); and Warren Dean, *The Industrialization of São Paulo, 1880-1945* (Austin: University of Texas Press, 1969).

43. See the interesting study by Frederick B. Pike, *Spanish America, 1900-1970: Tradition and Social Innovation* (New York: Norton, 1973).

44. Among the exceptions are Worcester and Schaeffer, *op. cit.*; Burns, *op. cit.*; and Pike, *op. cit.*

45. Gabriel A. Almond and James S. Coleman, *The Politics of the Developing Areas* (Princeton, N.J.: Princeton University Press, 1960), Introduction, Conclusion, and Appendices; Seymour M. Lipset, *Political Man* (Garden City, N.Y.: Doubleday-Anchor, 1960); C. E. Black, *The Dynamics of Modernization* (New York: Harper & Row, 1966), esp. pp. 90-94; W. W. Rostow, *The States of Economic Growth* (Cambridge, Mass.: Cambridge University Press, 1960); Karl W. Deutsch, "Social Mobilization and Political Development," *American Political Science Review*, 55 (September 1961), 494-5; Phillips Cutwright, "National Political Development: Measurement and Analysis," *American Sociological Review*, 28 (April 1963), 253-64; and Bruce R. Russett *et al.*, *World*

Handbook of Political and Social Indicators (New Haven, Conn.: Yale University Press, 1963).

46. Deutsch, *op. cit.*; Lipset, *op. cit.*; and Needler, *op. cit.*

47. See the parallel arguments in Glaucio Ary Dillon Soares, "Latin American Studies in the United States: A Critique and a Proposal," *Latin American Research Review*, 11 (1976), 51-70.

48. For some suggestive themes see Louis Hartz *et al.*, *The Founding of New Societies: Studies in the History of the United States, Latin America, South Africa, Canada, and Australia* (New York: Harcourt, Brace & World, 1964); and Lewis Hanke (ed.), *Do the Americas Have a Common History?* (New York: Knopf, 1964).

3
Latin American Populism: Some Notes on Periodization

Ronald C. Newton

One of the more bemusing qualities of the guild of Latin Americanists is its remarkable susceptibility to fads. Since the early 1960s, when the Latin American boom (of happy memory) first began, enthusiasms for the middle sectors, the democratic-Left, university student activists, nationalism, the reforming military, elites, corporatism, dependency, and now populism, have swept through the academic establishment in rapid succession like waves of Asian flu through Camp Gitchigoomie. They have left in their wake a handful of fully developed landmark statements as well as endless windrows of chaff through which today's beginning student must pick his weary way in search of enlightenment. I must therefore confess to considerable wariness in approaching the topic of populism—especially as many of the materials commonly deployed under this label are already familiar under other guises. After all, Vargas, Ibáñez, and Perón we first met as vaguely fascist "caudillos" (though Pérez Jiménez and Rojas Pinilla were merely "dictators"); the Peruvian Popular American Revolutionary Party (APRA) and the Democratic Action Party (AD) were the Democratic (or noncommunist) Left; and —God save the mark—Haya and Betancourt, Figueres, Bosch, and Múñoz Marín once formed an "Axis." It is almost as though the Latin Americanists, in a reversal of their spendthrift exuberance of the 1960s, were now (as the pop phrase goes) recycling their data.

For all that, populism as an intellectual construct has much to recommend it. It does not suffer from the parochialism that has characterized most of the enthusiasms cited earlier. On the contrary, it can be set in a comparative frame and made assimilable to studies of populist movements in other areas of the third world. Equally important, it accords well with the temper of these passionless days, for

---

Revised version of a paper presented at the Seventh National Meeting of the Latin American Studies Assn., Houston, November, 1977.

most of the ideological shading has been leached out of populism since the term first made its apperance in Latin American contexts in the late 1960s. It may be, of course, that this leaching results from the interaction of two sets of awareness: first, awareness of the great debacles into which populist movements have staggered through their own internal weaknesses and inept leadership (as in Brazil in 1964, Chile in 1973, and Argentina following the death of Perón in 1974); and second, awareness of the forms of military gangsterism that seem to have become the inevitable successors to such debacles. To anyone who persists in applying democratic norms to his evaluation of the affairs of Latin America, neither populism nor its most prevalent present-day alternative offers much joy. But precisely because it lacks a normative charge populism can better serve as what it is: an intellectual construct.

The principal elements of the populist style are, it seems to me: (1) the assemblage of political coalitions out of disparate interest groups, the latter usually weighted in favor of newer economic interests that have not achieved satisfactory representation through conventional political party structures; (2) the inclusion of social elements from both middle and lower classes—what is often created is a temporary transclass alliance; (3) an urban locus (on this point Latin American populism diverges sharply from earlier Russian, East European, American, and Canadian phenomena bearing the same name); (4) a proclivity for extraparliamentary tactics that run the gamut of public manifestations of support, supplications, threat, etc., and include the forging of vertical links to ambitious public men in power or on the threshold of power; (5) personalistic leadership, frequently drawn from decaying sectors of the old oligarchies, rarely if ever from the plebs; (6) great ideological incoherence, although insofar as ideology is present, it is nationalistic, anti-imperialistic, and usually antielitist; (7) an assumption of the permanence of capitalism, despite socialist rhetoric, and distributive economics, despite developmentalist rhetoric; and (8) corporatist sociopolitical structures (Latin American corporatism is far from being the autonomous system that commentators sometimes postulate; it is in fact an expression of the populist style: corporatist structures offer newly emergent or otherwise threatened groups the means to consolidate material and social position in the context of whimsical economic systems that are as likely to regress as to grow).

With the possible exception of the final point, the foregoing is a fairly conventional checklist. There seems to be less agreement, however, on the causal factors that have given rise to populist movements, or on those that have led to the general demise of the populist style. I should like, therefore, to attempt to synchronize our knowledge of populism with what we think we know of this century's larger transformation—in short, to rough in some periodizations that may, I hope, generate discussion.

Latin American populism is as old as the century. Although seldom placed among the classic populist movements, the first notable expression of the populist style was in fact *batllismo*, which arose in Uruguay after 1900 under the banner of José Batlle y Ordóñez and the Colorado Party. It bears most of the stigmata: *batllismo* was an urban coalition of middle- and working-class elements; at least until Batlle's death in 1929, leadership was highly personalistic; in creating the Uruguayan welfare state the Colorados provided a model of distributive economics to the rest of Latin America. And yet one is puzzled, for *batllismo* does not really square with our sense of what populism is about. Is this because *batllismo* operated and flourished in an environment of representative parliamentarism? Is it because *batllismo* did not serve as the vehicle of aggrieved protest of a repressed or disinherited majority? For, on the contrary, *batllismo* was born to power (as was Batlle himself); it presided over Uruguay's national organization; it held power under majoritarian rules; and it found political devices—the collegial system and the guarantee of one-third representation—that made it reasonable for the opposition, the Blancos, to remain more or less loyal. *Batllismo* was also fortunate in that it had no need to struggle against or measure itself against a preexistent oligarchic republic with claims to lineage, status, and stewardship of power.

All of this is, alas, in the past tense. As we know, the civic culture bequeathed by *batllismo* could not preserve the welfare state, and the transclass alliance that had sustained it, in the decay that overtook the Uruguayan economy after 1945. Since the mid-1960s this decay has accelerated, and has brought with it the collapse of parliamentarism and a succession of stand-pat military regimes, each more repressive than the last. Uruguay has dropped from the ranks of European-style social democracies and has rejoined Latin America and the third world. And its present-day dissidents, middle-class and working-class alike, dispossessed of their Eden, are now kin to all other Latin American populists.

Outside Uruguay, populist movements came as the successors to the oligarchic republics that had, in the course of the nineteenth century, accomplished national organization, created a working polity (based on a severely limited franchise), and presided over the development of export economies dependent upon the industrial powers of the Northern Hemisphere. The crisis of the old order came, of course, with the inability of the industrial powers to restore the world trading system after 1918. In many of the Latin American states the break came in direct consequence of the crash of 1929 and the calamitous decline in trade that followed. It should be noted, however, that in Brazil and Chile severe dislocations of the export economies during the 1920s had already called oligarchic hegemony into question and had provoked the first mobilization of the commonality's putative champions, including Prestes and the *tenentes*, Ibáñez, and Grove. In Mexico the Porfirian system—a peculiarly predatory and violence-prone version of oligarchic rule—was swallowed up in the cataclysm of the revolutionary years from 1910 to 1919; its restoration in the 1920s, though an ever-present likelihood, remained blocked by the conflicting rivalries of surviving victorious generals. In Argentina the *oligarquía* ceded power peaceably, if not gracefully, to the politicized middle class during World War I, only to attempt to reclaim it in 1930; Argentine populism would ultimately find its champion in Juan Domingo Perón. Populist episodes have also followed on the demise of predatory dictatorships, as in Guatemala after 1944 and the Dominican Republic after 1961. Except, arguably, in the cases of Uruguay (cited above), Bolivia after 1952, and Cuba after 1959, populist movements have nowhere *caused* the demise of the old order.

Although the depression and the Second World War represent the crucial period for the evolution of Latin American populism, the basic inventory of populist ideology and rhetoric had already been assembled in the 1920s. It derived from the University Reform, the personal interchanges of migratory intellectuals, and the program of APRA. The inclination of this generation of left-leaning intellectuals to follow orthodox Marxist strategy, to work first to bring into being the bourgeois revolution, provided a rationale to middle-class reformers who sought (when the military would permit them) to operate within the frame of conventional electoral politics, and to offer themselves simultaneously as tutors to the under class.

In the depression decade of the 1930s, however, populist movements took important new directions. They were determined by a number of factors. The first was the determination of economic leaders to diversify vulnerable export economies and to add import-substitution industrial sectors. These initiatives, of course, altered the structure of the work force, and added impetus to the cityward migratory movement. The elite circles responsible for the new economic directions also recognized the desirability of incorporating the new working-class elements into their structures of patronage; in only a few countries, such as Chile, were autonomous trade-union movements capable of opposition. Secondly, it also became clear in the 1930s that civilian middle-class reformers were unable to mobilize multiclass coalitions and through them to broaden participation in politics. The decade was notable, rather, for the beginnings of *military* populism. Some of the strongmen of the 1930s, to be sure, sought only to halt the drift of events or to demobilize threatening coalitions of the commonality (Justo, Benavides, Batista). Others, however, embarked on the riskier adventure of capturing or indeed creating under-class constituencies. Those attempting such a course included Ibáñez, Sánchez Cerro, Toro and Busch, Cárdenas (who had to fend off military colleagues as well), Vargas, and Perón. This mode reappeared after the Second World War in the careers of Pérez Jiménez, Rojas Pinilla, Odría, and Barrientos. Fidel Castro partook of the Haroun al Raschid style during his first years in power, when Cuba could briefly be described as a populist republic, and he has not entirely abandoned it even today. Nowadays, however, the only authentic practitioner is Panamá's Torrijos. Elsewhere, the present-day military regimes are headed by boards of directors of surpassing anonymity. The cult of personality cannot be allowed to flourish; an autonomous power base cannot be tolerated. As Perón's career so graphically demonstrated—and he surely served his brother officers as a *locus classicus*—the genie once released may not so easily be gotten back into the bottle again.

Today populism is rapidly receding into the past and is best treated as a historical phenomenon. Three countries—Mexico, Venezuela, and Costa Rica—have surpassed their populist phase and are carrying out their bourgeois revolution, by which I mean that the middle classes are governing with the assent, however achieved, of other social classes in order to effect as much modernization as material resources and present conditions of dependency will permit. Cuba is doing the same in the name of the classless society. Colombia's oligarchic structure is still largely intact, amazingly enough; it has survived the ambitions of Gaitán and the Rojas to create populist movements, not to mention the dissolvent effects of *la violencia*. A number of rudimentary polities have never attained the conditions of modernity necessary to sustain a populist episode: Honduras, El Salvador, Haiti, Paraguay. Nicaragua also falls into this category at the present; it will probably experience a populist episode when Somoza departs. The remaining countries—Brazil, Uruguay, Argentina, Chile, Bolivia, Perú, Ecuador, Panamá, Guatemala, the Dominican Republic—have all experienced extended populist episodes; in all, overt military repression or the threat of it keeps social divisiveness and fiscal fecklessness at bay.

Two concluding points: one is that the most depressing legacy of populism, or so it seems to me, is the destruction of parliamentarism.

Admittedly, the parliamentary institutions bequeathed by the oligarchic republics were predicated upon limited popular participation and grossly manipulated franchises; to be serviceable to newly exigent political sectors they would have had to be modified greatly. Nevertheless, as a general proposition it would seem that without instruments of horizontal solidarity and interest aggregation—i.e., disciplined parties in a legislative framework—any system is prone to fragmentation; this is particularly true when it is loaded with input demands that cannot be met from stagnant or fluctuating economies. A principal consequence of parliamentary disintegration has been the strengthening of the role of the chief exceutive.

The second concluding point is that the loose ad hoc multi-class coalitions of the populist style derive much of their nervous volatility from the oft-cited political uncertainty of the middle classes. These, in the more advanced polities, achieved consciousness of class identity and purpose only a few years, at most a generation, before the working classes and the urban under-classes appeared on the perceptual horizon. As C. Wright Mills observed long ago, a social class, like an entrepreneur, is subject to a kind of demonstration effect; it is not obliged to reinvent the wheel. By this I mean that Latin American middle classes are partly premodern (rentiers and professionals), partly modern (entrepreneurs, though many entrepreneurial functions are performed by foreigners or recent immigrants), and to a considerable extent postmodern (managers, professionals, tertiary-sector white-collar occupations). "So what?" I say to myself. Just this: the worship of *property* is not a constant of postmodern middle classes. It is rarely held in family trust; its greatest value may lie in the speculative uses that may be made of it in inflationary contexts. The postmodern middle classes can support a populist coalition even when their leaders make the most bloodcurdling threats against property. However, should the coalition be caught up in the typical cycle of demands for wage, tax, cost-of-living relief—should *income* be threatened, and with it *status*—then perhaps the coalition's most vulnerable components can be jettisoned. Or a military coup wearily acceded to.

Part 3
Group Politics and Democratic Pluralism in Latin America: Prospects and Weaknesses

4
Peasant and Worker *Sindicatos* and Democracy in Latin America

Neale J. Pearson

Only a small percentage of the working class and the peasantry of Latin America are organized. Perhaps 31 million or 10 percent of the estimated Latin American population of 307 million in 1976 are claimed as members of confederations, *sindicatos, ligas,* cooperatives, and other groups affiliated with or guided by Democratic Leftists, Christian Democrats, Communists, Socialists, and other groups. Many urban inhabitants have only recently migrated from rural areas and small villages, while others work in small shops and retain the attitudes and techniques associated with artisans and small shopkeepers. Industrialization, highway construction, and mass literacy programs have been so recent in many areas that groups that might be part of the proletariat or working class in other parts of the world are still tied to the countryside and near-feudal conditions or attitudes.

A high degree of inequality in landownership and political power characterizes the rural areas in which a majority of the population still lives. This concentration of land ownership in a few hands has contributed to the maintenance of nonegalitarian, nondemocratic societies resistant to change and plagued by (1) a comparatively low average level of living, although the elite landowning and industrialist classes may live in fantastic luxury; (2) great class distinctions between the favored upper class and the masses who lack access to the land; (3) little social mobility; and (4) a population skilled only in the performance, under close supervision, of very limited manual tasks and lacking training and practice in managerial and entrepreneurial work.[1]

While it is true that labor movements developed between 1900 and World War I in the export sectors devoted to mining, petroleum and meat-packing in Argentina, Chile, Mexico, Uruguay and Venezuela, the greatest development of *sindicatos* in both the urban and rural sectors has taken place since World War II as a consequence of a "revolution of rising expectations." The airplane, movies, television, and the transistor radio have paved the way for literacy programs and an increased political and social consciousness in many regions. Industrialization and agricultural modernization, however, have not erased the political, economic and social inequalities that marked the region before World War II (see Table 4.1).

This chapter examines the impact of European ideas such as anarchism and socialism on the labor movement, corporatism's impact on the labor codes promulgated between World War I and II, the impact of national revolutionary movements such as Aprismo, and recent hemisphere-wide labor and peasant organizations. The impact of different social and economic characteristics within nations is examined along with the need for a newer type of labor leader who seeks to improve the economic and social well-being of a particular group, but who also understands that the group's short-range goals are linked to the larger goal of an expanding economy benefitting other groups.

Impact of European and Other Ideologies on Latin American Trade Unionism

Organized labor and organized peasant groups have been highly political from their beginnings in the mid-nineteenth century, when immigrants brought anarcho-syndicalist, socialist, and later Communist-Bolshevik ideas from Great Britain, France, Spain, and Italy.[2] From the beginning there has been controversy over gradualism versus direct action, over the formation of craft unions versus industrialization and an accompanying proletariat, over the utility of collective bargaining and arbitration in the face of systematic persecution and hostility by the organized state. The controversy continues principally between the Inter-American Regional Organization of Workers (ORIT) and its rival, the Latin American Central of Workers (CLAT), over such questions as the type of unionism that should be built within the Latin America of the future, on the nature of outside assistance to unions, and the type of outsiders from whom assistance should be received. The ORIT and its long-term secretary general, Arturo Jauregui (1961-1973), who came from the Peruvian Aprista national revolutionary tradition, believes in a kind of "revolution through evolution." The CLAT and its predecessor, the Latin American Confederation of Christian Syndicalists (CLASC)—led from 1966 to the present by the Argentine Catholic activist, Emilio Maspero—argues in favor of changing the present political and economic order and is much more critical of the United States and the North American labor movement.[3]

Latin American labor and peasant movements did not escape

TABLE 4.1

Population and Per Capita Income of the Americas
in the Mid-1970s

Country/Territory	Est. 1976 Population (1000) [a]	Economically Active (1000) [b] 1974	Per Capita Income [b] 1974 ($US)
Argentina	25,030	10,115 [d]	1,476 (1976)
Bolivia	5,272	2,297 [d]	315 [c]
Brazil	107,613	29,557	723 (1973)
Canada	22,781	8,329	5,672 (1973)
Chile	10,584	2,607	588
Colombia	22,217	5,134	399 (1973)
Costa Rica	1,968	577 [d]	799
Cuba	9,252	2,633 (1970)	358 (1973) [c]
Dominican Rep.	4,697	1,350 (1976)	488
Ecuador	6,705	1,442	474
El Salvador	4,100	1,314	373 (1973)
Guatemala	5,853	1,884	382 (1972)
Guyana	818 [d]	225	525 [d]
Haiti	4,569	--	141 [d]
Honduras	2,749	568	306
Jamaica	1,998	817	1,093 [d]
Mexico	58,075	12,900	997 [c]
Nicaragua	2,153	476	650
Panama	1,668	488 (1970)	935
Paraguay	2,547	586 (1962)	457
Peru	14,819	4,974 [d]	620 [c]
Puerto Rico	2,951 (1975)	880	1,836 (1973) [c]
United States	215,000	93,240	5,941
Uruguay	3,064	971 (1975) [d]	935 (1973)
Venezuela	11,980	700	2,052

Sources: [a] Richard F. Staar (Ed.) Yearbook on International Communist Affairs (Stanford: Hoover Institution Press, 1976), pp. xix-xx.

[b] United Nations Statistical Yearbook, 1975, pp. 87-90.

[c] Calculated by dividing Actual or Estimated Gross National Product for that year by Estimated Population listed for the country in The Americana Annual, 1976.

[d] Calculated from data appearing in Foreign Economic Trends prepared by the United States Embassy for that country.

dependence on imported ideas until sectors of the middle class, especially university students such as Peru's Víctor Raúl Haya de la Torre, developed new analyses and solutions to the problems of their own countries.

Communists, although participating in bloody strikes by Chilean nitrate workers in 1925, by Peruvian petroleum workers in 1930, and by Colombian banana workers in 1938, did not direct nationwide organizations until the late 1930s, when the Communist International encouraged the formation of popular fronts in Chile and other countries and participated in the creation, on September 8, 1938, of the Latin American Workers Confederation (CTAL).

Socialists, Communists, and national revolutionaries of the Democratic Left were joined by Roman Catholic activists in the post-World War II period. The latter group was based on a progressive Catholicism that had its roots in two great encyclicals on social reform: Leo XIII's *Rerum Novarum* (1891) and Pius XI's *Quadragessimo Anno* (1931). Both encyclicals vigorously criticized atheistic socialism—which was to be expected—but they also denounced laissez-faire capitalism and Manchester Liberalism for their exploitation of workers. The two encyclicals vigorously affirmed that Christianity as a religion and the Catholic church as an institution had a right to be concerned with the problems of social justice, poverty, and the misery of the working class.[4] *Rerum Novarum* encouraged the development of "workingmen's associations" although not specifying whether they should consist of workers alone or workers and employers together. Contacts with the ideas of European Catholic social philosophers, such as Jacques Maritain, L. J. Lebret and Emmanuel Mounier, were also important along with the ferment associated with the Vatican II Council. Young Catholic Workers, students and—in a few cases—farm youths were organized into *Juventud Obrera Católica* (JOC), *Juventud Universitaria Católica* (JUC), and *Juventud Agraria Católica* (JAC) in Argentina, Brazil, and Chile. Efforts were made in the 1940s to organize Catholic unions in the textile, metal, and shoe and leather industries in several countries, along with Workers Circles (*Círculos Operários* in Brazil) that emphasized worker solidarity, literacy training, and credit cooperatives.

Probably the most important effort at total community development was the Rural Assistance Service (SAR), organized in the 1950s in Natal, Rio Grande do Norte, Brazil, by Dom Eugenio de Araujo Salles—now Cardinal Archbishop of Rio de Janeiro. SAR's activities included radio schools, literacy programs, and the establishment of *sindicatos* and cooperatives. SAR's success with the radio schools led to the creation of the government-financed Basic Education Movement (MEB), which enlisted the support of university students in many states in 1961-1964. However, MEB's use of the consciousness-raising (*conscientização*) techniques development by Paulo Freire aroused the anger of many conservative military officers and civilians because of references in the program to class struggle and the need to organize for change.[5]

In other states, such as Pernambuco, Rio de Janeiro, and São Paulo, priests organized Workers Circles, cooperatives and *sindicatos* that faced attacks in 1962-1964 by Francisco Julião's *Ligas Camponesas*, the Russian-oriented PCB and Chinese-oriented PC do B factions of the Brazilian Communist Party, and the Ministry of Labor of President João Goulart—all of which were trying to take over the state federations and the National Confederation of Agricultural Workers (CONTAG). Although post-1964 military governments modified the direction of the Brazilian labor and peasant movements after Goulart was ousted, many of the techniques developed by SAR and MEB were later used in Chile, Honduras, and other countries.

International Connections

Since their earliest beginnings in the 1850s, Latin American trade unions have had connections with different international labor and political organizations, which helped—and probably hindered in some cases—their development. Many Americans forget that the U.S. labor movement had similar political and ideological links in the last century.

Worker and peasant groups in Latin America have preserved political tones and ideological orientations much longer than in the United States because they have not achieved adequate living conditions and acceptance as groups involved in the decision making of a pluralistic society.

As early as the 1860s, Latin American affiliates of the International Workingmen's Association (IWMA, or the First International) existed.[6] Frequently they organized the early trade unions of many countries. Efforts by different ideologically inspired groups to create international confederations have been made on many occasions since 1907, when the *Federación Obrera Regional* (FORA) of Argentina sought to do this. Among the more important, albeit short-lived, groups were the Pan-American Federation of Labor, created in 1927 but dead by World War II; the Latin American Syndical Confederation (CSLA), organized at Montevideo in 1929 by Communist-controlled labor groups in conformity with Communist International policy, which called for a separate Communist-dominated labor movement; and the CTAL, organized in 1938 in Mexico. The CTAL was organized for two principal reasons: (1) the Communist International adopted a Popular Front policy of unity among groups fighting "fascism"; and (2) Mexican President Lázaro Cárdenas wanted support in order to fight the efforts of the international oil companies and the British government to isolate his regime because of its nationalization of the foreign-owned oil industry in March 1939.[7] Vicente Lombardo Toledano, secretary-general of the Mexican Workers Confederation (CTM), was elected president and stayed in the post for the twenty-five years of CTAL's existence. During World War II, Lombardo Toledano and the Communists in the CTAL leadership opposed strikes and urged labor to stay on the job so that production might be maintained against the "fascist enemy." However, social and economic unrest persisted during the war as workers sought to deal with inflation and the rising cost of mass transportation.

In Victor Alba's words:

> The labor movement emerged from World War II weakened, divided, and disillusioned, its idealism and its role as social reformer largely dissipated. In several countries, management took upon itself the task of pressing for such measures as social security and workmen's compensation, by way of averting the threat of strikes and heading off incipient revolutions. The unions . . . simply failed to keep pace with the advance of industrialization into new processes and new technologies—to the inevitable detriment of effective union action.[8]

Efforts to organize a rival to the CTAL and the World Federation of Trade Unions (WFTU)—dominated by Communists—resulted in the formation of the Inter-American Confederation of Workers (CIT) at a January, 1948, congress in Lima, Peru. The CIT was later transformed in January, 1951, into ORIT, which was composed principally of groups that left the WFTU to form the International Confederation of Free Trade Unions (ICFTU), such as the American Federation of Labor, Venezuelan Labor Confederation (CTV), Peruvian Labor Confederation (CTP), Costa Rican Labor Confederation (CCT), "Rerum Novarum," the Socialist-controlled unions of Chile's Chilean Labor Confederation (CTCh), and Canada's Trades and Labor Council. Within a short time, the Canadian Congress of Labor, the American CIO, the Mexican Labor Confederation (CTM), the Colombian Labor Confederation (CTC), and several federations in the then-British West Indies also joined ORIT.

"The most serious opposition to the ORIT in the early 1950s came from the Peronistas," according to Robert J. Alexander, one of the early students of the hemisphere's trade union movements.[9] The CIT and ORIT refused to accept Peronista unions because of the Argentine regime's authoritarian nature and instead accepted exiled and underground anti-Perón unions. In response, Perón used his labor attachés in Argentine embassies throughout the hemisphere to try to build a federation. By November 1952, the *Agrupación de Trabajadores Latino Americanos Sindicalizados* (ATLAS) was composed of small central labor groups in Chile, Colombia, Costa Rica, Nicaragua, Panama, Haiti, and Uruguay, and only one large group besides the Argentine *Confederación General del Trabajo* (CGT): the Mexican *Confederación Regional Obrera Mexicana* (CROM). Although ATLAS continued to function after Perón's ouster in September 1955, it was little more than a paper organization.

ORIT went through a severe crisis in the late 1950s and early 1960s over developments in Cuba, which will serve to illustrate the political problems faced by both national and hemispheric organizations. The Cuban Confederation of Workers (CTC) was one of the founders of the ORIT, yet, when a general strike called by the CTC against Fulgencio Batista's seizure of power in March, 1952, failed, the CTC entered into a "kind of armed truce" with the dictator that lasted until Fidel Castro's invasion of Cuba in November, 1956. In 1957-58, CTC leaders opposed a revolutionary strike against Batista because they felt it would lead to the destruction of the trade-union movement; Batista opposed a strike for different reasons. In Alexander's words, "The CTC leaders, therefore, did their utmost to suppress opposition to Batista within their organization. This kind of alliance between the CTC leaders and Batista tended to discredit the labor officials both inside Cuba and elsewhere within Latin America."[10]

After coming to power, Castro's regime ousted those leaders affiliated with the ORIT and sought to launch the Revolutionary Latin American Confederation of Workers. Castro's move failed because his group alienated most Latin American worker-leaders, when (1) the Communist-dominated *Central Unica de Trabajadores de Chile* indicated its interest in joining, and (2) the CTAL said it was willing to dissolve itself so that its affiliates could join Castro's new group.[11]

In 1954, former CTAL members, plus members of the IFCTU had established the *Confederación Latino Americana de Sindicalistas Cristianos* (CLASC). However, as Alexander notes: "The hemisphere's two principal Catholic-oriented national central labor bodies, the *Unión de Trabajadores de Colombia* and the *Confederación Costarricense del Trabajo Rerum Novarum* did not affiliate with the CLASC. Rather, they maintained their membership in the ORIT and ICFTU.

The only central labor bodies which belonged to the CLASC by the time of its Fourth Congress in Caracas in 1962 were small groups in Argentina, Chile, Venezuela, Panama, Peru and Jamaica."[12]

CLASC leaders "insisted that their organization was 'purely Latin American' in spite of the fact that most of its funds came from European Catholic sources," such as the German Christian Foundation, International Solidarity, and the Solidarity Fund of the World Confederation of Labor (WCL), into which the IFCTU transformed itself in November 1971.[13]

Emilio Maspero, CLASC's principal spokesman since 1966, claimed CLASC acted as a third force between the CTAL and Communist-dominated unions on the one hand and ORIT on the other. CLASC was critical of the ORIT and ICFTU because of their links with the AFL-CIO, the American Institute for Free Labor Development (AIFLD) and the United States State Department, though he was not similarly critical of the state of trade unions or the peasantry in Communist countries. In 1962 the IFCTU had dropped the word "Christian" from its title and eventually became the World Confederation of Labor (WCL). The change of CLASC to CLAT in 1971 was a natural, if delayed, consequence of the secular trend of the former Christian world labor movement.

Other manifestations of the importance of outside groups in shaping the destiny of Latin American unionism are the training programs of ORIT, CLASC-CLAT, and various international trade secretariats, such as the Postal, Telephone and Telegraph International (PTTI), political parties, and AIFLD.

In the words of one of the prime movers of democratic unionism in the hemisphere, Serafino Romualdi, founder of AIFLD:

> There was a time when a Latin American labor leader's primary qualification was his ability to sway listeners to his point of view through oratory. Today, he is becoming a source of constructive contributions for the development of the national economy, enabling wage earners to receive a greater share of the ever-growing fruits of their labor. This new type of labor leader cannot be improvised. . . . He must have deep within himself a burning desire to serve his fellow workers, and through them, his own country. But he must also acquire a great deal of technical knowledge and this requires specialized education and intensive study.[14]

Since the statistics on literacy and social infrastructure clearly indicate that the overwhelming majority of the population does not receive this training from the educational systems of its societies—and most Latin American business or government groups have not supported education of potential adversaries—it is only through AIFLD or the Social Promotion programs of the Roman Catholic Church that individuals can obtain this training. The following, by the country program director of the AIFLD in Peru from 1967 to 1969, is not an official statement of AIFLD policy but, rather, one insider's personal attempt to describe and explain an effort that I personally support after having observed similar programs in different countries since 1964:

> The AIFLD in Peru, through its worker [and peasant] education program, has tried to help the Peruvian unions educate the workers to their social tasks so that through a better grasp of the broad social picture, they can surpass their immediate class instincts. In a sense, labor's Centro de Estudios Laborales del Perú (CELP) in Lima has tried to do for the trade union movement what the CAEM has tried to do for the middle-class army professionals, who also had to rise above the traditional conservative view of their own class interests before they could be a key force for reform. In addition to the basic trade union subjects [such as labor history, labor education techniques, collective bargaining, threats to unionism and democracy, economic problems of industry and agriculture, development] the Peruvian unions have . . . insisted on including in the . . . curriculum several courses on social doctrine and economic development. The workers are taught that economic, social, political democracy must form an integral system.[15]

As of March, 1976, 2,008 labor and peasant leaders from seventeen Latin American and Caribbean countries had finished advanced training programs in Front Royal, Virginia, generally designed for the best students completing basic training courses in their own countries.[16]

The success of ORIT, AIFLD, CLASC-CLAT, and affiliated groups in organizing workers and peasants in the hemisphere is shown in Table 4.2.

Types of Organizations

One category of organization is a *sindicato* organized by politicians or government leaders as an instrument of patronage and for support at the polls. These groups, be they urban or rural, are organized by outsiders (middle-class city dwellers, intellectuals, professionals, students, and clergymen) in which low-status clients receive material goods, services, or access to land in return for personal services, obligations to work at lower than normal wages one or more days per week or month, and votes for the candidates of the *patrón, coronel* or local *jefe político*.

This type of organization has long been found in Argentina, Brazil,

TABLE 4.2

Economically Active Population and Membership in National
and Hemispheric Organizations by Ideological Orientation, 1975
(? Indicates Membership Unknown)

Country/ Territory	Econom. Active Pop. 1974[a] (1,000)	Groups & Membership(1,000)[b]		
		Marxist & Communist	ORIT	CLASC-CLAT
Argentina	10,115	MUCS - 1	CGEC-260 CTM - 56 Peronist CGT-62 Bloc not affilliated with any of above CGT-32 Bloc Affiliated with ORIT	ASA - ?
Aruba, Bahamas, Belize & 12 Caribbean Island States	?	?	Carib. Congress of Labor - 215	?
Bolivia	2,292	COB - 200	CNTCB - 5	ASB - 5
Brazil	29,557	Brazilian Confederations Not Permitted to Belong to International Groups. Seven Confederations with 7.5 million members have some links with ORIT		
Canada	8,329	Selected Unions No Federation ?	Canadian Labor Congress 1,900	CNTU -160
Chile	2,607	CUTCh Both groups outlawed Sept. 1973		CGT
Colombia	5,134	CSTO - 200	UTC - 800 and Church-oriented CTC (400) are both Members of ORIT	
Costa Rica	572	CGTC - 3.6	CCTD - 10	CTC - ?
Cuba	2,633 (1970)	CTC - 2,200 ANAP (Peasants) - 170	None	None
Dominican Rep.	1,350	CGT - 4.3	CNTD - 188	CASC - ?
Ecuador	1,442	CTE - 55 FTL - ?	CEOSL - 10 COG - ?	CEDOC 80
El Salvador	1,314	?	CGS - 27 UCS (Peasants) 185	CGTS - 3.5
Guatemala	1,884	FAG - ?	CTF-CSG - 30 FTG - ? MCI - 2.5 (Peasant)	CNT - ?

TABLE 4.2 (Cont.)

Country/ Territory	Econom. Active Pop. 1974[a] (1,000)	Groups & Membership(1,000)[b] Marxist & Communist	ORIT	CLASC-CLAT
Guyana	225	GAWU - ?	TUC - 47	GUYFED - ?
Haiti	?	?	UNOH - 35	FHSC - ?
Honduras	568	PCH Infiltrates Selected Unions	CTH - 58,000 ANACH - 30,000	CGT-FASH 1.8 UNC - 7
Jamaica	817	?	NWUJ+TUC 100 BITU - 100	None Independent
Mexico	12,909	UGOM - 7.5 CROM-CROC -120 each	CTM - 2,120	FAT - ?
Nicaragua	475 (1963)	?	CNT - 4 CUS - 9 CGT - 4	MOSAN-CTN- UTC - 2.5
Panama	488 (1970)	FST - ?	CTRP - 15	ASP-CIT-?
Paraguay	586 (1962)	?	CTP Exile CPT - 40	FTU - ?
Peru	4,974	CGTP - ? Velasco Alvarado Regime (1968-1975) sponsored CTRP and CNA; membership unknown; CNA claimed 1.5 million	CTP - 800	CNT - ?
Puerto Rico	880	?	FTPR - 150 FLTPR - 105	FUTPR - ?
United States	82,897 (1970)	NCFI - ? TUAD - ?	AFL-CIO - 11,507 UAW	None
Uruguay	1,012	CNT declared illegal 1973	CGTU - 15	ASU - 15
Venezuela	3,700	CUTV - ?	CTV - 1,300	CUSIC & CODESA MONTRAL - ?

Source: [a]United Nations Statistical Yearbook, 1975, pp. 87-90 and The Europa Yearbook, 1974, Vol. II, various pages.

[b] Compiled from various sources. The best source of data on Marxist and Communist groups is the Yearbook on International Communist Affairs published by the Hoover Institution on War, Revolution and Peace, Stanford, California

Chile, Guatemala, Honduras, Mexico, Nicaragua, Puerto Rico, and Venezuela. In the 1950s and 1960s examples also appeared in Bolivia and Peru.

In Bolivia, although the National Revolutionary Movement (MNR) had contacts before the 1952 Revolution with a few peasant *sindicatos* led by José Rojas of Ucureña in the department of Cochabamba, it spent much time and effort afterwards organizing peasant unions all over the country into a structure capped by the Confederation of Peasant Workers (CTC).

In the 1930s and the 1940s the Democratic Action Party (AD) in Venezuela, struggling simultaneously to establish a meaningful electoral process and to break the hold of the entrenched traditional elites on governmental power, began to organize the peasantry. After a *golpe de estado* brought AD to power in 1945, access to government and private land was granted to those peasant *sindicatos* organized by the party.

When the AD's Rómulo Betancourt government came to power in 1958 and began to push agrarian reform, it found that the threat of land invasions strengthened the opposition to other reforms and thus became a liability to the government. In the words of John Powell: "The peasant union movement was induced (although it required a purge of radical leaders to consolidate the decision) to renounce land invasion as a means of solving the land problem. Thereafter, local peasant union leaders concentrated on their brokerage and representational functions."[17] (See Table 4.3.)

TABLE 4.3

Representational and Brokerage Activities
of Local Peasant Leaders, Venezuela, 1961-1965

Activity	Percentage (N=118)
Meetings to Discuss Community Problems	80.5%
Helping Members Obtain BAP Credits	78.0
Petitions to Ministry of Education	69.5
Petitions for Land to Agrarian Institute	66.9
Petitions for Rural Housing Projects	66.1
Petitions for Penetration Roads	65.3
Petitions for Public Health Projects	65.3
Organization of Educational Programs	37.3
Organization of Social Events	36.4
Sponsoring Athletic Activities	24.6

Source: John Duncan Powell, "Venezuela: The Peasant Union Movement," in Henry A. Landsberger (Ed.) <u>Latin American Peasant Movements</u> (Ithaca, New York: Cornell University Press, 1969), p. 75.

In Brazil, the *Movimento dos Agricultores sem Terra* (Landless Workers Movement, or MASTER) began in 1958 as a genuine protest group of landless agricultural laborers in Encruzilhada do Sol, Rio Grande do Sul. It was, however, taken over by Governor (and later Federal Deputy) Leonel Brizola, who used it to mobilize votes for candidates of the Brazilian Labor Party (PTB) and to force landowners to sell land to himself or his friends.

In the Brazilian northeast, the first *Liga Camponesa* (Peasant League) was organized by tenants on the Galileia Plantation in Vitôria de Santo Antão, Pernambuco. When the owner and his son tried to evict them, the tenants were guided to Francisco Julião de Arruda Paula, a lawyer-politician landowner elected to the State Assembly as an alternate deputy for the Brazilian Socialist Party (PSB). Julião then transformed himself from a politician with a modest peasant following, for whom he provided limited services, into a charismatic leader manipulating modern publicity techniques that brought him national and international attention. Many of the leaders affiliated with Julião in other states were, in fact, large landowners seeking expropriation of the land of political opponents, either as a punitive measure or as a means of acquiring land for themselves. These "peasant" leaders provided their peasant followers with protection, dental, and medical services similar to those furnished by other traditional land-owner politicians.

In Mexico, the dominant Revolutionary Institutional Party (PRI) organized the National Peasant Confederation (CNC) to mobilize and channel the aspirations of peasants who previously participated in guerrilla groups led by "Pancho" Villa and Emiliano Zapata. The CNC has not always been a satisfactory broker for peasant demands because the lack of arable land, water, and low prices are frequently beyond its control. A consequence has been that toward the end of every presidential term, uprisings and occupation of public and private land erupt in different states. These incidents are staged to pressure an outgoing or incoming president to distribute land. Probable collusion exists between squatters and PRI/government officials. In 1963-1964, 1969-1970, and 1974-1976, clashes took place in Chihuahua, Hidalgo, Oaxaca, and Vera Cruz between state or federal police, landowners, and squatters who said they had been promised land by the PRI for many years. Although President Díaz's government distributed 12,307,000 hectares in 1964-1970—second only to the amount distributed by Lázaro Cádenas in 1934-1940—much of it was located in isolated desert areas without water. His successor, President Echeverría, expropriated several hundred thousand acres of irrigated land in northwest Mexico in late 1976 after squatters' occupations. Opposition by landowners and their allies in the Monterrey banking community resulted in the expropriations being nullified.

A second form of organization is the armed militia. Peasants in Bolivia, Brazil, Colombia, and Mexico and miners in Bolivia and Peru have organized paramilitary groups to defend themselves against the arbitrary actions of government officials, landowners, rural judiciary and the police—whom landowners or industrialists frequently control—or against the destruction of hired thugs who roam the countryside.

In Peru, the military regime of General Juan Velasco Alvarado organized the Central Organization of Workers of the Peruvian Revolution (CTRP) to compete with the Aprista-dominated Peruvian Workers Confederation (CTP) and the General Confederation of Workers of Peru (CGTP), organized by the Peruvian Communist Party three months before the October coup that brought in Velasco's reformist regime. Nevertheless, despite having received government support, the CTRP still ranked second to the CGTP as Peru's largest central labor organization, in part because the Velasco regime also treated the Communist-dominated group sympathetically. These two groups—plus the small Catholic-oriented National Worker's Confederation (CNT) and the new National Confederation of Agricultural Workers (CNA)—defended the government's June, 1975, austerity measure, which generated discontent among organized labor and peasant groups. The role of the CTRP and the CNA have been reduced since the August 29, 1975, coup that brought General Francisco Morales Bermúdez to power, while the influence of the CTP, which did not defend those austerity measures, has increased once again.

Urban worker and peasant unions also exist whose function is the protection and advancement of their interests against business organizations, government agencies, landowners, labor contractors, and rural middlemen. Peasant unions have also been concerned about the contractual practices of farmed land, crop prices, and owner-government determination of crops to be planted and their market prices. These groups are most numerous and active in Argentina, Brazil, Chile (before the September 1973, coup that ousted Allende), Colombia, Costa Rica, Guyana, Honduras, Mexico, Jamaica, Peru, Uruguay (before 1973), and Venezuela.

Peasant *sindicatos* may have been formed originally with the assistance of outside clergymen, political parties, or government officials, but many have grown sufficiently strong to remain somewhat independent of their founders and have improved their bargaining power from what was originally an unequal patron-client relationship. Probably the most successful examples are the Peasant Confederation of

Venezuela (CCV), the Banana Workers of the North Coast Federation of Workers in Honduras, and the Manpower Citizens Association (MPCA) in Guyana.

Factors Affecting the Success of Urban Worker and Peasant Groups

Several factors contribute to the success or limited achievements of these groups. No single factor is dominant. A complicated set of relationships is found, not the least of which is a nation's labor code and the conditions under which labor movements are permitted to operate.

1. Workers tend to be highly unionized in enterprises that are heavily capitalized and in which few alternate sources of products exist in world markets. The copper miners of Chile and Peru, the tin miners of Bolivia, the bauxite workers of Guyana and Jamaica, bank employees, and workers in the petroleum and steel industry come to mind. In the rural sector, wage or salaried employees, or multinational firms producing banana, coffee, and sugar, have become highly unionized. These groups can exert pressure on firms and governments dependent on foreign exchange earnings from primary products, in contrast to those workers in industries that have little impact on a country's export earnings.

2. Those agricultural or manufacturing establishments that concentrate large numbers of workers in one or a few locales are more likely to have employees who develop common interests. The traditional paternalistic bonds between owners and artisans or owners and peasants are weakened when owners live in a city or in another country and an administrator is in charge of a factory or *hacienda*. The administrators of a *hacienda* or *estancia* are frequently former workers and are psychologically unequipped to assume the paternalistic roles of the owner, and certainly have only limited power to make decisions that cost money.

The large-scale corporation frequently must resort to collective bargaining, not only because the old personal relationships are gone but also because employees are separated by a hierarchy of foremen, plant superintendents, and so forth.

3. Wages tend to be lower for workers in small shops or small agricultural enterprises in which the owner is neither physically nor psychologically separated from employees; *sindicatos* are less numerous because paternalistic favors and controls can be maintained. Wages are higher in large organizations with hierarchy and diversified work forces; these firms also show a greater tendency to have *sindicatos.*

These phenomena can be illustrated in two ways. In the mid-1960s

Henry Landsberger used 1964 data to calculate the following ratios for industrial employers plus self-employed artisans, compared to industrial wage and salary earners for different countries:[18]

United States	1:50
United Kingdom	1:35
France	1:10
Mexico	1:4
Venezuela	1:2
Ecuador	1:2/3

Another way of demonstrating this is to use data for manufacturing firms of different sizes in a single country. Table 4.4 shows that nearly 80 percent of the Brazilian manufacturing firms with less than 50 workers employed only 20 percent of the total manufacturing work force and paid only 14.7 percent of the total wages. On the other hand, the 3.8 percent of firms with more than 250 workers employed 51 percent of the work force and paid 59.9 percent of the wages. The data show that the larger the firm, the greater the ability and tendency to pay higher wages—a fact that *sindicato* bargaining representatives use to their advantage.

4. The formation and continued existence of organized worker pressure groups is related to the modernization process of a society. The increasing diversification and complexity of a society is dependent upon, and contributes to, increased literacy and a more complex social structure, leading to the development of different skills, including leadership and bargaining skills. We can see this to some degree in Tables 4.5 and 4.6, which deal with two groups of Brazilian states—one group in the underdeveloped northeast, the second in the more modern south. Some parts of São Paulo and Rio Grande do Sul have industrial complexes equal to those found in the United States and Western Europe. In the Northeast, only Recife, Pernambuco, has a large skilled work force, and that is due to a Volkswagen assembly plant and other factories established in the 1960s. Table 4.5 shows that the south has a greater ratio of urban and rural *sindicatos* per *municipio*, with larger membership per *sindicato* than the northeast, with the exception of Pernambuco, whose automobile, sugar, and textile industries are the largest and most unionized in the northeast.

Table 4.6 shows the southern states with higher population densities, higher literacy rates, and a greater number of Catholic and Protestant groups at the parish level than the northeastern states. Rio Grande do Sul has a lower population density than the other southern states be-

TABLE 4.4

Numbers and Wages of Employees by Size of Firm,
Brazilian Industries of Transformation, 1966

No. of Employees	No. of Firms	Total Employees	Total Wages (1,000)	Average Wages (Cruzeiros)
1-4	7,431	20,731	23,920	1,153.82
5-9	8,835	58,378	67,990	1,164.65
10-19	7,126	97,505	133,091	1,364.96
20-49	6,869	211,971	326,223	1,541.18
. . .	. . .	. . .	. . .	. . .
250-499	828	286,573	557,528	1,945.50
500-999	430	297,415	604,145	2,031.32
1,000 +	189	389,312	1,068,420	2,772.87
Totals	38,013	1,885,077	3,744,744	1,986.52 Aver.

Source: Calculated from data in Anuário Estatístico do Brasil, 1970 (Rio de Janeiro: Fundação IBGE, Instituto Brasileiro de Estatística, 1970), p. 145.

Note: Brazilian statistics separate metallurgical workers from industrial transformation workers for unknown reasons. In any case, metallurgical workers in the largest establishments --more than 250 employees--also earn higher average wages -2,783 Cruzeiros--than workers in the smallest establishments employing less than 50 workers-1,893 Cruzeiros. This data is calculated from material in the 1970 Anuário Estatístico do Brasil, p. 147.

cause its lower half is composed of huge cattle and sheep *estancias* covering more than 1,000 hectares (2,470 acres) each, and this land use dilutes the heavy population density found north and west of Pôrto Alegre, the state capital, and the interior agro-industrial city of Santa Maria. Santa Catarina still has many large forests.

In the northeast there was a great dependence on priests and lawyers in the formation of rural *sindicatos* and cooperatives through 1959-1964 because of the lack of rural schools and male teachers of a peasant or small-farmer background who were important leaders in the south during the same period. The importance of priests in the northeast is indicated by the fact that I found northeast *municipios* without priests and, in 1964-65, *municipios* with a priest and no *sindicato*, but not one *sindicato* that did not have a sympathetic priest advising the peasant leadership.

On the other hand, I found many small farmer and rural-worker *sindicatos* and cooperatives in the south that functioned without the aid

TABLE 4.5

Population, Municipios, Federations, and Sindicatos of
Urban and Rural Workers in Selected Brazilian Regions, 1969

Region and State	Population[a] 1960(1,000)	Municipios[b] 1960	Municipios[b] 1969[c]	Federations of Employers	Federations of Employees[d]	Urban Sindicatos No.	Urban Sindicatos Members[d]	Rural Worker/ Small Farmer Sindicatos[e]
Northeast								
Alagoas	1,271	69	94	2	1	32	17,794	14
Paraíba	2,018	88	171	3	1	36	8,519	50
Pernambuco	4,137	102	164	4	7	65	108,217	98
Rio Grande do Norte	1,157	82	150	3	2	50	12,582	59
South								
Guanabara (Rio de Janeiro)	3,307	1	1	15	28	102	347,415	0
Rio de Janeiro	3,403	62	63	4	6	117	101,919	33
Rio Grande do Sul	5,449	152	232	7	12	252	122,867	230
Santa Catarina	2,147	104	197	3	6	139	45,622	149(1971)
São Paulo	12,975	506	571	—	19	419	702,610	74

Sources: [a]Anuário Estatístico, 1970 (Rio de Janeiro, Fundação-IBGE Instituto Brasileiro de Estatística), p. 37.

[b]Anuário Estatístico, 1961 (Rio de Janeiro, IBGE-Conselho Nacional de Estatística), p. 413.

[c]Anuário Estatístico, 1970, p. 713. The increased number of Municipios in 1969 over 1960 is the consequence of the constant creation of new Municipios (desmembramento) by local and state authorities out of existing urban areas and surrounding rural areas because of (1) revenue-sharing legislation that guarantees each municipal government a guaranteed minimum income, and (2) political opportunities to become prefeitos, council members and municipal employees. The creation of a new Municipio, however, does not also mean the creation of a new sindicato. Therefore, the 1961 figures are used.

[d]Anuário Estatístico, 1970, pp. 556-557.

[e]Compiled by the author.

TABLE 4.6

Population Density, Literacy, and Social Group
Infrastructure in Selected Brazilian States, 1959-1960

Region and State	Population[a] 1960(1,000)	Density Per Sq. Km.[a]	Literacy 1950[b]	Catholic & Prot. Rel. Assns[c]	Ratio of Pop. to Each Assn.
Northeast					
Alagoas	1,271	45.8	24%	354	1/3590
Paraíba	2,018	35.8	29	572	1/3528
Pernambuco	4,137	42.1	32	1,425	1/2903
Rio Grande do Norte	1,157	21.8	32	427	1/2709
South					
Guanabara (Rio de Jan)	3,307	2,438.8	85	1,460	1/2265
Rio de Janeiro	3,403	79.3	56	2,019	1/1685
Rio Grande do Sul	5,449	19.3	66	2,756	1/1477
Santa Catarina	2,146	22.4	64	1,289	1/1665
São Paulo	12,975	52.3	65	7,329	1/1770

Sources: [a] Calculated from data in *Anuário Estatístico, 1970*, pp. 18 and 37.
[b] Calculated from data in *Anuário Estatístico, 1961*, pp. 359-360.
[c] Calculated from data in *Anuário Estatístico, 1961*, pp. 398 and 400.

of a local priest or protestant pastor. In fact, I visited *sindicatos* that functioned despite the opposition or indifference of local priests and pastors. The greater social diversity in those villages and rural areas with primary schools and male teachers meant a larger resource pool for local leaders.

Tables 4.4-4.6 also implicitly raise the question of increased political participation and the modernization process. It is sufficient to say that political participation—including the election of the opposition to federal, state, and local office—has been much greater in the south than the northeast for many years.

It is useful to compare literacy data and other statistics within a given country to similar information in another country. For this purpose I have used Venezuela, a relatively developed nation with a sophisticated peasant and industrial worker leadership that has been functioning since the late 1930s, and Honduras, a relatively underdeveloped nation whose union movement did not really begin until a banana worker strike against the United Fruit Company in May-June 1954 established the right to bargain collectively. Census data reveal that only 32.5

percent of the Venezuelan population was rural in 1950, compared to 76 percent of the Honduran population in 1961.[19] Although 48.7 percent of the Venezuelan population was illiterate in 1950, government programs reduced that number to 10.9 percent by 1965. In contrast, 46.7 percent of the rural Honduran population over ten years of age in 1974 was still illiterate.[20] See Table 4.7.

Table 4.7 also shows the higher levels of education of Venezuelan peasant leaders in the early 1960s, compared to the limited education of most Honduran peasant leaders in 1970-71.

Given the illiteracy of the Honduran peasantry in general, and the lack of schooling of peasant leaders in particular, how does one explain the formation of Honduran peasant pressure groups?

The rise and fall of the Arbenz regime in Guatemala (1951-54) coupled with an "enclosure movement" by Honduran and Salvadoran cotton farmers of public land and private land of dubious title created a land pressure unknown before World War II. Responding to these pressures, the Honduran Catholic church launched a radio literacy program in the

TABLE 4.7

Comparative Education of Peasants and Leaders in Venezuela and Honduras

Level of Education	Venezuela a (1961-1966)			Honduras	
	Asentados (N=191)	Leaders		1961 Pop. Over 10 Years[b]	1971 Peasant Leaders[c] (N=241)
		Local (N=118)	National (N=24)		
Illiterates	0	0	0	50.3%	0
No Schooling	66.5%	30.5%	0	0	40.9%
Some Primary (Ven.) 1-3 Years (Hon.)	23.6	45.7	4.1%	29.1	44.0
Four to Five Years	--	--	--	9.2	12.5
Complete Primary	1.4	18.6	61.5	2.7	--
Some Secondary or More	0.5	4.2	32.8	4.0	1.6
Unknown	--	--	--	4.7	--

Sources: [a]John Duncan Powell, "The Peasant Union Movement," p. 81. Asentados were residents of government agrarian reform settlements (asentamientos) from whom a sample was taken.
[b] Compiled from data in Problemas Económicos de Honduras (Tegucigalpa, D. C., Instituto de Investigaciones Sociales Facultad de Ciencias Económicas, Universidad Nacional Autonoma de Honduras, 1967), pp. 48-49.
[c] Martha O. Brown and Olga Elvir Hernandez, "Las Invasiones Campesinas Como Fenomeno Social en La Reforma Agraria," Tesis de Grado para Optar el Titulo de Trabajador Social, (Tegucigalpa, D. C., Universidad Nacional Autonoma, Noviembre 1971), p. 33.

departments of Choluteca and Valle on the Pacific Coast in 1960-1961.[21] Although originally intended to combat illiteracy, the People's Promotion Movement discovered the peasants' lack of organization and dependence on authoritarian local *caudillos*. Canadian priests, American Peace Corps volunteers, and Hondurans developed not only literacy programs but also credit unions and 1,000 homemaker clubs linked to international development agencies and urban allies—bypassing traditional paternalistic relations with the large landowners. In effect, the church and other agencies provided a technical knowledge and specialized education similar to that which Romualdi had called for in establishing the AIFLD to prepare new types of labor leaders. In the Honduran case, Christian Social Action organized an estimated 15,323 peasants into sixty-six peasant leagues affiliated with the National Peasant Union (UNC) by June, 1971.

In a parallel development, General Secretary Celeo González of the United Fruit Company's SITRATERCO union and other North Coast labor leaders met with Andrew McLelland, an associate inter-American representative of the AFL-CIO, to discuss organizing the peasants to protect the long-range self-interest of urban workers and to promote the economic and social welfare of the peasantry as consumers of industrial goods. Various peasant leaders were sent to basic training courses of ORIT and AIFLD in Guatemala, Costa Rica, Colombia, and Mexico, and to advanced training at the AIFLD center at Front Royal, Virginia. By mid-1973, the National Association of Honduran Peasants (ANACH) claimed 25,000 members in 300 subsections with about 5,000 paying entrance fees of 50 *centavos* ($.25) and monthly dues of 1 *lempira* ($.50).

From 1968 to 1972, the impact of modernization on Honduras further transformed economic and political forces in the country, even as it experienced economic difficulties in the Central American Common Market, a short-lived war with El Salvador, and the demise of a political agreement (the *Plan Político* of 1971) between the military, popular forces, and the traditional political parties. By 1972, *campesino* organizations realized that only extreme pressure tactics, such as threatened "hunger marches" and occupation of land bearing questionable title, gained a response from the government. In October 1975, the UNC and ANACH joined the Federation of Agrarian Reform Cooperatives (FECORAH) to form a United Peasant Front (FUC) whose immediate goals were the release of peasant leaders imprisoned as part of the government's reaction to land invasions and support for Lt. Colonel Mario Maldonado, the 1974-1975 director of the National Agrarian Institute, who supported the peasant demands for land.[22] Although Chief of State Melgar Castro later fired Maldonado for his alleged complicity in a plan to occupy unused public lands, Melgar Castro sought peasant support by replacing him with a director who continued the process of implementing the January, 1975, Agrarian Reform Law. Between January, 1973, and September, 1976, 44,700 families received title to 141,867 hectares of land. In 1977, the process of land distribution slowed as the agrarian institute underwent a change of top leadership, but the three principal peasant organizations in the United Peasant Front obtained agreement from the new INA leadership on June 24, 1977, that they would participate in INA's future planning and programs. As Table 4.8 shows, there is a high relationship between the organization of peasant groups belonging to ANACH and the distribution of land by INA between 1973 and 1976. The table shows that those regions and departments with many ANACH groups had more land distributed, while those regions and departments with few ANACH groups had little land distributed. Statistical tests would be even more valid if UNC data were available.

Labor Codes and Government Controls

A labor code has been enacted in nearly every Latin American nation, but—like most social legislation—was not the product of labor agitation for such but, rather, resulted from the coming to power of national-revolutionary or middle-class populist groups, such as the **Peruvian Apristas, or dictatorships that used the 1930 Model Labor Code** of the International Labor Organization as a model for their own purposes.[23] These codes have had two functions in the long run: (1) they guarantee labor the right to organize and establish minimum conditions of work, vacations, pensions, dismissals, etc.; and (2) they give the government control over bargaining or mediation processes as well as the power to recognize and regulate labor and peasant organizations. In effect, the codes were drafted by elites and not by workers or peasants; labor's power was coopted and subject to government control.

The political history and economic development of a nation determine the differences between countries and the variations within a given country. In Argentina, Robert Alexander notes that the Peronista experience contributed to the "negotiation of nationwide industrial contracts between organizations of employers and the national unions of their workers. . . . All attempts . . . to modify this pattern since 1955 have failed."[24] On the other hand, in Mexico and many other countries, collective agreements govern the petroleum, electric, and railroad industries nationwide but there are also regional contracts and contracts with individual firms.

TABLE 4.8

Relationship of Municipios with ANACH Groups Sending
Delegates to Seventh Intermediate Congress, September 28-30, 1977,
and Land Distributed in Amounts and Families, Honduras

Region and Departments	Percent of Municipios w/Delegates and Rank[a]		Percent of Land Distr. by INA & Rank 1973-1976[b]		Percent of Families Rec. Land and Rank 1973-1976[b]	
Aguán-North Atlantida-Colon	62.5%	1	31%	2	32%	1
Sula-Northwest Cortes, Santa Barbara & Yoro	50.0%	2	35%	1	26%	2
South Choluteca-Valle	28.0%	3	10%	3	14%	3
Northeast Olancho	18.2%	4	7%	4	8%	6
Western Copan, Intibucá, Lempira & Ocotopeque	13.4%	5	7%	4	4%	7
West-Central Comayagua, Franc. Morazán & La Paz	9.2%	6	6%	6	8%	4
East Central El Paraíso	5.6%	7	7%	5	8%	5
Totals	22.8% (63 of 276)		100% 141,867 Hectares		100% 44,700 Families	

Sources: [a]Percent of Municipios with Delegates Calculated from "Lista de Delegados Asistente a La VII Convencion Nacional Intermedia ANACH, Celebrada 28, 29 y 30 Septiembre 1977."

[b] Data on Land Distributed and Percent of Families Receiving Land within each INA Region is taken from a Table in *Plan Operativo Anual 1977* (Tegucigalpa, D. C., Honduras: Instituto Nacional Agrario, Junio 1977), p. 3.

A Spearman Rank-Correlation Test made for me by Roland Smith showed the following: ANACH Bases with Land: $r = .8214$ ($p = .012$)
ANACH Bases with Families: $r = .7143$ ($p = .036$)

In most countries, the structure and activities of unions are subject to government supervision. When unions need legal or official recognition before they can participate in collective bargaining or conciliation proceedings, governments control the leadership of those unions. In Brazil and many other countries, one finds a principle of institutional unity or union monopoly in the labor code that states that only one organization can represent each occupational group in a *municipio* or state. This principle can be and has been a real threat to the individual or group that dissents from the politics of the minister of labor, interior, or a national confederation. In Brazil, for instance, the term *pelego*, or "corrupt careerist," has been applied to those professional labor leaders who looked out more for their own interests and the interests of a government or firm interested in social peace than the interests of the members. In the words of one frank and cynical industrialist: "Don't think that the *pelegos* were created only by the [Vargas] government. We created them and we maintain them.... We will concede more benefits to workers represented by a *pelego*, because if we don't he may be replaced by some radical."[25]

In the Brazilian case, government officials insisted after the 1964 *golpe* ousting João Goulart that labor and peasant organizations comply with requirements that leadership posts be filled by genuine workers or peasants and not by outsiders. Given the fact that the government closely supervises the collection and disbursement of dues—and that most *sindicatos* are not self-supporting on the basis of membership dues alone—most *sindicatos* and federations need government approval to obtain the funds necessary to staff offices and hire attorneys to bargain with employers, or to represent individuals in court cases. In a few cases, such as Peru, labor leaders affiliated with the Aprista Party have worked underground for many years because of government harassment or refusal to grant juridical personality. In Honduras, groups affiliated with the Christian Democratic affiliated General Confederation of Workers (CGT) or the National Peasant Union have not been recognized by the Ministry of Labor and other government institutions. Their ability to function as brokers on behalf of their members is thereby reduced. A group must therefore be highly motivated ideologically if it is to operate "outside the law" and depend on dues of $.20 per month from workers or peasants earning $1.50 per day.

Internal Democracy and Leadership Turnover

Many American journalists and social scientists have been concerned about the lack of internal democracy within many U.S. trade unions, although they have not been as concerned about similar conditions within the bar and medical associations, the Farm Bureau, or the National Association of Manufacturers. In Latin America, some writers have been critical of Fidel Velásquez, long-term secretary-general of the Mexican CTM, who has held a position analogous that that of George Meany of the AFL-CIO—this in a society whose revolutionary rhetoric has included "no re-election" for the holders of elective political offices. One encounters similar criticism of Argentine, Brazilian and Honduran labor/peasant leaders, but few suggestions have surfaced as to how these leaders might gain the experience and bargaining skills of government or management officials.

Nevertheless, there is turnover in the leadership of many organizations and some opportunity for internal democracy that did not exist in the past—in great part because of the efforts of AIFLD and church-sponsored leadership training groups. In Brazil, for example, only five persons of twenty-four or 20.8 percent serving on the national executive committee of the Agricultural Workers Confederation (CONTAG) in 1965-68, were still in office in 1971. In São Paulo, only 14 (15.5 percent) presidents of ninety rural worker/small farmer *sindicatos* in 1965 were reelected in 1968 and 1971. It is difficult to determine how many may not have sought reelection because they were tired of their responsibilities or how many may have been pressured by labor or military officials not to run for office again. In any case, executive continuity was minimal.

Conclusion

Developments in communications, the spread of literacy, and the evolution of industry and agriculture in the twentieth century have brought profound changes to the economic, political, and social structures of Latin America. Worker and peasant *sindicatos* have evolved to where many of them, in Victor Alba's words:

> are no longer trade unions, as in years past, but industrial unions, with consequent problems—of organization, of administration, of relations with the state and with management organizations—that go beyond the knowledge and training of the peasant leaders. Unless they are represented by labor experts (who, by definition, cannot know or feel the life of the workingman, or reflect it in union negotiations), the unions need leaders who not only live the life of the union man, but possess intelligence, a breadth of knowledge, a certain economic and social vision, and diplomacy—and such men are of course rare.[26]

There is evidence that organizations such as ORIT, which elected José del Pino, a Venezuelan petroleum worker leader, as its new secretary general in April 1977 are adapting to the circumstances of what Alba called the Second Industrial Revolution, when multinational corporation power increased with industrial automation and agricultural mechanization in Andean, Central American, and Caribbean nations. Many organizations have not adapted to these new circumstances.

There are many honest leaders who resist the temptations of managerial or government bribery and extortion, but the *pelego* is "both cause and effect of bureaucratization which, being unplanned, has left orphaned the peasant turned industrial worker," to quote Alba.[27] Those *sindicatos* are most likely to survive whose leadership training courses stress democracy as both a goal and process, emphasize the role of *sindicatos* as instruments of social reform in both the short and long run, and give their leaders and members a greater understanding of the need for outside experts.

In many countries, labor disputes are handled constructively. Government bureaucracies employ lower- and middle-level administrators who do not remember or care about the ideological fights of the 1930s or 1950s and who may share the social justice values of the 1960s and 1970s.[28] Industrialists, agricultural entrepreneurs, middle-class academicians, and students need to know more about the history and conditions of the laboring and peasant classes in their societies and to accept their contributions to the welfare of their nation now and in the future. Given the implications of traditional belief systems of entrepreneurs who see their traditional worlds being "destroyed" and unable to adapt to newer circumstances, political creativity and "statesmanship" will be necessary if Latin American societies are to avoid the bloodshed characteristic of Guatemala and Chile in recent years.[29]

Notes

1. T. Lynn Smith, *Brazil, People and Institutions* (Baton Rouge: Louisiana State University Press, 1963), p. 318.

2. Robert J. Alexander, *Organized Labor in Latin America* (New York: The Free Press, 1965), pp. 7-8 and 18-24, and Victor Alba, *Politics and the Labor Movement in Latin America* (Stanford: Stanford University Press, 1968), pp. 30-197, are the best English-language sources of material on different European and North American ideas.

3. Carroll Hawkins, *Two Democratic Labor Leaders in Conflict, The Latin American Revolution and the Role of the Workers* (Lexington, Mass.: D. C. Heath and Company, 1973), is probably the best account of the differing ideas of Jauregui and Maspero.

4. Henry A. Landsberger, "Chile: A Vineyard Workers' Strike—A Case Study

Peasant and Worker Sindicatos *and Democracy*

of the Relationship between Church, Intellectuals, and Peasants," in Henry A. Landsberger (ed.), *Latin American Peasant Movements* (Ithaca: Cornell University Press, 1969), pp. 257-261, and Howard Wiarda, "The Corporative Origins of the Iberian and Latin American Labor Relations Systems," a monograph published by the Labor Relations and Research Center (Amherst: University of Massachusetts, 1976), p. 3.

    5. MEB, *Viver é Lutar (2a Livro de Leitura Para Adultos)*, Outbro 1963, was the second of several books used by MEB personnel in the Radio School Literacy Programs. One Fourth Army intelligence officer told me in August 1965 in Recife, Pernambuco, that the contents of this publication was sufficient to justify the coup that ousted Goulart. The booklet not only taught illiterates traditional words such as "house" and "school" but also included such concepts as "community," "justice," and "exploitation of Brazil by foreigners."

The first MEB publication, *Saber Para Viver*, never aroused any controversy, probably because of its modest political content.

    6. Alexander, *op. cit.*, p. 242.
    7. Ibid., p. 246.
    8. Alba, *op. cit.*, p. 210.
    9. Alexander, *op. cit.*, p. 251.
    10. Ibid., p. 255.
    11. Ibid., pp. 255-256.
    12. Ibid., p. 260.
    13. Hawkins, *op. cit.*, pp. 3-4, discusses the sources of funding of both ORIT and CLASC-CLAT in general terms but not in specific amounts.

    14. Serafino Romualdi, "AIFLD—An Experiment in Labor Education," in *Presidents and Peons, Recollections of a Labor Ambassador in Latin America* (New York: Funk & Wagnalls, 1967), p. 417.

    15. William A. Douglas, "U.S. Labor Policy in Peru—Past and Future," in Daniel A. Sharp (ed.), *U.S. Foreign Policy and Peru* (Austin: University of Texas Press, 1972), pp. 323-324.

    16. "Front Royal Graduates The 2000 Participant," AIFLE Report, April-May 1976, p. 3.

    17. John Duncan Powell, "Venezuela: The Peasant Union Movement," in Landsberger, *Latin American Peasant Movements*, p. 75.

    18. Henry A. Landsberger, "The Labor Elite: Is It Revolutionary?" in Seymour Martin Lipset and Aldo Solari, *Elites in Latin America* (New York: Oxford University Press, 1967), p. 288.

    19. Harry Kantor, *Patterns of Politics and Political Systems in Latin America* (Chicago: Rand McNally, 1969), p. 349, for Venezuela; figure for Honduras calculated from data in Cuadros nos. 17 and 18, *Problemas Económicos de Honduras* (Tegucigalpa, D. C.: Instituto de Investigaciones Económicos y Sociales, Facultad de Ciencias Económicas, Universidad Nacional Autónoma de Honduras, 1967), pp. 48-49.

    20. Dirección General de Estadística y Censos, *Censo Nacional de Población* (Tegucigalpa, Honduras, Tomo I, Noviembre de 1976), p. 58.

    21. Robert A. White, *Mass Communications and the Popular Promotion*

Strategy of Rural Development in Honduras (Stanford: Stanford Research Institute, 1976), p. 20, and Neale J. Pearson, "Peasant Pressure Groups and Agrarian Reform in Honduras Under Civilian and Military Regimes, 1962-1973," a paper presented at the Rocky Mountain Social Science Association, El Paso, Texas, April 25-27, 1974, p. 20.

22. James A. Morris, "Political Modernization in Honduras: The Evolution of Campesino Organizations," a paper presented at the Rocky Mountain Council on Latin American Studies, Tucson, Arizona, April 7-9, 1977, p. 5.

23. Alba, *op. cit.*, p. 212; Alexander, *op. cit.*, pp. 25-26; and Wiarda, *op. cit.*, pp. 11-16.

24. Alexander, *op. cit.*, p. 26.

25. Philipe C. Schmitter, *Interest Conflict and Political Change in Brazil* (Stanford: Stanford University Press, 1971), p. 129 footnote.

26. Alba, *op. cit.*, pp. 343-344.

27. Ibid., p. 343.

28. Wiarda, *op. cit.*, p. 35; on p. 41, he notes the need to analyze labor relations in revolutionary societies such as Cuba, Peru, Chile [during the Allende period], and Portugal.

29. On June 28, 1977, Fernando Larrizabal, president of the Honduran Cattlemen's Association (FENAGH), told me that he was convinced the Melgar Castro regime wanted to "liquidate" his "class." Larrizabal, who graduated with a bachelor's degree in agriculture from the University of Nebraska in the 1950s, has lived in both the "traditional" Honduran and "modern" North American agricultural and political worlds.

5
Women, Population Policy, and Democracy in Latin America

Iêda Siqueira Wiarda

In recent decades, and especially since the advent of a socialist Cuba, there has been an unprecedented outpouring of research and writings on Latin America. While this is certainly a welcome development, the portion of this research and writing specifically devoted to Latin American women is still miniscule and, more often than not, overburdened by myths and preconceptions that no longer—if they ever did—apply.[1] A well-known historian concluded, after a painstaking survey, that "the abundant literature on twentieth-century Latin America contains few references to the fundamental—even 'revolutionary'—changes now affecting over half its population: women."[2]

A brief examination of doctoral dissertations on Latin America just as clearly indicates that women have, until very recently, been totally neglected. Even the newer, "revolutionary" literature, largely written by men, has been remiss in its examination of some of the most "revolutionary" processes taking place in the role and status of women, in the open questioning of old traditions, in the emergence of a myriad of women's organizations, and in the unprecedented appearance of the female labor organizer, the female scientific researcher, and the female political leader. The militants' passionate discussions on the need for a revolution in the structure of Latin American society almost always concerns economic and political issues; practically no militant of note can be said to have paid much attention to the part women can and do play in both reforms and revolutions. Indeed, in this respect, "revolutionary" leaders are often accused by their ideological sisters as being among the most *macho* where women's issues are concerned.

Cuba is being specifically omitted from this survey. The author would like to acknowledge the very helpful comments of Judith F. Helzner, Pathfinder Fund; Susan Bourque, Smith College; and Kay Warren, Mount Holyoke College on an earlier version of this chapter. The author is solely responsible, of course, for whatever views and information are presented herein.

A similar situation exists in relation to population research and action and women. For a number of years researchers and activists in the population policy process have been seeking to implant family planning programs in Latin America and to find effective ways of reaching the "target" group, i.e., Latin American women in their fertile years. There has been considerable accomplishment, and a number of countries have now either a laissez-faire attitude toward family planning or even an official population policy program. The "implantation" of family planning is, however, far from realized. Often, the very countries that are the largest recipients of international funds for population-related activities are also the ones that seem the farthest from "democratizing"—from actually including women in the population policy process and/or actually reaching large numbers of fertile women.

This situation has caused much concern among the donors, especially in an era of shrinking foreign aid. The usual reaction aimed at remedying the apparent failure of the family planning "dollar" to strike a notable breakthrough in fertility patterns in the foreseeable future is to issue a call for more dollars—and further research. A burgeoning literature on various aspects of population policy and family planning service "models" has evolved. Yet, this very literature, while of undeniable value as a research and action tool, has failed to focus much attention on the women themselves. Thus, we have a paradoxical situation in which funds have been provided and research is being undertaken, and yet the ultimate recipients of these funds or the primary focus of this research, the women, have somehow been left at the margins.[3] Mentioned, yes, but never quite made an integral part of the whole population policy process from the international to the local or clinic level. Researched, yes, but again from a distance, often from an unadulterated "Western" point of view, and almost never dealt with as individuals whose motivations for or against a large family have a considerable "rational" component if viewed within their particular economic and cultural context. This chapter is devoted to suggesting some preliminary steps in the correction of this prevailing omission on the part of donors, researchers, and activists, and contributing some better understandings of Latin American women.

Regardless of the little attention they have received or the little significance they have been granted, the women's position is undeniably changing, though at different rates from country to country and even within the countries themselves. Evidence is mounting that women who regularly attend mass just as regularly disobey the church's teachings on contraceptive methods.[4] Women, who have the right to vote in all the countries, are beginning to run and to be elected to office. Nearly all the countries have liberalized their laws concerning divorce. Brazil, which likes to call itself "the most [meaning the largest] Catholic country in the world," finally adopted a divorce law in 1977. The Dominican Republic, another strongly Catholic country, has become a haven for "quickie divorces" for its own people and for Yankees in a hurry. Colombia, among the most "conservative" countries in the region, has had an extensive and multifaceted family planning program for years. Women are "invading" the universities and the professions in unprecedented numbers. And while the weight of the law is still overwhelmingly favorable to the *Latino*, this too is changing, and in slow and at times awkward ways the codes are being modified to take into account the actual changes in women's status.

Slowness, male dominance, and internal contradictions characterize the history of family planning for most Latin American countries. Examined together, what impresses the observer are the similarities rather than the differences in the timing, the patterns, and the evolution of family planning services.[5] Almost always, we find that the first doctors who showed an interest in family planning were familiar with the newest research abroad, were educated abroad, had experience or some training abroad, or were foreign medical missionaries. The earliest family planning efforts usually involved medical doctors who were interested in the physiology of reproduction, who were gynecologists and/or obstetricians, or who had heard about Margaret Sanger's efforts. They were a very small group of individuals, almost solely male, and their interest in family planning can only be described as of a purely medical nature. Thus, some of them might have been concerned with the social and economic implications of large families, but it would be accurate to say that above and beyond these considerations lay their *medical* interest in ameliorating pregnancy problems or, as scientists and researchers, in better understanding the complexities of the reproductive system.

These doctors were operating within a cultural context in which large families were the norm; the extended network of kin, the traditional framework of family relations; the predominance of *machismo*, the unchallenged reality; the undereducation and underemployment of females, the overwhelming condition; and Catholic and Iberian values, the historic and psychological understructure within which thoughts, actions, policies, groups, and individuals ultimately moved. It was thus not coincidental that the first organized efforts in the area of family planning moved from a purely individual medical concern to concerns that basically appealed to the strengthening of the family as well as to the reinforcement of the existing taboos, such as the condemnation and prevention of abortions.

In the post–World War II period, many physicians became familiar with the newest discoveries in contraceptive techniques. For those women in the upper and middle classes who could affort the costs involved, the prescription and use of contraceptives became fairly common. For the poorer women, there long existed traditional methods of avoiding or aborting births, but many of these were medically dangerous and subject to overwhelming social condemnation.

In a number of countries, the first organized efforts at family planning occurred because of medical, religious, and social concerns with the alarmingly high incidence of abortions in spite of all the legal and religious sanctions against their practice. Chile, which was among the first countries in Latin America to provide diaphragms to a very limited number of women as early as 1938 and which pioneered in IUD research in the late 1950s and 1960s, did not seriously consider family planning on a national basis until surveys showed the already high and growing abortion rate.

Several medical surveys documented what Chilean doctors had suspected for some time. These systematic studies, with slight variations, showed that mortality from abortion was higher than from childbirth. Victims of dangerous and nonmedical procedures, women were ending up in the hospitals and often dying. For Santiago, the figures were stark: abortions were estimated to make up 41.5 percent of all hospital admissions and to be responsible for 26.7 percent of the volume of all the blood dispensed. The suffering, the maternal mortality, and the public health costs were so high that they became a public issue. At about the same time these figures were being publicized, Dr. Ofelia Mendoza of the International Planned Parenthood Federation (IPPF) visited Chile and played a catalytic role in getting together physicians concerned with the epidemiology of abortion and thus establishing the first organized group interested not only in abortion but, more significantly, its prevention through famly planning. The Comité Chileno de Protección de la Familia was launched in 1962, and a small grant from IPPF helped it initiate family planning clinics in Santiago.[6]

Newer data (1970) for Chile indicated that induced abortion was still being utilized as a method of fertility control among women with one to three children who did not want to have any more children. This research further substantiated that women who practiced contraception regularly and effectively experienced fewer pregnancies and showed a lower abortion rate during a given period than those who employed ineffective contraceptives or none at all.[7] In short, in Chile an early awareness of the dimensions of abortion incidence had prompted the establishment of family planning clinics in the early 1960s, while the more recent surveys supported the claim of those who viewed contraceptives as a deterrent to abortions.

Similar surveys of abortions undertaken by Dr. Octavio Rodrigues Lima and a group of his medical students in Brazil also resulted in grants from the IPPF and the establishment of a private family planning association, the Sociedade Civil Bem-Estar Familiar no Brasil (BEM-FAM), in late 1965.[8] In both Brazil and Chile, as was true in most Latin American countries, the very names given these early organizations indicated a conscious attempt to legitimize their establishment as organizations devoted to the "protection," the "well being," and the "research" (the Costa Rican IPPF affiliate was named the Costa Rican Demographic Association) of the family. In no case do we find a Latin American organization and program that openly declared itself as antinatalist or in favor of offering medically safe abortions. Almost in every case, the justification was the strengthening of the family unit, be it by avoiding the dangers of or the need for abortion, by seeking a decline in the numbers of unwanted and subsequently abandoned children (e.g., in Venezuela), or by highlighting the increasing population density and its attendant problems (e.g., in Costa Rica).

But while these justifications might seem eminently legitimate and sufficient to some in the medical profession, to local demographers, to some religious and political elites of a given country, and to the indispensable international donors, in general they bore no link to the actual situation of the vast majority of the Latin American women. These were the women who sought abortion at great personal risk or the women who continued to find a large rational component in the very act of becoming frequently pregnant. More recent research, often undertaken by female Latin Americanists, is beginning to suggest that at the individual level and particularly for the poorer women, having a large family can be, and many times indeed functions as, a survival mechanism.[9] To women living close to the margin of subsistence, the only way to survive appears to be the effort to try to make the best of their precarious situation, with flexible family organization and patterns of sharing.

"Making the best of the situation" usually involves early motherhood and a large family. With few exceptions, the poor Latin American women have their first child close to the onset of puberty. Whether they are in a marital union or not, having a child forecloses further education or other training that might lead to more stable jobs and a lower-fertility future. More often than not, these women do not even have the luxury of an alternative—if they themselves do not form a union they are likely to continue living in the cramped shacks of their mothers or to eke out a meager subsistence bartering goods or services. The possibility of being pushed into the "easy life" of a prostitute is always very close.

Their male counterparts likewise have few opportunities for advancement. At best, they obtain unstable and ill-paying jobs; at worst, they face calamitous periods of unemployment. Such economic uncertainties make unions, legal or common, extremely vulnerable. Once a woman has had a child in early puberty, the possibilities of her breaking out of the "vicious circles of poverty" are very low. For her the best survival strategy—sometimes the only strategy available—is to have *more* children, often by several partners. In the short term, having a child may help strengthen a relationship and prompt the new partner to provide for his woman and her children. In the long term, children are likely to prove a good investment.[10]

In this context, children are *rationally* perceived as economical assets. They help with the family chores, they babysit for their inevitable younger siblings and thus make it easier for the mother to obtain employment, or they themselves work for pay or barter their services and thus bring precious money and goods into the family. In the absence of *real* (as distinct from the beautifully advanced legal provisions) welfare programs, the only welfare anyone can turn to is one of kin and children. "My children are my security" becomes a deeply felt refrain. To the men, children—especially sons—mean help in the fields or on the streets. To the women, children—of whatever sex—mean not only help but also a basis for claiming support from their men. So the woman keeps on getting pregnant. By the time she is so old that a new union is unlikely, she has children old enough to support her.

In the 1960s and early 1970s very few family planning organizations— and even fewer international donors—seemed aware of or interested in helping women break out of this symbiotic arrangement between a large family and economic conditions that fed upon and fostered the very need for large families. The order of the day for those organizations and their international sponsors was to concentrate on opening new clinics, in dispensing more pills, in inserting new IUDs in the naive expectation that young Latin American women would flock to the clinics and that, before long, by popular demand, the government itself would underwrite an extensive and nationwide system of contraceptive distribution. Among the rare exceptions to this general tendency to find in family planning a new panacea was the emergence of the Serviço de Orientação da Familia (SOF) in Brazil. SOF's history gives us some clues to the crucial role played by international donors in the way local organizations are shaped and either thrive or barely manage to survive.

Early in the 1960s, with the discovery of the pill already well known among medical circles, more organized efforts in the area of family planning took place. Among the most imaginative of these was that attempted by a small group of young Paulista women in 1963. Letitia Borges da Costa and her collaborators initiated a service that aimed at ministering to the broader needs of poor families, not just their need to limit family size. With modest funds and at first no help from abroad, this small group of young professionals, many of them women, sought to offer services mostly on a voluntary basis, charging only minimum fees to those who could pay. As the name indicated, they helped "orient" families to consider various ways of coping with their problems and of possibly breaking out of the vicious circles engendered by pitiful income and a large family. SOF's staff liked to call its approach "global." By this they meant an awareness that the people who sought the clinic had other basic concerns besides those simply related to reproduction. In most instances the SOF staff counselled men and women on contraceptives but, almost as often, the clients received advice on family budgets, nutrition, and the existing social security system. SOF thus saw its own role as much broader than one solely focused on family planning. In turn, this "global" approach appealed to many who had only a minor— if any—interest in family planning per se but who desperately needed help and advice on how to cope with everyday family problems.

The word spread and soon it was clear that SOF could barely keep up with the demand; by the end of 1966 five clinics were being operated. It was a modest beginning, but SOF seemed destined for a promising future. Even the Marxian and often non-Malthusian intellectuals of São Paulo saw the emerging organization as an entity with which they could empathize: the leadership and staff so clearly had the welfare of the lower classes and the strengthening of family ties at heart. It was hard not to be "for" SOF, and the organization was the first of its kind in Brazil to be declared, in 1968, an "agency of public utility."

Despite these accomplishments, SOF became an early victim of international donor agencies that were unwilling to risk a small amount of funding on indirect approaches to family planning. Because it insisted on pursuing its own broader interpretation of family problems rather than concentrating on preventing abortions or controlling population growth, SOF eventually lost the support of the IPPF. BEMFAM, which from its inception in 1965 stressed that contraceptives were deterrents to abortion and which narrowed its services to family planning, began to receive ever larger funds from abroad.

This is not the place to recount SOF's history or BEMFAM's expansion. Suffice it to say that BEMFAM has now over 100 clinics throughout Brazil—but it has failed to completely dispel the suspicion of many Brazilians that it is controlled by foreign funds and interests. As for SOF, it is interesting to note that this program, initiated and in part staffed by women, still exists in Brazil. It has a "good image" among those who know its "orienting services" and its "global approach," but it has languished for lack of greater financial support, especially from abroad.[11]

There is little doubt that external aid has been essential to the evolution of family planning in Latin America. In Brazil and Chile, for example, foreign aid was crucial in the organization of family planning clinics. In the Dominican Republic, U.S. initiative, commitment, support, money, planning, organization, and ideas were critical at every important phase of the program and without the United States there would probably be no public program. One observer went so far as to conclude that "in seeking to explain the nature and growth of the Dominican family planning program, one need not correlate a battery of socio-economic and demographic indicators. The answer is quite simple: The United States."[12]

The Dominican Republic is not an exception. Surveying the situation in the entire Caribbean region, Segal has affirmed that "external aid has been critical to the evolution of population policies."[13] It has come from national governments (e.g., the United States and Sweden), international organizations (e.g., IPPF, the United Nations Fund for Population Activities [UNFPA], and the World Bank), and "private" organizations (e.g., Ford and Pathfinder), often themselves recipients of and conduits for U.S. Agency for International Development (AID) funds. During the 1950s and early 1960s external aid came mostly from the IPPF and family planning foundations such as Pathfinder. This aid financed field trials of contraceptives in Puerto Rico, funded medical and clinical research, supported surveys on abortion incidence, and subsidized the first family planning clinics. Grants became available for social science research and evaluation of issues related to population, and the U.S. Census Bureau was active in improving census facilities in the Hemisphere. Post-partum services that carried a component of family planning orientation were fostered in large maternity hospitals, such as those in Venezuela.[14]

With the expansion of funds and the concomitant expansion of activities of family planning organizations in the 1960s, the role of "foreign" funds made available to these organizations came increasingly to be questioned. The fact that often international donors, such as IPPF, received the bulk of their funds from U.S. governmental or private largesse smacked of an attempt to "launder" funds and to screen the "Yankee" hand manipulating family planning services in Latin America. In some countries, most prominently in Brazil, the controversy generated by the sources of its funds and the motives of its donors cost the fledgling family planning organization much of its energies and moneys that otherwise might have gone into the operation of clinics. Furthermore, it forced BEMFAM to engage in a widespread public relations campaign to "educate" the country's elites as to the real benefits to Brazil to be accrued from the existence of family planning services.

Lost in the shuffle of charges and countercharges were those who should be receiving the services. Even at that early date, the indications were that clinics would indeed have plenty of clients if properly managed and located. In other words, there were enough women eager to avail themselves of contraceptives, and if they had been provided easily and freely at clinics, the women would have been there to obtain them. But the money and the staff of some IPPF affiliates had to be diverted to a campaign to ensure their very survival by educating the various countries' elites so that services and contraceptives would eventually be provided by the governments themselves.

Another consequence of the acrimonious struggle between those favoring family planning services and those who, for whatever reason, opposed what they felt was an "insidious population control" scheme manipulated from abroad, was that some family planning organizations became imbued with a "fortress" mentality. In an effort to close ranks and defend itself, the bureaucracy of the family planning organization became less open to criticisms from within, less tolerant of possible new visions on how to attain its goals, and more autocratic and centralized. With few exceptions, the governing bodies of those organizations became almost exclusively male, upper class, white, and medically-dominated.

For the women who were the *recipients* and *targets* of the few services that were provided, the confusion meant that their own particular perspectives and peculiar needs found no hearing within the family planning organizations. Complaints of discomfort with certain types of pills, for example, were routinely disregarded by the doctors who dismissed them as proverbial female malingerings. Little attention was paid to the need for privacy in these types of consultations. Often the women had to go through the indignity of disclosing their marital situations or the number of abortions they had had in a crowded clinic room. At other times, in the drive to make family planning appear as a bona fide medical and scientific endeavor, the dispensing of contraceptives had little to do with the personal situation or preference of the woman, and much to do with the doctor's particular professional research interests.

If, on the one hand, the struggles of the late 1960s did much to determine the shape and nature of the family planning organizations and, by inference, the way women were approached, on the other hand, the search for medical and social legitimacy for family planning services did accomplish a measure of "education" of the elites and eventually produced a more relaxed, laissez-faire attitude on the part of governments toward the operation of family planning organizations. In the Caribbean, where U.S. influence was powerfully felt, the late 1960s and early 1970s saw the emergence of the United Nations and the U.S. government itself as major donors, and government-to-government assistance became the prevailing mode. The local private associations became adept at playing off the old and new sources, at expanding their informational services, and at undertaking new clinical programs. More recently, with the proliferation and eagerness of new donors, it has become usual in the Caribbean for a government to negotiate family planning aid with a dozen different donors. There has been a new trend, pushed by recipient countries on the less-than-enthusiastic donors, to demand funds for fairly large and intricate health-care delivery systems, of which family planning represents only a small or token part.

In the interim years, more sophisticated censuses have been undertaken in several countries. Preliminary analysis of these censuses indicate that although birth rates are declining, rates of natural increase are going to remain high—2 percent or above for most countries—for at least another decade. Better medical care and a youthful population continue to swell the ranks of women of reproductive age. Even if these women opt for smaller families, there are *more* women and thus the potential for more babies. At the same time, the infusion of larger doses of foreign funds for family planning services has not been accompanied by a comparable growth in the number and quality of clinics, and even a cursory survey shows that in much of Latin America the services are either deficient or nonexistent. The easy conclusion is that family planning services have not had much impact on the rate of population growth, because for various reasons they have not been provided on a large-enough scale to reach a significant percentage of women of child-bearing age. Where population growth has shown a decline, it has usually been explained by reasons *other* than the availability of family planning services. Thus, in the Caribbean, emigration has served as a safety valve for the surplus populaton, but the signs are unmistakable that the freedom to emigrate, especially to the United States, is about to be drastically curtailed. In other countries—and Brazil comes prominently to mind—the rate of infant mortality has helped keep the rate of population growth within a declining curve that cannot be explained by the limited availability of family planning services.[15]

Thus, at a time when the international donors have become more numerous and the governments in Latin America have become less hostile to the use of contraceptives, the situation in most countries still has a long way to go in making family planning services available through a nationwide program that would reach most women of a fertile age. However tempting it is to blame these fundamental failures on the well-intentioned but misguided foreign donors, there are other reasons that help explain the uphill fight of family planning in most of Latin America. An allusion has already been made to the rationale that prompts a large family in a culture of poverty. Other explanations include the fact that many of the problems encountered by family planning activists stem directly from and are inherent in the laws that have failed to keep pace with the accelerated rate of modernization and the increasing sophistication of Latin American women. In fact, a case can be made that it has been largely these increasingly sophisticated women who have perceived their own plight and who have transcended the legal restrictions and contradictions that remain in most Latin American legal systems. But here again, one must proceed with caution because even the women themselves are hardly unanimous in their interpretations of their options.

Some examples will underline the contradictions both in the laws and among the women themselves. The Brazilian Constitution, as with most Latin American fundamental laws, assures legal equality of the sexes. In practice, equality of the sexes is not even the unquestioned ideal for all Brazilian women. As recently as early 1978, a prominent Brazilian female attorney expressed the opinion that "someone should be the head of the family; our laws and tradition dictate that this be the husband.... The woman should have the right to *aspire* to the same jobs as the men, *but within limitations*" [our italics]. Patriarchal customs and religious influences continue to view the woman almost solely in terms of her traditional role as mother and housewife. Even the most recent proposed modifications of the Brazilian civil code are viewed by long-time Brazilian feminists as "keeping women as second class citizens" because they include clauses that give the man the right to administer the family's finances or the right to choose a tutor for the children, and declare that "man and woman should collaborate in the marital union, but the final decision belongs to the husband." It is not surprising, then, to realize that only in 1977 did Brazil finally legalize divorce, one of the last countries to do so.

Some of Brazil's laws refer to the use of contraceptives, and here again the contradictions abound. The Law of Penal Contraventions prohibits the advertisement of contraceptives or abortion materials. The Code of

Medical Ethics provides that the doctor shall not, either "clearly or obliquely," advertise processes or treatment for avoiding pregnancies. Official Document no. 40 GB of January 1, 1970, of the Ministry of Health, states that the direct sale to the public of pharmaceutical substances and products used as oral contraceptives can be made only with a prescription from a qualified professional. The Opinion of the Federal Council of Medicine of November 5, 1967, states in its conclusions that the use of contraceptives is legal and ethical in Brazil. Draft Law no. 635 of 1975, which will institute the new law of Penal Contraventions, provides punishment for the "advertisement of abortion," eliminating the prohibition on the advertisement of contraceptives that the present law contains. As an expert in legal medicine concluded in a February, 1978, symposium, "Even though it appears that the government is now leaning towards a policy of family planning, it is necessary to make clear that none of the limiting clauses in our codes has been abrogated." Although Brazil approved the World Population Plan of Bucharest, which declared, Item No. 3: "The right to have access to contraceptives should not be a privilege of the wealthy and thus the State should make available information and methods which can be requested by low income families," Brazil still does not have a national program for family planning, and family planning remains a privilege of middle- and upper-income families.[16]

This explains why, even though a decade and a half ago Brazilian women already showed a preference for fairly small families by Latin American standards (2.6 children compared to 3.9 desired by Mexican women, for example),[17] many of them, due to the restrictions on advertisements, did not know anything about contraceptives. Despite the diffusion of this knowledge—mostly through oral means—the majority of Brazilian women who would probably use contaceptives often are unable to afford the costs. There are indications that the government may begin providing counselling and contraceptives through the national health care system within fairly restricted guidelines (for example, in cases of women subject to high-risk pregnancies), but these indications have not been in any way formalized or implemented. With the 1979 changeover of governmental administration in Brazil, it is unproductive to speculate on future policies. In the meantime, women are the primary group caught in the contradictions and dilemmas of an archaic system of laws and welfare that traditionally has given more rights to men than to women and that has specifically favored larger families by giving special subsidies for children. Women are also the primary group caught in the conflicts inherent in the Brazilian population policy, a conflict between the government's pledge to provide "information" so that the individual couple may make its own decision in regards to the number of desired children and the types of national values expressed in the II National Development Plan that states "Brazil still is among the underdeveloped countries . . . and as a sovereign nation it has the right . . . to let its population grow at a reasonable rate, in order to effect its development potential and its economic destiny."

Yet, what may be surprising in view of all these restrictions and the obvious government reluctance to include family planning among its priority programs is that recent data show that an overwhelming number of Brazilian women know about contraceptives and a growing number of them are already acting on the basis of this knowledge. In a recent survey, out of the 300 women interviewed, only 3 did not know at least one contraceptive method, including those that are by law prohibited in Brazil (IUDs). Actual use varied from 85 percent for those women classified as belonging to the upper classes to 41 percent for the poorest class. The motives for family planning, according to the survey, were the desire not to have more children and health and financial reasons. The majority of those who did not use contraceptives wanted to have more children or were afraid of health hazards. There was also a clear indication that a greater proportion of younger women knew *and* used some method. Finally, the number of younger women from the lowest strata knowing and using some method was considerably greater than the number of older women of the same socioeconomic strata. It should also be pointed out that this survey clearly indicated that most of the women were not aware of the legal restrictions or, if they knew, certainly did not obey them. The whole system whereby the pharmacist almost always sells without a prescription or even helps the woman choose her contraceptive makes the legal restrictions nearly unenforceable.[18]

Brazil is not at all unique in the way that its traditions, its laws, and its practices discriminate against women and relegate them to a "second class status." In Peru, for example, the constitution does not discriminate against women explicitly, and equality of the sexes appears to be an underlying premise of many of its provisions. This is true of individual guarantees as well as of the national and social welfare guarantees. Other basic or "organic" laws, such as decree laws and supreme resolutions, contain legal guarantees of the equality of men and women. However, there are many legal articles and provisions that are clearly discriminatory. In the Civil Code, the Law of the Family unmistakably perpetuates traditional cultural patterns of family life and thus places the woman in an inferior or less favorable position vis-à-vis the man of the family. Similarly, the Commercial Code places limitations on the capacity of the married woman to act in commercial matters, subjecting her to the decisions and authority of her husband, even in those cases in which she was the original possessor or inheritor of commercial properties. The same code reflects the traditional sex roles long in existence in employment patterns. These discriminations persist despite several changes in the codes. Almost paradoxically, even in the family laws women are discriminated against. We say "paradoxically" because the family is the one institution in Latin America where women have traditionally performed the greatest proportion of their activities and where the woman, supposedly, reigns supreme.[19] Yet, before the law, this "reign" is in fact fairly circumscribed in terms of the dictates and the authority of the husband.

Interestingly enough, it is among the women that there rests the greatest potential for eventual change and for faith in the ultimate "democratization" of the legal systems. In the words of two Peruvian lawyers who have been active in the International Council of Women, changes are slowly being introduced and:

> suggest that the roles available to and played by women are changing and will continue to change, and promise much hope that in the future, women will be co-responsible and a co-participant in decision-making with the men. . . . The dedication of 1975 as the "Year of the Peruvian Woman," the existence of a Commission to coordinate the initiatives favoring the equal rights of women, . . . and other recent changes suggest strongly that . . . the Peruvian woman may attain her rights and a dignity and role corresponding to her importance in Peruvian society.[20]

It is within the new generations that the expectations and the hopes are greatest, and these women are already showing a great deal of understanding for their own status and all the many hurdles still to be overcome. Among middle- and upper-class students and young professionals one hears family planning and even sterilization openly discussed, girls talk seriously about the possibility of childless marriages, and boys now debate the merits of careers for their female colleagues and girl friends. Their attitudes are refreshingly new, sometimes touchingly naive in their great hopes and their faith that barriers can be overcome with time and perseverance. It is within this group that one finds a disinclination to follow the "American" feminist movement because it is widely perceived as unsuited to Latin women— too strident and too radical, and to many it seems to be assailing the forms rather than the substance of discrimination, infused with myths, posture, and hangups that have little significance or are inappropriate for the Latin American context.

While the situation and the prospects for the upper- and middle-class Latin American women have definitely improved in recent years, one has to be restrained about making a similar assessment for the lower-strata women (the largest group numerically). They are still trapped in servility and unable to see, know, or even less use, the few legal guarantees that are available. They still have a very long way to go, though theoretically, with the expansion of education and service opportunities, they too will eventually break away from the cycles of poverty and high fertility behavior. In this connection, it is interesting to point out that help for the poorer women is coming mainly from their better educated, sophisticated, and well-placed sisters who already have found ways to influence and manipulate the prevailing value and political system to their advantage. Much is expected from these privileged pioneers and, hopefully, much will be obtained. They are the ones organizing women's groups and serving as spokespersons for the needs and problems of the voiceless, amorphous masses.

It is in this stewardship that one sees most clearly a blend of the old and new traditions in the Latin American milieu: the upper classes are defining the needs and serving as the sponsors and spokespersons for those below them in the social strata—just as they always did. The novelty is that the sex of the sponsors and benefactors, as well as those sponsored, is now female, whereas before, those involved on both sides of the equation were overwhelmingly male.

When thus viewed in context, population policy in Latin America is not altogether different from the picture that emerges in a number of other policy areas. There are also many common strands between the situations in one country and another. The similarities are often greater than the contrasts confronted in "democratizing" family planning—actually including women in the population policy process and actually reaching large numbers of fertile women. On one level, we noticed the catalytic role played by the foreign donors in the establishment and, later, in the shaping of family planning organizations, often with little regard for the local woman's basic needs and even less effort to involve women in the design and management of services. On other levels, we observed the contradictions inherent in legal systems that ideally opt for "equality" but which in practice, through the application of the code laws, perpetuate old traditions and inequalities.

Transcending even these inequalities of sex are the persistent inequalities among classes whereby, even for a single sex—women—some are, as they have always been, more equal than others. For upper-

and middle-class women, medical care and contraceptives are available; the same cannot be said for the lower-class women. It is thus not surprising that we inevitably end by turning to women who are already or are now becoming influential in policy making and that we expect some change and "democratization" to eventually "filter down." It is to these "elites" that we turn in the hope that they will serve as articulators, organizers, and leaders for lower-class women. It is they who must convince international donors and national activists that family planning, like all else, must be part and parcel of a greater range of services, adapted to local conditions, but above all aimed at involving rather than simply "helping" the "target" lower-class and high-fertility women.

We have questioned how any policy can be implemented or how any program can have any lasting impact without a greater involvement and participation of the major groups affected—in this case, the women. It is imperative that population program donors as well as the local recipient organizations become more meaningfully concerned with the ultimate "target" of all their efforts. Indeed, it is essential that as a first step we change our very semantics and begin considering women as individuals with individual needs and aspirations and no longer, as they have been for years, as "targets" of funds and programs.

It is equally important that women and their many contributions to family, community, and country be acknowledged, not only in the context of the past and the present, but also with some attempt at viewing future roles they may eventually play in countries that are experiencing the accelerating pace of modernization. By acknowledging women's manifold contributions to society, we can avoid the "target mentality," a mentality that considers women solely in terms of their capacity for pregnancy. Obviously if we consider pregnancy to be the sole problem, then it is only pregnancy that family planning programs will focus on. To many women—and men—this mentality and this blindness to women's other functions and roles in society appear to be the prevailing spirit behind the current guidelines for international (particularly U.S.) aid and for family planning programs in Latin America.

I venture to suggest that we must avoid this mentality because programs that simply and solely emphasize the childbearing and motherhood roles may be doomed to failure when the ultimate objective of the programs is supposedly to deemphasize those very roles, offering women the opportunity to exercise other functions besides motherhood, and eventually leading them to opt for smaller families. Thus exhortations to practice family planning for the purpose of raising happier, healthier babies are self-defeating if they focus exclusively on the goals of quality motherhood and neglect completely the nonreproductive roles that all women carry out as well.[21] In a similar vein we must attempt to look at women and family planning in the larger context of today's Latin America: a continent in the throes of fast-paced modernization with countries leapfrogging the several stages of development and striving to gain their own identity, sensitive to what they regard as their sovereign concerns, determined to solve their problems in ways compatible with their own particular historical experience and political and social institutions.

In closing, there are some fundamental questions still to be asked whose answers must await further research and deeper insights into the nature and problems of Latin American society. Among the thorny questions is that of abortion, especially since many of the Latin American family planning organizations emerged and have justified their existences on the grounds that family planning would be a means of preventing abortions. Abortion still reaches epidemic proportions in most of the countries of the region and yet, indications are that this is also the region where opposition to any liberalization of the sanctions against abortion is stronger than anywhere else.

Another question involves the fact that we are dealing with governments that, in general, have had few funds—and often less inclination—to spend toward a real expansion of human services. How can we then expect these governments to spend more on such a low priority area—by their criteria—as family planning? More fundamentally, how is it possible to "democratize" population policy—or any other policy area for that matter—when indeed the whole society is imbued with nondemocratic biases?

For too long we have concentrated on the smaller, more mundane questions. For too long, even after it became apparent that it was a false focus, emphasis has been placed on preventing abortions and pregnancies, rather than on opening up new alternatives for the young women of Latin America. For too long we have supported only those organizations that have narrowly focused on pregnancy as *the* problem—the same organizations that were at one time pioneers and innovators, but which have by now become overburdened by their own bureaucracy and overly identified with what Latin Americans perceive as "American" perspectives and approaches. For too long we have viewed women as "targets" of rather than as participants in the family planning process.

It is a relatively simple matter to work for the distribution of pills and other contraceptives. It is a much harder task to seek ways to provide women with proper motivation *not* to need or want to have more children. It is here that we find a chance for hope. There are a number of greatly expanding, imaginative, and sensible organizations that are interested in working out the problems of women and their families, as well as in providing family planning services. These organizations have, by and large, been ignored or neglected by the international donors and the already established family planning organizations that see that these other organizations, quite rightly, as potential rival "patrons" for the lower-class high-fertility women and rival recipients for the international donors' dollars. Many of these alternative organizations have existed for a number of years and have survived with minimal or no outside help through a great deal of devotion and ingenuity. Most of them are not bent on a nationalistic or pronatalist binge or hung up by other phobias, nor are they likely to reject, out of hand, help because it is coming from U.S. AID or other "population" donors. For example, most of these organizations would be more than happy to use appropriate materials on health, family, and crafts.

It is not too farfetched to suggest that if donor agencies had been willing to risk funding on such indirect approaches or if they had been willing to support broader interpretations of family planning (as exemplified by Brazil's SOF), they might have avoided some of the pitfalls and problems that continue to plague Latin American family planning associations. Donors might have found that the increased motivation for seeking fertility services on the part of women participating in these more-broadly focused programs yielded a far greater return on their investment than the returns obtained in the narrowly focused programs involving only contraceptive promotion and distribution. After years of disappointing returns for ever larger investments in narrowly focused family planning organizations, some donor agencies are now cautiously experimenting with indirect and broader approaches. Yet, even as we draw near the 1980s, the bulk of available funds are still too narrowly targeted.

For too long the magic "breakthrough" has been measured by the establishment of clinics or the higher number of contraceptive acceptors, with little attention being paid to the vast majority on *non-*acceptors: those women who have a perfectly rational motive for having more children, given the paucity of other alternatives for survival. The focus should have been here, on the failure to alter the rationale for large families and not on the myth of the ignorance or resistance to change among high-fertility women. It may well be that "democratization" of population policy is a chimera—that it must wait until the whole nature of Latin American society has changed and become "democratized." In the meantime, it is possible that we can help change the nature and focus of family planning. To the extent that we realize that alternatives to larger families can and must be provided, that high-fertility poor women can and must perceive themselves as involved in broadly defined population policies and programs, to that extent we are coming closer to achieving the goals of reaching more women and, eventually, of having them as participants and actors in a policy area that is intimately significant to them as women and as individual human beings. It is in this effort to help "democratize" the whole population policy process, from the reaching of fertile women to the creation of alternatives to pregnancies, and from the involvement of women in policy making to their participation in the actual implementation, that hope for the eventual "success" of family planning efforts in Latin America exists.

Notes

1. Asunción Lavrin, "Latin American Women's History, " *Latin American Research Review*, 13 (Spring 1978), 314-318.

2. Lewis Hanke (ed.), *History of Latin American Civilization*, 2 (Boston: Little, Brown and Co., 1973), 454.

3. Elsa M. Chaney, "Women and Population: Some Key Policy, Research, and Action Issues," in Richard L. Clinton (ed.), *Population and Politics* (Lexington, Mass.: Lexington Books, 1973), 233-246.

4. See, among others, J. Mayone Stycos, *Ideology, Faith, and Family Planning in Latin America* (New York: McGraw-Hill Book Co., 1971), especially chap. 16.

5. David Chaplin (ed.), *Population Policies and Growth in Latin America* (Lexington, Mass.: Lexington Books, 1971); Terry L. McCoy (ed.), *The Dynamics of Population Policy in Latin America* (Cambridge, Mass.: Ballinger Publishing Co., 1974); and Aaron Lee Segal (ed.), *Population Policies in the Caribbean* (Lexington, Mass.: Lexington Books, 1975).

6. Vivian Epstein-Orlowski, "Family Planning Programs and Dynamics of Agenda-Building in Costa Rica and Chile," in McCoy, *op. cit.*, chap. 11; and Thomas G. Sanders, *Family Planning In Chile, Part II: The Catholic Position*, American Universities Field Staff Reports, West Coast South American Series (February 1967).

7. "New Data on Abortion in Chile," *Forum*, 1 (October 1978), 11.

8. Howard J. Wiarda and Iêda Siqueira Wiarda, *The Politics of Population in Brazil: Public Policy and the Political Process* (forthcoming).

9. Helen I. Safa, "Women, Production and Reproduction in Industrial Capitalism: A Comparison of Brazilian and U.S. Factory Workers," discussion paper presented at the 1978 meeting of the International Studies Association, Washington, D.C.

10. Susan E. Brown, *Women and Their Mates: Coping with Poverty in the Dominican Republic* (New York: MSS Information Corporation, 1976); and Rae Lesser Blumberg, "Fairy Tales and Facts: Economy, Family, Fertility, and the Female," in Irene Tinker and Michèle Bo Bramsen (eds.), *Women and World Development* (Washington, D.C.: Overseas Development Council, 1976), 12-21.

11. For greater detail, see Wiarda and Wiarda, *op. cit.*

12. Howard J. Wiarda, "The Politics of Family Planning in the Dominican Republic: Public Policy and the Political Process," in McCoy, *op. cit.*, chap. 13. The quotation is found on p. 316.

13. Segal, *op. cit.*, 20.

14. Iêda Siqueira Wiarda, *Family Planning in a Democratic Context: The Case of Venezuela* (Columbus, Ohio: Mershon Center, Ohio State University, 1970).

15. Charles H. Wood, "Infant Mortality Trends and Capitalist Development in Brazil," *Latin American Perspectives*, 4 (Fall 1977), 56-65; and Thomas W. Merrick, "Population and Development in Brazil," *Hearings before the Select Committee on Population*, Ninety-fifth Congress, Second Session, 2 (1978), 399-420.

16. Iêda Siqueira Wiarda, "The Politics of Population in Brazil: The Women Dimension," in *Hearings*, ibid., 385-398; and Romy Medeiros da Fonseca, "Law and the Condition of Women in Brazil," in Columbia Human Rights Law Review (ed.), *Law and the Status of Women* (New York: Columbia Human Rights Law Review, 1977), 11-34.

17. Joseph A. Kahl, *The Measurement of Modernism: A Study of Values in Brazil and Mexico* (Austin, Texas: The University of Texas Press, 1968), chap. 5.

18. Raimar Richers et al., "O Planejamento Familiar e o Mercado de Anticoncepcionais no Brasil," *Revista de Administração de Empresas*, 15 (July-August, 1975), 7-20.

19. For some original insights, see Evelyn P. Stevens, "Marianismo: The Other Face of Machismo in Latin America," in Ann Pescatello (ed.), *Female and Male in Latin America* (Pittsburgh: University of Pittsburgh Press, 1973), 89-102; and Susan C. Bourque and Kay B. Warren, "Campesinas and Comuneras: Subordination in the Sierra," *Journal of Marriage and the Family* (November 1976), 781-788.

20. Carmen Rodríquez de Muñoz and Elsa Roca de Salomen, "Law and Status of Women in Peru," in Columbia Human Rights Law Review, *op. cit.*, 208, 211.

21. I am deeply indebted to Judith F. Helzner, Associate in Women's Programs, Pathfinder Fund, for suggesting some of the ideas developed in these last three paragraphs. See also Adrienne Germain, "Women at Mexico: Beyond Family Planning Acceptors," *Family Planning Perspectives*, 7 (September-October 1975), 235-238.

6
Political Parties, Opposition Politics, and Democracy in Latin America

Michael J. Kryzanek

The history of democratic party opposition in Latin America is much like the old saying, "always a bridesmaid, never a bride." Like the bridesmaid, political party opposition in Latin America has never achieved the recognition and acceptance that political parties out of power have attained in many advanced industrial democracies. More importantly, parties out of power have seen little in the way of electoral success, as they have continually been relegated to a secondary position, unable either to win national office or to retain power once in office.[1]

The practice of opposition party politics in Latin America is generally characterized by government-initiated harassment, incarceration, and repression, as authoritarian regimes have consistently shown an unwillingness to recognize the democratic institution of the loyal opposition.[2] Opposition party leaders constantly have to face the very real possibility that their organization may be declared illegal or forced underground, and their supporters subjected to the oppression of the governing regime. When parties are permitted to participate in electoral or legislative politics, they almost always have to face the problems of rigged elections or decree-made policy.

As a result of the serious risks and the demoralizing futility connected with opposition politics, political parties have been forced into a position of constantly preparing and waiting for an opportunity to achieve national power, only infrequently reaching that goal. With the opportunities for a full and fair role in national politics so limited, opposition parties have had to delay their quest for power until political circumstances permitted them to seek, and possibly even assume, the reins of government. As we shall see, the political circumstances in favor of successful democratic opposition are so scant and appear so seldom in Latin America that parties have remained on the fringes of national political power.

One of the more unfortunate aspects of the "bridesmaid" quality of oppostion parties in Latin America is that in recent years there has been a general lack of analysis of the position these organizations occupy in various political systems and their relationships to other opposition parties in this region.[3] It seems that the proclivity of military regimes in the 1970s and the heavy emphasis placed on economic modernization has shifted attention away from analysis of parties, opposition politics, and the condition of democracy in Latin America.

However, with the conclusion of the decade of the 1970s, it is the feeling of this author that a more thorough investigation of opposition political parties and their relationship to the establishment of democratic government is warranted. Signs pointing to the lessening of influence of military regimes, added to stronger cries for popular participation, democratic policy making, and human rights, suggest that political parties and democratic opposition may be entering into a new phase.

It is the aim of this chapter, therefore, to examine more deeply and perhaps shed new light on the current state of parties, opposition politics, and democracy in Latin America. Moreover, this chapter will seek to determine whether political party opposition is indeed entering into a new era, a more democratic era.

For the purpose of achieving a clearer analysis of democratic opposition politics in Latin America, political parties will be grouped according to four general categories. The categories describe not only the character of the political regime that opposition parties exist in, but also comment on the political behavior that the parties have shown as opposition participants in the regime. This attempt at categorization of opposition parties will then be followed by a concluding discussion of the effects of opposition status on political parties and the prospects for opposition parties and democratic politics in modern-day Latin America.

Throughout the discussion, and particularly in the remarks on the prospects for party opposition, there will be a conscious attempt not to lose sight of the book's major theme—the struggle for democracy in Latin America. The relationship between political party opposition and the state of democracy is indeed a significant one. Political parties in their role as critics and challengers of the governing regime provide an important means of determining the strength and vitality of the democratic process in Latin America.

If we are to make a judgment on the condition of democracy in Latin America, what better means of attaining such a decision than by examining those organizations that have struggled so long to establish the principles of political choice, open criticism, and a fair challenge of power?

Restricted Party Opposition: The "Survivors"

Perhaps the most common situation of political party opposition in Latin America is that in which numerous barriers are established in order to limit the influence of the party out of power. In countries where such "controlled" and restricted opposition can be found, political parties gauge "success" in terms of their ability to acquire the qualities of resilience and determination, since there is often little opportunity to effectively challenge the dominance of the governing regime.

In the restricted system parties are allowed to exist and function; they often run candidates in elections, hold seats in the legislature, and probably have a high level of influence within urban, peasant, and labor groups. However, this picture of activity and involvement must be counterbalanced by the fact that opposition parties in this restricted climate are usually not allowed to reach the pinnacle of national power.

The key axiom of politics in the restricted system is that the governing regime take every step necessary to debilitate the opposition short of destroying it. The government in the restricted opposition system is always conscious of its image in the outside world and does not want to appear to be overly repressive or dictatorial. This image of political tolerance cannot mask the fact that opposition parties must constantly bear the brunt of government-sponsored policies that lessen their influence and demoralize party activists.[4]

If and when parties are successful at gaining power, their ability to maintain that position is usually extremely weak. Quite often these parties are only able to remain in power for a brief period of time. The governing forces view opposition parties as unacceptable national decision makers and proceed to make certain that the organization remains in a secondary position.

The restricted party opposition system thus creates "survivors," party organizations that struggle to be active in national politics despite the fact that they face constant pressure from governing regimes. The life of the opposition survivors is one of continually facing the prospect of engaging in a brand of politics where the governing regime achieves the victories and receives the benefits of participation, while the opposition must endure frequent defeats and is forced to wait long periods for its success. In such a restricted opposition climate the "survivors" can only react to the antiparty policies of the regime in power by engaging in a "politics-of-the-future." As a result, the parties educate, recruit, propose, criticize, and organize all in an attempt to show the citizenry and the government that they remain a vital force and a political alternative for the future.

The political parties that are the opposition "survivors" in Latin

America clearly point up the hardships endured by organizations forced to wait decades for their opportunity to control the reins of power. Although it is possible to view restricted party opposition in countries like Brazil, Nicaragua, Bolivia, and Guatemala, it seems appropriate that we examine two of the most disturbing examples of political survival in Latin America—the Dominican Revolutionary Party (PRD) and the Peruvian Popular American Revolutionary Party (APRA or "Apristas").

The choice of the PRD and the APRA is based on the fact that these two parties have long histories of survival against restrictive governing regimes, but at the same time both parties have experienced limited political victory. As is expected with restrictive party opposition, the PRD and APRA have faced many more hardships than victories, and have, in the process, become the epitome of opposition survival in Latin America.

In the case of the PRD, the party spent thirty years in exile from the dictator Trujillo and was not given an opportunity to present its reform government to the people in a democratic election until 1962. Upon the landslide victory of its candidate, Juan Bosch, the PRD soon realized that the conservative forces would not tolerate the changes proposed by the Bosch government. The PRD and Bosch lasted only seven months in power, and through a military coup, were returned to "survivor" status and forced to wait for another opportunity to hold national power.

An attempt to regain power in 1965 through a violent civil war was a failure, as again conservative forces, this time supported by U.S. troops, were victorious. After 1965 the PRD waited and planned for another opportunity to regain power. The wait was not easy because the government of President Balaguer allowed the forces of repression to run free against PRD activists.[5] It was only recently, in the presidential election of 1978, that the PRD felt confident that it could win and replace the Balaguer regime. The PRD and its presidential candidate, Antonio Guzmán, were victorious, but not without difficulty. The military stopped the vote count when Guzmán was surging ahead and threatened to cancel the election. Extreme pressure from numerous sectors in the country and from the United States forced the military to reopen the vote count, but again the PRD witnessed new restrictions placed on its capacity to govern. Based on past experiences, it remains to be seen whether Guzmán will be allowed to remain a Dominican president or whether the PRD will be forced back into "survivor" status.

The opposition predicament of the APRA in Peru is similar to that of the PRD, but it provides an even stronger example of the difficulties encountered by political parties in a restricted opposition system. Under the dedicated party leadership of Víctor Raúl Haya de la Torre, the APRA organizagion has worked since the 1920s to bring moderate yet vigorous social-democratic reform to Peru.[6] Whenever the party was on the brink of gaining national power, the military, supported by conservative economic interests, moved in to quash the election and strip APRA of its victory. In 1931 and 1962 Haya de la Torre and APRA were denied entry to the presidential palace. On a number of occasions the party was forced into exile, most notably in 1948, when Haya de la Torre fearing government reprisals sought asylum in the Colombian embassy. Like the PRD, the history of the APRA is replete with instances of harassment, incarceration of its leaders, and repression. Through it all, though, APRA has remained a popular and surprisingly strong organization. APRA has solid ties to labor and peasant groups and appears to receive the largest amount of citizen support.

Also like the PRD, APRA has had to play the waiting game, waiting for another opportunity to move into the center stage of national politics. APRA's ability to wait and remain strong is the direct result of its leader, Haya de la Torre. Haya is the classic example of the "survivor." Now in his eighties, Haya continues to prepare APRA for another political battle. With presidential elections scheduled for 1980 and a preliminary constitutional assembly victory for the APRA in 1978, Haya de la Torre may be headed for yet another testing of Peru's restricted opposition system.

Superficial Party Opposition: The "Compromisers"

The second type of party opposition in Latin America is, in many respects, the most unusual and intriguing. The title "Superficial Party Opposition" suggests that certain political systems in Latin America have allowed party opposition to exist freely, but, at the same time, have either created elaborate rules of the game that make meaningful opposition extremely difficult or have so dominated the political system that successful opposition is impossible. In both cases the aim of the governing regime is to insure the continuance of the status quo. As for party opposition, it often leads dedicated activists to become "compromisers."

What one sees in such countries as Mexico and Colombia is a strange sort of democratic opposition. Parties are alive, functioning, and relatively free of government retribution, but once one scratches beneath the surface, it is a certainty that the democratic opposition system will be shown to be a facade with parties severely limited in their role as political antagonist. In countries where superficial party opposition is present, the governing regime needs the favorable image that opposition parties provide and indeed may even encourage the development of the party organization. This positive opposition climate is present only because those in power are satisfied that party opposition cannot influence the shape of politics or create destabilizing pressures. Opposition parties, in a real sense, are captives of this superficiality—they play the role of political challenger, but all along recognize that they are part of a compromise designed to legitimize a kind of guided democracy that will not permit them access to the central arena of power.

In Mexico, the Party of the Institutional Revolution (PRI) has a firm lock on national power and uses that hold to control opposition politics. The PRI's popularity in Mexico has come under sharp attack lately as a result of high voter abstention and stepped-up antigovernment demonstrations. Despite these problems, there is no doubt in the minds of the Mexican people that the PRI is an entrenched, well-run, paternalistic party that has created a divided and demoralized opposition.[7]

The success of the PRI at organizing the Mexican citizenry, providing personal favors, and dispensing public service has forced opposition leaders to reevaluate and readjust their challenges to the governing regime. Opposition parties such as the Party of National Action (PAN), the Party of the Authentic Mexican Revolution (PARM), the Popular Socialist Party (PPS), and the recently legalized Communist Party recognize the dominance of the PRI and have responded in ways that signal their acceptance of the status quo and their willingness to either support it or remain passive.

For example, political party leaders have on a number of occasions joined the government team after years of unsuccessful opposition.[8] Some party leaders have worked out informal arrangements with the government so that their voices may receive some hearing by the government.[9] Other party leaders, often after serious internal disputes, have decided that participating in elections is futile and have dropped out of the electoral arena. The presidential election of 1976 is a case in point. PAN, PARM, and PPS, the major opposition parties, did not run candidates against the PRI's José López Portillo. Only the Communists fielded a token presidential candidate.

The weakness and compromised nature of party opposition in Mexico has caused a degree of concern among PRI leaders. The party has felt a need to manipulate Mexican democracy in a way that presents the government in a favorable light. The PRI amended the Mexican constitution to allow for increased opposition participation in the Mexican congress even if opposition parties did not win a seat. The recent legalization of the Communist Party and the public encouragement of "responsible" opposition all point to the fact that the PRI desires party opposition as long as it is willing to compromise and accept the dominance and guidance of the governing regime.

The PRI, because of this nurturing of the superficial opposition system, has achieved the best of both worlds—it can rightly state that party opposition is given every opportunity to participate freely in Mexican politics, while at the same time the PRI knows full well that its control of Mexican politics makes a successful challenge to the governing regime remote. Perhaps the most important result of its opposition system is that the PRI feels it can declare itself a modern, democratic state, when, in reality, democracy is superficial and the primary agents of democracy have been forced to compromise themselves.

Perhaps an even more interesting example of superficial party opposition can be found in Colombia. Since 1958, with the signing of an agreement called the Pact of Sitges, the two dominant political parties, the Liberals and the Conservatives, have agreed to the practice of *alternidad* and *paridad*, and, as a result, have ushered in twenty years of controlled party politics and compromised political opposition that has come to be called the National Front.[10] *Alternidad* is an agreement by the two parties whereby the presidency of the country alternates every four years. After four years of a Liberal president, the Conservatives assume the presidential sash. Other parties are allowed to participate, but their presence has been frowned upon, and moreover, the Liberals and Conservatives are so dominant that a third-party challenge is often given little credence.

Once a party is in office, the other part of the agreement, *paridad*, is implemented. *Paridad* means that major cabinet positions are allocated on an equal basis to, in effect, share the responsibilities of governing (and of course to share the benefits as well). *Alternidad* and *paridad* have certainly served their purpose by insuring the dominance of the Liberals and Conservatives in the Colombian political system. However, the political compromise made with the formation of the National Front has not provided Colombia with the kind of aggressive, visionary, reform government that the country desperately needs. During the period of the National Front, Colombia lapsed deeper into international debt, gained a reputation for excessive corruption, saw a disturbing rise in inflation and unemployment, and witnessed increased internal pressure for change.[11] In short, Colombia, like Mexico, has become a country that superficially presents a picture of a quiet democracy at work, but, in reality, is covering up a system where opposition politics is severely compromised by two parties more interested in maintaining internal stability and their quasi-monopoly of politics and patronage than in fostering dynamic, efficient government.

The sense of security and control that *alternidad* and *paridad* provided was shattered in 1970, when the aged but popular general Gustavo Rojas Pinilla started his own party and challenged the increasingly suspect National Front government. Rojas lost in what many felt was a rigged election, but nevertheless it was clear from his popularity that the National Front opposition system was unacceptable to many Colombians.[12]

Since 1970, the National Front has broken down completely because the Liberal party took both the 1974 and 1978 presidential elections. However, the decline of this "guided democracy" has not stimulated participation or helped to form alternative political parties. In the election of 1978, two-thirds of the Colombians stayed away from the polls primarily because there was no viable opposition to the Liberals or the Conservatives.

The image that Colombia has developed as one of the few democratic countries in Latin America is well known. What perhaps is not well known is the state of its democratic opposition. The control that the Liberals and Conservatives sought with the National Front has weakened government and created widespread apathy. The Colombian citizenry thus has seen the interaction of two parties bent on compromise in order to preserve their dominance. In return Colombia has become one of the most troubled countries in Latin America, a superficial democracy.

Oppressed Party Opposition: The "Outlaws"

The discussion up to this point has stressed the fact that opposition parties are allowed to exist in Latin America but only under restricted or compromised circumstances. What will be presented in this section is an examination of those political systems where party opposition is actively banned or forced underground, and where parties who seek to challenge the governing regime become, in effect "outlaws."

Ever since political parties began playing a larger role in Latin American politics and challenging the traditional ruling elites, they have had to endure oppression and the very real possibility that they would not be allowed to practice their activities openly.

In recent years, opposition political parties have had to face increased pressure from authoritarian military governments seeking to eliminate any vestige of democratic practice. Unlike the restricted opposition system, where limits are placed on the attainment and maintenance of national governing power, in the oppressed opposition systems an effort is made to destroy democratic party challenges and rid the country of those organizations that foster alternative policy making.

It would be quite possible to discuss the oppression of party opposition in a number of Latin American countries, including Paraguay, Panama, Honduras, and of course Cuba, but for the purpose of this paper Uruguay and Chile seem to present the best examples of governing regimes serious about their desire to destroy party opposition.

In Uruguay, the entrance of the military into politics in 1973 created one of the most oppressive antiparty regimes in Latin America. Uruguay, which historically has had one of the strongest two-party systems in the region, moved into a new era where the National and Colorado parties were forced underground and made to endure what human-rights organizations feel is the most vicious attack on democratic opposition in Latin America.[13] Once considered to be the Switzerland of Latin America and the center for progressive and stable democracy, Uruguay has become a place where party leaders have either left the country or have remained to face the harsh actions of the generals.

Chile in the post-Allende period has also seen the dismantling of the party system. Parties like the major opposition Christian Democrats have had to accept government-imposed outlaw status and endure the indignities and the repression of the Pinochet regime.[14] In place of political parties stands a military dictatorship that has little commitment to democratic politics and a sad record of respect for human rights. Although the actions by the Pinochet regime have severely limited the Christian Democrats from mounting a counter-attack, the leadership of the party, with help from the church hierarchy and the human-rights policy of the United States, has been able to maintain the organization's visibility in Chilean society.[15] Party leaders hold on to the belief that the popular commitment to democratic practice will pressure the governing regime into restoring civilian rule and the system of loyal opposition, so long an integral party of Chile's political system.

The lessons of Uruguay and Chile point up the fact that oppressed opposition is by far the most serious problem faced by parties in Latin America today. The lure of a more ordered society, the speed of a directed economy, and the sense of permanence and stability that comes with appointed leadership, has done much to precipitate the rash of military governments in the 1970s and the subsequent oppression of party opposition.

If oppressed parties are to ever break out of the "outlaw" mold and be allowed once again to practice their art, not only must authoritarian governments tolerate their presence, but, more importantly, the Latin American populace must decide whether they prefer military regimentation to the disorder of politics, the slow compromised nature of economic development in a democracy rather than the speed of dictatorial rule, and the insecurity that comes with electoral change instead of predetermined leadership. The day may come soon when oppressed parties will be allowed to participate in national politics, but the real question of whether parties have the support of the people remains to be seen. Without that support, political parties in Uruguay and Chile will remain "outlaws."

Successful Party Opposition: The "Victors"

Political party opposition has certainly been presented as in a dismal state. However, the story of "survivors," "compromisers" and "outlaws" must be balanced with a presentation of those political systems where it is possible to view successful party opposition.

The attainment of an opposition system similar to that found in the United States or Western Europe is limited, with some reservations, to Venezuela and Costa Rica. Both these countries take pride in the fact that the principles of loyal opposition are firmly established and working well. In both countries it is possible to see opposition parties win national power away from the incumbent, hold power for a number of years, and implement alternative policies, without fear of retaliation from the other side.

Since 1958, when the dictator Pérez Jiménez was overthrown, Venezuela has been a model of successful and prosperous democracy. At the heart of Venezuela's successful opposition system is the Democratic Action Party (AD) and Christian Democratic Party (COPEI).[16] With the fall of Pérez Jiménez not only did Venezuela experience an uninterrupted period of stable democracy under a series of AD presidents, but from 1968 to 1973 Venezuela saw its first change of party power and the ascension to the office of the presidency of the COPEI candidate, Rafael Caldera. When out of power, both parties have assumed the role of loyal opposition—criticizing, challenging, offering alternative programs—but always in a manner that is not disruptive of the fragile democratic process.

Similarly, Costa Rica, since the revolution of 1948 against the dictator Rafael Calderon, has seen the formation and development of a two-party system where oppositon politics flourishes. After 1948, the two major parties, the more liberal Party of National Liberation (PLN) and a loose coalition of more conservative parties called the Unity Party, have opposed each other in the presidential and congressional elections without incident.[17]

The PLN, like the AD in Venezuela, has won more than its share of presidential elections since 1948, but the Unity Party has not been shut out. The current Costa Rican president, Rodrigo Carazo, is of the Unity Party, and he narrowly defeated the candidate of the PLN in the 1978 election.

The success of party opposition in Venezuela and Costa Rica is an encouraging sign in a region where political "out" groups are usually treated with so little respect. But the fact that opposition politics does thrive in these two countries should not distract us from some problems in the opposition system that create questions about the success of party politics and the achievement of the democratic institution of loyal opposition.

Perhaps a more precise way to define the party system and, in particular, the party opposition system in Venezuela and Costa Rica is to use a term found in the language of state and local politics in the United States. The term often used to describe a state where two competing organizations exist, but one exerts a dominent influence over the other, is called a modified one-party system. In Venezuela, where the AD is dominant, and in Costa Rica, where the PLN is consistently strong, a modified one-party system seems to have developed, as party opposition has only an occasional opportunity to gain national power. The opposition candidate has to be exceptional (as in the case of Caldera) or the circumstances have to be right (as in the allegation of corruption directed at the PLN in Costa Rica) in order for the opposition to have a chance of electoral success.

Besides the modified nature of the two-party system in Venezuela and Costa Rica, opposition parties in these countries also seem to have a more narrow socioeconomic or regional base of support. Both the COPEI and the Unity Party cannot yet claim to be national or mass parties, but they have support in certain clientele. Finally, the tradition of paternalism remains strong in these countries, so that once a party gains power and begins to dispense public service, it is difficult to convince people to change party patrons. The success of the AD and the PLN is owed largely to their image as the force behind national liberation and economic modernization.

Despite these disclaimers, the achievement of a democratic opposition system in Venezuela and Costa Rica must not be minimized. In Venezuela and Costa Rica, the heritage of paternalism, military intervention, regional and class differences, and limited practice in the art of democracy has not deterred party leaders from developing a democratic opposition system that can serve as a model for other republics in the region. Both countries have proven that opposition politics can be structured in a more democratic manner without the restriction, superficiality, or oppression found in other countries.

The Effect of Political Party Opposition in Latin America: Four Problems

The categorization of party opposition in Latin America presented above is not complete without a more general analysis that cuts across the diversity present in democratic opposition groups and analyzes the problems common to parties that occupy positions as policy critics and political challengers of existing governing regimes. By presenting an analysis that concentrates on the effect that opposition politics has on the political party hierarchy and operation, it will be possible to see that parties face not only the prospect of becoming "survivors," "compromisers," and "outlaws," (and perhaps "victors") but also can expect to encounter four problems that create internal disarray and disillusionment.

Tactical Disagreements

The most obvious problem facing political party opposition in Latin America is the inevitable disagreements that arise over how best to challenge the governing regime. Many opposition parties unable to win and maintain national power find themselves groping for some means of effectively counteracting the actions and policies of the government. When an opposition party finds that the electoral process is a fraud, the legislative body is impotent, and the avenues of public communication are censored or closed, it soon becomes obvious that the party has few opposition options available, short of armed revolution. Faced with so many obstacles to effective opposition, party leaders almost constantly bicker over the "correct" opposition position and the "most effective" means of challenging the government.[18]

To remain visible amidst these restraints, opposition parties have in recent years encouraged voter abstention, initiated general strikes, and directed world attention to their political system. However, these actions are designed mainly to voice anger against the government, and they do little to bring about substantial internal change. In the end, the opposition party must realize that, without the institutionalization of democratic political opposition in many Latin American states, the tactical options available to parties will be slim and generally ineffective.

Ideological Disputes

Alongside the tactical disagreements, opposition parties also face disputes of a more serious nature. Through the years, many parties, after experiencing fruitless opposition efforts, have entered into an introspective phase in which party leaders and theoreticians debate the merits of retaining a particular party philosophy. Although there is no general rule on the outcome of these internal ideological debates, there is some evidence from the more moderate liberal democratic opposition parties that the failures they encounter have caused a shift to the Left and a reevaluation of democratic practice and reform.[19] After seeing electoral fraud and police repression, and after experiencing periods of exile and military rule, it is not surprising to witness parties engaging in discussion as to whether they should reject previously held democratic positions and move to a new set of principles that better match the realities of politics to their state.

Oftentimes these debates cause more furor than the bickering over tactics, primarily because they strike at the heart of the party's reasons for existence. Even more importantly, these ideological disputes, especially those that bring into question the possibility of effective democratic government, make clear the dilemmas facing democracy in Latin America. Opposition parties that have engaged in this debate know that the real question is not whether to run candidates in an election or endure police intimidation; the real question is whether to hold on to democratic principles and the vision of a democratic state in the future.

Factionalism

When disputes arise over the method of opposition to the government and the correct ideological posture, factionalism within the party is usually not far off. Many of the opposition parties in Latin America have experienced, or are experiencing, internal cleavages that are a direct result of conflicts over tactics or philosophy. There have been instances where the egos of the party leaders have precipitated a separation, especially with respect to the division of "spoils" in the leadership hierarchy. In the main, though, opposition parties have experienced factionalism primarily because they cannot agree on how best to criticize and challenge the governing regime.

Factionalism is perhaps the most serious result of party opposition in Latin America. Unable to effectively oppose the government, rent by ideological disputes, political parties begin to break off into rival bands of activists who still want to replace the government, but now, rather than speaking with one voice and from one direction, present a wide spectrum of beliefs and policies.[20]

What often occurs as a result of this factionalism is that, if elections are held, the government faces not one or two strong opponents but a whole host of parties that fight the government, and themselves. In some political systems of Latin America there have been attempts to create large opposition coalitions, but these have often failed because of an inability to find common tactical and ideological ground. In a real sense factionalism takes the job of oppression away from the government. Rather than the government having to actively weaken the democratic opposition, parties often weaken themselves. Unfortunately the end result is the same—a feeble opposition voice.

Morale Problems

If the party can avoid factional disputes and agree to a set course of action, it is by no means free of the problems that face opposition groups. The most insidious result of party opposition in Latin America is the atmosphere of despair and fear that it instills among dedicated opposition activists.

After years of party opposition, individuals who have worked to replace a particular governing regime may simply feel that victory is impossible, that the risks are too high, and that if the party would take power it might not be able to hold it or would cause an internal war that could destroy the country. With options such as these, it is no wonder that party opposition is not a popular occupation. Once-proud leaders of the opposition have either gone into exile, live quietly underground, publicly renounced politics, or have accepted jobs within the government. Many opposition party leaders see the futility of their efforts and the very real danger to them and to their families. It is certainly possible for an opposition to overcome tactical, ideological, and personal problems through the art of compromise and individual sacrifice. The morale problem, though, runs much deeper than the others. Opposition party leaders, when faced with the prospect of remaining on the outside of the political arena and being branded as criminals, oftentimes choose to leave politics, with all its frustrations and dangers. The fact that political party opposition still remains in Latin America is a credit to the bravery and perseverance of its leaders. for every determined party leader, however, one can find others whose morale has dropped so low that they have left the fight forever.

Prospects for the Future

Political party opposition in Latin America has been presented in the press as an "endangered species" in the kingdom of Latin American politics. Faced with various forms of government sponsored repression, intimidation, and control, party opposition has been forced to live on the fringes of politics with little influence and often in great danger. In only a few isolated instances is it possible to see a vibrant opposition system in Latin America.

Despite this gloomy picture, it is possible to examine a few hopeful signs that point to a resurgence of party opposition and perhaps a strengthening of democratic practice in Latin America.[21] One of the more visible changes in the status of party opposition is the effect that President Carter's human-rights statements have had in Latin America. Although the Carter policy has been heavily criticized by military governments, there is a new feeling of optimism present among opposition leaders and a complementary wariness of U.S. pressure and critical world opinion on the part of authoritarian governments. The 1978 presidential election in the Dominican Republic is a case in point. Most observers credit the Carter resolve on human rights and democratic government with forestalling the military from trying to influence the presidential election that was clearly won by the opposition party candidate Antonio Guzmán. Statements made by President Carter and Secretary Vance that the United States would not look favorably on the corruption of the democratic election process appear to have caused the military to back away from its intervention and allow the election results to be tabulated. It remains to be seen whether Guzmán will be allowed to hold power for any length of time, but the actions of the Carter administration not only bolstered the PRD opposition but sent a signal to other opposition groups that outside pressure can strengthen the internal position of a political party.

A less-publicized change in the Latin American political scene that may benefit the status of party opposition is the decline in popularity and confidence in modernizing ability that the military now receives in the region. In recent years the military has been touted in many circles as the only effective force for modernization and stability. The claim made by the generals that they will be able to bring to Latin America administrative efficiency, a sense of social discipline, and a well-ordered political state was viewed as particularly well adapted to the needs of Latin American development.

In the last few years, however, criticism of military governments has become widespread, and, not surprisingly, some Latin American countries are returning to a civilian democratic form of government. Peru and Ecuador are good examples of countries where the military has lost the support of the people and, in the process, has heightened the chances for opposition parties to once again compete for national office.

The Peruvian people in particular never developed a strong feeling for the military and their left-leaning modernizing efforts. The Peruvian generals were often seen as overbearing, corrupt, and inaccessible. When it was reported, for example, in the world press that Peru was near bankruptcy and engulfed in military mismanagement, increased pressure was placed on the generals to open up the political system and allow for new elections. The main beneficiaries of this pressure are the opposition parties, who now have another opportunity to gain power and manage Peruvian affairs.

The unpopularity of military governments is not necessarily as widespread elsewhere as it is in Peru and Ecuador, but it can be said with confidence that throughout Latin America military leaders have not been able to create an atmosphere of support within their respective countries. Civilian political leaders continue to be viewed as more competent, more honest, more humane, and simply more likeable. Should military unpopularity intensify in Latin America, it can only lead to the resurgence of political party activity and, more importantly, the reinstitution of democratic government.

Finally, looking into the future, party opposition can be seen as entering a more favorable period, primarily because, in this author's opinions, the vision of democratic government remains fixed in the minds of many Latin Americans. Relying purely on an impressionistic analysis of the current state of Latin American politics, democracy continues to show a surprising resilience in the face of the most unfavorable conditions. There is no doubt, though, that military governments are still numerous and strong and remain committed to retarding the growth of democratic institutions and practice. Although these conditions of political control persist, it is possible to see, at the same time, increased demands for a revival of the electoral process, angry antigovernment demonstrations, critical newspaper reporting, heightened citizen activism and, perhaps most important, the renewed popularity of political party organizations.

It is not my intent to conclude this paper with a glowing account of the prospects for parties, opposition politics, and democracy. Political party organizations, as proponents of the principles of loyal opposition and the democratic system, are still in what can be called a recuperative state—they have been dangerously ill in recent years and need a long period of revitalization and support before being declared fully healed.

Nevertheless, signs do point to the fact that this may be a crucial juncture in the life of parties, opposition, and democracy in Latin America. The military cannot be expected to lie down and die, nor can the people be expected to rise up in democratic revolution. What can be predicted with some certainty is that parties and party leaders will press more vigorously than ever before to reassert their presence and their dedication to the principles of democratic government. Democratic party opposition has never been an easy occupation in Latin America, but as we enter the 1980s it seems that the conditions may be right for a return to democratic government. Only time will determine whether the military is on the decline and popular pressure ushers in civilian-run democracies. What is certain is that political parties will be at the forefront of this revival and, in many respects, will be responsible for its success or failure.

Notes

1. The seminal article on Latin American party opposition is Robert Dix's "Latin America: Oppositions and Development," in Robert Dahl, *Regimes and Oppositions* (New Haven: Yale University Press, 1973).

2. The most detailed study of Western democratic opposition and the practice of loyal opposition can be found in Robert A. Dahl, "Patterns of Opposition," in Robert Dahl, ed., *Political Opposition in Western Democracies* (New Haven: Yale University Press, 1966).

3. Some of the more well-known and more significant studies on opposition are Charles D. Ameringer, *The Democratic Left in Exile: The Anti-dictatorial Struggle in the Caribbean 1945-1959* (Coral Gables: University of Miami Press, 1974); Paul Lewis, *The Politics of Exile, Paraguay's Feberrista Party* (Chapel Hill: University of North Carolina Press, 1966); and Donald Mabry, *Mexico's Acción Nacional—A Catholic Alternative to Revolution* (Syracuse: Syracuse University Press, 1973).

4. The mechanics of a restricted system are discussed in my own study of Latin American opposition. See Michael J. Kryzanek, *Political Party Opposition in Latin America: The PRD, Joaquín Balaguer and Politics in the Dominican Republic 1966-1973* (Ph.D. dissertation, University of Massachusetts, Amherst, 1975).

5. See Michael J. Kryzanek, "Diversion, Subversion and Repression: The Strategies of Anti-Opposition Politics in Balaguer's Dominican Republic," *Caribbean Studies* (Winter 1978).

6. Harry Kantor's work on the Aprista movement remains the basic text for investigating Haya de la Torre and the APRA organization. Harry Kantor, *The Ideology and Program of the Peruvian Aprista Movement* (Berkeley: University

of California Press, 1953). See also Grant Hilliker, *The Politics of Reform in Peru: The Aprista and other Mass Parties of Latin America* (Baltimore: Johns Hopkins University Press, 1971).

7. The most recent analysis of the Mexican political system can be found in Kenneth Coleman's *Diffuse Support in Mexico: The Potential for Crises* (Beverly Hills: Sage Publication, 1976); and Salvatore Bizzarro's "Mexico's Government in Crises," *Current History* (March 1977).

8. Two works that discuss the "cooptation" efforts of the PRI are Bo Anderson and James D. Cockroft, "Control and Cooptation in Mexican Politics," in Irving Louis Horowitz, Josué de Castro and John Gerassi, *Latin American Radicalism* (New York: Vintage Books, 1969); and Kenneth F. Johnson, "Ideological Correlates of Right Wing Political Alienation in Mexico," *American Political Science Review* (September 1965), pp. 656-664.

9. See Alejandro Portes, "Legislatures and Authoritarian Regimes—The Case of Mexico," *Journal of Political and Military Sociology* (Fall 1977), pp. 185-201.

10. The most complete study of the National Front is Robert Dix, *Colombia: The Political Dimension of Change* (New Haven: Yale University Press, 1967).

11. The current difficulties facing Colombia caused massive violent demonstrations in 1978. See *The New York Times* (September 14-15, 1978).

12. There were signals as early as 1967 that all was not well with Colombian democracy. See Ronald H. McDonald's "Political Protest and Alienation in Voting: The Case of Colombia," *Inter-American Economic Affairs* (Autumn 1967), pp. 3-22.

13. The Inter-American Commission on Human Rights of the Organization of American States charged the Uruguayan government with "wholesale violations of human rights, including arbitrary arrest, torture and murder of political prisoners." See the *Washington Post* (June 29, 1978). Also see the analysis of the *Washington Office on Latin America,* entitled "Uruguay—Five Years of Military Rule" (June 1978).

14. Current analysis of the Pinochet regime is overshadowed by a desire by many to investigate the demise of Salvador Allende. The best study of post-1973 Chile can be found in Frederick M. Nunn's "Military-Civilian Relations in Chile—The Legacy of the Golpe of 1973," *Inter-American Economic Affairs* (Autumn 1975), pp. 43-58.

15. The Chilean Catholic church in a real sense has replaced political party opposition in that country. See Kenneth Longton and Ronald Rapaport's "Religion and Leftist Mobilization in Chile," *Comparative Political Studies* (October 1976), pp. 227-308.

16. Daniel H. Levine, *Conflict and Political Change in Venezuela* (Princeton: Princeton University Press, 1973), contains a fine analysis of the interaction between the AD and COPEI in Venezuela.

17. Burt H. English, in *Liberación Nacional in Costa Rica: The Development of a Political Party* (Gainesville: University of Florida Press, 1971), presents the most recent study of the major party in Costa Rica and also the state of the democratic system in that country.

18. See my study of the problems encountered by the opposition PRD in the Dominican Republic, "Political Party Decline and the Failure of Liberal Democracy: The PRD in Dominican Politics," *Journal of Latin American Studies* (May 1977), pp. 115-143.

19. See Susan Bodenheimer, "La Crises del Movimiento Social Demócrata en América Latina." *Estudios Internacionales* No. 12 (enero-marzo 1970). Also, see Howard J. Wiarda's "The Crisis of the Latin American Democratic Left," *Dissent* (November-December 1969), pp. 529-536.

20. Russell Fitzgibbon comments on the problem of party factionalism in an article entitled "Seven Dilemmas of Latin American's National Revolutionary Parties," *Orbis* (September 1970), pp. 443-462.

21. For a discussion of the human rights issues from the Latin American perspective see Howard J. Wiarda's "Democracy and Human Rights in Latin America: Toward a New Conceptualization, *Orbis* (Spring 1978), pp. 137-160.

7
Democracy and Elites in Latin America

Jack W. Hopkins

Introduction

The continuing struggle for democracy in Latin America, viewed from the perspective of the late 1970s, might appear to be rather the death throes of democracy. Rarely in modern times has that region's political landscape seemed more devoid of even moderately open, democratic governments. An inventory of freely elected, constitutionally legitimate governments includes barely a half-dozen states, even when a rather parsimonious definition of democracy is employed. The observer biased toward democratic politics might despair at the current scene.

At best, of course, measurement of democracy poses an extraordinarily difficult task, one permeated by subjective considerations and criteria.[1] However, regardless of the criteria, whether one uses procedural norms (e.g., free elections, extent of participation, legal safeguards of individual rights, etc.) or substantive norms (e.g., social and economic pluralism and reasonable equity in the distribution of wealth), Latin America in general falls short on democratic achievement.

One might argue that taking a long, historical perspective on Latin American politics makes the contemporary situation relatively less unattractive. In comparing past and present, one must contrast woefully undeveloped political and economic systems and frequently tyrannical past governments with today's situation, where numerous regimes, as Busey puts it, "make no pretense of constitutionality and offer no legal justifications for their governance by unmasked force,"[2] even though substantial development and modernization in other respects have occurred. The reader must judge which situation is more palatable.

A volume such as this, focusing upon the continuing struggle for democracy, must perforce include an examination of the various groups that have affected that struggle in complex ways. This chapter is a survey of the role of elites in the development of democracy in Latin America.

In many respects, the concepts of democracy and elitism clash philosophically with each other even under ideal conditions. To an important degree, democratic government and its accompanying notion of representativeness (difficult though that is to define) suggest a natural antagonism toward the reality of elite control. Although the two concepts are not contradictory, except perhaps in the purest form of democracy, their relationship is rarely a comfortable, complementary arrangement. But we must study the high strata of societies because, among other reasons, as Lipset and Solari observe, "it is clear that regardless of differences in social systems, one of the requisites for development is a competent elite, motivated to modernize their society."[3] And some have argued that the elite should be given the main credit for preserving and defending democratic government and concepts in many countries against the authoritarianly inclined masses.

Under other than ideal conditions, as in a less developed area such as much of Latin America, certain elites may find it extremely difficult to function effectively while respecting the constraints of democratic government. In much of Latin America, serious obstacles exist in the way of the development of democratic government and a supportive role for elites within a democratic system.

First, there appears to be a weak consensus, if any, among Latin American elites about the desirable form of government. Various elite groups—the military, intellectuals, business and economic leaders, political party leaders, and bureaucrats—have seldom in the recent period reached any but the most tenuous agreement on the form of government and the proper nature and scope of participation in its politics. Anderson has observed that democracy has never been legitimated in Latin America.[4]

Second, elite ambivalence about democratic government frequently has left such governments weakened and in a highly vulnerable position. Common indeed are the cases where the elite has either apologized for authoritarian actions on the part of supposedly democratic governments or covertly or overtly encouraged military overthrows of such governments when such coups d'état served their purposes.

For example, despite the difficult communication barriers that exist between military men, intellectuals, and civilian politicians, Imaz notes that:

> resort to the Armed Forces as a source of legitimacy has ended by being a tacit rule of the political game in Argentina. This is an aspect of political life of which nobody expressly approves, but from which all the political groups have profited at least once. All will publicly deny this rule, but in

private Argentine politicians cannot ignore that, at one time or another during this quarter of a century, they have all knocked on the doors of the garrisons.[5]

Astiz has noted, in reference to Peru, "only a handful of those who participate actively in politics question the principle of the military as referees of political disputes; what different people question at different times is the choice the military make."[6] The problem extends to recently democratic nations such as Venezuela. As Rafael Caldera observed, "Venezuelans are so accustomed to make the army arbiter of the political contests that at each moment the most varied groups for the most dissimilar ends attempt to involve the army in new adventures to change our political reality."[7]

Another version leaves a perilously weak democratic government immobilized because of ideological rigidity on the part of the political elite in the legislature, political parties, or other strategic structures. The rigid, doctrinaire divisions of factions of Argentine political parties, leading to splits of old parties and the rise of new ones, provide an example of the problem. Ideological rigidity of factions within the old Unión Cívica Radical (UCR) party—the Conservative Unionists on one hand and the left-wing Intransigents on the other—led in 1957 to a formal split of the UCR into two distinct parties, the Intransigent Radical Civic Union and the People's Radical Civic Union, and the two bitterly fought each other. A major issue was the question of broadening the scope of participation to insure *peronistas* a full political role.

Finally, major barriers to change exist in the social, economic, and political systems of Latin America and impede the development of the infrastructure necessary for an effective, symbiotic relationship between elites and democracy. These several obstacles to the development of democracy in Latin America and the role of the elite in that process will be considered in what follows.

The Problem of Analysis

Hazardous indeed is the journey into studies of power, decision making, and elites in society. Research and speculation about the "ruling class," the "ruling elite," the "power structure," or the "power elite" have all been based on the assumption that there exists in every polity "an identifiable minority that makes most of the important decisions that shape the lives of the majority."[8] Various approaches have characterized the literature, ranging from the Marxist (economic elites constitute the ruling group), through the stratification theorists (the upper class rules in its own interest, and is superior to political and civic leaders), to the pluralist school (rejecting the assumption that some particular ruling elite must exist and searching for an understanding of how political decisions are made by diffused forces in society). One frequently is left with an uncomfortable conclusion that political decision making remains a rather amorphous, highly complex, and typically mysterious process in which it is often difficult, and sometimes impossible, to determine the extent of involvement of the key participants. Such uneasiness is compounded by the environment of decision making in Latin America. Whether one employs the reputational method, sociobackground studies, role theory, or the analysis of decision making and events as a means of arriving at determination of patterns of elite influence, many analytical questions remain.

Relatively little systematic and rigorous research exists on elite groups in Latin America. The important gaps in this field of Latin American studies are somewhat surprising, given the generally acknowledged strategic role played by such elites. In part, such gaps resulted from the tendency of many scholars to allow generalizations to outrun data. The haste to provide explanations of political, economic and social phenomena frequently led students of Latin America to accept uncritically many descriptions of the causes and relationships of such phenomena. That tendency left us, as far as most countries of Latin America are concerned, without adequate answers to even the most elementary question—who are the elites? Even the descriptive dimension has been explored inadequately. When coupled with underdeveloped research into closely related areas, such as research on pressure groups, decision making, and public administration, the absence of sound data of this type assumes crucial importance.

For example, there is as yet no substantiation of the common assumption that the key to behavior may be found in a group's socioeconomic background. Perhaps social background data often is used indiscriminately because conclusive evidence of the actual relationship between background and attitude is lacking.[9] Obviously, the possible gulf between attitude and ultimate behavior in or out of office may also be great.

However, as Beck and Malloy[10] suggest, concentration on control will facilitate more accurate identification of elites and aid in avoidance of many of the problems typically associated with descriptive elite studies. The focus on control naturally leads to consideration of the role of potential elites in the processes of change. Unless attention is given to the existing power configuration of a polity and the behavioral norms of the elite, understanding of the probability of potential elites exercising their potential will be deficient. Other key variables, which Beck and

Malloy consider secondary, are elite perceptions and the techniques and mechanisms for maintaining an elite position.

The Beck and Malloy typology of elites, which included three basic ideal types (the divided and permeable elite, the unified and impermeable elite, and the divided and impermeable elite) seems highly serviceable for structuring elite analysis. The closest approximation to typical Latin American elites (to the extent that a typical elite structure may be found) would appear traditionally to be the divided and impermeable types. In this variety, no coherent unified groups exert pervasive control, although there are definite centers with autonomous power potential, and members do tend to come from the same socioeconomic caste or class strata. Other characteristics are a definite lack of mobility from constituencies. The lack of agreed-upon principles of open and peaceful-interest competition reinforces a tendency toward intraelite conflict. It would appear that the characteristic coup d'état in many Latin American political systems is a logical outlet or means of resolution of such conflicts. Contrast this view with that of Kling, who interpreted violence and the military coup as a consequence of the closure of various paths to power (economic or political) to certain groups in society.[11] Anderson has suggested that new power contenders are not admitted to the elite arena until they have demonstrated their power capabilities, and that old ones will not be eliminated.[12]

A number of recent coups appear to indicate a trend toward further disintegration of shifting and transient elite coalitions and alliances. Peru is perhaps the best example, and the political strategies of the armed forces as the critical power factor in Peruvian politics provide a case in point. After the 1962 coup, which annulled the election of that year, the military junta took a number of measures to mollify the upper classes of Peru. For example, repressive action was taken against labor and *campesino* organizations that were creating problems for the traditional upper classes. Even after the military relinquished power, following new elections in 1963, they remained deeply involved in the decision-making process in the Belaúnde Terry administration. The overthrow of Belaúnde in 1968 was followed by expropriation of the controversial La Brea and Pariñas oil fields of the International Petroleum Company and a land reform program that went further toward neutralizing the power of the traditional landholding classes than other reform efforts. The military since 1968 have considered themselves to be the developmental elite of Peru and on occasion that role has brought them into conflict with groups that traditionally have been close allies.

Another example of the changing nature of traditional elite coalitions may be seen in Venezuela. It has become increasingly clear that the "oligarchy" in that nation can no longer depend on a special relationship with the military that existed with and before Pérez Jiménez. Less and less do the armed forces appear to play a critical role in policy formulation and decision making, or even seem inclined to do so.[13]

Too many elite studies of Latin America, as Welsh points out, fail to examine leaders in their environmental context, despite the host of theoretical formulations that call attention to nonpolitical dimensions such as economic, social, and cultural factors.[14] Welsh's call for "continual and systematic interplay" between broad generalizations and specific case descriptions is especially pertinent. He criticizes the prevailing tendency of leadership studies "to attribute functional significance extra-empirically to formal positions in government or political party hierarchies." Yet the nature of the decision-making process being what it is, the researcher, as a practical matter, must often make such assumptions pending much more thorough understanding of how decisions actually are made.

The implicit assumption of functional significance is evident in a number of studies of political leadership in Latin America. In Cochrane's and Agor's studies of the Chilean Senate, in my study of Peruvian bureaucrats, in Imaz's work on the Argentine military leadership,[15] at least an implicit assumption of the significance of these particular leadership groups is an underlying theme. In defense of that assumption, one could point to the critical role of the Chilean Senate in hamstringing the reform legislation of President Eduardo Frei's Christian Democratic administration and a similar situation during Allende's government from centrist and rightist parties; to the strategic role of the Peruvian bureaucracy in the administration or maladministration of agrarian reform, education, and developmental program under President Belaúnde Terry; and in the case of Argentina, to the continuing role of the military as arbiters of national politics in that nation, a role amply demonstrated by repeated intervention since 1930. The least that can be said in defense of such studies is that they are an essential preliminary step toward further analysis.

The Role of Elites

But this is not the place for an extended critique of elite studies nor for the development of a research agenda. Rather, my purpose is essentially to review the ways in which elites have been involved in both positive and negative ways in the development of democratic government in Latin America. For this purpose, I must use a broad definition of both the concepts of "development" and "elites." Employed in the broadest sense, development encompasses not only the positive notions of ever broadening differentiation, modernization, political participation, and integration, but also the negative notions of unintegrated differentiation, regression, and political decay.[16]

As far as the concept of elites is concerned, there is basic agreement in recent studies of elites that power is the central phenomenon in the idea of the elite. Generally, "elites" is used to refer to "functional, mainly occupational, groups which have high status (for whatever reason) in a society."[17] However, strict adherence to the notion that actual control over decision making (as distinguished from "power" or notability) is essential to eliteness, may force the omission of groups with apparently strong potential for control if not indirect influence on decision making. That view also tends to delimit the scope of decisions to those of paramount importance to the overall society (whether that be city, region, or nation) and fails to accommodate analyses of lower-strata "elites." The latter, of course, may be exercising comparable control at their own level. Thus "high status" or "eliteness" must be defined in relation to strategic structures of the society.

The Corporative Society and Redundancy

Wiarda has proposed the corporative model to recognize and account for the peculiarly Iberian experiences in the formation of the social and political systems of Latin America.[18] If valid as a framework—and the description is persuasive—that interpretation provides a valuable outline of the nature of the environment within which the various elite groups in Latin America function in maintaining the traditional order under developmental pressures.

> Why and how do the traditional social and political forms—and the legal and constitutional framework that help give them legitimacy—hang on so tenaciously? One important answer, it would seem, is the maintenance, even in the present and increasingly modern era in Latin America, of corporate social and political structures, reinforced by a political culture that stresses hierarchy, authority, status, and patronage. The corporative framework helps maintain this traditional structure, but at the same time provides for change through the process of cooptation of new social and political units into the administrative units of the corporative system. The corporative way of achieving change thus helps preserve the status quo while at the same time defusing discontent through gradualist and incremental accommodation to new pressures. It helps keep the pressures for change within check by minimizing the possibilities for disruption or revolution. The corporative framework may respond to modernization and adopt some of its ways, but it also provides for the preservation of traditional attitudes and traditional institutions.[19]

Given the philosophical and pragmatic stresses between elitism and democratic government, the corporate structure that Wiarda describes may pose a serious barrier to certain types of change. For an effective, symbiotic relationship ever to develop between elites and democracy, a special kind of accommodation is necessary. Although the corporate structure and the elite guardians of the framework typically seek to accommodate change through the process of cooptation, that strategy may prove insufficient in periods where incremental concessions simply fall short of ameliorating the causes of discontent. The strength of the corporate structure may lie in its capability for melding the demands of modernization with the traditional arrangements, but its accommodative ability may prove too fragile or too brittle to confront and manage truly revolutionary movements and forces.

In such situations, where general violence is directed against the dominant groups, the accommodative cooptation may fail. Mexico, perhaps, offers an appropriate example of such a case; when the safety valves of the corporate structure could not accommodate the revolutionary pressures, the structure was temporarily swept away. However, the political system that followed the revolution, to a large extent, confirms the staying power if not the complete validity of the corporate structure. Since the Revolution, Mexico's dominant *Partido Revolucionario Institucional* (in effect, the embodiment of the new elite) has served to direct and moderate the developmental process, tightly controlling participation in politics and admitting or coopting threatening contenders through incremental and generally conservative accessions of influence. Whether that strategy will continue to be effective in the face of steadily mounting discontent and widespread challenges remains problematical. In Cuba, the revolutionary pressures of Fidel Castro and his followers on the elite structure, which had resorted increasingly to authoritarian rule, led to the collapse of the Batista regime and to wholesale replacement or exile of the former elite.

Even in the absence of the traumatic paroxysm of revolutionary violence, a society may find its critically important elite dropping out. **Scott has spoken of the serious loss of Argentina's elite during the past** decade and a half, in which a "brain drain" of major proportions has resulted in voluntary emigration of thousands of professionals, intellectuals, and other potential participants in the developmental process.[20] The loss may be virtually irreplaceable and the maturation of competing forces that could serve as countervailing factors in the political process is further retarded.

The cases of Mexico, Cuba, and Bolivia suggest what may be the critical aspect of societies with a corporative structure. As Wiarda observes, commenting on the "multiple currents" described by Newton,[21] reconciling these diverse pressures "is often an incredibly difficult juggling and balancing act, not only because of the increasingly diverse interests represented but also because no common consensus or bases of legitimacy any longer exist."[22] To a large extent, the capacity of the corporate society to graft on and assimilate new structures and functions may not be sufficient to build the kind of protective redundancy that serves as a cushion in times of great stress.

Lacking such redundancy (such as viable opposition political parties, accommodative constitutional and statutory provisions, a reasonably autonomous judicial system, and a broad array of supportive institutions such as interest groups and a free mass communications network), the juggling and balancing act may fail to defuse extreme situations and the lack of integration may become fatal for the elite structure. In such situations, an apparent ideological rigidity on the part of participants and diverse interests in the corporate structure mitigates against a search for pragmatic solutions and aggravates the vulnerability of democratic governments.

The essential problem may be that the corporate structure, while it appears to be capable of almost indefinite absorption and assimilation of contending forces, deliberately attempts to act as controller of the assimilative process so as to keep it always within acceptable limits. That is, *the marketplace of ideas and interest is not free but managed.* The necessity for official legitimation (through licensing, recognition, or legal approval) inhibits the full development of competing forces and institutions, and therefore these elements are not capable of providing the protective redundancy when needed.

Traditional Elite Coalitions

"In the beginning the landed oligarchy had the money and practically all the social prestige; the church had the truth; the military had the guns—all the stuff of political power. There were no middle class, political parties, labor unions, or bureaucracy—nothing except the political punch of the Unholy Trinity."[23] In much of Latin America, the rapid change and the concentrated onslaught of challengers to the old order have produced what Scott has called a "cultural lag."[24] No longer can the traditional bonds that tied together the mutual interests of the landowning class, the military leadership, and the church be taken for granted. That alliance formed a classical power elite; a reasonable consensus existed about both the proper role of government and the nature and scope of political participation. The traditional solid front of that power elite has been shattered in country after country, and the previously allied factions of that elite have increasingly come into conflict with one another. As the development process has unfolded, the mutually supportive role of the different traditional elite sectors has disintegrated.

This type of change came about in various forms. In Peru, for example, the military after 1968 attacked not only transnational corporations and their landholdings, but the problem of Peruvian-owned latifundia as well. The traditionally comfortable relationship between the army and the landholding elite collapsed as the interests and long-run objectives of the military developmentalists and that elite came into conflict.

This new developmental stance of the military amounts to a third phase in the changing role of the armed forces elite in Latin America. The first phase, following the obviously critical function of the military in the wars for independence, was essentially a mutually supportive role with the other key segments of the power elite—the landowners and the church. The second phase might be described as one in which the armed services filled a moderating role, in which the divergent interests of the traditional elite and its growing competitors were reconciled frequently by direct but temporary military intervention. The current phase in the role of the military casts the armed forces in leadership roles as planners, promoters, and directors of the modernization process. The political and economic systems of several Latin American states were subjected to severe strains as the military leaders chose to take on the development task directly. In Brazil since the overthrow of Goulart in 1964, in Peru since the coup against Belaúnde in 1968, in Chile since Allende's fall in 1973, in Argentina since the ouster of Illia in 1966, among other countries, the military unabashedly has determined to direct rather than moderate the developmental process. Further, the attitude of the armed forces leadership about the duration of their intervention has shifted. From the view that intervention is a transient, temporary corrective, the military has taken an open-ended attitude regarding the return of "normal politics."

Needler points out that several major studies (by Baker, Lieuwen, Finer, and Thompson), essentially conclude that military self-interest has been the most significant factor in Latin American coups d'état.[25] Needler observes that:

> Institutional-interest motives thus appear invariably present in institutional seizures of power. System-level causes, e.g. class struggle, may on occasion be the ultimate prime movers in the process that leads to a coup;

but while they have great explanatory power in the history of some coups, they are not of frequent enough applicability to serve as a general explanation of the military seizure of power.[26]

Valid though these conclusions may be, perhaps they miss the main point: why the military intervenes may be much less important than what the military does after securing power. And the role of the armed forces as a critically important elite group, with serious implications for the continuing struggle for democracy, seems likely to expand in the future.

The Democratic Left

In any study of the political elite of Latin America, prominent attention must be given to the relatively small number of leaders who initiated, sparked, and maintained the struggle for democracy against strong opposition. There are many examples throughout much of Latin America (mainly *aprista*-type parties, led by men such as Haya de la Torre of Peru, Juan Bosch of the Dominican Republic, and José Figueres of Costa Rica), but one of the most noteworthy is the "generation of '28" of Venezuela. Much of the ideology and patterns of political thought in contemporary Venezuela derive from the protest of this group against the dictator Juan Vicente Gómez. Among the leaders of the "generation of '28" was Rómulo Betancourt, who played a critical role in the formation of the precursor party of Acción Democrática and later served as Venezuela's president. The willingness of Betancourt and others to join with the armed forces to overthrow the government in 1945 and again in 1958 suggests a more complex character of the democratic left than might be commonly assumed. Taylor comments:

> As it has existed in Latin America, the democratic left has preferred due process wherever possible, not only because this attributes value to transactional politics rather than to the massing of arms, but also because it gives credibility to a commitment to benevolence. The democratic left has not been weak or non-ideological. In general it has been nationalist, comparatively institutional, and relatively subtle. It has not always succeeded when it has had its first opportunity in national power, and in some countries it never has had a chance at power at all. When generally it has been staffed by men of good will, it also has had its scoundrels.[27]

The willingness of the elite of the democratic left to resort to force may be seen in a number of instances, including José Figueres' volunteer army against the *Republicano* government in Costa Rica, the Apristas in

Peru, and others. Despite such occasional tactics, however, the leaders of the democratic left have played what is probably an indispensable role in political development in Latin America. Comparing Colombia and Venezuela, Taylor concludes that "the essential difference between the two countries appears to have been the presence (or lack) of a leadership committed to the establishment of a democratic left regime."[28] He goes on to say, "In a society in which the participation 'crisis' is virtually impossible of resolution, since purely democratic processes normally are regarded as conferring the opportunity for license rather than of self-restraint, it appears that the essential critical variable is intent by leadership."[29]

Until the elite of the democratic left make an unequivocal and permanent commitment of their intent to participate and govern democratically, democratic governments stand on shaky ground. Yet, of all the political leadership in Latin America, the leaders of the democratic left parties come closer to being consistent advocates and defenders of democratic government. Where they have resorted to violence, it has been after the most extreme provocation and against the most tyrannical regimes. Their commitment to democracy, both procedural and substantive, has been more steadfast under trying conditions than that of any other elite group.

Other Elites

The role of elite groups other than the political leadership and the military elite is far more elusive and difficult to assess. Yet their importance should not be minimized because the elite in other sectors serve essential functions in developing (or retarding) the supportive societal infrastructure, providing (or closing) avenues of upward mobility, and facilitating (or impeding) economic and political participation.

These critical roles may operate in various ways. Analyzing the industrial elite in Argentina, Chile, and Colombia, Cardoso observes that "effective control of the enterprises is still exercised on a family basis and through the selection of persons who enjoy the 'confidence' of the shareholders in the light of non-professional criteria and relationships."[30] Although Cardoso's study was limited to three countries, his observations would apply well to other societies. In Brazil, for example, despite a generally fluid social mobility pattern, the *parentela* and other institutions for mutual benefit and control serve to limit open recruitment, participatory management, and economic development, all of which support democratic government.

The potentially strategic role of religious elites in the development of democracy in Latin America can hardly be denied. The Roman Catholic Church throughout the modern history of Latin America has occupied a pivotal position in society, and the church hierarchy has not been at all reluctant, as a general rule, to exercise its influence.

However, for many reasons, the religious elite have failed overall to fulfill their potential as a force promoting democracy. The early church's close identification with the ruling classes as an agency of the crown created permanent difficulties in terms of its relating to societal needs. Its deep involvement in the widespread struggles between liberals and conservatives in Latin America left most of the hierarchy aligned with the conservative forces and this relationship equipped the Church poorly for confronting the social and economic problems of the modern period. As Vallier has observed:

> The traditional Church, especially during the past fifty years, has in one Latin American country after another encountered trends and events that are forcing its elites to recognize a state of bankruptcy. The credits of the Church, built up over the years through political coalitions, a permissive morality, property involvements, and other worldly promises, are largely depleted.[31]

These comments are not intended to suggest that the church has reacted entirely monolithically to society's challenges. Although the dominant elements in the Catholic hierarchy have generally aligned themselves with the status quo—and, in effect, retarded democratic development—reformers and dissidents in a number of countries (notably Chile and Brazil) have tried to transform the traditional church. These individuals and groups, basing their actions on such social encyclicals as *Rerum Novarum*, *Quadragesimo Anno*, and *Mater et Magistra*, and the proposals of the Second Vatican Council, have allied themselves with *campesino*, liberal, and leftist movements in the effort to swing the church's strengths in the direction of change. Although the overall record of the religious elite has not been encouraging, there is still the possibility that the church may become a major force in support of democratic government.

The evidence supports no firm assessment of the role of the cultural elite or the intellectuals in the struggle for democracy in Latin America. Part of the difficulty in evaluating their roles is inherent in the diffuse and amorphous nature of ideas and their effect upon political attitudes and development. Another complicating factor lies in the definition of boundaries that delineate the cultural elite from other sectors. In Latin America, the frequent overlapping of professional roles adds to the problem; the philosopher-politician, the poet-president appear far more plausible in the Latin American context than in the United States.

Yet one might easily conclude—again recognizing the flimsiness of the evidence—that the Latin American cultural elite have been something less than champions of democracy. Bonilla pessimistically observes that:

> Ideological failure has stemmed not only from the disconnection with reality but from a failure of faith. Even the handful of luminary *pensadores* who have thought most deeply about the identity and fate of Latin America have alternated between black pessimism and ingenuous self-congratulation; intellectuals have never had more than a faltering conviction that Latin America was truly a promised land.[32]

The evidence is not convincing that the cultural elite have functioned as a major force in the continuing struggle for democracy. The university in Latin America seems far removed from policy-making councils. But the contemporary observer may indeed stand too close to judge that.

The relation of the labor elite to politics and to the struggle for democracy in Latin America appears somewhat inverted. Where organized labor has exerted significant influence upon politics, likely as not that influence was derived not so much from labor's demanding it on the basis of strength as from grants of power or encouragement from political leaders. As Landsberger recounts,[33] in country after country, mass trade unionism was almost handed down to labor. Foresighted political leaders—Perón in Argentina, Vargas in Brazil, the leaders of Acción Democrática in Venezuela, Obregón in Mexico and others—recognized the potential power of mass labor unions, encouraged their organization, anticipated their needs through legislation, and built the unions as sources of support.

In several instances, labor has clearly affected the outcome of political situations—Perón's dramatic rise to power provides one of the best examples. The Mexican labor charter, incorporated in the 1917 constitution, resulted partly from the recognized strength of labor, but even then it was not a concession wrested by labor itself. Landsberger holds that labor's aims are less revolutionary, ideological, and long-range than they are "mundane ones: short-range, limited, economic, and not primarily the total reconstruction of society."[34] One might conclude that it is unlikely that labor would serve as a major factor in the struggle for democracy as a political objective. However, to the extent that improvement in labor's economic condition builds an essential foundation for a viable democratic system, one could be more sanguine. Unfortunately, political science has no really adequate methods of measuring that relationship.

Conclusion

In attempting to develop a reasonably balanced perspective on the role of elites in the continuing struggle for democracy in Latin America, one is struck anew by the tangled web that makes up the body politic. Consideration of any segment of society in isolation, whether it is the bureaucracy, the military, the peasants, or others, yields a fragmented result, certainly not wholly satisfactory. The complex relationships that exist in any society inevitably lead to contradictions when one attempts to assess roles and the effectiveness with which various segments carry out their roles. Even when analytical efforts, such as the massive study of Venezuelan political change by Bonilla, Silva Michelena, and others,[35] attempt to apply quantitative analysis to qualitative questions, the result still seems to provide only a very partial understanding.

When one moves to an evaluative question, such as "Have the elites failed?", the answer inescapably must be largely subjective and to a certain extent ethnocentric. Judging the progress of Latin America toward democracy may require the application of inappropriate standards and criteria that have a poor culture-fit. It may be true, as Anderson has suggested, that democracy has never been truly legitimated in Latin America. And therein may lie the root problem— the abyss between the ideal and real. The success or failure of Latin American elites should be measured against the standards, ideals, and goals that the Latin Americans have set for themselves. By that measure, the record of most Latin American elites has fallen short.

Notes

1. The interested reader may explore the problem further in the series of articles by Russell H. Fitzgibbon, "Measurement of Latin-American Political Phenomena: A Statistical Experiment," *American Political Science Review* 45 (1951), 517-23; "How Democratic is Latin America?", *Inter-American Economic Affairs* 9 (Spring 1956), 65-77; "A Statistical Evaluation of Latin American Democracy," *Western Political Quarterly* 9 (1956), 607-19; (with Kenneth F. Johnson), "Measurement of Latin American Political Change," *American Political Science Review* 54 (1961), 515-26; and "Measuring Democratic Change in Latin America," *Journal of Politics* 29 (February 1967), 129-66. See also Ernest

A. Duff and James F. McCamant, "Measuring Social and Political Requirements for System Stability in Latin America," *American Political Science Review* 62 (December 1968), 1125-43, as an example of a study employing more "objective" data, such as census and economic information, as the basis for judgment.

2. James L. Busey, *Latin American Political Guide*, 16th ed. (Manitou Springs: Juniper Editions, 1975), p. 3.

3. Seymour Martin Lipset and Aldo Solari (eds.), *Elites in Latin America* (New York: Oxford University Press, 1967), p. viii.

4. Charles W. Anderson, *Toward a Theory of Latin American Politics* Occasional Paper no. 2, Graduate Center for Latin American Studies, Vanderbilt University, February, 1964.

5. José Luis de Imaz, *Los que mandan* (Albany: State University of New York Press, 1970), p. 88. Translated by Carlos A. Astiz.

6. Carlos A. Astiz, "The Military Establishment as a Political Elite: The Peruvian Case," paper delivered at the 1969 Rio de Janeiro Round Table, International Political Science Association.

7. As quoted in *The Guardian*, March 19, 1977, p. 13.

8. Constantine Menges, *Ruling Elite Theories and Research Methods: An Evaluation* (Santa Monica: Rand Corporation, December 1968), p. 9.

9. Lewis Edinger and Donald D. Searing, "Social Background in Elite Analysis: A Methodological Analysis," *American Political Science Review* 61 (June 1967), 428-45.

10. Carl Beck and James Malloy, *Political Elites: A Mode of Analysis* (Pittsburgh: Archive on Political Elites, University of Pittsburgh, n.d.).

11. Merle Kling, "Toward a Theory of Power and Political Instability in Latin America," *Western Political Quarterly* 9 (March 1956), 21-35.

12. Charles W. Anderson, *Toward a Theory*.

13. Philip B. Taylor, "Thoughts on Comparative Effectiveness: Leadership and the Democratic Left in Colombia and Venezuela," Special Studies, Council on International Studies, State University of New York at Buffalo, August 1971, p. 2.

14. William Welsh, "Methodological Problems in the Study of Political Leadership in Latin America," *Latin American Research Review* 5 (Fall 1970), 3-33.

15. James D. Cochrane, "The Chilean Senate, 1961-1965: A Profile," (unpublished paper); Weston H. Agor, "The Senate in the Chilean Political System," in Allan Kornberg and Lloyd D. Musolf (eds.), *Legislatures in Developmental Perspective* (Durham: Duke University Press, 1970); Jack W. Hopkins, *The Government Executive of Modern Peru* (Gainesville: University of Florida Press, 1967); and José Luis de Imaz, *Los que mandan* (Buenos Aires: Editorial Universitaria, 1964).

16. See Fred W. Riggs, *Prismatic Society Revisited* (Morristown: General Learning Press, 1973) and Samuel P. Huntington, *Political Order in Changing Societies* (New Haven: Yale University Press, 1968).

17. T. B. Bottomore, *Elites and Society* (New York: Basic Books, 1965), p. 8.

18. Howard J. Wiarda (ed.), "Law and Political Development in Latin America: Toward a Framework for Analysis," in *Politics and Social Change in Latin America: The Distinct Tradition* (Amherst: University of Massachusetts Press, 1974), 199-229.

19. Wiarda, p. 210.

20. Robert E. Scott, "Political Elites and Political Modernization: The Crisis of Transition," in *Elites in Latin America*, pp. 117-45.

21. Ronald C. Newton, "On 'Functional groups,' 'Fragmentation,' and 'Pluralism' in Spanish American Political Society," *Hispanic American Historical Review* 50 (February 1970), 27, as quoted by Wiarda, p. 217.

22. Wiarda, p. 217.

23. Edward J. Williams and Freeman J. Wright, *Latin American Politics: A Developmental Approach* (Palo Alto: Mayfield Publishing Co., 1975), p. 143.

24. Scott, "Political Elites and Political Modernization: The Crisis of Transition," in *Elites in Latin America*, p. 121.

25. Ross K. Baker, *A Study of Military status and Status Deprivation in Three Latin American Armies* (Washington: American University Center for Research in Social Systems, 1967); Edwin Lieuwen, *Generals vs. Presidents: Neomilitarism in Latin America* (New York: Frederick A. Praeger, 1964); S. E. Finer, *The Man on Horseback* (New York: Frederick A. Praeger, 1962); William R. Thompson, "Explanations of the Military Coup," (Ph.D. diss., University of Washington, 1972), as cited by Martin C. Needler, "Military Motivations in the Seizure of Power," *Latin American Research Review* 10 (Fall 1975), 63-79.

26. Needler, p. 72.

27. Taylor, "Thoughts on Comparative Effectiveness."

28. Ibid., p. 41.

29. Ibid.

30. Fernando H. Cardoso, "The Industrial Elite," in *Elites in Latin America*, p. 109.

31. Ivan Vallier, "Religious Elites: Differentiations and Developments in Roman Catholicism," in *Elites in Latin America*, p. 194.

32. Frank Bonilla, "Cultural Elites," in *Elites in Latin America*, p. 241.

33. See Henry A. Landsberger, "The Labor Elite: Is It Revolutionary?," in *Elites in Latin America*, pp. 256-300.

34. Ibid., p. 264.

35. See Frank Bonilla and José A. Silva Michelena, *A Strategy for Research on Social Policy* (Cambridge: MIT Press, 1967) and subsequent volumes in *The Politics of Change in Venezuela*.

Part 4
Has Democracy Failed?

8
Democratic Political Development and the Alliance for Progress

William L. Furlong

Introduction

The Alliance for Progress was a major attempt by the United States and Latin America to alter the course of history, both present and future. Like most grandiose plans, it fell far short of many of its goals. Although Latin America has historically been ignored by U.S. policy makers, the alliance was a principal foreign-policy platform of the Kennedy administration.

One of the factors that played an extremely important role in motivating the U.S. decision to become involved in Latin American affairs was the fear of the expanding influence of communist and Third World powers in Latin America. Nixon's disastrous trip to Latin America in 1958 and Castro's takeover of Cuba in January of 1959 led many Americans to believe that Communism was running rampant in Latin America. It was felt that unless some very spectacular changes took place, all of Latin America would turn to Communism. It was, in part, this fear that spurred the creation of the Alliance for Progress. The need to divert Latin American countries from Communism was a theme consistently urged on the U.S. Congress to obtain funding for AID projects prior to and during the alliance years.

Castro's takeover of Cuba in 1959 notwithstanding, some U.S. foreign-policy experts remained optimistic regarding the development of democracy in Latin America. Events in Venezuela, Colombia, Argentina, and a number of other countries had moved them toward more viable democratic governments, which had impressed numerous influential North Americans.

The late 1950s and the early 1960s saw the downfall of many political tyrants. Juan Perón left Argentina, Marcos Pérez Jiménez was out of Venezuela, Gustavo Rojas Pinilla was ousted from Colombia, and Rafael Trujillo was on his way out in the Dominican Republic. The only smudge in this otherwise bright picture was in Cuba, where Castro took over Batista's old personalistic dictatorship in 1959. So, although the fear of Communism pervaded U.S. perceptions of Latin American politics, there was also hope for a new dawn of democracy during the period in which the Alliance for Progress was formulated and implemented.

U.S. policy makers believed that it was in our own interests to help, protect, and support the more democratic governments in Latin America, and at the same time to stimulate industrial and social development in these countries so that the benefits of modernization might raise the quality of life at all levels of society. Both North American and Latin American founders of the Alliance for Progress believed that improvements at the social and economic levels would also be associated with a broadening of political participation on all levels of society; this, in turn, would eventually strengthen democratic concepts, principles, and overall democratic practices throughout the region.

Despite this belief and the early optimism of the 1960s, the misreading and misunderstanding of political developments were probably the single largest failure of the Alliance for Progress. Founders of the alliance hoped that Latin American governments would move progressively toward more representative democracy. They believed that, with economic and social development, democratic political development would surely follow. However, this notion was unrealistic, given Latin American culture and politics. Although social, economic, and political development are intertwined and affect each other, economic and social development do not necessarily bring about political democratization. In a real sense the dislocations and strains put on traditional culture by social and economic changes threaten the growth of democracy rather than foster it. As the disenfranchised-poor majority demanded increased participation in the power structure and a "bigger piece of the economic pie," status-quo structures reacted by trying to obstruct those forces rather than reform existing institutions and processes into more democratic ones.

Basic Elements of the Alliance for Progress

Although the Alliance for Progress Charter turned out to be basically an economic and social document, as approved by the Punta de Este Conference in 1961, the Kennedy administrators formulated it and saw it as a program that would also help to establish and to further the role of democratic government and institutions within Latin American society. It is important to remember that the major political goal of the Alliance for Progress was to direct the desires for change into a democratic framework, procedure, and orientation. President Kennedy stated it this way: "For our unfilled task is to demonstrate to the entire world that man's unsatisfied aspiration for economic progress and social justice can best be achieved by free men working within a framework of Democratic institutions."[1]

Many of the social and economic ideas for the Alliance for Progress came from Latin American intellectuals and politicians who were also concerned about developmental problems, but the major emphasis for a democratic approach to the solution of these problems probably came from the Kennedy administration. A number of progressive, democratic Latin American leaders supported this democratic emphasis, while other people, such as President Juscelino Kubitschek of Brazil and his "Operation Pan America," and Latin American economists such as Raúl Prebesch, José Mayobre, and Felipe Herrera, and a number of other noted Latin American intellectuals and politicians introduced and supported economic and social modernization aspects of the alliance and suggested sufficient redistribution of the wealth to meet some of the rising expectations of the people in the area.[2] Kennedy, on the other hand, put his trust in progressive democratic governments and political parties in Latin America to produce change. He attempted to direct his influence where he could toward democratic regimes and to ignore and punish those regimes that were less than democratic.

Kennedy's diplomatic recognition policy during the early 1960s is an example of this approach. All the countries that experienced military coups after Kennedy came to office were not recognized diplomatically for some time. In this manner, the Kennedy administration tried to express a negative attitude toward military governments. In contrast, immediate recognition and guarantees of aid and support were granted to democratically elected governments. Although in the past the withholding of diplomatic recognition had weakened and even brought about the collapse of some Latin American governments, it had little impact on any regime during the Kennedy period. Nevertheless, it did at least give some indication that the Kennedy administration would support democratically elected regimes and democratically oriented political parties over other types of governments and parties. Kennedy also had plans for other programs to impress and push Latin America to more democratic orientations. "At times Kennedy even thought it might be useful to convene a 'club' of democratic presidents for regular meetings in Puerto Rico or Florida. He hoped that the less democratic presidents might be stimulated to work on reform in order to make the club; but the idea presented obvious problems, and nothing came of it."[3]

Despite the strong democratic commitments of the Kennedy administration, the final document for the Alliance for Progress program, the charter of the Punta de Este Conference, formally placed most of its emphasis on social and economic programs, rather than on democratic procedures and democratic political development. The twelve points of the Alliance for Progress Charter were:

1. Sustained annual economic growth
2. Some equalization and redistribution of national income
3. Diversification of national economic structures and orientations
4. Acceleration of industrialization throughout the whole region
5. Improvement of the level of agriculture and productivity
6. Acceleration of agrarian reform programs and land redistribution
7. Educational programs to eliminate adult illiteracy and to improve elementary education
8. Increase in health benefits and health programs
9. Expansion of low-cost housing
10. Attack on the inflation problems of Latin America
11. Economic integration and work toward some type of a common market orientation in Latin America
12. Improvement in cooperation of trade policies throughout Latin America and throughout the whole Western Hemisphere

It was believed by many people in the Kennedy adminstration, as well as by the Latin American officials who signed the Alliance for Progress Charter, that social and economic change and improvement would, at the same time, improve democratic institutions and processes throughout Latin America. This proved to be a false hope. In many ways, the expectations raised by the Alliance for Progress did just the opposite: they weakened and in some cases greatly damaged many democratic procedures, political parties, and institutions within Latin America. There are many reasons why democracy was not strengthened during this period of time and why it was very difficult to create democratic orientations in Latin America, given the culture, society, historical attitudes, and the traditional political systems with which the alliance had to work.

Cultural Traits that Impede or Inhibit Democracy

It was unrealistic for the United States to believe that the goals of the Alliance for Progress could be fulfilled in such a short time period. It was also overly optimistic to expect Latin America to alter its basic social, economic, and especially its political structure within this time frame and with the minimal incentives given by the alliance to do so.

Historically, Latin America had strongly resisted major social and political changes, although economic evolution had been significant in a number of Latin American countries during the first half of the twentieth century. Therefore, the stream of history was against any major alterations in these systems. Although many elements of democracy and free government had been practiced in many Latin American nations from time to time, and in some countries for extended periods of time, in the majority of nations in this region democracy was more of an exception than a rule most of the time.

Russell Fitzgibbon's studies, which have since been extended by Kenneth Johnson, have isolated some of the elements of democracy that have been perceived to exist and that do exist in Latin America today.[4] However, given its political history, and the disrupting effects of social and economic change upon its society, it is not surprising that there are fewer democratic governments and institutions in Latin America today than there were in 1960.

In addition to this historical legacy, there are a number of cultural traits that act as impediments to the growth and practice of democracy throughout Latin America.[5] The cultural trait of "personalism" is one of the most important of these. In most Latin American political systems and political parties, commitment and loyalty are based upon a leader's personal attachments and charisma. Commitment is not based on loyalty to a nation, to a constitution, to a system, or to an ideology. This creates, therefore, a condition where those in power have all of the rights and where the opposition or those out of power are considered to behave conspiratorally instead of creating a so-called loyal opposition. Bargaining and compromise are, therefore, considered negatively, and it is not unusual for deliberate obstructionism by opposition forces to take place in order to prevent those in power from receiving credit for positive programs. Thus, political conflict and competition for power take on a zero-sum game orientation and occur between personalistic groups and between strong personalities without any accepted set procedures, game rules, or constitutional frameworks.

This type of system leads to and reinforces the development of elite cliques that compete for power with their own means and procedures. This competition for power seldom includes the majority of the population, and when it does, it is in a personalistic fashion. A charismatic leader, a *caudillo*, can appeal to the electorate and thus gain office and power through democratic means. Nevertheless he and his clique may or may not be committed to a democratic way of maintaining power and working with the opposition. In many cases they will attempt to crush the opposition in order to reduce its competition for power in the future.

In contrast to the above, an open democracy requires loyalty to the system, or a constitution, and/or a process that includes the ability to bargain and to compromise. Without these elements, democracy, in the U.S. sense, cannot function. Men must be controlled by law and not be beyond its reach. Personalism, however, places men above the law and does not restrain them either by procedure or by constitutional means. In the past the *caudillo* has been the creator of law and constitutions and has been the servant of neither. For this reason, as well as others, there have been numerous constitutions in Latin America since its independence. Some countries have had more than twenty constitutions, or an average of one every seven to eight years. It can thus be seen that, where personalism means more than democratic procedures or constitutionalism, and commands more commitment than any to the whole political system, it acts as an impediment to the development of democracy as it is usually defined within a U.S. framework.

There is another cultural factor that reinforces this, known as transcendentalism. Included in this concept is the idea that goals and written commitments have a future orientation and do not apply to procedural commitments and substantive orientations in the present. Thus, a society accepts that constitutions written and ratified by a political regime do not necessarily mean that they will be implemented or followed. It merely indicates a commitment to future goals and an orientation to higher-level standards. The function of the constitution differs greatly from that of the United States; in Latin America, words speak louder than actions. A constitution is therefore a legitimizer for the present, not a procedural guide or a power map of current reality, and is not a binding document upon the behavior and actions of the political elite in the present.

In addition, transcendentalism is related to fatalism, another strong cultural trait. Latins generally accept political reality without trying to change it. This trait is revealed in a number of everyday language terms such as *Así es la vida* ("Such is life"); *Qué va hacer?* ("What can you do?"); and *Si Dios quiere* ("If God wills it"). This trait results in general acquiescense and apathy toward government and particularly toward any major changes in the system. It also leads to some paradoxical political behavior. For example, after a democratically elected president takes office, in many cases people will go into the streets and cheer their new president in a very nationalistic manner and with great emotional fervor. When, two years later, a military coup ousts their popularly elected president and places instead a military colonel or general in the seat of power, the people will again take to the streets in an emotional, nationalistic fashion and cheer their new president with equal zeal. Many times the imposed president will be as popular and be considered as legitimate as was the popularly elected president.

Those out of power, and, particularly, the majority of the population who are not directly involved in the political system, have in the past done little to change the above procedures and, in reality, believe that they can do little to affect the system.

A very fundamental cultural orientation that greatly differentiates Latin and Anglo-American attitudes toward government is the theory of the creation of government itself. In the Anglo-American–John Locke sense, government is created by a social contract. The people of the society band together and create a government over which they are still the sovereign. They then have the right to alter the government and to re-create a new government in any point in time. In contrast, the Latin looks at government as a corporatist entity. That is, government exists and has always existed along with society and is an organic element of the society. This includes the idea that government is to an extent out of the reach of the society as a whole. The people neither created it nor have much control over it because it evolved as society developed and is an organic part of society. This orientation then produces considerably different political behavior on the part of the Latin in contrast to his Anglo-American counterpart.

One further element that has had an interesting impact in Latin America is the cultural trait of tangible materialism. Historically, Latins have claimed to reach higher spiritual goals and not be tainted by the crass materialism that infects North American society. (The best single example of this orientation is Rodó's book, *Ariel*.) This concept indicates that the Latin elite, the educated and professional people, are above the quest for material possessions. Nevertheless, as middle classes developed in Latin America and as consumer goods became more available to the Latin Americans, a type of materialism did develop.

American scholars like John J. Johnson, hoped that as middle classes developed in Latin America, they would adopt a value system similar to the value system of the Anglo-American middle classes, and that, armed with this value system, the middle classes would then press for democratic institutions, procedures, and political systems. Despite this concept, as middle classes did develop after World War II, they did not develop those middle-class values described by Johnson or outlined by Seymour Lipset in his book *Political Man*. Instead, the middle classes developed a great appetite for foreign-produced consumer goods, while their political and social values became attached to the old elite values of Latin America. In consequence, the middle classes sought the benefits of modern, developed, and industrialized society and, at the same time, maintained the values of a traditional political elite developed in the eighteenth and nineteenth centuries. This paradox and conflict of values have not aided in the development of democratic institutions or procedures, but, in reality, have impeded their development. The middle classes in many cases will do anything to maintain their prerogatives and comforts of life, including selling the political systems to the military or any other power that will prevent their loss of status, income, and material goods. Consequently, the development of middle classes, rather than reinforcing and improving democracy in Latin America, have, in reality, hindered, impeded, and diminished the possibility of the formulation of democratic systems.

Up to now, we have discussed some cultural characteristics that impede and conflict with democratic orientations and philosophy. However, the cultural trait of individualism reinforces in many ways various aspects of free government and democracy within Latin America. For the Latin American, the individual is very important and is protected very carefully. To the Latin, there is a special, inherent uniqueness to each individual. Therefore, his uniqueness must somehow be reinforced and protected by the society. As a consequence of this attitude and orientation, many elements of free government have consistently continued to exist throughout Latin America even in times of severe dictatorship. In other words, freedom of expression, of religion, of movement, and other such freedoms have been protected throughout much of the history of Latin America. These elements have at times been lost to authoritarian and dictatorial governments, but in most cases not for any extended period of time. In early 1977, the Inter-American Press Association met in Colombia and condemned ten Latin American countries for their lack of freedom of the press. Censorship and other repression comes and goes in most of these nations; but, nevertheless, an element of freedom continues to exist and a commitment to such freedoms continues even in the harshest dictatorships in Latin America. While other elements and characteristics of the culture mitigate against democratic procedures and orientations, the cultural trait of individualism seems to reinforce some of the free-government aspects of democracy.

On the other hand, it could be argued that individualism also restricts democracy. It does so as personalistic leaders, *caudillos*, and others who gain power put their individualistic stamp on that power. They create a unique regime that is generally accepted. But as each regime is accepted, it also stands above the law and creates its own constitutions, its own rules, and its own procedures. Therefore, the trait of individualism creates a continuing conflict within the mind of the Latin on how to protect the individual and at the same time create a government that is unique to the personalistic leader who is protecting his individualistic orientations and special way of doing things.

This discussion does not purport to deal with all of the cultural aspects of Latin America and could be argued to be somewhat one-sided. Nevertheless, it does indicate some of the problems of creating democratic institutions, procedures, and political systems in Latin America, and it can give at least some insight into why the Alliance for Progress was unable to create a more democratic framework in Latin America. It must be remembered, however, that a number of other factors also impeded the development of democracy in Latin America. These factors include such things as the lack of institutionalization of competing and democratic elements of the political systems and within the political parties; the vast power and historical political roles of the military throughout Latin America; the traditional dominance of the president; the disruptive effect that economic and social change have on any society; the lack of legitimacy of most regimes because they are based on raw power; the dislocating aspect of vastly increasing political participation and its impact on the traditional social and political structure of a nation; intervention from outside; and the more recent argument, that of *dependencia*, which blames the industrial countries for the nondemocratic and underdeveloped state of Latin America. For these and many other reasons, democracy did not develop during the period of the Alliance for Progress.

Cultural Traits and Communism

Many of the same cultural traits that inhibit the development of democracy in Latin America also inhibit the growth of Communism and a Marxist ideology for Latin America. For example, personalism and a commitment to personal and kinship ties usually inhibit the development of a strong attachment to an ideology such as Marxism. A Fidel Castro may develop and use his personalism and charisma to adopt Communism as his major ideology; in this type of a situation the people might follow him. In other words, personalism can work both ways. Personalism can help or inhibit democracy or Communism, depending on a leader's ability to manipulate these types of symbols and political systems and inspire the people to follow him.

The development of cliques and strong kinship ties that relate to a personalistic approach to politics usually make it difficult for people to become committed to anything except personalism itself. Therefore, a strict ideology like Communism has little appeal to the vast majority, thus obstructing its aceptance. However, traits such as the inability to bargain and compromise, and the attitude that opposition is conspiratorial rather than loyal, do reinforce the communistic tendency to crush opposition and establish a totalitarian type of government.

The cultural trait of transcendentalism also impedes the development of Communism in Latin America. People are used to hearing promises and being told that some goals are attainable with one leader, party, or ideology or another. But the people are also convinced that many of these utopian ideas will not be realized because of the past promises that never were fulfilled. Consequently, many of the programs and utopian alternatives given by Marxist promises fall on deaf ears in Latin America.

The cultural trait of individualism also stands in direct contrast to much of the known communist practices throughout the world. Many well-educated Latins see through communist promises and are aware of the real conditions that exist throughout the communist bloc, where the state becomes much more important than the individual. This directly conflicts with their attitudes and commitments to individualism and the protection of the inner self. These commitments to free government and freedoms for the individual tend to diminish the appeal of a communist solution in Latin America.

In contrast to the above, the corporatist belief in government tends to support a more communistic approach to politics on the part of many Latins. The organic belief in the state—the acceptance that the government exists outside the control of the individual and subjects the individual to it—would benefit a communist approach. Therefore, the paradoxical condition exists between the belief in the state and the belief in the individual among many Latin Americans.

An additional cultural trait that might inhibit a communist approach or solution to government would be that of fatalism and apathy. Communism preaches that man can overcome his environment and that the proletariat and the peasants should rise to overthrow the imperialistic, capitalistic system. However, tradition indicates that the peasant and the laboring class can have little impact on the political system. Consequently, although the idea might sound good, at the same time it might be rejected by many of these people because it seems so completely unreasonable and outside of the realm of their reality.

Due to the above conditions and cultural traits, it might be suggested that the majority of governments in Latin America for the foreseeable future will neither be democratic nor communistic. It appears that instead they will follow the traditional path of mild to repressive authoritarianism with some elements of free government creeping in and out of various political systems over a period of time. What has occurred in Latin America over the past decade will continue to occur over the next decade. That is, the military will continue to direct and control or at least influence most of the governments of Latin America. Democracy and democratic forms, institutions, and procedures will continue to exist in the minority of Latin American countries. Freedom of speech, press, movement and other such freedoms, such as of religion and free education may continue in many areas controlled by authoritarian governments, as well as still continue in the democratic systems.

In other words, Latin America will continue to follow along its own path of political development, each nation finding unique patterns. Pat Holt stated it this way: "We have to remember, however, that the choices in all of these matters are up to the Latin Americans. We can help clarify the factors involved, but the future of Latin America is going to be determined in Latin America, not in Washington—or in Moscow either, for that matter."[6]

We now turn to a more specific evaluation of some direct impacts that the Alliance for Progress had on particular countries and the effect of these programs on democratic orientations, procedures, and institutions throughout Latin America.

The Alliance and the Countries

Let us reiterate the importance that democratic political development had for the promoters and initiators of the Alliance for Progress in the United States. For example, one of the leading Latin Americanists in the Kennedy administration, Lincoln Gordon, believed that without democratic development. "The Alliance then will become simply another American aid program, but not a cooperative process for bringing about a real change in the actual standards of living, in the prospects for their future rapid improvement, in the sense of participation and progress for all classes and regions of national communities, and in the security of civil liberties and the institutions of representative democracy."[7] Nevertheless, "Kennedy's Latin American policy was thus a wager on the capacity of the progressive democratic governments and parties of Latin America, with properly designed economic assistance and political support from the United States, to carry through a peaceful revolution.[8]

It was therefore extremely important to the founders of the alliance that democracy be one of the end products. However, there were never any real criteria for judging countries on a democratic basis or for identifying programs that would lead to more democratic development. Consequently, although the commitment for democratic institutions and processes was stated and considered important to the alliance, in reality any progress towards that goal was difficult to measure, and it was even more difficult to set criteria for giving or withholding aid to programs in the individual countries.

An interesting picture develops when one looks at where aid was sent between 1961 and 1967. The five countries receiving the most total aid were Brazil, Chile, Colombia, Mexico, and the Dominican Republic.[9] If one looks at recipient nations in per capita terms, however, different countries appear on the list. The countries receiving the highest per capita aid from 1961 to 1966 were Panama, the Dominican Republic, Chile, Bolivia, and Costa Rica. Chile and the Dominican Republic make both lists as major recipients of aid monies. The next-to-lowest recipient in per capita aid was Mexico, and very close to it were Argentina and Uruguay.[10]

It is rather paradoxical that some of the countries receiving the lowest per capita amount of aid in the first six years of the Alliance for Progress were countries that are classified by most Latin Americanists as being quite high on the democratic scale, Mexico and Uruguay. On the other hand, some of the countries receiving some of the higher rates of aid received it in periods of time when they were less democratic than they had been prior to the reception of large amounts of aid. Brazil and the Dominican Republic, and to a lesser extent Bolivia, are examples of this condition.

For example, in the Dominican Republic, the Juan Bosch regime, which lasted from February 1963 to September 1963, was in power really too short a time to receive much aid and little was given. On the other hand, after the 1965 U.S. invasion of and intervention into the Dominican Republic, it became the highest per capita and most significant recipient of aid and support from the U.S. government.[11] Not only was per capita aid extremely high, but AID sent many of its best administrators and program advisors to the Dominican Republic to develop and improve conditions there. Nevertheless, the Dominican Republic, under the guidance of Joaquín Balaguer, has become one of the most authoritarian Latin American republics in the 1970s. President Balaguer has become one of the most astute and ruthless politicians in Latin America. He runs the Dominican Republic much like his predecessor, Rafael Trujillo, who in reality was his political teacher.

Brazil is another interesting example of this paradox. The presidencies of Janio Quadros and João Goulart reflect the condition of U.S. nonsupport for democratically elected presidents and democratic governments. In contrast, the United States gave very strong support to the military government that overthrew the democratic government in the 1964 coup. In other words, the United States will support democratically elected governments who are favorable toward the United States but will not support democratically elected governments who fall out of favor with U.S. policies. According to statistics, the Brazilian government received at least twice the amount of aid from 1964 to 1969 than it received from 1961 to 1964.[12]

The most obvious of these paradoxes is the example of Chile. Although Chile was one of the most aided nations during the 1960s, there are a couple of major occasions where deviation from support for this democratically elected government occurred. Levinson and de Onis state that in 1969, when President Frei of Chile needed some strong support and aid because he had become unpopular due to his taxation programs, wage and social investment programs, and land reform programs that were implemented under the alliance, he was turned down in his request for foreign assistance by AID. On the other hand, during the same period of time, Brazil, who had not put into effect any of the alliance's recommended social and political programs, received even more aid from the United States.[13]

The culmination of all of this, of course, is reflected in the U.S. orientation toward and subversion of the Salvador Allende regime after 1970 in Chile. Although President Allende had been elected through democratic procedures and was running a democratically styled government, the United States helped bring on his demise with financial aid and moral support to his opposition forces. The military forces that intervened in Chile in 1973 and assassinated President Allende destroyed most of the democratic infrastructure of that country.

On the other end of this paradox lies Mexico. Although Mexico has been one of the most stable Latin American governments for over the last fifty years and has run a democratic type of government in Latin America, it received the lowest amount of per capita aid in Latin America next to Haiti. Here again, other factors are involved as with the countries mentioned above, but nevertheless the United States found it very difficult to fully support and aid this democratically oriented government with a functioning democratic institutionalized process and commitment to free government. The author realizes, of course, that many people do not classify Mexico as democratic; nevertheless, the Johnson study in 1975 placed Mexico as the third most democratic nation in Latin America,[14] which is fairly consistent with the previous studies of 1965 and 1970 that placed Mexico as the sixth most democratic nation.[15]

The case of Colombia is probably the single most successful example of democracy and aid under the Alliance for Progress program. Colombia became a showcase of democracy and alliance programs and ended up receiving nearly the highest per capita amount of aid. The political system developed under a unique plan, the National Front, which allowed the two major political parties to compete politically, but assured them both of specific shared powers and a share of the presidency every other term.

Many of the economic and social programs in Colombia were only moderately successful. Per capita agricultural production declined, and only small amounts of land were redistributed. Education was improved, low-cost housing built, and private investment was increased. The major problem, however, was that about 75 percent of the AID money going into Colombia was used for balance of payment problems and short-term budget deficits. This deprived the social and economic projects of their much-needed capital.[16]

Politically, the alliance bought time for Colombia to work out its problems.[17] Although electoral participation declined during the National Front period, the system stabilized, and violence and threats of coups decreased significantly. For the period 1960-1975, Colombia was identified as one of the five most democratic nations in Latin America.[18]

The case of Bolivia is one of the most difficult of all to analyze. Bolivia since 1952 has received one of the highest amounts of per capita aid from the United States of any country in the world. Bolivia continued to receive high per capita amounts of aid during the Alliance for Progress period. The amount of aid given to Bolivia changed little between 1961 and 1964 and between 1964 and 1967[19] despite the fact that during 1961-64 the government was democratically elected and the later government was run by a military junta headed by an air force general. It has been the aid program that has significantly affected Bolivia's ability to survive with any degree of viability. Yet it was not the aid that created the democratic processes or the lack thereof, but conditions and orientations within the country itself, as well as commitments to such forms by the leaders of that country. So, although Bolivia went through a period of transition in 1964 and again from 1969 to 1972, U.S. aid and commitment to Bolivia continued relatively unaltered through most of that period of time. Nevertheless, Bolivia today is not very democratic, although it is more open and more free than most of its neighbors.

This section has tried to illustrate that the United States has had a very difficult time in supporting political development and democratization in Latin America. It has been very difficult, if not impossible, to make loan commitments, judgments, and even diplomatic recognition policy on whether a government is democratic or non-democratic, whether it is free or whether it is repressive. On the other hand, it has been indicated that the United States at times did not support democratically elected governments who might have policies that were contrary to its own; but in reality the United States supported those military juntas that overthrew the democratic regimes. It has also been shown that U.S. aid programs and projects under the Alliance for Progress have strongly aided governments that were not democratic. It can be argued, therefore, that although the United States was committed to democratic development in Latin America, that commitment was one of words rather than actions and deeds.

It can also be argued however, contrary to the dependency theory, that Latin America is responsible for its own destiny and that no matter what the United States does within a limited framework, Latin America will find its own future and its own way of political development.

Dr. Harry Kantor was one who believed that Latin America would find its own routes to democracy through the creation and development of viable political parties. He was of the opinion that native political parties of the *aprista* type would be able to create strong institutional commitments to democratic forms and procedures and that these commitments would eventually work themselves into the whole political system and thereby create more democratic governments in the long run.

Venezuela is a good example of how this could happen. Venezuela had had probably one of the most undemocratic histories of any nation in Latin America. It had been plagued with ruthless and personalistic as well as repressive dictatorships. For many years there were practically no institutions, forms, or behavioral patterns that could be considered democratic. Nevertheless, Venezuela since 1958 had been able to establish one of the most stable democratic systems within modern Latin America. Many people are convinced that this is due to the very strong political party system in Venezuela and the parties' commitment to democratic forms and procedures. Dr. Kantor would argue that here is an example where the institutionalization of political parties has in reality brought about a democratic condition in a Latin American country previously very low on the democratic scale.

Another example that could be used is that of Costa Rica, which, with its strong party system, has been able to develop and function as one of Latin America's strongest and most viable democratic systems since 1948. Power has been exchanged from party to party and individual to individual without violence and without military interference.

Other examples include those of Mexico and Colombia, which have been discussed above. Mexico and the development of the institutionalized political party, the PRI, has developed its own fashion of democracy which, although somewhat authoritarian and at times repressive, is still one of the most open and one of the most committed to development within a democratic framework in Latin America. Colombia has also worked out its own special type of democracy whereby the National Front shares power from one party to the other.

On the other hand, the countries of Uruguay and Chile, which up to 1970 had been considered the most democratic countries in Latin America, have since had their party systems dissolved and outlawed. Despite nearly fifty years of political party institutionalization in those two countries, internal problems and domestic crises caused the military to intervene and overthrow the democratic governments and implement very authoritarian and repressive regimes. The political parties have been unable to reverse this situation and for the foreseeable future will have no political influence or power.

One of the most outstanding examples of military-civilian party opposition exists in Peru. The Aprista Party of Peru is one of the strongest political parties in Latin America and has a history of continuity as long as most other parties. Despite this fact, the Aprista Party has never been able to obtain political power and rule the country. In some cases it has been forced to cooperate with the military and in other cases go into opposition against military governments. Despite all of this, the Apristas have never been able to institutionalize democracy in Peru. It is even doubtful that they would democratize the system if they did assume power, because Peru is a country where military coups and political violence have been such a central element of the political system.

Conclusion

The above argument indicates the difficulty that parties as well as other institutions can have in developing democratic orientations and governments in Latin America. Tradition, history, culture, and other factors remain so strongly ingrained that democratic solutions to Latin America's problems must truly come from inside. Or, as Pat Holt has stated, "The institutions which people devise to make their societies work are peculiarly and intimately a matter of domestic concern. If they are to be practical, they have to evolve out of a people's own experience, and what works in one set of circumstances is unlikely to work in another. Outside advice is likely to be mistaken and certain to be rejected.[20]

The belief by the founders of the Alliance for Progress that somehow the United States, through political, social, and economic development could strengthen democracy in Latin America was at least naive if not misguided. For although an outside country might be able to create industry, hospitals, and educational systems in a country, a nation's political system must evolve from within. Without commitment from within, a foreign country could only impose its own ideas and systems through military rule, and this, of course, has not worked very well in Latin America with regard to U.S. intervention in the past. Consequently, it must be Latin America that decides on the degree of democracy and the commitment to freedom that each country will develop and allow to exist. Programs of democratization can be supported from the outside, but not transferred and imposed from outside countries without internal support and commitment for those programs.

Probably the most singular failure of the Alliance for Progress was its inability to increase the degree of democracy and freedom in Latin America. Nevertheless, the commitments to human rights, to democracy, and to freedoms should not be given up, and, where possible, programs that will support these types of orientations should be funded and supported strongly by the U.S. government. But this is a question of policy that must be decided with each and every case in each individual nation. The United States must have the flexibility and foresight to support democratic elements when they do appear.

Notes

1. John F. Kennedy, "Alianza para Progreso," *Department of State Bulletin*, April 3, 1961.
2. Arthur Schlesinger, Jr., "The Alliance for Progress: A Retrospective," in Ronald G. Hellman and H. Jon Rosenbaum (eds.), *Latin America: The Search for a New International Role*. New York: Halsted Press, 1975, pp. 60-65.
3. Ibid., p. 63.
4. "Revised Fitzgibbon-Johnson Index: Reputational Democracy in Latin America: 1945-1970," table 12, in James W. Wilkie, *Statistics and National Policy*, Supplement 3 (1974), UCLA Statistic Abstract of Latin America. Los Angeles: University of California, UCLA Latin American Center, 1974, p. 482; and Kenneth F. Johnson, "Scholarly Images of Latin American Political Democracy in 1975," *Latin American Research Review*, vol. 11, no. 2, Summer 1976, pp. 129-140.

5. A very good statement on cultural traits and some of their political implications is found in Jon P. Gillin's article, "Some Signposts for Policy," in Richard N. Adams (ed.), *Social Change in Latin America Today*. New York: Vintage, 1960, pp. 14-62, esp. pp. 28-47. A good book that covers cultural traits as well as historical and traditional aspects of society and their impact upon social, economic, and political development is Howard J. Wiarda (ed.), *Politics and Social Change in Latin America: The Distinct Tradition*. Amherst: University of Massachusetts Press, 1974.

6. Pat Holt, "Survey of the Alliance for Progress: The Political Aspects" in U.S., Congress, Senate, Committee on Foreign Relations, Subcommittee on American Republics Affairs. *Survey of the Alliance for Progress: Compilation of Studies and Hearings of the*..., 91st Cong., 1st Sess. Washington, D.C.: GPO, 1969, p. 30.

7. Lincoln Gordon, *A New Deal for Latin America*. Cambridge: Harvard University Press, 1963, p. 111.

8. Schlesinger, *op. cit.*, p. 62.

9. Harvey S. Perloff, *Alliance for Progress: A Social Invention in the Making*. Baltimore: Johns Hopkins Press, 1969, p. 55.

10. Ibid.

11. U.S., Congress, Senate, Committee on Foreign Relations, Subcommittee on Western Hemisphere Affairs. Hearings, *United States Policies and Programs in Brazil*, 92nd Cong., 1st Sess. Washington, D.C.: GPO, 1971, p. 167.

12. Ibid., pp. 159-187.

13. Jerome Levinson and Juan deOnis, *The Alliance That Lost Its Way: A Critical Report on the Alliance for Progress*. Chicago: Quandrangle Books, 1970, pp. 206-207.

14. Kenneth F. Johnson, "Scholarly Images of Latin American Political Democracy in 1975," *Latin American Research Review*, vol. 11, no. 2, Summer 1976, p. 137.

15. "Revised Fitzgibbon-Johnson Index," *supra* note 4.

16. *Survey of the Alliance for Progress: Colombia—A Case History of U.S. Aid* in *Survey of the Alliance* . . . , U.S., Congress, Senate, *op. cit.*, pp. 667-853.

17. Ibid., p. 671.

18. "Revised **Fitzgibbon-Johnson Index**," and Johnson, *op cit.*

19. Perloff, *op. cit.*

20. Holt, *op cit.*

9
Development Strategies and the Decline of the Democratic Left in Latin America

Paul H. Lewis

The Democratic Interlude

As the decade of the 1960s opened in Latin America there was great hope for the future of democratic reform parties. To well-wishers like Tad Szulc, the disappearance from the political scene of such *condottiere* as Juan Perón, Getúlio Vargas, Gustavo Rojas Pinilla, Marcos Pérez Jiménez, Anastasio Somoza, Manual Odria, and Fulgéncio Batista—all of whom had fallen from power between 1954 and 1960—signalled the "twilight of the tyrants." Indications were, Szulc proclaimed, "that democracy, so late in coming and still taking its first shaky and tentative steps forward, is here to stay in Latin America."[1]

Events within the next few years seemed to bear out such optimism. Imagine how the political scene in Latin America might have looked to a follower of the democratic Left on, say, Columbus day, 1961. Rómulo Betancourt, one of the great figures of the democratic Left, presided in Venezuela. His good friend and colleague, Victor Paz Estenssoro, was in power in Bolivia. Arturo Frondizi, a nationalist and democrat, headed the government in Argentina. Brazil had just gone through the bizarre episode of Quadros's resignation, and a rather tense moment in which military interventionists were forced to back down; but constitutional government was continuing under João Goulart, head of the Labor Party. Honduras, one of the more backward countries, was enjoying, under Ramón Villeda Morales, her first democratic government—replete with agrarian reform, a labor code, and laws regulating foreign investments. In Colombia, reform liberals were in power, under Alberto Lleras Camargo. Panama had just had the most honest elections ever held in that country. Chile, Costa Rica, Ecuador, and Uruguay were under conservative administrations, but were still in the democratic camp. And in Mexico, Adolfo López Mateos was nudging the PRI back to the left of center.

All in all, the forces of democracy and reform had reason to be satisfied, and there were signs of more progress to come. Fidel Castro had not yet declared himself a Communist. Meanwhile, his land reform, anticorruption campaign, and defiance of the United States evoked general sympathy. In the Dominican Republic assassins had eliminated the hateful figure of Rafael Leonidas Trujillo, thus opening up possibilities for reform there. In Peru, that great patriarch of all Latin American democratic reform parties, APRA, was favored to win next year's elections. Only El Salvador, Guatemala, Haiti, Nicaragua, and Paraguay—all marginal countries—remained as reactionary dictatorships, and even they were shaky. Finally, in the United States, which had supported military dictators in the past, there were signs of change. A new administration, under John F. Kennedy, had taken office. Promises of massive economic aid and moral support for democratic reform governments were in the air.

Yet, in a very short time the optimism was gone. In 1962 Frondizi was toppled by a military coup in Argentina, and the Peruvian military nullified APRA's victory in Peru. In 1963 military coups ousted democratic governments in the Dominican Republic, Ecuador, and Honduras. In 1964 military men took over in Bolivia and Brazil. Meanwhile, Castro had broken definitively with the democratic Left and proclaimed a Marxist-Leninist dictatorship in Cuba. And in the United States, Kennedy's assassination resulted in the Lyndon Johnson administration, which went back to the old policies of browbeating and indifference.

To be sure, the democratic Left continued to make gains here and there. New Peruvian elections held in 1963 resulted in a victory for Fernando Belaúnde Terry and his center-Left *Acción Popular*. But that only split the democratic reform forces, for APRA, sensing a competitor in Belaúnde, joined with the conservatives to block his programs. Eventually Belaunde fell, in 1968, to be replaced by a Left-wing military dictatorship. Another kind of democratic reform party seemed to be on the rise when Eduardo Frei and his Christian Democrats swept the 1964 elections in Chile. But again a coalition of the Left and the Right hamstrung his efforts. By 1970 the Christian Democrats had declined in popularity and were quarreling among themselves. Accordingly, they were replaced in power by a Socialist-Communist alliance headed by Salvador Allende. The same story was repeated in Guatemala, where the *Partido Revolucionario*, led by Júlio César Méndez Montenegro, won the 1966 elections. It spent the next four years vainly fighting off attacks by the extreme Left and Right. Unable to deliver on its promises, the PR was defeated in 1970.

By the mid-1970s only three countries remained in the democratic camp: Colombia, Costa Rica, and Venezuela. And even in those countries there were signs of trouble. The Colombian Liberal Party, the National Liberation Party of Costa Rica, and *Acción Democrática* were bitterly divided into moderate and radical wings. Signs of institutional ossification were evident, and a new generation of political activists was impatient with the gradualism of the democratic reform approach. In the rest of Latin America military dictatorship was the rule. Even long-established democracies such as Chile and Uruguay had succumbed. Sometimes, as in Peru from 1968 to 1976, the military followed policies advocated by the Left; but more often those dictatorships were sympathetic to the Right. In either case they were dictatorships, and it was democracy that now stood at bay.

How can we account for such a reversal of fortune in such a short time? Conspiracy theories will not do. The United States may have been involved in the Brazilian and Chilean coups, just as Communists may have influenced the military men who took over in Peru, but in every case the government that fell had lost the support of key political groups: not just the military, but also businessmen, farmers, the church, the middle classes, party leaders, and even some of the labor unions and peasants. Moreover, the inability of the United States to prevent the military from intervening in Argentina, Honduras, or Peru, despite her protests, indicates that the Latin American political process is much less amenable to outside influence than many people suppose. At the same time, the failure of the democratic Left in the mid-1960s was too universal to be dismissed as only a series of coincidences. Rather, it is our contention here that economic causes lay at the bottom of that failure, and that they were of such a nature that the downfall of the democratic Left was practically inevitable.

In order to explain this, let us begin by positing the following assumptions about the crisis. First, the backbone issue of contemporary Latin American politics is how to achieve economic development and thereby close the gap in living standards with the industrialized nations. Second, the larger Latin American countries actually made much progress toward this goal in the first four decades of our century, but since World War II the process has stalled out. It is this stagnation, coupled with a rapidly growing population and "rising expectations," that is raising political tensions. Third, the cause for this stagnation lies in Latin America's deviation from the classical model of development followed by Western Europe, North America, and Japan. This is now being recognized by many Latin Americans themselves. Fourth, there are three broad, general strategies being offered by modern economists to get Latin America out of her cul de sac. Each strategy has political ramifications, two of which lead to dictatorship. Fifth, the strategy consistent with the democratic approach was tried by the center-Left parties and failed, which suggests that democracy and development may be incompatible in the modern world.

The Classical and Latin American Models

Let us begin by contrasting the classical and Latin American development models in order to understand where the latter deviates. That will help to pinpoint the specific problems that any new development strategy must grapple with. Obviously, there is no time here to go into detail concerning the particulars of British, German, French, U.S., or Japanese development. We will restrict ourselves to indicating useful sources in a footnote and will use instead the composite picture of classical development drawn by W. W. Rostow in *The Stages of Economic Growth*.[2]

Rostow's terminology is familiar to all students of development. First comes the stage in which the "preconditions for take-off" are laid down. Those include: (1) the establishment of political order under a leadership class dedicated to development; (2) the commercialization of agriculture and improvements in mining, in order to increase production for export; and (3) a significant rise in exports to pay for industrialization and certain internal improvements—roads, ports, railroads, schools—that facilitate commerce and productivity.

Second, there is the "take-off" stage, characterized by a rise in both exports and investment. Now, however, industries are developed to process local primary goods for the world market. For example, instead of exporting only raw wool or cotton, a country may begin to sell textiles as well. With the earnings from these new products investments are now possible in heavy capital goods industries—iron, steel, chemicals, and machinery—to raise productivity even further in export industry and agriculture.

The third stage is the "drive to maturity." As before, exports lead the way to growth and the volume of investment continues to rise. But now the emphasis is on the capital-goods sector, which begins to develop to the point where it is possible to export machinery, tools, electrical equipment, and the like. The country has now become a major power in world trade. Business at home is large-scale and sophisticated. Most of the labor force is in industry and lives in the cities. The general level of wealth in the society is rising, and as it does so the domestic market takes on importance.

Finally, there is the stage of "mass consumption." The domestic market is now greatly developed. Social attitudes supporting hard work, sacrifice, and productivity have given way to demands for greater consumption and leisure. Labor unions win higher wages and shorter hours for workers, while the social-welfare state makes its appearance to guarantee the buying power of consumers. Highest growth rates are in consumer-goods industries and services.

Certain features stand out in this classical model. First, growth is *export-led*. The ever-intensifying cycle of reinvestment, up through the drive to maturity, hinges on earnings from exports. Second, the main source of investment capital is domestic savings. Rostow does not deny that state investment of foreign capital may aid in the development process, but the main burden must be borne by a domestic entrepreneurial class. That is the way in which modernizing values are best percolated through a developing society. Third, up to the last stage of development, social values emphasize production, savings, and sacrifice. The domestic market is secondary, and both consumerism and social welfare are practically absent.[3] Fourth, political consolidation and unified leadership are essential. Investment and entrepreneurial talent would be discouraged by unstable social and political conditions.

Now let us turn to the Latin American model. By the mid-nineteenth century the Spanish American republics were beginning to emerge from the political chaos of the post-Independence period. Powerful centralizing dictators, backed by powerful domestic and foreign economic interests, were suppressing the petty regional *caciques*. Brazil, of course, had always enjoyed relative stability under her emperor. But in either case the second half of the century saw a process of development taking form that approximated the classical stage of the "preconditions for take-off." Mining and agriculture received larger investments, and the export of both increased considerably in volume. Financed largely by foreign capital, but also to some extent by local entrepreneurs and the state, railroads and telegraph lines were laid down, ports were modernized, banks were started, and the beginnings of industrialization were evidenced by the appearance of meat-packing and food-processing plants. From Mexico to Argentina new modernizing elites were talking the gospel of "Positivism," which promised a materialist paradise as the reward for social order and scientific technique.

If foreign capital and state enterprise were playing greater roles in Latin America than they did in the classical model, that did not mean that domestic entrepreneurs were lacking. Particularly in Argentina and Brazil, a growing middle class of manufactures and merchants had begun to take on importance. Moreover, the Latin American model conformed in one critical aspect to the classical model at this stage: growth was export-led. Indeed, by the turn of the century Latin America's share of world trade was only slightly less than that of the United States, and that volume was to triple between 1890 and World War I.[4]

It is during World War I that the two models begin to diverge. Still in the phase where primary products are exported in exchange for imports of industrial consumer goods, the Latin American economies received a shock when wartime mobilization shut off manufactures from Europe. Moreover, this came at a time when Europe's war needs required even larger purchases from Latin America. The inflexibility of demand for certain consumer goods in Latin America created a potentially lucrative market, while large earnings from exports provided the capital needed to take advantage of it. Thus, local industry expanded into the vacuum left by the Europeans. The result was a quantum leap for Latin American manufacturing, but note the difference in the stimulus to growth: unlike the classical, export-led model, industry in Latin America increased to meet *internal* demand. Furthermore, the largest gains were in the consumer-goods sector.

After the war the old trade pattern reasserted itself temporarily as cheap and better-made foreign goods came back to the market. But then the Great Depression hit, once more disrupting trade. This settled once and for all the question of whether industry would supplant agriculture as the chief economic activity in Latin America. As the industrial nations cut back their purchases of raw materials, Latin America's export earnings plummeted. The commercial agricultural sector simply collapsed. At the same time, without export earnings it was impossible to import. Once again, then, foreign industrial goods became scarce. And, once again, local industry expanded to take up the slack. It seems a paradox, perhaps, that amid the wreck of Latin America's traditional economy the 1930s witnessed a dynamic upsurge in the number of industrial enterprises, in the volume of investment and output, and in the industrial labor force.

This time, too, governments turned a favorable ear to the demands of the local manufacturing sector. Industrial growth meant jobs for the rural migrants who streamed into the cities to escape the depressed conditions of the countryside. It also meant for nationalist intellectuals and military officers the road to national power and prestige—as the example of the fascist powers, then in the ascendancy in Europe, amply demonstrated. Lastly, industrial growth meant saving on precious foreign exchange through import substitution. In brief, industrialization based on import substitution became a panacea—almost an ideology. In its more extreme claims, it became a gospel of autarky.

Again, let us look at the process. Import substitution-type growth was *inward-looking*. And it was oriented toward consumer-goods production. Rather than seeking to promote foreign trade it was aimed at avoiding foreign trade. Its purpose was to exclude from the domestic market any foreign product that could be produced locally, whether or not that local product was cheaper or better made. An industry, once established, could usually count on government protection in the form of tariffs, import quotas, subsidies, or currency exchange restrictions.

Obviously this type of growth has no built-in dynamism. The new Latin American industries did not have to be efficient or competitive: they were guaranteed a market. It was more important for a businessman to have good political connections than entrepreneurial skill. The lack of inner dynamism was not noticed at first, however, for there were so many possibilities for satisfying the local market for consumer goods. The growth of cities in the 1930s and 1940s, and the increase in the urban working and middle classes as industry and government expanded, all added new consumers to the marketplace. Moreover, there were spurts of prosperity during World War II and the Korean War as foreign demand rose for raw materials.

While the consumer goods industry expanded, so did government services and the government payroll. Industry could not grow fast enough to absorb the enormous wave of rural migrants that swelled the cities during the depression, so much of the new urban population was unemployed. The sudden growth of cities also brought the usual social problems: inadequate housing, sanitation, educational facilities, transportation, and police protection. It was a volatile situation, and the Latin American governments can hardly be censured for trying to tackle those problems by increasing public spending for social welfare and by hiring tens of thousands of the jobless as state employees. Nevertheless, the result was to create prematurely (according to the classical model) a welfare state whose costs could not be afforded by a society still in the early stages of industrialization. Every peso spent on social insurance schemes, or on redundant government workers, or—for that matter—on consumer goods was a peso that could not be put into long-range investment.

In sum, the Latin American model has attempted to leap from the "pre-conditions for take-off" directly into the "mass consumption society" without passing through the difficult and demanding stages of "take-off" and "drive to maturity." Soon the contradictions in the deviant model would begin to make themselves felt. The welfare state and the consumer society can be sustained only by a fully developed, highly productive, and efficient consumer-goods industry. By the 1950s the larger Latin American republics were, in fact, nearly self-sufficient in consumer goods—although how productive or efficient those industries were is a separate question. But the next requirement is that the consumer goods sector be, in turn, sustained by the existence of an equally developed capital-goods—or heavy-industrial—sector. And that was what Latin America lacked. There lay the cruel contradiction in import substitution-type development: the Latin Americans had attempted to free themselves from dependence on foreign imports, only to discover that the more independent they became in consumer goods the more they became dependent on the importation of foreign capital goods. And those capital goods were very expensive.

The strain would not have been so great if the Latin Americans had been in a position to pay for capital-goods imports by increasing their exports. Unfortunately, however, Latin American industry was inefficient and uncompetitive. It could exploit the domestic market behind protective walls, but it was not in shape to fight for its share of the world market. As for the traditional export products, a shift in investment capital from land to industry during the 1930s, the failure to mechanize when rural labor migrated to the cities, and government attempts to raise revenue by taxing exports had combined to keep the agricultural sector stagnant. On top of that, the discovery of many synthetics, the rise of competitors in Africa and Asia, and the tendency of industrial nations to spend proportionally less on agricultural products as income rose tended to result in unfavorable terms of trade. Thus, Latin America not only lacked a capital-goods sector to undergird her consumer-goods industry, but she was unable to earn the foreign exchange either to invest in one or to purchase such goods abroad in sufficient quantity.

Once the local consumer-goods market was saturated, and once the wartime prosperity was over, the limitations of import substitution became painfully apparent. The possibilities of inward-oriented growth had reached their limit. Now the economy began to stagnate. As it did, social tensions began to build up.

Now the question becomes: what is the way out of the current dilemma? Unfortunately, there is no consensus among Latin Americans, or anyone else, as to how healthy growth might be restored. Three main strategies have been offered: monetarism, moderate structuralism, and radical structuralism. For reasons that should become clear presently, both the monetarist and radical structuralist alternatives are—in the Latin American context—incompatible with democracy. The moderate structuralist strategy is the one associated with the democratic Left. The reasons for its failure, and consequently the failure of the center-Left reform parties, will be analyzed next.

Moderate Structuralism: The Democratic Reform Approach

The structuralist position has been developed most cogently by a group of economists attached to the Economic Commission for Latin America (ECLA), a United Nations agency. Most prominent among them is Raúl Prebisch. In both its moderate and radical forms, structuralism rejects the classical model of development and insists that inward-directed growth will work. Structuralists point to the impressive gains in industrialization that import substitution brought in the past, and they predict that a heavy-industrial sector can be developed in the same way. All that is needed is to remove certain "structural bottlenecks" in the society. That, however, will require state action. There is no denying that political tempers may rise as a result.

Heading the list of structural reforms is the elimination of the agricultural bottleneck, or the problem of "inelastic supply." Agricultural production has lagged behind industry since the 1930s, at the same time that the urban population has been growing. The result is higher food prices, a main contributor to inflation. Also, low agricultural output results in less export earnings and a decline in the capacity to import needed capital goods. For the structuralist, the fault lies in the traditional land-tenure system, with its vast, semi-feudal estates on the one hand, and its tiny, subsistence-level peasant plots on the other. The *latifundio*, which needs only to produce enough to keep its owners living well, does not try to be efficient or to maximize production. The intensively cultivated *minifundio* provides only a bare living. Its impoverished owners cannot afford machinery or modern tools and fertilizers, so it produces no surplus. The structuralist answer, then, is to consolidate the *minifundios* into cooperatives; and to expropriate the *latifundios* and turn them into cooperatives or else put heavy taxes on unused land. The predicted results are that production will rise, lowering food costs in the cities; more foreign exchange will be available through an increase in exports; and rising rural incomes will create a domestic market that will stimulate industrial expansion.

Another structural problem is the export bottleneck. It is related, as we have seen, to the agricultural bottleneck. But even if agricultural production could be raised, structuralists reject the current attempts to increase foreign trade. "External demand for basic commodities no longer has pride of place and is replaced by internal demand," claims one ECLA publication. "From . . . the standpoint of the allocation of resources, this change supposes that a substantially larger proportion of resources is directed toward the production of goods and services for home consumption."[5] This view proceeds from the assumption that in the international division of labor those nations that occupy the industrial "center" get rich at the expense of the primary-goods producers at the "periphery." Peripheral nations become the serfs. Moreover, to depend primarily on imports of capital goods means that more production must be sent abroad as exports to pay for them, leaving less to use for raising domestic living standards. Thus, the import substitution approach must be taken to develop heavy industry. However, Latin American countries may open up greater possibilities for import substitution by setting up regional common markets, thereby treating Latin America as a whole as one big domestic market.

Next, there is the incomes bottleneck, or the maldistribution of wealth. It has been estimated that the richest 5 percent of the population accounts for about 30 percent of all consumption. Moreover, the rich pay almost nothing in taxes. Most government revenues are derived from indirect sources, which bear heaviest on the poor. Insufficient revenue, in turn, leads to constant deficits in the government's budget. Those are then covered by printing more money, thus resulting in more inflation. Structuralists propose to attack the incomes bottleneck through tax reforms and income redistribution. Heavy taxes on the rich will provide money for government investment, and better-financed welfare schemes will raise the buying power of the lower classes.[6]

Obviously the structuralists foresee a larger role for the state in the development process than the classical model would advocate. It is the state, not private enterprise, that will take the lead in planning, capital formation, and investment. Only a powerful, centralized government will be able to undertake successfully an agrarian reform, income redistribution, nationalization and expropriation, the control of foreign capital, and a host of other reforms too numerous to discuss here—such as the restructuring of the educational system. Because what is clear is that the structuralists propose nothing less than a social revolution, a substantial shift in economic and political power from the upper and middle classes to the lower class. That revolution may come about gradually, through the use of indirect measures such as the taxing power, as the moderate structuralists wish. Or, as the radical structuralists prefer, it may take the form of immediate, wholesale confiscation of property, backed by the coercive power of a revolutionary party.

As Prebisch observes, the younger generation of Latin Americans is less interested in efficiency and productivity than in social justice. That may strike economists as romantic and impractical, but, in the last analysis, politicians—not economists—choose the development strategy to be followed. And, in the name of social justice, development will have to be financed by forced internal savings derived from socializing the income sources of the rich and by restricting the upper and middle classes' consumption. But this may not be so impractical as it seems, Prebisch says, because by shifting wealth downward to the great mass of the underprivileged a vast potential market will be created to stimulate domestic industry.

Moderate structuralists differ from the radicals both in the scope of their proposed changes and in their methods. The radical is out to create a "people's republic"; the moderate prefers something resembling Scandinavian democratic socialism. Democratic reform parties such as APRA, *Acción Democrática, Liberación Nacional,* and the Christian Democrats try to work out reforms by playing consensus politics. They emphasize proudly their multiclass nature and reject the communist theory of inevitable class conflict and Armageddon. Instead of resorting to bloody revolution and the dictatorship of the proletariat, they seek to induce social change gradually through fiscal incentives and government spending. Consensus is built around an appeal to the national welfare, to which all interests must sacrifice if the country's economic independence is to be won. Joseph Grunwald observes that "a primary objective of the 'structuralists' in the implementation of their difficult long-term program is to create a national consciousness and an almost religious spirit for economic development. In this manner it is hoped to create the conditions that will make possible cooperation from all sectors of the community and will bring forth the needed sacrifices by all groups: the sacrifice of additional consumption by the great masses of the community; the sacrifices that are entailed in agrarian reform, tax reform, and a greater role in general for the landowning and business groups."[7]

In the meantime, the national consensus is preserved by a careful balancing of sacrifices with concessions. The military's budget won't be cut, but it will be directed to community action programs instead of weapons. Landowners need not lose all their possessions if they agree to modernize production and take better care of their workers. Labor unions will receive government protection, but are expected to moderate their wage demands. Businessmen must accept the government's social legislation and pay fair wages, but property and profits are safe so long as they are exercised responsibly. Nor is this sort of consensus-building seen by the sincere moderate reformer as mere opportunism. On the contrary, to him it reflects his commitment to democratic procedure— indeed, it is his educational mission to teach the art of compromise to Latin American societies that have suffered violence too long. This, says Charles Anderson, is the essence of democratic politics as practiced by such figures of the center-Left as Betancourt, Belaúnde, Figueres, Frei,

Lleras Camargo, and Villeda Morales.[8]

The trouble with such an approach is that it tries to practice democracy in societies that have no patience with democracy. The upper classes are frightened, and view any concession as a breach in the political dam. If their way of life is threatened with extinction, what does it matter whether the executioner is a democratic politician (read, "demagogue") or a Communist commissar? As for the lower classes, how can they be expected to wait for slow, piecemeal change, when radical agitators fan their expectations and hold out the prospect of violent revolution as the instant solution for every grievance? In that sort of atmosphere consensus-building and moderation seem like mere opportunism, if not outright treason.

In the end, impatient and exasperated onlookers—often former friends—turn on the democratic reformers. As early as 1963, Victor Alba predicted that the future belonged not to the center-Left parties but to military technocrats and/or Marxist-Leninist intellectuals. The blame, he said, lay in the democratic reformers themselves, for they lacked a true commitment to social change. Led by the educated and well-born, such movements were little more than humane offshoots of the old oligarchy. Their politicians were, at bottom, only paternalists who, faced with the choice of instigating a real revolution or knuckling under to vested interests, preferred the latter. Thus, Alba excoriated them for their "weakness," "social conformity," "lack of political imagination," and "intellectual cowardice."[9]

No doubt the indictment was overstated and unfair. Yet, even friends of the democratic Left have been embarrassed by the increasing conservatism of some of its traditional spokesmen, as well as by their opportunistic tactics. For example, whatever the purpose may have been APRA's collaboration with the reactionary Odristas during Belaúnde's administration did much to hurt the credibility of the center-Left. So did the participation of many democratic reform parties in the School for Political Education in Costa Rica, which was funded by the CIA. In any case, Alba's tirade proved to be prophetic, for today military technocrats are in power in most of Latin America, and Marxist-Leninist intellectuals have supplanted the democratic Left as the main opposition force.

The Alternatives: Radical Structuralism and Monetarism

Having explained the demise of the democratic Left, it only remains to show why the military technocrats and Marxist-Leninist intellectuals, in particular, inherited the battlefield. Radical structuralism—the strategy of the authoritarian Left—is easier to explain. Its model is that of the USSR, or some other communist variant. That model has the advantage of being the only historically-tested successful alternative to the classical model. It requires no abandonment of inward-directed, import-substitution-type development. The structuralist preference for state action receives here its most extreme emphasis, the entrepreneurial spirit that motivates the classical approach is substituted by a ruthlessly determined revolutionary elite, and a command economy—organized according to a central plan—permits the experiment to be sealed off from the corrupting influences of foreign capital and trade. Totalitarian dictatorship, not democracy, has thus become the inevitable ramification of structuralism. Any lingering appeal that democracy might have had for the Left in Latin America was lost when Salvador Allende's regime came crashing down. Whatever lessons it may have taught others, the Chilean experience convinced radical structuralists that democratic institutions and procedures only put weapons in the hands of the reactionaries.

That leaves the monetarists, whose program leads to the opposite extreme. Monetarism seeks to return to the classical model, but admits that this can be accomplished only through much sacrifice. If one assumes that Latin America's problems stem from leaping directly from export agriculture (the "preconditions for take-off" phase) to mass consumption and the welfare state, then the society will have to reduce consumption and forego many services in order to save the capital to go back and underwrite the intermediate stages of growth. That means belt tightening. Moreover, in conformity with the classical model, monetarists believe that private enterprise must play the leading role. In their view, state-directed development gets too bogged down in politics, whereas for economic efficiency there is no substitute for the free market. But to create a climate in which private enterprise can flourish, labor unions, peasants, and party demagogues will have to be prevented from disrupting the social order. Also, in addition to restricting consumption at home, it will be necessary to produce more for export, so as to help in the process of capital accumulation. The agricultural sector must be encouraged by lifting price controls on food and by devaluing the currency to make exports cheaper, all of which will put profits into the pockets of the hated *"oligarchy"*—for land redistribution is compatible neither with productivity nor a favorable investment climate. As for industry, new investments and credit will be shifted away from previousy subsidized and projected consumer-goods manufacturing to capital goods and selected products that are able to compete on the world market.

Now, it may be asked, where is the provision for social justice in this scheme? Can the desperately poor in Latin America really be expected to defer consumption, put aside their rising expectations, for the generation or more that the classical model will take to work itself out? What of the businessmen who own the consumer-goods industries, or the workers who depend on those industries for jobs, or the middle class employed in the government or the service sector? What becomes of them during the painful period of readjustment? Structuralists are correct in pointing out that even if monetarism ultimately brought prosperity, the transition phase will be attended by business failures, unemployment, and lower living standards. Could any democratic politician run on such a platform?

Certainly not, and that is why orthodox economists like Roberto Campos of Brazil and Adalberto Krieger Vasena of Argentina willingly accepted posts in military regimes. Such men prefer the constitutional arrangements of Great Britain or the United States, but as pragmatists they understand that democracy is unlikely to flourish in Latin America for some time—save in countries with peculiar advantages, like oil-rich Venezuela. Therefore, it is to the authoritarian variant of the classical model—the examples of Germany and Japan, with their fusion of military, capitalist, and technocratic elites—that monetarists now turn. As with structuralism, monetarist strategy in Latin America today seems to lead inexorably to dictatorship: but of the Right, not the Left.

Latin Americans may deserve a better set of choices than communism, authoritarian capitalism, or the turbulent chaos of moderate structuralism—let us call it "dynamic stagnation"—but, unfortunately, there does not seem to be any.

Notes

1. Tad Szulc, *Twilight of the Tyrants* (New York: Henry Holt & Co., 1959).
2. W. W. Rostow, *The Stages of Economic Growth* (Cambridge: University of Cambridge, 1961). Other useful sources on classical development are: E. L. Bogart, *The Economic History of the United States* (New York: Longman, Green & Co., 1915); J. H. Clapham, *Economic Development of France and Germany, 1815-1914* (Cambridge: University of Cambridge, 1968); Phyllis Deane, *The First Industrial Revolution* (Cambridge: University of Cambridge, 1965); Robert E. Ward, ed., *Political Development in Modern Japan* (Princeton: Princeton University Press, 1968); Theodore S. Hamerow, *The Social Foundations of German Unification, 1858-1871*, 2 vols. (Princeton: Princeton University Press, 1969); William W. Lockwood, ed., *The State and Economic Enterprise in Japan* (Princeton: Princeton University Press, 1965).

3. This is less true of the United States, where, despite constant advances in the export trade, the home market remained paramount. Nevertheless, it may be argued that the expanding frontier played a role similar to that of colonial markets and spheres of influence in the European and Japanese cases.

4. Adalbert Krieger Vasena and Javier Pazos, *Latin America: A Broader World Role* (London: Ernest Benn, 1973), 23-24.

5. Economic Commission for Latin America, *Development Problems in Latin America* (Austin: University of Texas, 1970), xix-xx.

6. Economic Commission for Latin America, *Towards a Dynamic Development Policy for Latin America* (New York: United Nations, 1963), 4-5, 11, 15, 32, and 69. Also, Raúl Prebisch, *Change and Development: Latin America's Great Task* (Washington: Inter-American Development Bank, 1970), 88-89, 112-113.

7. See the discussion in Joseph Grunwald, "The Structuralist School on Price Stabilization and Economic Development: The Chilean Case," in A. O. Hiroschman, ed., *Latin American Issues: Essays and Comments* (New York: Twentieth Century Fund, 1961), 122-123.

8. Charles W. Anderson, *Politics and Economic Change in Latin America* (New York: Van Nostrand Reinhold Co., 1967), 111-114.

9. Victor Alba, "Latin America's Future Leaders," *New Republic*, 21 September 1963, 12-13.

10
Leadership and the Failure of Democracy

Lee C. Fennell

Introduction

The story of democracy in Latin America often seems to be a contradiction between support in principle and failure in practice. Throughout the century and a half since independence, pluralistic or liberal democracy has been the most consistent and widely shared notion of the desirable political system.[1] There always have been advocates of competing ideologies, to be sure, but none has come even close to replacing the historically rooted commitment to the idea of democracy. In the twentieth century, this commitment has been manifested in political changes that brought more democratic regimes into being in many parts of the hemisphere. Some of them were relatively short-lived; others lasted many decades and were widely interpreted as indicating that democracy had really "taken root" in practice as well as in principle.

But, with depressing regularity, periods of expanding democracy seemed to be followed by periods of reaction and dictatorship.[2] In the 1970s, even what had appeared to be two of Latin America's most firmly rooted democracies, Chile and Uruguay, were replaced by military regimes. This recurring failure, even in those countries where social and economic conditions seemed most propitious for democracy, has long stimulated efforts at explanation. Events of the 1970s have intensified these efforts.

Explanations of the failure of democracy in Latin America have been extremely varied. Most, however, seem to fall into one of three general categories, depending upon whether they place emphasis upon cultural conditions, social and economic structures, or particular political groups. Each of these will be touched upon very briefly, after which the case will be argued for an alternative explanation.

Some Common Explanations

Cultural themes are found among both some of the oldest and the most recent attempts to explain Latin American politics. U.S. writings during the early decades of the twentieth century often attributed the unstable and frequently undemocratic nature of Latin American politics to a "Latin temperament," which was itself variously assumed to result from some combination of genetic and geographic fate. Ironically, long after this mode of explanation was no longer intellectually fashionable in the United States, similarly fatalistic cultural explanations were put forth by some Latin American writers. A cultural basis for the failure of democracy is also central to the "corporative" model of Latin American politics that has gained a considerable following in the 1970s. In essence, this argument maintains that the individualism, structured competition, and subordinate role of the state that are at the core of pluralistic democracy are antithetical to the Iberian value structure, which has persisted since the middle ages and was brought to the new world with the Conquest. Consequently, advocates of the corporative model argue that, despite rhetoric to the contrary, democracy is not really desired by the Latin American political elites.[3]

Structural explanations can be generally divided according to whether they are based upon liberal or Marxist assumptions. The former type were particularly popular in the 1950s and early 1960s among U.S. scholars. Basically, this type of argument maintains that the major impediment to democracy in Latin America is the traditional class structure. The most important step toward democracy, from this point of view, was the expanding size and growing influence of the "modern" middle class.[4] For those whose structural explanations have a Marxist foundation, however, this class is not the answer but rather the problem. This view derives both from the traditional role of the bourgeoisie in Marxist theory and, in the recently fashionable "dependency theory," from the class's linkages to an international economic system dominated by the major capitalistic economies.[5]

The third general category of explanation focuses upon individual social groups believed to be responsible for the failure of democracy. Historically, the large rural landowners, the *caudillos*, or an often ill-defined "oligarchy" have usually been viewed as the major culprits. In recent years, concomitant with a greater incidence of military coups and an increasing duration and severity of military governments, the armed forces have been frequently portrayed as the major enemy of democracy in Latin America. In terms of the groups singled out for attention, explanations of this type may seem little different from those in the structural category. They differ, however, in that here the groups are treated more or less in isolation, whereas in a structural explanation they are seen as part of a broader framework of causality.

For all their differences, the various explanations touched upon above share several important characteristics. For one thing, they all tend to treat politics as the dependent variable, assuming that what goes on politically in a country is the byproduct of cultural, economic, or social forces. Secondly, their portrayal of Latin American "democrats" tends to fall at one of two extremes: the latter are seen either as champions of democracy whose tireless work is repeatedly thwarted by a hostile environment, or as individuals who may use the language of democracy but who really do not want a democratic political system. Moreover, none of these approaches offers a truly adequate explanation of why democracy succeeds in some Latin American countries and fails in others, or why, in a particular country, it often appears to succeed for a while and then fails.

An Alternative Approach

In an effort to more adequately account for these intraregional and intracountry variations, this chapter will treat political behavior as an independent variable and will look not at democracy's overt enemies but at its ostensible friends. This is not to deny the importance of contextual influence; rather, it is denying contextual determination. Agreeing with Giovanni Sartori that "wrong ideas about democracy make a democracy go wrong,"[6] the central argument of this paper is that the attitude toward opposition held by democratic leaders is a crucial but often overlooked variable in explaining the success or failure of democracy. The assumptions underlying this proposition are that (1) free political competition is the most central characteristic of democracy; (2) democratically competitive politics requires certain attitudinal as well as structural conditions; (3) the attitudes of political leaders are of particular importance in the success or failure of a political system; and (4) the attitudes and behavior of political leaders are especially important in new political situations where orientations and expectations appropriate to the new context are being formed.

Opposition is widely recognized as a central and defining characteristic of democracy. As a reflection of this importance, the forms, patterns, and style of opposition in democracies have been the focus of a considerable amount of careful research.[7] Many of these works have added important new insights into the role of opposition in democratic politics. Nevertheless, the tendency to focus solely upon the opposition groups themselves and to emphasize structural and behavioral rather than attitudinal aspects results in only a partial picture of the process.

The freedom of opposition and the effective organization of this opposition is a necessary but not sufficient condition for stable democracy. Opposition must not only be allowed; it must be accepted. Acceptance in this sense means that the leaders of government accept not only the fact of opposition or the abstract principle of competitive politics but also the legitimacy of the specific opposition groups and the interests they represent. Such an acceptance, in turn, requires a degree of tolerance and willingness to compromise that often has been absent in Latin American interpretations of democracy. A recent work on democratic theory sums up this argument well:

> Citizens of a democracy must tolerate opposition even when presented by vicious or stupid men. In the heat of political strife, with important issues at stake and all one's energies engaged, it will often appear that only sheer thick-headedness could lie behind an opposition so stubborn and blind as that one faces. If one's opponents clearly are not ignorant or stupid, it is tempting to conclude that they are evil men, driven by selfishness, ambition, or other base motives. To the government, so it must often seem. Sometimes it will be so. But central to a democratic system is the general conviction that, whatever the motives or beliefs of the conflicting parties, governing decisions cannot be determined prior to the participatory process, but only through the process. And if the process itself is to go on, the several members of the community must be internally disposed to tolerate every kind of opposition, notwithstanding the irritation and anger it may cause.
>
> This disposition is manifested through the practice, not merely the profession, of great self-restraint. A democrat believing sincerely that his opponents are thoroughly and absolutely wrong must still live and work with them, permit and even encourage their participation in the self-governing process of the whole.[8]

This tolerance requires a great deal of self-restraint in words as well as in deeds. The swiftest and most dramatic death of democracy comes, of course, when a democratically chosen government uses its strength to forcefully eliminate specific opponents or all opposition. When this occurs, it is usually justified by alleging that the opposition lacks true legitimacy and that the governing group is the only real representation of "the people." Even when the governing elites lack either the power or the will to forcefully eliminate opposition, however, the rhetoric of intolerance can, over time, just as effectively lead to the collapse of democratic governments. The process is slower and less dramatic, but the result is often equally fatal to democracy.

Importance of Elite Attitudes

The emphasis throughout this paper is upon the attitudes and orientations of political leaders rather than of the general population. This is not to deny the important role of the citizen in a democracy, nor that mass attitudes and experiences can be either an asset or a detriment to the success of democratic politics. Rather, it reflects the belief that the political elites have a considerable amount of influence upon the success or failure of democracy independent of the conditions prevailing in the larger society. As Joseph LaPalombara has argued, the political culture of the elites "may be compatible with political democracy even where values espoused by the masses are not particularly democratic and where other organizations in society are not democratically run."[9] Similarly, of course, elite attitudes may be less compatible with democracy than might be conditions in the larger society. The crucial importance of elite political culture is twofold: (1) political leaders are the ones who actually engage in competitive politics and, thus, their behavior determines the nature of the interaction, and (2) through their rhetoric and their actions, members of the political elite set a "tone" of politics that tends to be followed by the general citizenry.[10]

The influence of elite attitudes upon the general population is particularly crucial in a radically new political situation, where past experience offers little guidance for either interpretation or behavior. Under such circumstances, political leaders not only set the tone but actually define the situation for a great many of their followers. This can be seen quite clearly in the wake of a successful revolution, but it is no less true when rapid but peaceful change has produced a new political landscape with few familiar guideposts.[11]

The foregoing arguments can be summarized and specified as follows. The leaders of many of Latin America's "democratic" movements have failed to recognize (or accept) the centrality of tolerance of opposition in a democratic polity. Despite a formal and often quite sincere commitment to the principle of democracy, their concept of democracy thus often lacks a crucial component. Upon achieving power, these leaders often speak not only as though their party and administration are the *best* representatives of the people, but as though they are the *only* legitimate representatives of the people. Either explicitly or by strong implication, they thus suggest that the former administrations and the interests they represented, which are now likely to be the major opposition groups, lacked not only representativeness but fundamental legitimacy as well. Whatever may be its historical validity, this is perhaps not a politically inappropriate argument if made by a revolutionary leader who has overthrown the former regime by force. But from a leader pledged to democratic principles who achieves power peacefully because members of the former administration adhered to at least some minimal set of democratic rules of political competition, it seems to be a singularly inappropriate stance. The opposition, with its roots in the former administration, reacts sharply to such condemnation by a group it "allowed" to take power. Quite apart from differences over policy or ideological orientations, this type of attack on the legitimacy of the opposition is likely to produce angry feelings that the new government is violating the rules of the game under which it assumed office. There also is an important influence upon the rank-and-file supporters of the new government. When democracy is little more than an appealing abstraction in the minds of many, or when its meaning is undergoing rapid change, their "working definitions" are going to be taken from the leaders they support. The result is that the followers of the "democratic" leaders in power will tend to equate democracy with intransigent pursuit of their own partisan interests and the opposition will increasingly see the new "democracy" as little more than a political fraud. The dynamics of this situation lead to increasing intransigence on all sides, a resulting political immobilism, and—quite often—an eventual military coup de grace for an already moribund democracy.

The test of any analytical approach is in its utility to help to explain individual cases. Although space precludes a detailed analysis of individual countries, the remainder of the chapter will briefly examine within this framework two prominent examples of the failure of democracy in Latin America. The two cases, Argentina from 1916 to 1930 and Chile from 1970 to 1973, are a half-century apart and represent quite different stages in the evolution of democracy. There are, however a number of important similarities.

Argentina, 1916-1930

The election of 1916 brought the middle-class Unión Cívica Radical to national power and its long-time leader, Hipólito Yrigoyen, to the presidency. It represented the triumph of more than twenty years of struggle and is widely interpreted as the beginning of Argentina's brief "golden age" of democracy.[12]

Since the mid-nineteenth century, Argentine politics had been dominated by an elite whose power was based upon agriculture and export. The period was characterized by what Dahl refers to as "competitive oligarchies" rather than a single hegemonic group,[13] but conflicts tended to be resolved through a tradition of private compromises, or *acuerdos*, rather than open conflict. There was a considerable amount of economic growth after 1880 as well as significantly progressive legislation in such areas as education. But tradition, legal barriers, and electoral fraud shut out the middle and lower classes from effective political participation.

As a result of economic growth, urbanization, and heavy European immigration, new political groups emerged demanding entry into the political system. The Unión Cívica Radical, formed in 1891, was the most persistent of these parties and, over the years, came to be the most prominent symbol of the struggle for democracy. Hipólito Yrigoyen, leader of the UCR since the mid-1890s, was an advocate of democracy but believed it could only be achieved by revolution. His platform over the years was a vague call for "national reparation," the only specific contents of which were free elections and respect for the national constitution. He refused numerous offers to participate in the government, choosing instead to lead his followers upon many conspiracies and several widespread but unsuccessful attempts at armed rebellion.

By the end of the first decade of the twentieth century, the governing elites had become convinced that the only way to maintain the prevailing system was to expand it so as to incorporate the increasingly restless middle class. This led to a government-initiated electoral reform, a reform upon which opposition leader Yrigoyen's counsel was sought and that made possible his victory in the next presidential election. Even after this reform was in effect, Yrigoyen favored abstention and rebellion over open electoral participation. But his intransigence was increasingly unacceptable to other leaders in the party, now that they saw the chance of campaigning and winning office, and Yrigoyen himself finally agreed to seek the presidency in 1916.

Thus from 1916 until 1922 and again from 1928 until he was overthrown by the military in 1930, Yrigoyen was a constitutional president whose election was facilitated by the "oligarchy's" electoral reform and who had long portrayed himself as a champion of democracy. But throughout his years as president Yrigoyen's rhetoric, and to some extent his behavior, continued to be more appropriate for a revolutionary leader than for a democratically elected head of state.

Many examples could be cited, but a few will have to suffice. Yrigoyen was fond of saying that his government was the first legitimate government of Argentina. Not just the first popularly elected government, which it probably was, but the first legitimate government, which it surely was not. He also persisted in using the pre-1916 imagery of a struggling *causa* (the UCT) against an evil and powerful *régimen* (the former governments and the interests now represented by the major opposition). After the UCR's national victory in 1916, Yrigoyen continued to maintain that those conservative administrations still in control of many of the individual provinces were all without legitimacy.

While he generally respected the formal rules of democracy, Yrigoyen's behavior as well as his words betrayed an intolerance that attacked the basic legitimacy of the opposition. He repeatedly insulted congress, where members of the opposition still retained influence, by sending his annual message in writing with an aide rather than presenting it as a personal address, which had long been the tradition. The first year, on the date for the annual message, he sent only a curt note saying he had been too busy correcting problems left by the prior administration to have time to prepare the message. And although federal intervention to overthrow provincial governments had a long history in Argentina, Yrigoyen utilized this tactic more frequently and with more overtly partisan motives than his predecessors.

In the name of democracy and "national reparation," Yrigoyen and his close followers spoke—and often acted—with the arrogance and intransigence that might have been expected had they in fact overthrown the *régimen* by force. But under the actual circumstances, the result was the reinforcement of a narrowly partisan notion of democracy among Yrigoyen's followers and a growing alienation on the part of the opposition. This lack of tolerance produced a growing reactive intolerance not only among the conservative opposition but also among opposition groups such as the Socialists, which before 1916 had also opposed the *régimen*.

The Radical Party itself experienced a deepening cleavage during Yrigoyen's first administration between those who shared his approach and those who favored a more conciliatory stance toward groups associated with the prior governments. This schism resulted in a formal split into two parties in 1924, during the presidency of Marcelo T. de Alvear, who was supported by the dissident "antipersonalist" (anti-Yrigoyen) Radicals. During the next four years, the Yrigoyen intrasigent Radicals became the major opposition to Alvear's UCR administration.

Yrigoyen won reelection against an antipersonalist candidate in 1928, but was overthrown two years later by Argentina's first military coup since the mid-nineteenth century. The immediate cause of the overthrow was governmental inaction in the face of a rapidly deteriorating economic situation. But the stage had been set over a number of years as Yrigoyen's leadership produced a misunderstanding of democracy among his followers and a growing frustration and cynicism among his opponents.

Chile, 1970-1973

Whereas popular democracy had been a novel idea in Argentina in 1916 when Yrigoyen came to power, it was well established in Chile in 1970 upon the election of Salvador Allende. In Chile, 1970 was to have been the beginning of a peaceful transformation to socialism. But there were a number of parallels. Like Yrigoyen, Allende was able to win the presidency because his opponents were willing to respect the electoral rules of the game despite their anxiety about what the new government might bring. And because it was a new stage in the country's political evolution, Allende, like Yrigoyen, had an especially important role in defining the new political situation. There were other important similarities, but first a brief review of Chilean politics up to 1970 is in order.[14]

From the early nineteenth century, Chilean politics had been more stable than was typical of Latin America. Initially this was primarily the result of competent leadership by a tolerant oligarchy that successfully coopted rising members of the middle class. There were intermittent periods of instability, but this tradition of flexibility and cooptation laid the foundation for a twentieth-century democracy that grew to have widespread support and that became a source of pride for many Chileans.

But even into the 1960s, the social system underlying this political democracy was quite traditional in many respects—particularly in the rural areas. This had been one of the sources of strength of the political system, for changes had come more gradually and peacefully than in many neighboring countries. But it also was a weakness, for it provided an added basis for revolutionary rhetoric in the midst of a functioning democracy.

It had been fashionable even for non-Marxist parties such as the Christian Democrats to renounce capitalism in name if not in practice by the mid-1960s. Allende, a national senator of the Socialist Party for many years, had sought the presidency without success on three previous occasions and ran again in 1970 as the candidate of *Unidad Popular*, a coalition of Communists, Socialists, and minor leftist parties. His pledge was to bring socialism to Chile through peaceful means while maintaining a democratic political system. Allende received 36.2 percent of the vote, a narrow edge over the conservative National Party's Jorge

Alessandri but far short of the majority needed for election. Under such circumstances, which were quite common in Chile's multiparty system, the constitution provided that the congress should choose the president from between the top two candidates. Congress thus had the constitutional prerogative of choosing Alessandri, who have been president from 1958 to 1964 and who would clearly have been the safer choice in the eyes of many legislators. But despite this constitutional latitude, there had evolved a tradition of choosing the candidate with the largest popular vote. A sufficient number of members of other parties, particularly the Christian Democrats, followed this tradition in 1970 and Allende was named president. But the action came only after the Marxist candidate agreed to formally pledge that he would not violate Chile's democratic political system.

The attempt to move a nation rapidly toward socialism was bound to create dislocations and produce opposition. There is considerable evidence, however, that it was not the specific economic policies that provided the catalyst for the massing of opposition that led to the overthrow of the government and Allende's death in 1973. There was widespread multiparty support for the nationalization of certain major industries and for a comprehensive land reform; even those who did not favor them in principle often seemed convinced that they were necessary for the survival of the basic system.[15] With a carefully planned and executed program of reforms, where the policies at any given time were designed to generate sufficient support to counteract specific opposition. Allende most likely could have accomplished these and many more of his basic economic goals.[16]

But this was not Allende's approach. Instead, he insisted on speaking as though a revolution rather than a period of reform was taking place. Despite the election outcome and the Statute of Democratic Guarantees that had been required before congress would name him president, Allende acted as though he had a broad mandate to drastically and permanently alter the structure of the nation's political system. This challenged not only the tangible interests but also the past accomplishments, beliefs, and fundamental legitimacy of major sectors of the opposition. The result of this revolutionary rhetoric and continuing attack upon an institutional structure that had widespread multiclass support was increasing unification of the opposition and alienation of many would-be supporters.[17]

Allende's revolutionary rhetoric also may well have contributed to difficulties in economic areas such as land reform. Land redistribution had been taking place in Chile for some years and there was general support for its accelerated pace under Allende's administration. But, although Allende himself seemed committed to peaceful and legal means, many of his followers were not. It perhaps cannot be proven that Allende's rhetoric contributed to the problem of illegal seizures of land, but it is certainly reasonable to assume that he played an important role in providing cues—however unintentional—regarding what would be appropriate behavior along the Chilean road to socialism. What is clear is that these illegal seizures, often directed against small amd medium-sized farms, and Allende's failure to protect landowners against them, were seen by many as a serious violation of the true *via chilena*.

One could cite many additional examples of gratuitous revolutionary rhetoric and its counterproductive impact upon the economic goals of the Allende administration. The way he came to power carried with it a commitment to the protection of Chile's prevailing political system and the various groups and interests which composed it, and even had he ignored this ethical obligation Allende lacked the support to forcefully impose basic structural changes. The rhetoric was therefore both inappropriate and unrealistic; it did, however, challenge not only the immediate interests but the very legitimacy of the opposition and contributed in a very significant way to the downfall of his regime. "Thus Allende failed because he lacked the power to impose a revolutionary socialist regime yet insisted on employing the rhetoric of revolution."[18]

Conclusion

Few question the sincerity of either Yrigoyen or Allende in his commitment to the abstract notion of democracy. Yet each played a significant role in the failure of the democratic regime over which he presided. The central arguments sketched out in this paper obviously need to be tested in more depth and in other national contexts, including those where democracy has succeeded as well as where it has failed. But the evidence so far does strongly suggest that leadership is a crucial but often overlooked factor in explaining the success or failure of democracy in Latin America.

The role of leadership is especially important in situations where democracy has been little more than an abstract ideal or where its interpretation is changing rapidly, as occurs when there is a sudden expansion of political participation. The personalism common to Latin American politics has on occasion been used by skillful leaders in such circumstances to transfer traditional loyalties "from a charismatic to a rational pattern of legitimacy which includes respect for opposition."[19] But this seems to have been the exception, and analysts typically have failed to recognize or examine in depth "the ways in which leadership behavior may *undermine* effective adjustment" to a new political situation.[20]

We would thus agree with Greenstein that it is not just the "heroes" of history, those who altered the course of events through extraordinary talents, who should be studied. "The Great Failure is equally significant: an actor's capabilities may be relevant to an outcome in a negative as well as a positive sense."[21] There have been many great failures in the history of Latin American democracy. Some of these, at least, appear to have failed largely because they held the wrong ideas about democracy.

Notes

1. Democracy, of course, is a term that has been used to describe radically different and often incompatible types of political systems. When not otherwise defined, the term "democracy" in this paper will refer to what is typically called pluralistic or liberal democracy but which, Dahl argues convincingly, might better be called "polyarchy." This is the usage most consistent with both institutional arrangements and tradition in Latin America, however often it may seem to have been otherwise in practice. For useful typologies of democracy, see Barry Holden, *The Nature of Democracy* (New York: Barnes & Noble, 1974), chap. 2; and Robert D. Putnam, *The Beliefs of Politicians* (New Haven: Yale University Press, 1973), chaps. 13-14. The most comprehensive statement of Dahl's argument is found in his *Polyarchy* (New Haven: Yale University Press, 1971).

2. This cyclical pattern makes particularly hazardous the temptation to base long-term projections upon short-term trends in Latin American politics. Thus, a number of books published in the late 1950s and early 1960s that, on the basis of the previous few years, were predicting the flowering of democracy in the hemisphere were quickly outdated by the resurgence of military regimes in the 1960s. The pessimistic projections typical of the 1970s may similarly be refuted by events. Among those who have attempted to explain the rhythm of military coups is Warren Dean, "Latin American Golpes and Economic Fluctuations, 1823-1966," *Social Science Quarterly*, 51 (June 1970), 70-80.

3. See Howard J. Wiarda, "Toward a Framework for the Study of Political Change in Iberic-Latin Tradition: The Corporative Model," *World Politics*, 25:2 (January 1973), 206-235. Among recent country studies analyzed within this framework is Martin Weinstein, *Uruguay* (Westport, Conn.: Greenwood Press, 1975).

4. Perhaps the most widely known work reflecting this perspective is John J. Johnson, *Political Change in Latin America* (Stanford: Stanford University Press, 1958).

5. For bibliographic analyses of the voluminous literature on the dependency theory, see Ronald H. Chilcote, "A Critical Synthesis of the Dependency Literature," *Latin American Perspectives*, 1:1 (1974), 4-29; and C. Richard Bath and Dilmus D. James, "Dependency Analysis of Latin America: Some Criticisms, Some Suggestions," *Latin American Research Review* 11:3 (1976), 3-54.

6. Giovanni Sartori, *Democratic Theory* (Detroit: Wayne State University Press, 1962), p. 5. Sartori's insights are particularly appropriate for Latin American which, as he describes Italy, is in many respects "a frontier zone of the West" (p. vii).

7. Some of the best works on this theme can be found in two volumes edited by Robert Dahl, *Political Opposition in Western Democracies* (New Haven: Yale University Press, 1966) and *Regimes and Oppositions* (New Haven: Yale University Press, 1973). See also Rodney Barker (ed.), *Studies in Opposition* (London: Macmillan, 1971); Barbara N. McLennan (ed.), *Political Opposition and Dissent* (New York: Dunellen, 1973); and articles published in the British journal *Government and Opposition*.

8. Carl Cohen, *Democracy* (Athens: University of Georgia Press, 1971), p. 186.

9. Joseph P. LaPalombara, *Politics Within Nations* (Englewood Cliffs, N.J.: Prentice-Hall, 1974), p. 497. See also Arend Lijphart, *The Politics of Accommodation* (Berkeley: University of California Press, 1968). The contrary and more conventional view that successful democracy depends upon compatible social structures and general culture is well argued by Harry Eckstein, *Division and Cohesion in Democracy* (Princeton: Princeton University Press, 1966).

10. See Fred I. Greenstein, "The Impact of Personality on Politics: An Attempt to Clear Away the Underbrush," *American Political Science Review*, 61:3 (September 1967), 629-641; James V. Downton Jr., *Rebel Leadership* (New York: Free Press, 1973); and Putnam, *op. cit.* The general lack of attention to this important variable in the study of Latin American politics is perhaps reflected in the failure of elite political culture to appear among fifteen criteria used to measure democracy in the well-known reputational assessments begun by Russell Fitzgibbon more than thirty years ago. For the latest in this quinquennial series, see Kenneth F. Johnson, "Scholarly Images of Latin American Political Democracy in 1975," *Latin American Research Review*, 11:2 (1976), 129-140.

11. Greenstein, p. 637.

12. For an introduction in English to the Radical era and events leading up to it, see David Rock, *Politics in Argentina, 1890-1930* (London: Cambridge University Press, 1975); Peter H. Smith, *Politics and Beef in Argentina* (New York: Columbia University Press, 1969), and *Argentina and the Failure of Democracy* (Madison: University of Wisconsin Press, 1974); and Carl Solberg, *Immigration and Nationalism; Argentina and Chile, 1890-1914* (Austin: University of Texas Pres, 1970).

13. See *Polyarchy*, especially chap. 3. Robert Dix says that Argentina from the 1860s to 1916 and Chile from about 1833 to 1920 were among "leading examples of limited-participation aristocracies" in Latin America. See Dix, "Latin

America: Opposition and Development," in Dahl's *Regimes and Oppositions*, p. 268.

14. For political background on Chile in English, see, among others, Federico G. Gil, *The Political System of Chile* (Boston: Houghton-Mifflin, 1966), and James Petras, *Politics and Social Forces in Chilean Development* (Berkeley: University of California Press, 1969). Because of the emotionalism surrounding the Allende period, as well as its recentness, polemics still far outnumber careful analyses and even the latter are seldom without strong ideological bias. For a sampling of accounts of the 1970-1973 period from varying ideological perspectives, see Les Evans (ed.), *Disaster in Chile* (New York: Pathfinder Press, 1974); Kenneth Medhurst (ed.), *Allende's Chile* (London: Hart-David MacGibbon, 1972); Robert Moss, *Chile's Marxist Experiment* (Newton Abbot, England: David Charles, 1973); Philip O'Brien (ed.), *Allende's Chile* (New York: Praeger Publishers, 1976); James F. Petras and Morris H. Morley, *How Allende Fell* (Nottingham: Spokesman Books, 1974); and Paul M. Sweezy and Harry Magdoff (eds.), *Revolution and Counter-Revolution in Chile* (New York: Monthly Review Press, 1974). A detailed documentation of events in Chile from 1969 through 1974 can be found in Lester A. Sobel (ed.), *Chile & Allende* (New York: Facts on File, 1974).

15. Robert R. Kaufman, *The Politics of Land Reform in Chile, 1950-1970* (Cambridge: Harvard University Press, 1972), analyzes the strategies of land reform and the degree of success in pre-Allende administrations.

16. On general reform strategy, see Samuel P. Huntington, *Political Order in Changing Societies* (New Haven: Yale University Press, 1968), chap. 6. For a good, brief discussion of the prospects for reform and how these were ignored and eventually undermined by Allende, see Brian Loveman, "Allende's Chile: Political Economy of the Peaceful Road to Disaster," paper presented at the 1974 Annual Meeting of the Latin American Studies Association.

17. Unable to bring about the changes by force, Allende's political program would have required existing institutions to voluntarily alter themselves to the point of destruction. But, as Loveman notes, "suicide to accommodate the Popular Unity government was not to be expected of the opposition" (p. 6).

18. Loveman, p. 11.

19. Dix, p. 296.

20. Downton, p. 12. Emphasis added.

21. Greenstein, p. 635.

Part 5
Is Democracy Still Viable?

11
Ideological Dependency and the Origins of Socialism in the Caribbean

Anthony P. Maingot

Introduction

Students of Third World societies are substantially agreed that the various models of dependency that emerged in the 1960s have contributed to a deeper understanding of their condition of underdevelopment. Dependency is not only an economic condition; it is also political and intellectual in nature. It is increasingly clear, however, that many students of dependency have so politicized the *models* of dependency that they can only produce heavily ideological and moralistic *theories* of dependency. Not only is the heuristic and operational value of the model reduced, but also two quite serious distortions become integral parts of these value-laden theories of dependency:

1. A focus so narrow that it tends to interpret only certain types of elites and decisions as dependent. The focus varies with the political-ideological predilections of the particular author, though generally speaking radical or revolutionary elites are not seen as dependent.
2. A denial of any decision-making capabilities and options to the "dependent" Third World elites—all decisions are seen as direct consequences of a wide-ranging dependency, a dependency that is cause for moral indignation.

This chapter advances the proposition that dependency is a structure; it therefore permeates all layers of the elite groups participating in the society, whether radical-revolutionary, reformist-revolutionary, or status-quo in outlook. This proposition is based on the notion that colonialism is also a structural condition, the main characteristic of which is the continual dependence on external models for internal solutions. This dependence characterizes all groups of the colonial society and often most dramatically those radical-revolutionary or reformist groups that wish to change the society's colonial situation. Socialists are no less than free enterprise advocates dependent on external ideas; to ignore this reality is to weaken the utility of the model for understanding underdevelopment.

Approached in this way, the model helps us understand which options are open to the native elites and how and why they opt as they did or do. The proposition is developed through an analysis of stages of early Socialist party organization in the Caribbean with special emphasis on Cuba, Trinidad, and Jamaica.

Ideological Dependence of Cuban Socialism

Spanish immigrant laborers first brought radical ideas to Cuba. These syndico-anarchists continued to have close ties with their Spanish homeland and the movements there. Especially important in the tobacco industry, their ideas spread to Key West and Tampa as the industry migrated to those mainland centers. Not surprisingly, the first Socialist party would be organized by a Cuban, Diego Vicente Tejera, whose residence in Spain and Paris exposed him to both the misery of the working classes of those countries and the socialist intellectuals who addressed themselves to possible solutions.[1] Tejera's major works were written in Paris (in French) and even after his return to Cuba, his closest intellectual associates were to be found in radical circles of Key West and Tampa. Neither Tejera's Partido Socialista Cubano (est. 1899) nor the one that followed its demise in 1900, the equally short-lived *Partido Popular*, had any impact on the Cuban laboring classes. For one, these classes were too deeply divided on ethnic grounds, native Cubans resenting the Spanish workers.[2]

The origins of the Cuban Communist Party (in 1925) showed just how persistent was the dependency of radical elites on foreigners. Although the guiding spirit was undoubtedly the Cuban, Julio Antonio Mella, and to a lesser degree, Carlos Baliño, foreigners played an important role in the organizing stages: Mexicans, Yiddish-speaking Poles (a translator was needed for these early meetings), and Spaniards.[3] Crucial financial aid came from the Communist Party USA, and there is little doubt that the Cuban Communist Party accepted the leadership of Moscow's Comintern from the very inception (even though membership was not granted until 1928.) Mella himself had a deep mistrust of any and all national bourgeoisie, especially the reformist ones, and looked upon the Third International and Moscow as the "pivot" (to use his words) of all Latin American socialist movements. He continually sought "inspiration" from that source.[4] According to Robert Alexander the lines of communication ran Moscow-Paris-New York-Havana.[5] Two crucial decisions taken during the early phases of this Communist Party indicate its close dependence on external factors: the initial working alliance between two new labor unions (the *Confederación Nacional Obrera* and the *Federación Obrera de la Habana*), allied in 1925 to the new Communist Party, split after the Stalin-Trotskyite rift in the USSR. Cuban Trotskyites (who controlled the *Federación Obrera de la Habana*) left or were expelled from the Cuban Communist Party and formed the *Partido Bolchevique Leninista*. The leaders of this movement were under no illusions as to their condition of dependence. "The Trotskyites felt," Victor Alba notes, "there could be no revolution in Cuba so long as socialism remained a minor force in the United States, because of the island's economic dependence on the United States."[6]

If splits within the Cuban movement reflected the situation in the Soviet Union, so did the Cuban Communist Party posture regarding vital national problems. Such a problem was the Negro question in Cuba. There can be no argument that the Cuban Communists were the first to really deal with that burning issue in Cuba and the first to make a truly concerted effort to change a shameful state of affairs. But their efforts did show a high degree of dependence on the Soviet Comintern's posture: the Negro question was to be dealt with as a "national" rather than a "racial" question; consequently, "self-determination" was called for in the "Black Belt" of Oriente Province. The Cuban approach was identical in goals, and even wording, with the posture adopted by the Communist Party USA on the Negro question in the United States.[7] Throughout the 1930s leaders of the Communist Party USA, such as Earl Browder, Robert Minor, James W. Ford, and William Z. Foster, were frequent guests and speakers at various activities of the Cuban Communist Party. Similarly, Cuban Communists—especially after the Comintern ordered, in 1934, a shift from the "Third Period" to a "Popular Front" stance—were frequently in the United States. In 1936, Blas Roca, Secretary-General of the Party, went so far as to tell the *New York Times* that he was in the United States in order to ensure "continued financial aid" from the U.S. Communists.[8] The behavior of the Cuban Communist Party, including its "critical support" of the Batista regime (1940-1944), was quite in keeping with the "Browderite" program of national unity mandated by the Comintern for the Communist Party USA and its hemispheric peers.

To conclude: the first decade and a half in the life of the Cuban Communist Party showed a high degree of programmatic and financial dependence not only on the Comintern but also on the Communist

Party USA. This was part of a broader dependence of Cuban society on the United States. One fundamental aspect of this U.S.-Cuban relationship was the fact that the absence of a significant American socialist party left the Cuban Left with no major representation beyond the Communists.[9] The absence of a significant American socialist party was paralleled by the absence of an effective Second International.[10] This absence of a socialist alternative to the Comintern-directed Communist movement made Cuban dependence qualitatively different from that of the incipient socialist movement in the British West Indies. The case of Trinidad is illustrative.

Trinidad

Although there were certainly individuals in the nineteenth century whose radical views earned them the reputation of being "socialist," the first significant socialist political organizer, Captain Andrew Cipriani, did not come onto the political scene until after World War I. Cipriani became president of the moribund Trinidad Workingmen's Association in 1919, and, within a decade, it was the largest and best organized labor movement in the British West Indies. He affiliated the association with the British Labour Party and the Labour and Socialist International, and was regularly present at the biennial empire conferences of the British Labour Party.

Cipriani and the other leaders were all creoles and the issues they addressed were local ones, but their dependence on the British Labour Party was clear. Here is Cipriani speaking to a conference of the British Labour Party:

> [In Trinidad] the voice of the people, the voice of the working man is never heard at all, and therefore I look forward to a Labour Government in office and in power, for a change in this unfair and un-British treatment meted out to us . . . and I am to remind my friends in the Labour Party . . . I am entitled to a satisfactory and sympathetic hearing . . . looking to you for help and support.[11]

The next stage in the development of Trinidad's radical movement came in the 1930s, when a considerable rise in labor consciousness led to active trade union organization, and such organizations were legalized in 1932. But the 1932 ordinance made no provision for the right of peaceful picketing, nor did it give unions immunity against action in tort—both part of Great Britain's union legislation since 1906. The deep-rooted dependence of the Trinidad Left was again evidenced when Cipriani's association refused to register as a union as a protest—a decision taken on the advice of the International Department of the British Trade Union Congress.[12]

It is interesting to speculate on the consequence of Ciprani's decision not to register as a trade union. This is the period when the two most significant groups of workers—in oil and sugar—were joining two newly registered unions: the Oilfield Workers' Trade Union (OWTU) and the All-Trinidad Sugar Estates and Factory Workers' Trade Union. Power seemed to pass from Cipriani's hands into those who grabbed the leadership of labor rather than, as Cipriani did, enter the political arena where—given the colonial structure of the government—there was simply no room to maneuver.

This became obvious in 1937, when the pent-up frustrations of labor in Trinidad and the West Indies exploded into violence. Uriah Butler, a Granadian who migrated to Trinidad at age 30 and who had been expelled from the Trinidad Labour Party in 1936, emerged as the rough-hewn but effective leader of the activists in 1937. Although his "British Empire Workers and Citizens Home Rule Party" had barely 100 paying members at the time, Butler's aggressive agitation for bread-and-butter issues struck a respondent note among union and nonunion labor.[13]

The dependence of Cipriani on British legalistic approaches to labor was *part* of the problem. Butler had no such restrictions and could fit his methods to the local needs—including the racial ones, for instance, by flailing out against the South Africans on oil company staffs. Cipriani's attempt to emulate the British Labour Party's structure did not conform to the islands's fast changing economic scene. By not converting the Trinidad Workingmen's Association into a legal union and making it a branch of his labor party, Cipriani paved the way for the effective separation of trade unionism (the labor movement) from parliamentary politics in Trinidad.

This permitted, by 1956, a totally pragmatic, nonideological politician, Eric Williams, to organize and launch a racially-based political party (the PNM, People's National Movement) without association with the union structure and leadership. This, in turn, permitted Williams to exclude from party membership any radicals whose outright loyalty he doubted. Given the Indian-black division that had already crystallized, the unions had no alternative but to support the predominantly black PNM.

The Island's Marxist-Leninists organized into the West Indian Independent Party (WIIP). Their dependence on the emerging black nationalist Williams is evident in their thirty-seven-page memorandum to the Constitution Reform Commission of 1955, where they could do no better than to quote Eric Williams no less than fifteen times![14] This Marxist-Leninist group never really went much beyond being a small "discussion circle," despite their continual efforts at political participation.[15] Despite the labor struggles of the late 1930s, despite the dramatic changes in labor practices wrought by the U.S. "occupation" of the island during World War II, and its labor-intensive construction and maintenance employment on the military bases, and despite their occasional use of black nationalist rhetoric, the radical ideologue on the island found it difficult to break his intellectual dependency on foreign models. Note the eulogy of one of the shining lights of the island's Marxist-Leninist circle, Quintin O'Conner, written by a prominent colleague:

> the decisive influence on Quintin's career as a trade unionist was ... John Jagger, President of the National Union of Distributive and Allied Workers of the United Kingdom who visited Trinidad in 1939 ... [until his death he relied] for unfailing guidance on "The History of Trade Unionism" by Sidney and Beatrice Webb and inspired by a picture and the always remembered words of Lenin.[16]

The dramatic consequences of this ideological and practical separation of radical trade unionism leadership from ongoing parliamentary politics can be witnessed from various election results. In 1956, general elections for the Legislative Council, the WIIP contested only one out of a possible twenty-four seats. Its candidate received 3.8 percent of the vote in that district. In 1961, they ran no candidate. In the 1966 parliamentary elections, the radical groups ran under the banner of the Workers and Farmers Party (WFP) and ran in thirty-five out of thirty-six constituencies. Their total vote was 3.46 percent, not electing a single member: this, despite running such well-known radical figures as Lennox Pierre, C. L. R. James, Eugene Joseph, George Weekes, Basdeo Panday, Stephen Maharaj, and John Kelshall. The figures from the first elections after the island's independence, shown in Table 11.1, tell a dramatic story.

All these men had long histories of direct or indirect ties with the labor movement and were a mix of black, Indian, colored and white Trinidadians. Politics had already become a racial matter in which ideology played a minimal role. No better evidence of this can be had than the fate of the United Labour Force (ULF), a "popular front" of labor union-based radicals that competed in the 1975 elections. Led by a charismatic Indian lawyer, Basdeo Panday, the ULF won ten out of thirty-six seats—all in heavily Indian areas formerly controlled by the

TABLE 11.1

Parliamentary Elections, 1966

W.F.P. Candidate	W.F.P. %	P.N.M. %	D.L.P. %
Lennox Pierre	.355	54.6	40.9
Eugene Joseph	.891	88.9	4.5
C.L.R. James	2.8	53.8	40.8
George Weekes	4.9	28.06	51.2
Basdeo Panday	3.5	15.0	65.8
Stephen Maharaj	5.5	39.2	53.9
John Kelshall	1.2	49.9	46.2

Indian-based DLP (Democratic Labour Party). In early 1977, a group of Marxist-Leninists united in a semisecret organization called NAMOTI (National Movement for the True Independence of Trinago)[17] carried out a coup within the ULF hoping to carry the membership of the major trade unions with them. The final outcome of this schism is still in doubt, but Panday's assessment is interesting. "These armchair ideologists," he told the press, "have no conception of how our people feel and think. They mislead themselves into believing that the working class care what is happening in China, Cuba and the Soviet Union or that our people are ready to accept, lock, stock, and barrel these foreign systems."[18]

The schism within the ULF seems quite in keeping with the history of Trinidad politics: a trade union leadership heavily dependent on foreign models of politics and state organization, but little in tune with the popular sentiments of the masses. The grip that race and ethnic allegiances have on the island's politics seems stronger than ever in 1977. The Puerto Rican model of development ("industrialization by invitation"), adopted by the ruling PNM, has had moderate success, in part, no doubt, to the vast sums available from the island's oil wealth.

The ideological dependence of early (and later) socialist organization has been shown to be crucial in the cases of Cuba and Trinidad. This dependence can be seen in other prominent Caribbean cases. In the case of Guyana (formerly British Guiana), it is important to note that Marxist-Leninist leader Cheddi Jagan was educated not in England but in the United States. The importance of both the elements of race and ideology are evident in the career of Jagan, as it is in that of so many West Indian leaders. The first thing he became very conscious of in the United States, Jagan notes in his autobiography, was the question of color, for him an entirely new experience: "I, too, had imbibed the psychology of fear which had gripped the U.S. Negro."[19] Already exposed to Marxist thought in the United States, Jagan's ideological maturing came from his travels to Trinidad to meet radical labor union and political leaders, of whom he writes with amazing candidness: "These were some of the 'gods' I then worshipped." Jagan soon declared his People's Progressive Party (PPP) a Marxist-Leninist movement, tightly aligned with Moscow. But even the long-standing ideological and institutional association with the USSR has failed to shift Guyanese politics from its basic ethnocentric characteristics.

The strength of racial and ethnic attachments in Guyana, as elsewhere in the Caribbean, are such that they have led to several crucial "schisms" in the history of Caribbean socialism. George Padmore, first black member of Moscow's Comintern, broke with the Comintern in the early 1940s on fundamentally racial grounds.[20] And Aime Cesare's break with the French Communist Party in 1956 was not a break with Marxism but with the white French Communist Party and Stalinism.[21] In a way, the neo-Marxist theories of Frantz Fanon can also be interpreted through an understanding of the racial factor,[22] and the wide acceptance of Fanon's race-based theories are further indication of the "ideological permeability" of the area.

Jamaica

The Jamaican case illustrates the various themes of ideological dependency and the tenacity of the race question. Contrary to the effects of the late 1930s labor unrest in Trinidad, in Jamaica they had a significant result: the emergence of a true, charismatic trade unionist called Alexander Bustamante (né William Alexander Clarke in 1884) and of his half cousin, a politically oriented intellectual lawyer called Norman Manley. Politics and labor unionism were tied together from the beginning. The history of Jamaican politics since that time has been the history of the counterpoint between Bustamante and Norman Manley, a counterpoint between Bustamante's nonideological populism and Manley's intellectual socialism. This counterpoint produced a solid two-party system but also a propensity to violence. "The Bustamante-Manley polarization,"notes Rex Nettleford, "is seductive. The rival cousins, each with undoubtedly major talents, have provided an excellent scenario for the nation's political drama."[23]

While both Manley and Bustamante organized on the labor front,

Manley moved politically, and his People's National Party (PNP) was the first serious Jamaican effort at a mass-based political party. In 1940, the party was declared a socialist party. To Manley, socialism meant "a fundamental change . . . a demand for the complete change of the basic organization of the social and economic conditions under which we live."[24] Manley included in his definition the notion that "all means of production should in one form or the other come to be publicly owned and publicly controlled." Not surprisingly, a fundamental characteristic of Manley socialism was its foreign intellectual origins. As Nettleford notes, part of the motivation was "the exposure of a few bright self-made intellectuals to Fabian socialist thought then current in Britain. Sir Stafford Cripps of the British Labour Party's left and Gollancz's Left Book Club publications were important intellectual and inspirational sources in the Jamaican genesis and adoption of the creed."[25] While clearly the labor unrest of the late 1930s played a major role in awakening native leadership, the foreign ideological influence was crucial in giving it a perspective. Equally crucial is the sequence: ideology *followed* organization, it was not the basis of it. Under attack from members of the colonial government, Manley, as early as 1940, noted that it was the socialism of Norway, Sweden, Ireland, Denmark, New Zealand, Australia, and the British Labour Party that was the PNP's ideal. In the mid-1950s Manley wrote that he was a democratic socialist, which was the essence of British socialism, "and that is the socialism to which I subscribe."[26]

Despite Manley's demonstrated adherence to democratic principles—an adherence that led in 1952 to the expulsion from the PNP of some of his most important leftist allies on grounds that they had formed a Marxist caucus within the PNP—Manley and the PNP were vulnerable on two grounds: (1) the "foreign" origins of the party's philosophy and (2) the PNP was a party of socialist, middle-class "Brown men." As George Eaton has noted:

> Bustamante . . . elected to fight the P.N.P. on the issue of which they were most vulnerable and one which they themselves had interjected, namely, ideology. . . . Socialism was equated with Communism, and Communism meant tyranny and slavery. Besides, as the P.N.P. was also the party of the urban middle classes . . . a P.N.P. victory would mean tyranny and slavery.[27]

With Bustamante's Jamaican Labour Party (JLP) pushing a populist line and the radicals within the PNP at bay, the PNP's commitment to socialism weakened over the years, but not its ideological dependence.

Only the focus shifted—to the Puerto Rican model of development through import substitution. Socialism would not be pushed to the forefront until the 1970s, with the electoral victories of Norman's son, Michael Manley, and the outcome of that new initiative is far from decided. The bitter battles within the PNP in 1977 between the so-called moderates and the radicals are reminiscent of the battles of the early 1950s and center, now as then, around the charges of "ideologies alien to the party."

Conclusion

Early socialist thought and organization in these three Caribbean islands have been characterized by a heavy ideological dependence on external sources. Yet these early socialists were struggling to put an end to Western colonialism, to one form of dependence. Any distinction between one form of dependency and the other involves a matter of political-ideological preference, not a sociological distinction. Sociologically, both dependencies stemmed from a similar structural condition, a condition that can best be analyzed through a *model* of dependence rather than any value-laden theory. The question is not "dependence or independence" but, rather, what kind of dependence and how that dependence either increases or decreases native elite power for national purposes. In other words, does dependence promote or hinder development and modernization?

Those who pose an ideal "independence" against "dependence" are obviously unacquainted with Marxian dialectics as they reflect on the modernization process. To quote from the *Manifesto of the Communist Party* (1848):

> The bourgeoisie has through its exploitation of the world market given a cosmopolitan character to production and consumption in every country. ... In place of the old local and national seclusion and self-sufficiency, we have intercourse in every direction, universal inter-dependence of nations. And as in material so in intellectual production. The intellectual creations of individual nations become common property. National one-sidedness and narrow-mindedness become more and more impossible, and from the numerous national and local literatures there arises a world literature.

The dilemma between an ideological or moral stance on dependency has parallels in the moral stance on imperialism. A sociological realization of some of the positive features of imperialism need not depend on retrograde social theory—it is in fact an integral part of liberal and radical Western thought—as Table 11.2 indicates. It was no

TABLE 11.2

On the Positive Effects of Western Imperialism

Liberal Thought	Radical Thought
"Future historians will say, I think, that the greatest event of the twentieth century was the impact of the Western Civilization upon all other living societies of that day . . . touching chords in human souls that are not touched by mere external material forces -- however ponderous and terrifying." (A. J. Toynbee, "Encounters Between Civilizations," Harper's Magazine, April 1947, p. 290)	"England, it is true, in causing a social revolution in Hindustan (India), was actuated only by the vilest interests . . . But that is not the question. The question is, can mankind fulfill its destiny without a fundamental revolution in the social state of Asia? If not, whatever may have been the crimes of England, she was the unconscious tool of history in bringing about that revolution." (Karl Marx, "The British Rule in India," The New York Daily Tribune, June 25, 1853)
	"England has to fulfill a double mission in India: one destructive, the other regenerating -- the annihilation of old Asiatic society, and the laying of the material foundations of Western society in Asia." (Karl Marx, "The Future Results of British Rule in India," The New York Daily Tribune, August 8, 1853)
"A plausible case can . . . be made for the proposition that the future will look back upon the overseas imperialism of recent centuries, less in terms of its sins of oppression, exploitation, and discrimination, than as the instrument by which the spiritual, scientific, and material revolution which began in Western Europe with the Renaissance was spread to the rest of the world." (Rupert Emerson, From Empire to Nation. Boston: Beacon Press, 1962, p. 6)	"The conquest of Algeria is an important and fortunate fact for the progress of civilization. . . . After all, the modern bourgeois, with civilization, industry, order, and at least relative enlightenment following him, is preferable to the feudal lord or to the marauding robber, with the barbarian state of society to which they belong." (Friedrich Engels in Northern Star, January 22, 1848)

less a sociologist than Marx himself who understood that the bourgeoisie "draws all, even the most barbarian nations into civilization" and, by creating enormous cities, "rescued a considerable part of the population from the idiocy of rural life." Marx's approach, Shlomo Avineri notes, enabled him to dissociate moral indignation and social critique from historical judgment.[28] This is the task awaiting many dependency theorists, for, in the final analysis, the central question in politics remains not whether the ideas are original or borrowed but how well they serve the people.

Notes

1. Cf. Jose Rivero Muñiz, *El primer partido socialista cubano*. Universidad Central de Las Villas, 1962.

2. Carlos Baliño, who in 1925 was instrumental in founding the Cuban Communist Party, resigned from *Agrupación Socialista de la Habana* in 1909 because of that group's pro-Spanish worker stance. (cf. *Pensamiento revolucionario cubano*. La Habana: 1971, pp. 279-281).

3. Hugh Thomas, *Cuba*. New York: Harper and Row, 1971, p. 577.

4. Cf. "Mella y la Unión Soviética," in Raquel Tibol, *Julio Antonio Mella en El Machete*. Mexico: Fondo de Cultural Popular, 1968, pp. 76-96.

5. Robert Alexander, *Communism in Latin America*. New Jersey: Rutgers University Press, 1957, pp. 36-41.

6. Victor Alba, *Politics and the Labor Movement in Latin America*. Stanford: Stanford University Press, 1968, p. 290.

7. Alexander, *Communism*, p. 276.

8. Quoted in Thomas, *Cuba*, pp. 712-713.

9. After the defeat of the "revolutionary" movement of 1934, the Cuban Left was absorbed by the Communists, especially as the latter became more respectable in Cuban and U.S. eyes. It is hard, in hindsight, to regard the *Autentico* party of Grau San Martin and Prío Socarrás as anything more than patronage-distributing electoral machines. Eduardo Chibas' *Ortodoxo* party was more populist than socialist.

10. The Second International (the Socialist International) was fundamentally a Western European organization; the U.S. socialists played a minor role in it. Established in Paris in 1889 (Marx's First International had expired in 1876), it went out of existence during World War I and reemerged in 1923 under the name "Socialist Workers International," only to again be dissolved by World War II. It came back into existence in 1951 under its original name, the Socialist International. It has until recently lacked the influence of its archrival, Moscow's Third International.

11. Quoted in C. L. R. James, *The Life of Captain Cipriani* [1932].

12. Cf. *Trinidad and Tobago Disturbances, 1937*. Report of Commission.

Port of Spain: Government Printing Office, 1938, p. 40.

13. Even though Mr. Cola Rienzi was general president of the OWTU and of the All-Trinidad Sugar Estates and Factory Workers' Trade Union, the colonial authorities regarded Butler as the functional leader of the workers and Rienzi as "without question Butler's accredited emissary." (*Trinidad and Tobago Disturbances, 1937*, p. 58).

14. Lennox Pierre and John La Rose, *For More and Better Democracy*. Trinidad: 1956. The authors were encouraged no doubt by the fact that the island's best known radical, C. L. R. James, had returned to work with the PNM as editor of its newspaper, *The Nation*.

15. In 1965 they were calculated to number fifteen. Cf. *Report of the Commission of Enquiry into Subversive Activities in Trinidad and Tobago*. House paper no. 2, 1965, p. 19.

16. Lennox Pierre, *Quintin O'Conner, A Personal Appreciation*. Trinidad: 1959, pp. 4-5. It is not clear just how thoroughly these radicals had studied their Marx. An English trade unionist recalled hearing the *Communist Manifesto* referred to as by Marx and Lenin by a member of this group (F. W. Dalley, *General Industrial Conditions and Labour Relations in Trinidad*. Trinidad: Government Printing Office, 1954, p. 67).

17. This group was led by some well-known radical labor leaders, viz. Raffique Shah, Lennox Pierre, Clive Nuñez, Joe Young, and George Weekes.

18. The *Express*, Port of Spain, August 11, 1977, p. 1.

19. Cheddi Jagan, *The West on Trial*. London: Michael London, 1966, p. 49.

20. James R. Hooker, *Black Revolutionary. George Padmore's Path From Communism to Pan-Africanism*. London: Pall Mall Press, 1967.

21. Aime Cesaire, *Lettre à Maurice Thorez*. Separata, *Presence Africaine*, 1956.

22. In other words, a necessary prelude to understanding Fanon's *Wretched of the Earth*, which deals with the Algerian Revolution, is a reading of his *White Masks, Black Skins*, which deals with his youth in Martinique and education in France.

23. Rex Nettleford, *Manley and the Politics of Jamaica*. Jamaica: ISER, 1971, p. 70.

24. Quoted in Rex Nettleford (ed.), *Manley and the New Jamaica, Selected Speeches and Writings, 1938-1968*. London: Longman Caribbean, 1971, p. 61.

25. Nettleford, *Manley and the Politics of Jamaica*, p. 35. Strachey's *Why I Should Be a Socialist* and the Red Dean's *Act Now* were best sellers among Jamaicans.

26. Nettleford, *Manley and the New Jamaica*, p. 89.

27. George E. Eaton, *Alexander and Modern Jamaica*. Jamaica: Klingston Publishers, 1975, pp. 106-107.

28. Shlomo Avineri, *Karl Marx on Colonialism and Modernization*. New York: Doubleday & Co., 1968, p. 3.

12
The Struggle for Democracy and Human Rights in Latin America: Toward a New Conceptualization

Howard J. Wiarda

The number of books and articles on Latin America describing the "struggle for democracy" there runs into the legions, and, in much current foreign policy discussion, the issues of the protection of human rights and U.S. relations with authoritarian regimes have received a great deal of attention.[1] This chapter deals with these issues with special reference to the Iberian and Latin American context, and raises the troubling questions of whether democracy and human rights are everywhere the same and universal, whether they are relevant in the same sense to all societies and time frames, and, hence, whether grounds exist for the hope of exporting democracy and human rights to other lands and culture areas.

The difficulty is that terms like "democracy," "human rights," "representative rule," "pluralism," "freedom," "participation," "social justice," and the like mean different things, convey different connotations, or enjoy differential legitimacy in different societies. Moreover, even in a single society, obviously including the United States, these concepts may change over time, relating generally to broad-scale cultural, socioeconomic, and political transformations. We have long been acutely aware of such differences of meaning with regard to the "peoples' democracies." What this chapter suggests is that within the "West" these concepts and terms of reference may also imply, in the distinct societies, some quite different meanings and understandings.

Neither adequate grounds for moral judgment nor the bases for an enlightened and rational foreign policy can be established until these differences are clearly understood. Although the focus here is on Iberia and Latin America, and what democracy and human rights mean in that culture area, the discussion also has relevance with regard to the same or

The comments of Keith Rosenn and Iêda Siqueira Wiarda are gratefully acknowledged. A somewhat briefer version of this chapter appeared in *Orbis*, 22 (Spring 1978).

similar issues in Africa, Asia, and perhaps elsewhere.

In offering such a macrofocus, this paper at times necessarily glosses over the various nuances, national variations, and ambiguities that exist, elements that must be taken into consideration in any final and definitive analysis of the subject. Obviously the situation of democracy and human rights in present-day Colombia, Costa Rica, and Venezuela is different from that of Argentina, Chile, and Paraguay. Although we must certainly be cognizant of these variations and differentiate carefully between the diverse nations of the area, as well as how they change over time, the emphasis here is more on the common and continuous features. Our purpose is to offer a way of thinking about the meaning and practice of democracy and human rights in Iberia and Latin America as distinguished from the North American conception, and to present an ideal-typical construct that stresses the similarities in the Iberic-Latin political culture as compared with that of the United States, rather than emphasizing the distinct national patterns within the area. Sound policy, of course, demands that each country be looked at on an individual basis, but before that an understanding must be achieved of the common context in which such individual variations take place. The present paper is conceived, therefore, not as a set of concrete prescriptions to be applied in individual cases but, perhaps more fundamentally, as an essential prelude before any such policy measures can be intelligently thought about.

Democracy and Human Rights in Iberia and Latin America: Applying a North American Perspective

In 1945 the Inter-American Conference on the "Problems of War and Peace," meeting at Chapultepec, Mexico, adopted a resolution calling for the international protection of human rights. At the Bogotá Conference in 1948, in addition to adopting the Charter of the Organization of American States, the Latin American nations also adopted the American Declaration of the Rights and Duties of Man, a document based largely on the United Nations Universal Declaration of Human Rights, to which the Latin American states are also signatories. And in their own constitutions the Latin American nations have consistently enshrined the principles of republican government, separation of powers, and human rights.[2] Based on such documents, we often assume Latin America means the same things in the use of such terms as in the United States.

A useful starting point for the discussion of just how "democratic" is Latin America and how its interpretations of "human rights" may be dfferent from that of North America are the influential, periodic surveys of "democracy" and its "progress" in Latin America by Russell H. Fitzgibbon and his collaborators.[3] The following criteria, among others, are included in their definition and measures:

1. The degree to which freedom of the press, speech, assembly exist
2. Whether there are free elections and honestly counted votes
3. Whether there exists freedom for political party organization, party opposition in the congress, and freedom for opposition groups generally
4. Whether there is an independent, coequal judiciary and congress.
5. The degree of public awareness of accountability for the collection and expenditure of public funds
6. Whether there exists civilian supremacy over the military
7. Whether there is freedom of political life from ecclesiastical controls
8. The strength of independent local government
9. Whether there is representative, participatory, pluralist, democratic government

Few of us would disagree with these values and institutions. But it may be argued that is so because the concepts and criteria used correspond closely to the liberal, Lockean, Anglo-American tradition and polity. The Fitzgibbon definition, to which most of us in the United States subscribe, has in it a powerful Montesquieuian, Jeffersonian, Madisonian bias. It is based on contract theory and the civil law tradition. It stems directly from the (North, *sic*) American Constitution and the Bill of Rights. Its model is the independent yeoman and individualist of the New England ideal, grassroots democracy and popular (electoral) participation, separation of powers and of the military and ecclesiastical realms from the political, and a pluralist and egalitarian polity with a hallowed tradition of respect for individual human rights. The question is whether these fundamental characteristics apply equally and in the same sense to Iberia and Latin America, or whether instead they represent a peculiarly U.S. set of expectations and practices inapplicable in culture areas other than our own.

A second difficulty with the Fitzgibbon formulation, in addition to its ethnocentrism, is that it ignores those features in the Latin American constitutions, at least as prominent as the "liberal" and "democratic" aspects, that enshrine authoritarian rule, corporate privilege, and constitutional and legal restrictions on human rights. Reserving further discussion for later, let us for now emphasize that authoritarian rule in

Latin America does not, as much of the literature implies, mean necessarily a usurpation of the laws and constitution but often a new emphasis on those features that the Fitzgibbon criteria ignore.[4]

Third, there is no sense in the Fitzgibbon studies that "freedom of the press," "elections" "opposition," etc., may mean something different in Luso-Hispanic civilization and law than they do in the Anglo-American, or that they may exist at distinct levels of popular acceptance and legitimacy. Keeping in mind the ups and downs, and vicissitudes within nations as well as variations between them, let us examine the Fitzgibbon criteria individually, both as a way of examining what Iberia and Latin America generally understand by these terms and how these understandings are distinct from those of North America.

1. Freedom of the press, speech, and assembly. These freedoms are a part of the Latin American legal and constitutional tradition, and some countries, to a greater or lesser degree, have striven to uphold them. But even allowing for the formal presence of such freedoms in Iberia and Latin America and their implementation in some countries in ways that parallel that of the United States, it is also clear that the meaning of these terms in the Iberic-Latin culture area implies different understandings and expectations than in the North American one. These liberties do not enjoy the hallowed place they do in the U.S. Bill of Rights, nor are they enshrined as inviolable principles. To a far greater degree than in the United States, freedom in Iberia and Latin America also implies obligations and duties, including the obligation to obey those in authority. Liberty carries with it the obligation for self-censorship and the exercise of prior restraint.

The lists of human and social rights contained in the constitutions, or injunctions to democracy and representative rule, constitute aspirations and future goals for the society to achieve. They are not presumed to correspond to actual operating reality, nor is any regime expected to live up to them completely. Frequently the human rights (*derechos*) must be subordinated to even more fundamental corporate group rights (*fueros*), the notion of the "common good" (generally as defined by the state), and the even higher-order requirements of natural, eternal, or, if one wishes, divine law (although even in Catholic Latin America the latter is seldom explicitly invoked). There is, in short, a hierarchy of laws that command differential obedience, and what in the United States are considered fundamental rights in Latin America often occupy a third or fourth order of priority. Human rights are respected and honored, but they may be subordinated to such perceived higher-order priorities as the unity and integrity of the state. Hence, when the two conflict, it is individual human rights that most frequently give way.[5]

Not only can these freedoms be consigned to a lower rung on the hierarchy but there are other provisions contained in the Iberian and Latin American constitutions (for example, "emergency" clauses and those providing for the declaration of a "state of siege") that make it possible to suspend them altogether, sometimes indefinitely. Freedom of the press or of assembly may legitimately be curbed if the peace and order of the nation are threatened. Of course there are abuses of these clauses and degrees to which they are practiced. But the point is that historically the rights contained in the U.S. Constitution have in Latin America seldom been considered inalienable. It is the state itself, rather, that is the arbiter and dispenser of both rights and justice. What the state conveys, obviously, it can also revoke. Further, even in those habeas corpus, writ of personal security, and *amparo* cases where an individual or group challenges the suspension of human rights, it is the state itself, acting in the name of some higher order "common good," that must ultimately decide.[6]

2. Elections. Electoral politics and elections have also become both important and imbedded in Latin American law and constitution. In Colombia, Costa Rica, and Venezuela, and in some other countries in other times, competitive elections have become a regular part of the political process. But in most of the countries, even in some of those mentioned, elections do not necessarily convey definitive legitimacy to a regime or individual for a prescribed term. Alternative routes to power, such as the skillfully executed coup d'etat or the heroic guerrilla struggle, remain open and also carry the potential for achieving legitimacy.[7] Further, even when the electoral results are accepted in principle, numerous legal and constitutional means exist to nullify their impact. The election in Brazil in 1960 of João Goulart, who was allowed to assume the presidency only after agreeing—temporarily, as it turned out—to the transfer of most of his authority to the congress, provided a dramatic case in point.

When elections do occur and they do count, additionally, seldom is there a genuine choice between alternatives; rather it tends to be the Bonapartist model that is followed. That is, elections often take a plebiscitary form, they frequently are used to ratify a government in power more than to provide real choice, or party pacts and accords are employed to provide for continuity (and monopoly) and to exclude other challengers. Of course genuinely competitive elections do occur, but even in those countries often thought of as "democratic" (Colombia, Venezuela, Costa Rica, and perhaps Mexico and the Dominican Republic), one is also struck by the tendency frequently toward oligopoly and accord within and between the major parties and hence the shutting off of possible alternatives. In these ways two potentially conflicting functions may be served at once: the oppostion and the ruling groups may have the "democratic" campaign both can agree is necessary, and the government "party" will generally "have" its election.[8]

3. Party freedom and loyal opposition. Freedom for opposition groups and parties is generally allowed in principle in Latin America, but, like the others already mentioned, this freedom is often constrained and subject to higher priorities. These constraints derive from both the legal-constitutional framework and the overall political culture.

The law and constitution provide the executive with ample power to limit opposition political party activity or to suspend opposition functions altogether. The more liberal and democratic regimes of Latin America have seldom been inclined to use the full gamut of these powers at their disposal, but the power is there nonetheless. Second, there is often relatively little "party politics" in the Anglo-American sense. One can easily overdo the differences but they remain important nonetheless: in the U.S. system, parties are usually viewed as at the center of politics, carrying out many and important functions, and providing about the only legitimized route to power. In Latin America, in contrast, and again with several notable exceptions, parties operate at the margin of the public law, frequently enjoying neither respect nor much legitimacy. The hurly-burly and chaos of party competition is frequently viewed as intolerable; divisive party politics are seen as detracting from the unity and coherence of the state. Hence, a "technocratic" regime devoid of "politics" (and parties) is usually much preferred.

Under the organicist, monistic conceptions that so pervade Iberia and Latin America, thirdly, opposition by definition is often viewed as subversive, traitorous, and to be dealt with harshly. A "loyal opposition" is thus almost a contradiction in terms. Finally, even where parties are organized, the party label is often avoided. One forms a "movement" or "civic action association," but seldom a "party." The parties tend to become official appendages of the regime in power, bureaucratic state machines, or national patronage agencies; rarely do they maintain an independent existence. Terms like "party freedom" or "opposition freedom" must be understood in this light.[9]

4. Independent, coequal congress and judiciary. Checks and balances à la Montesquieu exist in the formal law and constitutions of Latin America, but in that same law and constitution, as well as hallowed tradition, centralized, unitary control is also enshrined. The extensive power of the executive, in the "Caesarist" or "imperial" traditions, and

the weakness and lack of independence of courts and legislatures, are familiar features of Latin America. Though lip service is often paid to "separation of powers," and though in some countries legislatures gained prominence, the prevailing pattern has been presidential predominance.[10]

The strong executive is neither a quirk, aberration, or sign of Latin American "underdevelopment." It is the logical outgrowth of the assumptions on which the polity is based. For, under the prevailing "organicist" conception, government is "natural" and "good," not "unnatural," "bad," and therefore to be distrusted as in the historic U.S. conception. If government is natural and good, there is little need to limit or check and balance it. One should not therefore look for a coequal congress or courts in a system where that has not been the tradition, in law, constitution, or history.[11]

5. Accountability in the collection and expenditure of public funds. A quite sharp distinction is made in the United States between the public and the private weals. Abuses occur, but the fact we are incensed when a congressman or vice president enriches himself in public office is indicative of the strict separation we seek to maintain. Our model of the good public servant is that of the Burkean savant idealized in our civics courses: fair, responsible, serving the public interest, and strictly segregating private and public affairs.

In the Iberic-Latin patrimonialist tradition, no such sharp separation exists. The lines between public and private are blurred. Historically, both "private" and "public" wealth were considered a part of the ruler's domain. Land, mines, and trading contracts could be granted in trust to individuals for development, but the crown always expected to receive a share of the profits and it reserved the right to receive back the grants it had made. Moreover, the granting of lands, a charter, or virtually any service involved mutual obligations and generally the payment of a fee. For any official document to be expedited required another, often monetary, favor in return. This, of course, is not to imply that North Americans are by nature "honest" and Latin Americans not. But it is to say that "honesty" may mean different things in different contexts and that in the prevailing patrimonialist concept of Latin America no strict separation is possible between private and public weals. Any scale that purports to measure "accountability" in the collection and expenditure of public funds must take these differences into account.[12]

6. Civilian supremacy over the military. The concept of civilian supremacy over the military is a major premise of the Anglo-American polities, but it is often circumscribed in Latin America or even nonexistent. One must not, of course, overstate the differences, for the

military influence in this country has probably long been stronger than we usually presume, and in Latin America there are usually constitutional injunctions against the military exercising political functions. However, in Latin America, first, no strict separation exists between the military and civilian spheres. What we refer to by the hyphenated term "civil-military relations" implies a dichotomy that in Latin America does not always exist. The military is often the strongest "party," a fact recognized by both civilians and military men, with the result that most political conflicts take the form not of a civilian versus military struggle but of competing factions that overlap and crosscut the civilian and military spheres.

Second, the military in Latin America is no mere "interest group" in the U.S. sense but is an integral part of the bureaucratic system and inseparable from it. Stemming perhaps from the role of the military orders in the formation of the Spanish nation, the army is one of the fundamental props and backbone of the state system, with a hallowed and elevated position and special prerogatives and functions. Even in the more democratic countries, the military has consistently acted at or close to the surface of power. The military, additionally, by law and constitution, has certain "higher level" priorities to preserve order and tranquility, maintain domestic peace, and exercise a "moderating" role in national affairs. The military serves almost literally as a "fourth branch of government," with a certain duty and obligation to step into politics under certain circumstances. That the military stepped into power in Argentina, Brazil, Chile, and Uruguay should not be entirely surprising; what is shocking and repugnant especially in Chile is what the military did *after* it came to power.[13]

7. Freedom of political life from ecclesiastic controls. Much of what was said for the military also applies to the church: (1) the church is intimately a part of Iberian and Latin American culture, in terms of both the philosophic base of the political order and the frequent fusion and reinforcing aspects of Catholicism and the legal, educational, and social systems. (2) The church, like the army, is often a part of the state system and inseparable from it, with special obligations in the administration of schools, orphanages, and hospitals and the defense of public morality and order. (3) The church is not a mere interest group but bears certain primary responsibilities in the political realm. Despite the sometimes formal separation of church and state in the Latin American constitutions, the reality is more ambiguous. The principle of "freedom of political life from ecclesiastic controls" is either meaningless or requires further refinement.[14]

8. Strong, independent local government. This principle too derives

from the Anglo-American tradition, particularly the oft-romanticized model of New England's town meetings. But it is not an appropriate measure for Latin American "democracy." (1) Despite difficulties of implementation, the Latin American pattern has been one of centralized, administrative rule from the top rather than much grassroots participatory democracy from the bottom. (2) As in most nations whose administration is based on precepts of the Napoleonic Code, little power has ever been devolved upon the local units; rather, most local officials are appointed and power is concentrated in the central state. (3) There is little expectation at either local or national levels that local government can or should be effective. The national regime must usually respect local charters where they exist and it has some obligation to listen to local demands. But virtually all decisions are made in the capital city, and programs are implemented by the national government through its local agents. Local governments themselves have no power to tax or to devise educational or any other important local programs. Nor by history or law is there much expectation that they should.[15]

9. The existence of representative, participatory, pluralist, democratic government. Again, few of us would argue with these principles. The difficulty is that what Iberic-Latin civilization means by these terms frequently varies from Anglo-American:

A. "Representation" in Iberia and Latin America means not just geographic representation and one-man/one-vote but often implies also representation of society's major functional or corporate groups. Although lip service (and sometimes more than that) is paid to the principles of equal representation, group rights and corporate elites frequently receive preferential treatment. The mere fact of birth does not necessarily carry with it the right to representation; rather that is "earned" through a "civilizing" process that usually means incorporation into one of society's recognized component groups. Hence the importance often of functionally representative legislatures, councils of state, or special access for those groups with "juridical personality," or the mixture of corporate and individualistic modes of representation.[16]

B. "Participation" also takes place through, generally, officially recognized and sanctioned agencies, not necessarily on the basis of free associability. Hence the importance often of official parties, trade unions and the like, and the sanctions often used against unofficial and unrecognized groups.[17]

C. "Pluralism" may also exist in Latin America but it is usually a system of limited pluralism rather than the freewheeling laissez-faire pluralism of Tocqueville and the United States. The plural groups are often structured and controlled; an infinite multiplicity of groups, uncontrolled, "out there" will not do. To be accepted as one of the groups permitted to bargain in the political process requires more than an informal, ad hoc association; often it requires official licensing by the state and, hence, limits on the pluralism in contrast to the open-ended and untrammeled pluralism of the United States.[18]

D. What "democracy" means in the Iberic-Latin context is treated more fully in the next section. Suffice it here to suggest that while democracy is honored in Latin America and has been established in some countries in some time periods, it, too, represents more an ideal to strive for than a reflection of actual operating reality. Further, "democratic rule" is not necessarily incompatible with elitist rule and hierarchical, pyramidal, nonegalitarian structures of society and polity.[19]

It is clear from the foregoing that the commonly used measures of "democracy" and "political rights" in Latin America are strongly culture-bound. They derive largely from the Anglo-American constitutional model, which is often far removed from Latin American culture and reality. Indeed, what such indices purport to measure, democracy, is not being measured at all; instead, what is actually gauged is the presence or absence of U.S. institutional molds in Latin America. Naturally, using such criteria, Latin America shows glaring deficiencies. Hence, to my mind, not only are the measures faulty, but the questions raised are the wrong ones. A set of measures that seeks to assess Latin American democracy on its own terms rather than by U.S. criteria, and which hopefully does begin to pose the right questions, is offered in the following section.

But before condemning the earlier indices entirely to the ashcans of outdated and ethnocentric models, it should be said that these measures do have some relevance for Latin America. For probably all the Latin American nations in fact represent a blend of both the corporatist-organicist-patrimonialist features highlighted here and the liberal, republican, representative ones based on the Anglo-American model. There are, thus, two sets of institutional pillars on which the Iberic-Latin state systems rest. Sometimes fused, sometimes parallel but largely untouching, these two institutional foundations continue to exist side by side.[20] Any attempt to measure Latin American democracy, therefore, must take both traditions into consideration, and the criteria we use must reflect the composite, sometimes hodge-podge mix of both the historic organicist concepts and the newer liberal-democratic ones.

Toward a New Definition of Democracy and Human Rights in Latin America

Given the differences of meaning outlined above, let us proceed to a new definition of democracy and human rights in Latin America that takes into account both the distinctive features of the Iberic-Latin political tradition and the newer fusions. This definition has been fashioned in the form of a set of measureable indicators substitutible for the Fitzgibbon indices and based more on indigenous Latin American criteria than those derived from a foreign model. They provide not only a gauge for measuring Latin American democracy on its own terms but also a handy checklist to determine when a government oversteps its democratic legitimacy and is thus likely to be challenged or overthrown. It must be recalled that the model presented is an ideal-typical construct and that a fuller exposition would be required to account for the considerable variations between countries as well as within countries over time.

1. Strong, personalistic, executive leadership, *caudillo* or Bonapartist rule, is not only permissible but expected. The president may rule in an authoritarian fashion but not a totalitarian one. He should be strong and paternalistic, but not a tyrant. The president is only partially limited by a separate congress, courts, or constitution; equally important are the corporate group rights, or *fueros*, serving to check unbridled authority and the restraints imposed by moral law. By "moral law" is meant not the vague pragmatism of "situational ethics" but a higher eternal and natural law as articulated in Christian doctrine or in somewhat more secularized standards of "right" behavior beyond which strong leaders are constrained not to go. The index we use to measure the limits on presidential power must, therefore, take into account the widespread acceptability of authoritarian, paternalistic rule, as well as the fine line that often distinguished authoritarianism from the unacceptable forms of tyranny and totalitarianism.[21]

2. Although the principle of "separate, coequal" branches of government has not been so firmly established or desired in the Latin American tradition as in that of the United States, it does exist. This provides an example of the "mixed" or "overlapping" nature of the Latin American systems already mentioned. The congress is not coequal but it does have some important advisory, consultative, and representa-

tive roles, corresponding to the historic functions of the ancient *cortes*. The executive may be dominant, but the congress can still make life difficult for him; and if he rules entirely without a parliament, he runs the risk of alienating public opinion.[22]

The same applies to a government that rides roughshod over its own national court system. Any government that comes to power, especially if it is by extraconstitutional means, must immediately resolve its legitimacy problem. No court can entirely frustrate a government determined to pursue a particular action and willing to use force to accomplish it; much less would any court interpose itself to prevent an armed insurrection aimed at overthrowing an existing government. But, though circumscribed, judicial review and a functioning court system do often serve as checks on unbridled executive rule; further, the courts have a certain power in their ability to confer legitimacy on de facto regimes. A court may issue accords legitimating a regime in return for guarantees to observe human rights, preserve or restore the constitution, or even maintain the independence of the judiciary itself. Governments of doubtful legitimacy may thus be nudged toward greater commitment to respect constitutional rights, although of course broad political support for such moves is also necessary.[23] Hence, while the principle of *separate* and *coequal* power among the three branches is not always an established or accepted principle of Latin American government, the courts and congress do have some autonomy and power. An index that measures these relations in terms of the Latin American conception of the role and functions of the courts and congress, rather than from the point of view of the United States, would be both useful and feasible.

3. Free speech, free press, and freedom of assembly are also principles of Latin American constitutionalism, but they can similarly be limited for the "common good." Freedom is not an absolute but implies, to a far greater degree than in the United States, predeterminate bounds. Nor should one mistake the formal constitutional enactment of such rights, designed as goals and aspirations rather than actual operating realities, for their implementation. In addition, the laws and constitutions of Latin America give the executive broad discretionary power to declare a state of siege in times of emergency and suspend the usual guarantees. These emergency powers, however, are not intended to extend to violations of the human person. Nonetheless, the terrible centrifugal forces that have torn and continue to tear these societies apart are such that in Latin American constitutional law, the political rights that might otherwise seem inviolable must legitimately give way before the need to preserve the state itself.

At the same time the Latin American nations are signatories to a number of international documents for the protection of human rights. These include the United Nations Charter, the Universal Declaration of Human Rights, the Charter of the Organization of American States, and others. These encompass both political and human rights (fair trial, habeas corpus, freedom of speech, etc.) and social and economic rights (right to work, to food, health care, etc.). Further, although liberalism and republicanism—and the basic liberties usually associated with them—represent probably still a minority strain in Latin America, the force of this tradition is nonetheless important and cannot be entirely ignored. Finally, if it is inappropriate to judge the human rights credentials of various Latin American governments by U.S. criteria, one may employ their own criteria. A case in point is Paraguay, where a state of emergency has been in effect almost continuously since 1947. Clearly in this case the emergency laws are being abused to maintain in power an unpopular authoritarian regime, take measures that are disproportionate to the actual emergency, and systematically violate the human rights of the opposition to the regime. In this case it seems particularly appropriate for the Paraguyan Bar Association—and perhaps us as well—to issue a formal condemnation of the continued abuse of the emergency laws.[24] For here it is clear that both by North American and Paraguyan criteria, human rights violations have been widespread.

4. Although the Latin American tradition provides for strong centralized rule with little power given over to local government, a history of respect for the rights of local, state, or regional entities also exists. Frequently such local "rights" are enshrined in long-standing charters, sometimes in the constitution itself, providing for varying degrees of autonomy from the central government. There are numerous "center-periphery" issues that revolve around the autonomy question, perhaps most dramatically expressed in present-day Spain in the conflict over Basque and Catalan aspirations for independence from national policy emanating from Madrid. The centralization of power in Brazil at the expense of state prerogatives involves a related issue; so do the incomplete efforts of the central government in Peru to extend its control over the more isolated interior.[25] This conflict between center and periphery constitutes one of the major arenas of Latin American politics, although this is somewhat different from elevating the strength of representative government at the grassroots level into an index of democracy. To the extent a Latin American government respects local or regional *fueros* it is considered "democratic"; when it rides roughshod over local rights and fails to care for those living in the periphery, it risks losing its "democratic" legitimacy.

5. Closely related to the issue of local and/or regional "rights" is the

matter of corporate group rights, or *fueros*. While few Latin American executives are strongly restrained by congressional or judicial limits on their power, they are "checked" by the major corporate "power contenders" that are a part of their respective systems. These groups, the *fuerzas vivas* or *intereses creados*, include the army, church, economic elites, organized labor, bureaucracy, university students, and others. These are not merely "interest groups" in the U.S. sense, but the more fundamental vertebrae or set of corporate pillars on which the entire governmental superstructure rests. The concept is more a feudal, semifeudal, or traditional Luso-Hispanic conception than it is a reflection of North American interest-group pluralism.[26]

Any president who comes to power must respect the autonomy, as contained in their charters and organic laws, of the varied corporate pillars on which the government—any government—rests. This implies a certain respect for the church and the "concordat" (if such exists) signed between the state and the Vatican; for the university and its charter of autonomy; for landed, commercial, and industrial interests; and perhaps above all for the armed forces, their organic law and specially privileged position as the ultimate arbiters of national affairs, their special courts and immunities, and their direct access to policy through the *casa militar*. Any civilian president must be wary if he intervenes in the internal affairs of the military, for that is to invite the reverse process. More recently, corporate group rights have been extended to workers, peasants, and women. Obviously the power of these various groups is unequal, helping to explain the differential treatment of them by the state. But generally, a government is considered democratic to the degree it respects the corporate group *fueros* of society's component units; to the extent it rides roughshod over them it not only violates basic rights but runs the risk of its own overthrow.[27]

6. A government hence is viewed as democratic to the degree that it is pluralistic and that all elements enjoy autonomy from arbitrary authority and a considerable measure of freedom of action and movement. By "pluralism" we mean not the laissez-faire hurly-burly of the largely unrestricted U.S. interest-group struggle, but a sense of "limited pluralism" in which the various groups, while controlled, restricted, and often elaborately regulated by the state, nonetheless enjoy a certain contractually defined independence from it.[28] A system is pluralistic in Latin America insofar as it allows or safeguards centers of power other than itself: the family, the local entity, the *hacienda*, and various religious, cultural, educational, philanthropic, and professional agencies, to say nothing of the municipal, regional, and corporate groups already alluded to, which are designed to promote the rights and

interests of their members and protect them against unwarranted encroachments from the state or other groups. Some of these groups, such as the family, local community, or church, are considered to be prior to the state, in theory at least, in terms of both history and natural law. Except in emergencies (and even then there are some safeguards), these are sacrosanct institutions against which no government may move unless it is willing to sacrifice the loyalty and support of the group affected. A government that antagonizes several groups by violating their rights can, and likely will, be overthrown.

7. In addition to these corporate group rights, the government is also obligated to protect the basic human rights of individual citizens. These individual rights are not necessarily conceived in the same way or afforded the same elevated position as in the U.S. Constitution, although through such devices as the writ of *amparo, segurança,* habeas corpus, and cassation, individual rights receive some protection. Even more fundamental, because it stems from the natural law, is the obligation of government to leave people alone, respect their individuality, and protect the inviolability of the human person. While authoritarian rule of a paternalistic sort may be permissible or even desired, a regime or police agency that beats up its own people is not. The use of torture and killings as instruments of state policy, the turning of the police or army loose on hapless trade unions, students, or opposition elements, summary trials and executions, and the beating of women, priests, and children are clearly outside the bounds of acceptable behavior. The cumulative effect of such violations may undermine the legitimacy of a regime. Batista, Trujillo, Pérez, Somoza, and the Chilean regime are cases in point; Brazil seems to be skirting the edge.[29]

8. Government must be both "representative" and "participatory," but in the Latin American sense of those terms. It must be representative of "society," meaning those groups (church, army, labor, elites, etc.) that have been duly recognized by the state and given official sanction as legitimate "power contenders" in the system. These groups are usually represented in the cabinet, congress, or council of state, through the ministries and state agencies, and with special access to the centers of decision making. The state must also provide for "participation" through a generally officially sanctioned network of associations for workers, farmers, women, and so forth. To the extent it allows such "representation" and "participation," a government may be considered "democratic"; but to the degree it closes off or stifles such legitimate group life, it may lose its democratic standing. Note, however, that not all elements are represented in this scheme (e.g., unorganized peasants,

Indians, or urban marginals), nor is the principle of one-man/one-vote necessarily applicable.[30]

9. While government must be "democratic" in this sense, that is not always incompatible with top-down or elitist rule. The pervasive presence of notions of hierarchy and authority often implies that deference is given to those with a perceived "natural" right to rule. The elites, however, are obligated not to abuse their privileged position. They must provide charity and benefices to the poor and, while retaining social distance, respect the rights and individuality of those beneath them in the social scale. They may be patronizing and paternalistic but they cannot ignore or entirely disdain their workers, peasants, or servants. Transferred to the national level, that means an obligation also to accommodate and absorb the rising social forces, not close them out, as in Nicaragua and Paraguay. In classic patron-client fashion, now extended from the *hacienda* to the state agency, the patron enjoys a preponderance of rights but the situation cannot be entirely one way. The clients also have their rights, and a patron or government that ignores or abuses them may face the loss of loyalty usually given in return for various favors. The cumulative loss of his clients' services and loyalty spells trouble for any patron, including the great national patron, the government itself.[31]

10. A new criteria for democratic legitimacy in Latin America involves the requirement that government provide for both economic development and social justice. "Development" and "social justice" have become part of the ideology of the area and closely linked to its concept of democracy. The older conception that people must be poor, live in wretched housing, and see their children diseased and with bloated bellies because "poverty is good for the soul" or the church has obligated them to accept their station in life, is dead or dying. The "revolution of rising expectations" has come to Latin America; any government must deliver in the way of housing, health services, food, jobs, etc.—or else! Democracy in Latin America has thus been redefined to encompass social and economic criteria as well as political ones—though the precise nature of the regime that brings social justice and economic growth is left open and the models used (including varying forms of populism and/or syndicalism) may, again, be quite distinct from those of the United States or Western Europe.[32]

11. The right of rebellion. A government that oversteps the bounds of permissible behavior, outlined above, rides roughshod over natural law and rights, concentrates all power in its own hands, violates the contracts and *fueros* governing corporate associational life, becomes

brutal and oppressive, and becomes, in short, a tyranny, deserves to fall. The right of rebellion is as much a part of the historic Latin American political tradition as is the obligation to obedience. Against an "unjust tyrant" the citizen has the right and duty to resist, go outside the system, and seek to replace it. But even here, certain ground rules apply. Faced with widespread popular opposition, the tyrant has an obligation to resign instead of seeking to stay in office and thus provoking further bloodshed (e.g., Perón, Batista); such barbarism as the napalming of rural villages and the unleashing of a terror campaign against the opposition has consistently been considered illegitimate and self-defeating. But the opposition is also obliged to play by the rules: the right of asylum for officials of the outgoing government must be respected, the right to go into exile should be allowed, and reprisals should be avoided. In short, the final measure of democracy in Latin America is the right to rebel against "the system" if that system proves tyrannous, abusive and ineffective.[33]

Nowhere in this listing of characteristics for measuring democracy in Latin America is the notion of a formalized, constitutional "separation of powers" or "checks and balances" given central focus, nor do elections, political parties, and the like, constitute the chief criteria. Of course in some countries presently and others in the past elections do make a critical difference, but it must be reemphasized that elections are not the only legitimate route to power and certainly do not, by themselves, constitute an adequate measure of "democracy." The criteria developed here seek to go beyond the older, largely U.S.-based procedural gauges of democracy to encompass what Latin America most often means by that term and to develop criteria that derive from the context and tradition of that culture area instead of being imposed from the outside.

But while the concepts and criteria developed here derive from what is even now probably the dominant tradition in Latin America, it is no longer the only one. For alongside the historic tradition here briefly characterized as organicist, patrimonialist, and corporatist (in the broad political-cultural sense) has grown up a genuinely liberal and democratic one. These two models (which help give rise to the "two Spains" concept, for instance) may exist side by side within a given country, sometimes wholly separate and sometimes overlapping, considerably complicating our measures of "democracy" as applied to Latin America. The situation is complicated further, in Peru, Portugal, Cuba, by the superimposition of a third and socialist overlay upon the other two. Any assessment of democracy's presence or absence in Latin

America must keep in mind both the distinctively historical and cultural meaning of those terms in the area, and the newer conceptions that have recently emerged.

Conclusions and Implications

This study began with the question of whether democracy and human rights are everywhere the same and universal. The answer as applied to Iberia and Latin America is both yes and no. Neither the nations of Latin America nor Spain and Portugal have much trouble agreeing with the human rights principles set forth in various international charters; and there was probably no hypocrisy in King Juan Carlos' message to the U.S. Congress that his goal was to "perfect" Spanish "democracy," or in President Ernesto Geisel's labeling Brazil a "relative democracy." At the same time, one must be cognizant of the impact of what Lucian Pye once termed the "world culture,"[34] largely Western, which forces dependent countries like those in Latin America to redefine themselves in our terms instead of their own historical ones, to be judged by our criteria of democracy and human rights whether they wish to or not and whether that is even functional, given their own distinct cultural and political traditions.

It is also clear from this discussion that key terms like "representation," "participation," "pluralism," "democracy," and "rights" frequently mean something different in Iberia and Latin America, carry different connotations, or imply distinct expectations, than is the case in the Anglo-American context. One must bear in mind the hierarchy and differential importance of distinct bodies of law in Latin America, that human rights (*derechos*) may occupy a different level of importance than is true in U.S. law, that individual human rights are often subordinated to corporate group rights (*fueros*), and that both of these may be subordinated to the "common good" or the necessity of maintaining the unity and integrity of the state.

The sweep of the analysis given here is broad and the model presented an ideal-typical one. It is a heuristic device and is not meant to correspond to reality in every instance. However that should not blind us to the numerous qualifiers and variations that must be recognized. At one level a macromodel such as this is useful as a means of alerting us to the general parameters of a major issue area, but for specific policy recommendations we must also take into account both national variations and within-nation differences over time. A dynamic component must be incorporated, so the model is less deterministic than it somestimes appears.[35] We must be alerted to the human-rights versus intervention dilemma and must weigh carefully the mechanisms that produce successes in our efforts to promote human rights and those that produce backfires. We must further distinguish among types of human rights: those involving freedom from government violation of the person, social and economic rights, and democratic political freedoms. For the first of these there exists considerable international consensus and hence, it may be hypothesized, some possibilities for policy successes in the human rights area; for the second, there is less consensus on the means to achieve these goals and, hence, probably less chance of success; for the third category (the main topic of discussion here) there is still less agreement and, hence, probably even slimmer chances of success.

We conclude with a series of caveats. We must, I think, be skeptical of U.S. journalists and public officials who insist on interpreting Latin American democracy entirely through their own cultural and political concepts. The "liberalizing" and "democratizing" currents and "struggles" of which they frequently write or on which they ground policy decisions are often valid up to a point, but they tend frequently to be based on superficial readings derived from North American criteria rather than Latin American ones. The fact that political parties exist in Spain, for example, and elections held, is insufficient by the criteria developed here to describe Spain as a "democracy." But the reverse also holds. Because the Latin American systems do not always correspond to U.S. notions of democracy, we have frequently been quick to brand them as "failures." The fact is that in many cases they are simply practicing a type of democracy that is reflective more of their own historical and traditional understanding of that term than the Anglo-American conception.

So, too, with human rights. What constitutes a violation of human rights in one context may not be such in another, or is seen in a different light, or may have another meaning. Further, these conceptions may change over time relating to broader developmental changes and giving human rights a different meaning in one epoch or in one group of countries than in another. The *fuero*, for instance, will mean something different as the particular group grows in strength or the balance between competing groups is altered. Hence, in the case of both "democracy" and "human rights" a conception is needed that derives from Latin American understandings and not our own culture-biased views. The concepts discussed here represent a first step in that direction. Hence, we must distinguish between what the United States conceives of as human-rights violations (and that often become issues reflective primarily of U.S. domestic politics), and those violations that reflect actual Latin American disenchantment with their own governments' actions, which may be on somewhat different grounds. Care, caution, and sensitivity to the cultural and political differences involved are required. That may lead us both to a greater understanding of how the Latin American political systems actually do function, and to less a sense of despair when Latin American politics evolve in directions that do not correspond to our own conception of democracy.

We can and should be in favor of democracy and human rights in Latin America (as well as at home!), while also differentiating between the several categories of human rights, understanding how they apply in different countries at distinct stages of development, and remaining sensitive to the differences of meaning and interpretation of these concepts in societies other than our own. We cannot impose our conceptions on nations where human rights and democracy are conceived in a different light without considerable damage being rendered to them and to us. We must come to grips realistically with the fact that distinct culture areas have different understandings of these concepts and their relative importance.[36] At the same time, the criteria of democracy and human rights offered here give us a handle to grasp, a means to support human rights while also being sensitive to the cultural differences existent. Hence, for the policy maker as well as the scholar the same caveats apply: prudence, discretion, empathy, and a sophisticated understanding of quite different social and political traditions.[37] For, if we are to cease being the policeman of the world, we probably cannot, unless with great modesty, circumspection and sensitivity, presume to be its political and moral superior either.

Notes

1. Amnesty International has issued numerous reports on human rights violations in Latin America; the *New York Times* has published several recent accounts on the issue; the Department of State has submitted to the House International Relations Committee some detailed reports on human rights conditions abroad; various congressional hearings have been held; the report of the Commission on United States–Latin American Relations (the "Linowitz Commission") urged a stronger emphasis on human rights; and, of course, the president and his key advisers have referred repeatedly to human rights protection as a cornerstone of U.S. foreign policy. But see also Marshall D. Shulman, "On Learning to Live with Authoritarian Regimes," *Foreign Affairs*, 55 (January 1977), 325-38; and William P. Bundy, "Dictatorships and American Foreign Policy," *Foreign Affairs*, 54 (October 1975), 51-60.

2. For the background, see Kenneth L. Karst and Keith S. Rosenn, *Law and*

Development in Latin America (Berkeley: University of California Press, 1975).

3. Russell H. Fitzgibbon, "Measurement of Latin American Political Phenomena: A Statistical Experiment," *American Political Science Review*, 45 (June 1951), 517-23; Fitzgibbon, "A Statistical Evaluation of Latin American Democracy," *Western Political Quarterly*, 9 (September 1956), 607-19; Fitzgibbon and Kenneth F. Johnson, "Measurement of Latin American Political Change," *American Political Science Review*, 54 (September 1961), 515-26; Fitzgibbon, "Measuring Democratic Change in Latin America," *Journal of Politics*, 29 (February 1967), 129-66; Johnson, "Measuring the Scholarly Image of Latin American Democracy, 1945-70," in *Statistical Abstract of Latin America*, 17 (Los Angeles: UCLA Latin American Center, 1976); Johnson, "Scholarly Images of Latin American Political Democracy in 1975," *Latin American Research Review*, 11 (Summer 1976), 127-38; and Johnson, "Research Perspectives on the Revised Fitzgibbon-Johnson Index of the Image of Political Democracy in Latin America, 1945-75," in James W. Wilkie and Kenneth Ruddle (eds.), *Quantitative Latin American Studies* (Los Angeles: UCLA Latin American Center, 1977), 87-91. In the more recent formulations, Johnson usefully distinguishes between Latin American democracy per se and the various nations' reputations for democracy as perceived by the U.S. scholars surveyed. He has also introduced a number of other qualifications to remove some of the ethnocentrism from the original index.

4. See the comment of Dale Furnish: "Military governments . . . are an accepted part of the legal system"; they also govern "through laws and acts constrained by custom and constitutional privilege," in "The Hierarchy of Peruvian Laws: Context for Law and Development," *American Journal of Comparative Law*, 50 (Winter 1971), 91-120.

5. The best brief discussion is John Henry Merryman, *The Civil Law Tradition: An Introduction to the Legal Systems of Western Europe and Latin America* (Stanford: Stanford University Press, 1969); also, the special edition of the *American Journal of Comparative Law*, 5 (Winter 1971), dealing with "Law and Development in Latin America."

6. Karst and Rosenn, *op. cit.*, part 2, esp. 232ff.

7. Charles W. Anderson, *Politics and Economic Change in Latin America* (Princeton: Van Nostrand, 1967), chap. 4.

8. For one such case, see Steven Ussach, "The Portuguese Presidential Election of 1958" (Unpublished paper: University of Massachusetts, Dept. of Political Science, 1974).

9. Douglas Chalmers, "Parties and Society in Latin America," *Studies in Comparative International Development*, 7 (Summer 1972), 102-30; Robert Dix, "Latin America: Opposition and Development," in Robert A. Dahl, *Regimes and Opposition* (New Haven: Yale University Press, 1973).

10. Glen Dealy, "The Tradition of Monistic Democracy in Latin America," in Howard J. Wiarda (ed.), *Politics and Social Change in Latin America* (Amherst: University of Massachusetts Press, 1974), 71-104; and James Busey,

"Observations on Latin American Constitutionalism," *The Americas*, 24 (July 1967), 46-66.

11. Guenter Lewy, *Constitutionalism and Statecraft During the Golden Age of Spain* (Geneva: E. Droz, 1960).

12. Patrimonialism is discussed in Reinhard Bendix, *Max Weber: An Intellectual Portrait* (Garden City: Doubleday, 1962), 334-60; also Sidney M. Greenfield, *The Patrimonial State and Patron-Client Relations in Iberia and Latin America*, Occasional Papers Series no. 1, Program in Latin American Studies, University of Massachusetts, Amherst (October 1976).

13. On the military's place and role, see Lawrence Graham, *Portugal: The Decline and Collapse of an Authoritarian Order* (Beverly Hills: Sage, 1971); Alfred Stepan, *The Military in Politics: Changing Patterns in Brazil* (Princeton: Princeton University Press, 1971); and Robert A. Potash, *The Impact of Professionalism on the Twentieth Century Argentine Military*, Occasional Papers Series no. 3, Program in Latin American Studies, University of Massachusetts, Amherst (April 1977).

14. Fredrick B. Pike, *The Conflict Between Church and State in Latin America* (New York: Knopf, 1964); Henry A. Landsberger (ed.), *The Church and Social Change in Latin America* (Norte Dame: University of Notre Dame Press, 1970).

15. Lawrence Graham, "Latin America: Illusion or Reality?," in Wiarda (ed.), *op. cit.*

16. Howard J. Wiarda, *Corporatism and Development: The Portuguese Experience* (Amherst: University of Massachusetts Press, 1977); more generally, "Toward a Framework for the Study of Political Change in the Iberic-Latin Tradition: The Corporative Model," *World Politics*, 25 (January 1973), 206-35; and F. Pike and T. Stritch (eds.), *The New Corporatism: Social and Political Structures in the Iberian World* (Notre Dame: University of Notre Dame Press, 1974).

17. Howard J. Wiarda, "The Corporative Origins of the Iberian and Latin American Labor Relations Systems," *Studies in Comparative International Development* 3 (Spring 1978), 3-37.

18. Juan Linz, "An Authoritarian Regime: Spain," in E. Allardt and Y. Littunen (eds.), *Cleavages, Ideologies and Party Systems* (Helsinki: Academic Bookstore, 1964), 291-341. In an otherwise provocative article, Philippe Schmitter has confused the issue by presenting corporatism and pluralism as polar opposites, when, in fact, pluralism may exist in either corporatist or liberal polities. "Still the Century of Corporatism?," in Pike and Stritch, *op. cit.*

19. As derived from Roman law and Thomas Aquinas, as well as modern secular theorists Gumplowicz, Mosca, Pareto, Michels; see the discussion in Wiarda, "Corporatist Theory and Ideology: A Latin American Development Paradigm," *Journal of Church and State*, 20 (Winter 1978), 29-56.

20. John J. Bailey, "Pluralist and Corporatist Dimensions of Interest Representation in Colombia," in J. Malloy (ed.), *Authoritarianism and Corporatism in Latin America* (Pittsburgh: University of Pittsburgh Press, 1977); J. A. Morris and S. C. Ropp, "Corporatism and Dependent Development: A Honduran Case

Study," *Latin American Research Review*, 12 (1977), 27-68; and Linn A. Hammergren, "Corporatism in Latin American Politics: A Reexamination of the Unique Tradition," *Comparative Politics* (July 1977); as well as Howard J. Wiarda, "Corporatism in Iberian and Latin American Political Analysis: Criticisms, Qualifications and the Context and 'Whys' of the Debate," *Comparative Politics*, 10 (January 1978), 307-12.

21. Linz, *op. cit.*, has most clearly drawn the authoritarian-totalitarian distinction.

22. W. Agor, *Latin American Legislatures* (New York: Praeger, 1971).

23. Keith Rosenn, "Judicial Review in Latin America," *Ohio State Law Journal*, 35 (no. 4, 1974), 785-819.

24. The document is reprinted in Karst and Rosenn, *op. cit.*, 235ff; see also Hector Fix Zamudio, "Latin American Procedures for the Protection of the Individual," *Journal of the International Commission of Jurists*, 9 (December 1968), 60-95.

25. Karst and Rosenn, *op. cit.*, intro.; Hammergren, *op. cit.*

26. Ronald C. Newton "On 'Functional Groups,' 'Fragmentation,' and 'Pluralism' in Spanish American Political Society," *Hispanic American Historical Review*, 50 (February 1970), 1-29.

27. Howard J. Wiarda and Harvey F. Kline, *Latin American Politics and Development* (Boston: Houghton-Mifflin, 1979), intro.

28. Linz, *op. cit.*; David Collier and Ruth Berins Collier, "Who Does What, To Whom, and How: Toward a Comparative Analysis of Latin American Corporatism," in Malloy, *op. cit.*

29. See especially "Proceedings of the 67th Annual Meeting of the American Society of International Law," *American Journal of International Law*, 67 (November 1973), 198-226.

30. Wiarda, *Corporatism and Development* . . . , chaps. 2, 3, 4, and 11.

31. Emilio Willems, *Latin American Culture: An Anthropological Synthesis* (New York: Harper and Row, 1975), chaps. 5, 14, and 17.

32. Charles W. Anderson et al., *Issues of Political Development*, 2nd ed. (Englewood Cliffs, N.J.: Prentice-Hall, 1974), part 3.

33. The literature is vast, ranging from Saint Thomas to Fidel Castro's "History Will Absolve Me." See also Manuel Giménez Fernández, *Las doctrinas populistas en la independencia de Hispanoamerica* (Seville, 1947); and Lawrence E. Rothstein, "Aquinas and Revolution," paper presented at the Annual Meeting of the American Political Science Association, Chicago, September 2-5, 1976.

34. In Pye and Verba (eds.), *Political Culture and Political Development* (Princeton: Princeton University Press, 1965), intro.

35. These more dynamic features of change and modernization are treated in other writings: Wiarda, "Toward a Framework . . . "; *Politics and Social Change* . . . ; and *Transcending Corporatism? The Portuguese Corporative System and the Revolution of 1974* (Columbia: Institute of International Studies, University of South Carolina, 1976).

36. Fortunately there are signs that those responsible for policy have begun to

grasp these differences; see, for example, the speeches of Cyrus R. Vance, "Human Rights Policy," and Warren Christopher, "Human Rights: Principle and Realism," both published by the Bureau of Public Affairs, Office of Media Service, U.S. Department of State.

37. Both sound policy and adequate grounds for moral judgment in this area must be based on a clear understanding of the broad cultural differences existent. A thorough, factual dossier on democracy and human rights in specific countries is also required. This chapter helps provide a theoretical understanding of the issues involved and, hence, serves as a necessary prelude to policy; the reports of the Department of State and those growing out of the congressional hearings on human rights in specific countries provide the essential data base. But for those involved in policy who may have already grasped the distinct conceptions involved and who have the factual materials at hand, the dilemma is no longer a lack of understanding but what to do about governments that violate democratic norms and human rights even on their own indigenous terms: what levers can be manipulated, what mechanisms are appropriate, how can human rights and democracy be encouraged without involving unwarranted interference in another nation's internal affairs? Those issues, however, must constitute the subject matter of a separate paper.

13
Democracy and the Bureaucratic State in Latin America

Lawrence S. Graham

Beginning with the decision of the Brazilian military to end by force the regime of João Goulart in 1964 and to impose its own style of governance over a vast country, authoritarianism has been on the rise throughout Latin America. One by one popularly elected governments across the region have been eliminated, until in the late 1970s only two states in South America continue to adhere to the norms of regularly held competitive elections: Colombia and Venezuela. The record for all of Latin America is not much better when we add the smaller Spanish-speaking states in the Caribbean and Central America to this list, for there only one clear cut addition can be made: Costa Rica.

A new departure in Latin American politics has accompanied this rise in the number of military governments: the determination of the military as an institution to retain power on the grounds that it possesses a far greater capability than civilian forces to cope with the issues of continued socioeconomic change and the political activation of the lower sectors of society in urban and rural areas. As the military governments have sought to lay the foundation for long-lived authoritarian regimes, they have, with varying degrees of success, attempted to restructure radically civilian politics and society. Where consolidation of prolonged military rule has become a reality, however, each has had to broaden its power base to survive. For to confront effectively day-to-day issues in implementing economic, political, and social policy, the ruling military has found it necessary to incorporate selected civilian elements into their regimes to stabilize their control and to institutionalize their power. As a consequence a series of bureaucratic states are emerging throughout the hemisphere.

In seeking to attain simultaneously the illusive goals of sustained economic growth, regulated social change, and political order, junior and senior officers have increasingly turned to representatives of their own industrial communities and new middle-class professionals with training in economics and the management sciences for advice and assistance. In discussions of these developments the cases most frequently cited are Argentina (1966-73, 1976-present), Brazil (1964-present), Peru (1968-present), and Chile (1973-present). In each the initial decision by the military to intervene with the intent to decisively change the country's political environment and the distribution of power and resources in civilian society has been accompanied by wide-scale disillusionment with electoral politics as a suitable device for confronting and responding to socioeconomic change and mass political activation.

Whether or not these military governments will survive over the long-term as viable regimes is another question. The initial attempt by the Argentine military to rewrite the rules of the political game in 1966 failed, largely because Onganía, his successor Levingston, and their supporters failed to structure an effective new government that could break the stalemate in Argentine politics and impose and carry out a new set of political, economic, and social policies. Thus in 1973, when power was returned to the civilians, a policy of national reconciliation was declared in an attempt to span the Peronista–anti-Peronista cleavage and Juan Perón was finally permitted to return to his native land. But "national reconciliation" proved to be no more successful than Onganía's policy of rule without political parties and his attempt to destroy once and for all their mass political base. In the absence of a feasible alternative the military reluctantly reintervened in 1976 to remove Perón's widow from power. Since then, General Videla has been struggling to resolve a problem no previous regime has been able to overcome successfully: how to balance conflicting legalist and hardline factions within the military; how to reduce the level of political violence without engendering civil war while working out an accommodation among contending civilian political forces; and how to cope with continued economic stagnation and decline.

For those who would base their projections of Latin America's political future on the Argentine case, the future is bleak indeed: the perpetuation of a "conflict society,"[1] increased polarization of social forces as larger numbers of people are mobilized by political parties, further economic stagnation because of the inability to move beyond the limits imposed by the exhaustion of industrial development through import substitution, and continued regime instability as one "partial" government—civilian or military—follows another. Such arguments state persuasively the thesis that military rule becomes little more than a holding action and that, once the military returns to the barracks, politics are resumed with a vengeance, and the potential for open, sustained conflict, without necessarily moving to the level of civil war, is heightened.[2]

The Brazilian case, when compared with the Argentine one, points in yet another direction: the consolidation and continuation of authoritarian rule under military leadership. After more than a decade of rule, the Brazilian formula of limited pluralism and regulated political conflict has served to insure continuity in government and the peaceful transferral of presidential power from one military leader to another. Whereas there really is little difference among the conclusions political analysts have reached about the Argentine stalemate and none can foresee any easy exit from the conflict society that has become such a fixed part of the Argentine scene, this is not the case with Brazil. Since 1965, assessments of the military regime have diverged widely. During the initial phase, when military rule was being consolidated, optimists argued that the military had intervened only out of necessity and would return power to the civilians once the system was "purified" of its previous excesses. In turn, "realists" challenged the validity of this interpretation, because they saw in the postcoup situation a new power equation emerging in Brazilian politics and, as time passed, they became increasingly pessimistic about the prospects for a revival of democratic forces within the country.[3] By 1970 the debate shifted away from discussion of when the military would return to the barracks to whether or not the new authoritarian order could survive over the long run.[4] Those who have argued no have cited the various within-regime crises over presidential succession as an example of the inherent instability of the regime due to its narrow basis of political support and have called attention to the nonideological, pragmatic appeals made to privileged elements of Brazilian society: the ability to promote economic growth, to limit the inflationary spiral, and to insure continued salary increases for middle-income groups.[5] Others have singled out the capacity of the new regime over the long haul to structure a limited pluralism in which unacceptable power contenders have been effectively excluded from the system, and the ability of Brazil's new rulers to shift the political game away from an open arena (characterized by institutional tension between presidential and congressional centers of power and free-wheeling political parties) to a closed one confined to bureaucratic institutions belonging to the state.[6]

Whatever the position adopted by analysts after a decade of military rule in Brazil, one thing is certain: whereas the Argentine military failed in the late sixties to consolidate a new power basis in national politics and to establish meaningful control over the state apparatus, the Brazilian military succeeded. The key to this success lay in the accommodation worked out within the military institution whereby recognition was given to the need to share power with civilian groups and to build a conservative military-civilian ruling coalition. The mechanism for accomplishing this became the Brazilian War College (the *Escola Superior da Guerra*), where it was realized that the military had a mission beyond its own officials: to socialize key civilian sectors into accepting its outlook on national development and security.[7] By the mid-seventies, after a period of confrontation and crisis among groups accepted and recognized as legitimate power contenders within the regime (such as the hardline and Sorbonne military officers, São Paulo and Rio de Janeiro industrialists and businessmen, and professional economists and planners), a tacit agreement was reached between influential military and civilian officials: to continue in power and to head off what were for them the frightening prospects of regime collapse and a return to the centers of state power by various opposition groups, it was essential to broaden the regime's ruling base to include representatives of the industrial community and new middle-class professionals with training in economics and the management sciences. The growth of the professions, they discovered, if coupled with the provision of an adequate number of new jobs in a mixed economy where lines between public and private economic operations had become blurred all the more, could become a stabilizing force in consolidating the new political, social, and economic order.

The modern bureaucratic state, so often discussed in the scholarly literature in North America and Western Europe, thus has become reality in the Brazilian setting. Above all else it is today an effective device for a middle-range developing industrial state well along the road to achieving the goals of an industrialized society and of recognition on the world scene as an independent force. Within this state those in the upper sector who accept this regime as legitimate have achieved a good deal of autonomy and freedom of action, while the lower sectors of society have for all effective purposes been depoliticized and had their concerns excluded from the decision-making centers of government. One of the great strengths of this particular state apparatus is its size, its diversity, its amorphousness, its lack of accountability, and the diffusion of power whereby those within the system share the responsibility of rule and accrue advantages without really having access to the governing team at the top, centered in the Office of the President of the Republic.[8]

Those, then, who would base their projections for the future of Latin American politics on Brazilian experience call attention to the disastrous experience with populism and newly developing mass-based political organizations in the late fifties and early sixties and conclude somewhat pessimistically that this kind of bureaucratic-authoritarian regime, while not desirable in terms of an ideal world, is a very effective mechanism for promoting "constructive capitalism," for defending economic freedom and a certain range of political liberties for the privileged, "productive" elements of society, and for responding to the needs of sustained economic growth, regulated social change, and political order. The rationality of the new state structures, coupled with the values of economy and efficiency and the fear of chaos and social upheaval by the masses, all contribute in the eyes of those analysts to explain why, for the foreseeable future, they see this state model as the only alternative to a conflict society (the Argentine model) or to fundamental social revolution and the consolidation of a Marxist-Leninist state (the Cuban model).

Despite the very different national environments existing in Brazil and Chile, there is a parallel between the two military governments. In attempting to arrive at a successful formula for governing Chile, having destroyed by force the Allende government and dismantled the institutional apparatuses that had long given form to Chilean democracy, the Pinochet regime has looked favorably on the Brazilian experiment in building and maintaining a bureaucratic-authoritarian state, as a model suitable for adaptation to the Chilean context. As such, at the present time, Chile's military government requires not separate analysis but is best understood by first analyzing from a comparative perspective the strengths and weaknesses of the post-1964 Brazilian regime.

Such is not the case with the Peruvian experiment. Granted there occurred within the Peruvian military institution the same disillusionment with populist political formulas as a suitable device for promoting socioeconomic change and for sustaining increased national productivity, while responding to mass mobilization through political party organization. But, for the first eight years of rule by the Peruvian military, it appeared as though the political outcome there would be quite different.[9] The academic label most commonly used to describe the new regime has been "populist-authoritarian" or some similar equivalent, in contrast to the bureaucratic-authoritarian model so widely discussed by those who would base their projections for the future of South America on Argentine and Brazilian experience.

The irony is that once Peru's new military rulers had reached the limits of their capacity to declare a revolution and had dismantled definitely the old social, political, and economic order, in building a new state apparatus they found a power base confined to the military institution excessively narrow. Above all else, their inability to replace the old economic order with a new one that could be made to function in productive terms brought about displacement of the initial governing team from the centers of power. The shift from the Velasco Alvarado government to that of Morales Bermúdez in 1975, while no less military in nature, signalled movement away from a populist-authoritarian regime model to one that is best characterized as bureaucratic-authoritarian. To implement a radical series of new social, economic, and political policies required a much different kind of state apparatus than that they had inherited. While the military has made real strides in some areas of Peru in developing new agrarian structures, in others it has become quite apparent that the replacement of private ownership of large, commercialized plantations with state enterprise has not been sufficient to allocate more rationally agricultural resources, much less to maintain previous levels of production. All too late, officers identified with the Velasco Alvarado government discovered how difficult it was to convert a state bureaucratic apparatus, largely manned by the same civilian personnel as previously, from patronage, clientelistic, employment-oriented functions into entrepreneurial ones. State capitalism required state functionaries of a vastly different sort and they were in very short supply.

As the Morales Bermúdez government has had to face up to hard economic realities—serious food shortages in basic commodities, uncontrollable inflation and frequent devaluations, a decline in industrial activity, and deterioration in exchange earnings from commercial agriculture—it has opted for bureaucratic-authoritarian solutions rather than populist-authoritarian ones. To have consolidated a populist-authoritarian regime would have required sharing power with newly activated rural and urban lower-sector groups mobilized by the military themselves through the *Sistema Nacional de Apoyo a la Mobilización Social* (SINAMOS).

The initial thrust of the Peruvian revolution was in the direction of building support among hitherto excluded urban and rural lower-sector groups: squatters in Lima in satellite "cities" on the fringes of the metropolitan area, and peasants who responded positively to the military's lead in agrarian reform. But it soon became apparent that the mobilization promoted by SINAMOS to undercut the mass-basis of the old populist parties—especially the Apristas—would bring into national politics new uncontrollable mass elements. Ultimately, the more conservative officers feared that this would introduce into an already tenuous regime a distinct set of political aspirations and demands that could not be dictated to but would have to be bargained with.

Nevertheless, what decided the SINAMOS question was not so much the new mass equation it suggested but the economic crisis and the failure of concepts of the industrial community and participatory management to offer a viable alternative to previous forms of economic organization. The displacement of the reformist military and the emergence of more conservative officers at the forefront of the military government signaled a shift in the direction of accommodation with what remained of the Peruvian industrial and business community, a dismantling of those schemes in rural and urban areas designed to promote mass mobilization, and an expanded role for civilian professionals: economists, planners, engineers, and the like. Whether or not Morales Bermúdez will be any more successful in riding out the present crisis remains in doubt, but—in a way not dissimilar to the Brazilian crisis in 1968 at the time of President Costa e Silva's illness[10]—the chances are likely the military will muddle through and remain in control because of the absence of any alternative acceptable to them. A military departure from the centers of power in Peru would require acceptance of a condition that hitherto has always been refused: the formation of an Aprista government.

Projections from these three cases—Argentina, Brazil, and Peru—all augur poorly for the future of democracy in South America. What about the other governments on the continent? Chile has already been accounted for within the framework provided by Brazil. The same applies to Uruguay, where, for all effective purposes, the country has become a client state of Brazil. Bolivia is best accounted for within the context of the populist-authoritarian model. The difference between this case and that of Peru is that the Bolivian revolution preceded the military's assumption of power and no regime since 1952 has been able to govern without consideration of politically activated mass elements in the countryside and in the mining areas. There, consequently, the option of moving in the direction of a bureaucratic-authoritarian regime is simply not possible. The remaining two cases where the military is also in control represent carry-overs from earlier political styles now superseded on the rest of the continent: rule by military junta until a new alternative government can be arrived at, in Ecuador, and rule by military *cuadillo*: the Stroessner regime in Paraguay.

As noted at the outset, the only two South American cases at the moment that deviate from these patterns are Colombia and Venezuela. Yet, they are frequently dismissed as of little consequence for the remainder of the continent, or for the hemisphere for that matter. The Colombian system is most commonly seen as the continuation of a nineteenth-century two-party development, the Liberal-Conservative split, and as an example of successful elite survival and manipulation of national politics when faced with mass mobilization.[11] The Venezuelan case is usually explained away on the grounds that it alone has been able to afford the excesses of populism because of the margin given to incumbent regimes by the country's oil income, which makes available to all regimes sufficient public funds and resources to meet the demands of the most vocal sectors—be they Left, Right, or center.

At this particular point it would behoove us to retrace our steps in time a bit, before discussing the Venezuelan case, since the point of departure in each of our four cases is the crisis of populism. There is, however, a difference in the nature of the response to these crises. The crisis of populism and the development of mass-based political party organizations, to a point where they brought into national politics unacceptable mass elements from the standpoint of established power groups, engendered authoritarian breakthroughs in Argentina, Brazil, and Peru and convinced modern military establishments in those countries of the necessity of seizing power for the purpose of retaining control indefinitely. In Venezuela the crisis of populism and mass-based party development led to the formation and consolidation of a progressive, democratic regime.

Following the end of World War II, the preferred political formula for promoting socioeconomic change and sustained increases in national productivity while responding to mass mobilization through political party organization was populism. Although there are some notable exceptions—viz., Juan Perón's *Movimiento Justicialista*—populist political formulas coincided for the most part with the articulation of democratic ideals, with the belief in the superiority of the Western democracies as an appropriate model for national development, and with acceptance of the premise promoted by the United States that the greater the progress in socioeconomic development the more likely would the consolidation of political democracies throughout the Western Hemisphere become. Despite the return to business as usual after World War II on the part of U.S. firms active in Latin America and the opening up of the region to vast new prospects for investment, due to the near economic collapse of Great Britain and the absence of other competitors, the ideals of the Good Neighbor policy and the favorable image created by the Roosevelt administration lingered on. As that image began to wane, it received a substantial boost from the Kennedy administration. Certainly the events in Cuba and the outcomes of the Castro revolution presented a challenge to the prevailing orthodoxy, certainly there continued to be national sectors denouncing U.S. imperialism and calling for more radical solution to the issues of economic development and social change, but for the most part political leaders and influentials opted for the channelling of public debates and controversies over governmental policies through the structure of liberal democratic regimes imitating Western political models.

Many, if not most, conservative groups felt that their interests could best be protected under constitutional regimes that established certain basic rules for the political game and yet opened up the way for the entrance of others into national politics in a manner that made possible the accommodation of those interests and demands to their own, which had already been established and institutionalized in preceding periods. Certainly everyone realized that the times were changing. The old formulas of either aristocratic republics, in which national elites ruled on behalf of quiescent masses and defined for them their own best interests, or of dictatorships in which military *caudillos* imposed their personal conceptions of national unity and interest over the nation, were no longer sufficient.

Further experimentation with new kinds of authoritarian states, modeled after the European experience of the interwar period and adapted to meet conditions peculiar to the Western Hemisphere, was no longer acceptable. The two classic cases of such experimentation are Getúlio Vargas's *Estado Novo* and Juan Perón's mass-movement regime. Vargas's "new state" alluded unsuccessfully to the transferral into the Brazilian milieu of European concepts of a Corporate Society—first articulated in mass political terms by Mussolini in Italy and later "purified" by Salazar to fit the requirements of conservative Catholic thought and his desire to keep a society of limited participation alive in Portugal. Perón's regime, formed at the end of the war and maintained in isolation for a decade afterwards, constitutes really the only instance in the Americas where Mussolini's techniques of mass mobilization were used successfully. Dispensing with the language of corporatism and replacing it with his own doctrine of *justicialism* and his own definition of a "Third Position," in international affairs, Perón built a revolutionary-mass-movement regime under the auspices of a single, official populist party organization.

Equally unacceptable were Marxist-Leninist formulas for achieving revolutionary breakthroughs. While the revolutionary Left, with varying degrees of strength and representation in the various republics, aspired to the construction of a socialist society—like the conservatives—most of them opted for strategies of working within an ostensibly democratic mold in which a solid working class base could be built. For them, populist political formulas were seen as a device for creating a politicized urban working class with a mass consciousness, in much the same way conservatives saw the very same formulas as a means for dealing with newly activated lower-sector elements in urban and rural areas and for incorporating them into national politics, while minimizing their impact on their own privileges and economic interests.

In hindsight, from the perspective of the 1970s, it is all too easy to see the failings of populism as a nonviable political formula that could not last for an extended period of time. Nevertheless, it did serve to provide a framework through which political mobilization of the urban and rural masses could occur. Only in Argentina did mass mobilization under populist political formulas coincide with the structuring of a civilian-dominated authoritarian regime. Elsewhere in Latin America it was primarily an urban-based movement that coincided with democratic experiments. When it has involved groups in rural areas, as in Peru and Venezuela, these have been agricultural workers in commercial enterprises linked to the national economy, with an already well-developed consciousness of national politics.

Before turning to the particulars of the Venezuelan case and how populism led there to the institutionalization of a democratic, rather than an authoritarian order, populist-style politics also need to be viewed in wider comparative perspective. At the most general level the first characteristic of populist movements and political styles in the four cases under discussion—Argentina, Brazil, Peru, and Venezuela—is one that sets aside this political phenomenon when it appears in Latin America and southern Europe from other world areas. There it has been essentially an urban phenomenon linked to the involvement of large numbers of lower-sector individuals in national politics and oriented toward their incorporation into an urban life style offering a wide range of social services unavailable in rural areas. This is what makes so similar current Portuguese and Greek politics, now in the midst of a new experimentation with democratic rule, when compared with, say, Brazilian politics (1946-64) and Peruvian politics (1956-68). In other world areas populism has been primarily an agrarian movement.[12] While also tied to mass mobilization—although in rural rather than urban areas—those movements have had quite a different time orientation: the defense of a simpler rural culture and life style in the face of the onslaught of wider societal changes triggered by rapid industrialization.

Second, populist politics entail a coalition-building strategy in which a new set of political leaders of middle class origin successfully mobilizes a disposable mass of individuals, drawn from heterogeneous backgrounds, into a single mass movement that aspires to taking command of the state apparatus for the purpose of redistributing more equitably economic benefits accrued from the marketing of mineral resources and agricultural products on the world market and from industrialization. Linked to these redistributory demands are others for social services hitherto unavailable to large groups in the population: schools, medical care, water, electricity, sanitation, low cost mass transit, and the like.

In order to build a majority coalition, however, populist coalitions must develop as wide an appeal as possible and pick up support from groups other than those of working-class origin. The third ingredient, then, has been the use of nationalist and antioligarchic symbols that have an appeal also to new middle-class sectors whose access to the centers of power has also been restricted by previous governments. Articulating a fervent nationalism, these movements stress the negative impact on national society of foreign imperialism, the positive aspects of a new national identity transcending previous divisions and cleavages in national society, and the active role the state can and should assume in regulating the economy and society to insure more equitable benefits for all—in the form of jobs and social services.[13]

The fourth characteristic is organizational: as mass movements, populist coalitions are inherently instable. Loyalty to the movement is built largely in emotional and personal terms through the appeal to the public for the correction of past injustices and social ills. In each instance, at the core of the movement is a dominant personality whose leadership style is most effectively demonstrated in mass assemblies and in the ability to turn out the people for periodic public meetings to demonstrate the degree of popular support for the leader and his movement. At middle-range levels, this emphasis on the personality of the leader—Juan Perón, João Goulart, Haya de la Torre, Rómulo Betancourt—is transmitted to a series of lesser coalitions and political figures who, while loyal to the head of the movement, have their own particular clienteles. The whole structure of the movement, then, is centered around personalist appeals, the development of exchange relationships involving the delivery of support in exchange for social and economic benefits, and the cultivation of both positive and negative political sybmols that promote continued emotional involvement in the movement and a sense of psychic reward for participation in what is perceived to be a collective effort at building a new society and a new state.

It is in this wider context that one must consider the formation of new mass-based political party organizations and why some political parties proved to be capable of transcending populist-style politics and developed disciplined party organizations, while others remained essentially ephemeral electoral coalitions whose viability as mass movements disappeared quickly in the face of organized opposition from the armed forces. There are four cases that can shed light on this question from within the range of countries selected for attention here: the Brazilian Labor Party (PTB), *Acción Popular* (AP, Belaúnde Terry's electoral organization for winning the 1963 Peruvian elections), Haya de la Torre's Peruvian Aprista Party (APRA), and *Acción Democrática* (AD, the Venezuela organization of the democratic Left, led by Rómulo Betancourt). The first two turned out to be temporary organizations, easily dismantled once the military took power and imposed new, durable authoritarian regimes. The last two, in contrast, have been successful in developing core organizations that, while unable to command the allegiance of a majority over time, have been able to survive the vicissitudes of military rule and to continue to constitute major political forces to be contended with by any government in Peru or Venezuela. Yet, all four have engaged in a populist style of politics in periods of democratic rule when there has been a disposable mass electorate to contend with (in Brazil, 1950-64; in Peru, 1956-68; and in Venezuela, 1945-48 and 1958-present).

The difference between the Aprista Party and AD, and the others is to be seen in terms of two variables: ideology and leadership style. Both the Apristas and AD are identified clearly with the ideology of the democratic Left. Although the democratic Left in Latin America was a much discussed political force throughout Latin America during the 1950s,[14] most political scientists have since assigned this family of parties and political leaders to the historical archives. As viable national forces only three party organizations within these groups survived intact into the seventies: the aforementioned two and José Figueres's *Liberación Nacional* in Costa Rica. What sets them aside is a social-democratic-party ideology that is distinctly Latin American and appropriate to their own national realities. While they do manifest a certain similarity in terms of social policy with social democratic forces in Western Europe, none has imported its ideology from a Western European setting and sought to impose it over an alien reality. To capture this dimension effectively, one really must begin with the works of Haya de la Torre, since his are the most complete, and then move on to capture the vision of a democratic society articulated by all three—Haya, Pepe Figueres, and Rómulo Betancourt—in terms appropriate to their own national settings.

The first difference, then, between AD and APRA, on the one hand, and the PTB and AP (*Acción Popular*), on the other, lies in the formers' intense commitment to the democratic ideal despite all costs: the determination not to take power in their respective republics until they had first obtained victory at the ballot box, commitment to a bargaining-style politics in which their concept of a modern state and a more just society would not be superimposed over others by force, concern with the comon man and social justice, and the willingness to stand behind their ideals at times when opposition to and suppression of their organizations has been the greatest.

The second difference, leadership style, is to be seen in the personalities of Haya and Betancourt. Both men are responsible for the transition of their organizations from revolutionary mass movements bent on the radical transformation of society by force into democratic party organizations. The contrast between APRA in 1930, in 1945, and in 1960 is enormous and it reflects the internal transformation of the party imposed by Haya in response to external conditions and the evolution of his political thought.[15] The same can be said of AD in 1936 (then known as ORVE, the *Movimiento de Organización Venezolana*, and soon thereafter as PDN, the *Partido Democrático Nacional*), in 1945 and in 1960. Beginning as a revolutionary opposition movement, it took power in 1945 as the single most important mass political movement in Venezuela, with the determination to build a new society quickly and irreversibly—only to lose control to the military in 1948. During the following era of prolonged military rule (first under Lt. Col. Delgado Chalbaud, 1948-50, and then Gen. Marcos Pérez Jiménez, 1950-58), Betancourt initiated a process of internal change. Realizing the necessity of altering the party's tactics and resolving the inconsistency between a revolutionary commitment, on the one hand, and the articulation of democratic ideals on the other, AD after 1958 became a very different party organization.[16] Under the Betancourt presidency (1959-64), the party accord worked out in 1958 with the Republican Democratic Union (URD) and the Christian Democrats (COPEI) was maintained and strengthened and an era of reform and reconciliation in national politics set in. Perhaps the most critical moments of all came in 1961 and 1962, when the insurgency movement peaked, and in 1967, when having lost the election Betancourt led the party into the opposition where, rebuilt and reorganized, it came back to win the 1973 election. Without entering into all the details of what was entailed in building and maintaining a democratic order after 1958, the accomplishments of Venezuela by 1977 were impressive in a continent where military regimes were on the upswing: the insurgency movement of the Left had been neutralized; the traditional power contenders on the right had added their support to the maintenance of a democratic order; AD had negotiated away its hegemony, in exchange for support from the other major parties for democratic politics, and had functioned for five years (1968-73) as a loyal opposition; and the country had passed through nationalization of the petroleum industry without serious national trauma or international repercussions.[17]

Only in facile terms can Venezuela's accomplishments in the political realm be dismissed. The crucial factor in the institutionalization of a democratic order lay not in the extensive economic resources provided by the country's oil revenues, as some would argue, but in the realm of human choice: how political leaders in the major parties (AD, URD and COPEI) responded to the various crises spanning the years following the end of World War II. If economic progress has been an important condition shaping Venezuela's political experience after 1958, the same point needs to be made in considering the Brazilian case after 1964. If petroleum is the great national resource of Venezuela, then it is the huge industrial complex emergent in greater São Paulo (the largest in Latin America and one of the most important in the world) that is Brazil's great strength, just as it is the extensive fertile land of the Argentine pampas with its wheat and beef production that is the foundation of Argentina's economy. All three countries—Argentina, Brazil, and Venezuela—have extensive national resources of their own to draw upon as they have fixed their aspirations on becoming modern, industrial states with a commercialized agriculture and integrated market structure. Yet of the three, only Venezuela has pursued its economic options in the context of building a democratic order in which sustained socio-economic progress is being coupled with policies of maximizing human growth and the potential offered by the average citizen.

Despite all its imperfections—and these are not to be denied in a political environment where the excesses of populism are often only too visible—the Venezuelan experiment with democracy needs to be held up as a beacon of hope at a time when so many analysts of Latin American politics, within the region and outside, have concluded that corporatism and authoritarianism are an inseparable part of the region's cultural legacy and determinants of the region's future.

I know of no more fitting tribute to Harry Kantor than to end on this note, since it is through his tutelage years ago that I gained insight into the vitality of the democratic tradition in Latin America. At this moment, when it is least visible and when so many on the Right and the Left have despaired of the ideal of more just and equitable societies and of the provision of adequate housing, food, schooling, and health care for the average citizen in a context of freedom, ever becoming reality, it would do us all good to remember that the citizens of the Anglo-

American states in the Western Hemisphere have no monopoly on the articulation of democratic ideals and aspirations. There is Latin American tradition other than that called corporatist or authoritarian that continues to survive despite all odds. When the present moment of despair experienced by so many throughout Latin America passes by, there may well come another day when the ideals and hope of social democracy may yet become reality. It is for that day that we must all work.

As of early 1979, the economic crises confronting the present governments of Brazil, Chile, and Peru and the social forces in movement within Nicaragua, coupled with the expectations and hopes revived by the Carter Administration's human rights policy, raise the possibility of a revival of this hemisphere's democratic forces. With the proper combination of internal and external pressures throughout Latin America we may well be on the verge of experiencing a breakdown in authoritarian governance as we move into the 1980s. The skeptic would do well to consider the recent experience of Portugal, Greece, and Spain; the activist, to analyze carefully the conditions leading to the collapse of institutionalized authoritarian orders elsewhere and what is required to promote democratic outcomes.[18] Whether or not all this comes to pass, of course, remains to be seen, but once again the forces supporting democracy are on the move, and it is my great hope that these developments will come to fruition.

Notes

1. The phrase "conflict society" is taken from Kalman H. Silvert's *The Conflict Society: Reaction and Revolution in Latin America* (New York: American Universities Field Staff, 1966).

2. The most effective argument developed from Argentina's experience and using its political outcomes as a model for the future is Guillermo A. O'Donnell, *Modernization and Bureaucratic-Authoritarianism: Studies in Latin American Politics* (Berkeley: Institute of International Studies, University of California, 1973).

3. The "optimistic" view of Brazilian politics after the coup is best represented by Lincoln Gordon, the U.S. ambassador to Brazil at the time, and others who were instrumental in bringing about rapid U.S. recognition of the new regime and in providing it with monetary support and other forms of aid during the regime's early years. In contrast, the "realists" were confined largely to the academic community. For these conflicting perspectives, consult Gayle Hudgens (Watson), "Our Monster in Brazil—It All Began with 'Brother Sam'," *Nation* 224:2 (January 15, 1977), pp. 51-54; and the various articles published by

James W. Rowe, "Revolution or Counterrevolution in Brazil?" *American Universities Field Staff Reports Service*, East Coast South America Series, 11:4-5 (1964); "The Revolution and the 'System': Notes on Brazilian Politics," *American Universities Field Staff Reports Service*, 12:3-4 (1966); and "Brazil Stops the Clock," *American Universities Field Staff Reports Service*, 13:1-2 (1967). The Watson article draws on previously unavailable materials in the Lyndon B. Johnson Presidential Library at the University of Texas. For a detailed analysis of the U.S. role in the coup and involvement in the consolidation of the new regime I am indebted to Dalmo de Abreu Dallari's analysis of Johnson's White House papers contained in this collection.

4. The best cross-sampling of this debate is to be found in Alfred Stepan (ed.), *Authoritarian Brazil: Origins, Policies, and Future* (New Haven: Yale University Press, 1973).

5. For example, see the concluding article by Juan J. Linz, "The Future of an Authoritarian Situation or the Institutionalization of an Authoritarian Regime: The Case of Brazil," in Stepan.

6. Effective statements of this view are contained in Fernando Henrique Cardoso, "Associated-Dependent Development: Theoretical and Practical Implications," in Stepan; and Paul Israel Singer, "O 'Milagre Brasileiro': Causas e Consequências, *Cadernos de CEBRAP*, No. 6 (São Paulo: Centro Brasileiro de Análise e Planejamento, 1972).

7. For a discussion of the role of the ESG and military-civilian interaction see Alfred Stepan, *The Military in Politics: Changing Patterns in Brazil* (Princeton: Princeton University Press, 1971) and Luigi R. Einaudi with Alfred Stepan, "Latin American Institutional Development: Changing Military Perspectives in Peru and Brazil," Rand report R-586-DOS (Santa Monica, Calif., 1971).

8. A useful discussion, which pulls together in summary fashion the various decision-making levels in the contemporary Brazilian state, is to be found in Jerald A. Johnson, "Brazilian Bureaucracy and Politics: The Rise of a New Professional Class" (Ph.D. diss., University of Texas, 1977).

9. Abraham F. Lowenthal (ed.) provides a good overview of these developments in the preface and introductory chapter to his book, *The Peruvian Experiment: Continuity and Change Under Military Rule* (Princeton: Princeton University Press, 1975). See also Einaudi and Stepan.

10. For a discussion of the 1969 presidential succession crisis consult: Ronald M. Schneider, *The Political System of Brazil: Emergence of a 'Modernizing' Authoritarian Regime, 1964-1970* (New York: Columbia University Press, 1971).

11. Edwin Corr reviews the established literature in Colombia and covers these views quite well in his extended essay, *The Political Process in Colombia*, Monograph Series in World Affairs, vol. 9, no. 1-2 (Denver, Colorado: University of Denver, 1972).

12. While my analysis of populism does not agree entirely with that provided by Ghita Ionescu and Ernest Gellner (eds.) in *Populism: Its Meaning and National Characteristics* (New York: Macmillan, 1969), the distinction Ionescu

draws between the Latin American region and other world areas is essentially valid if one adds the southern European states to that categorization. The case in point would be Mario Soares and his Socialist Party in Portugal, which is essentially a case of populist-style leadership and populist organization of a mass movement/electoral coalition that is primarily urban based.

13. These last two points—the nature of the populist coalition and the basis of mass appeal—have been adapted from Torcuato di Tella, "Populism and Reform in Latin America," in Claudio Veliz (ed.), *Obstacles to Change in Latin America* (London: Oxford University Press, 1965), pp. 47-74.

14. For a useful overview of the political parties encompassed by the democratic Left and a positive view of this political force during the 1940s and 1950s see Robert J. Alexander, "The Latin American Aprista Parties," *Political Quarterly*, 20 (1949), pp. 236-47. While written in 1949, this article exemplifies this view as it continued to be articulated in the 1950s.

15. Since it is not appropriate here to enter into a detailed discussion of the changing role of the Aprista Party, the reader may wish to pursue this point further by consulting Peter F. Klarén, *Modernization, Dislocation, and Aprismo: Origins of the Peruvian Aprista Party, 1870-1932* (Austin: University of Texas Press, 1973).

16. The two most complete accounts of this evolution are to be found in Robert J. Alexander, *The Venezuelan Democratic Revolution: A Profile of the Regime of Rómulo Betancourt* (New Brunswick, N.J.: Rutgers University Press, 1964), and John D. Martz, *Acción Democrática: Evolution of a Modern Party in Venezuela* (Princeton: Princeton University Press, 1966).

17. For an excellent overview of Venezuelan politics and a general discussion of these developments, see David E. Blank, *Politics in Venezuela* (Boston: Little, Brown and Company, 1973).

18. An indispensable source for this kind of comparative analysis is Juan J. Linz and Alfred Stepan's four-part study, *The Breakdown of Democratic Regimes* (Baltimore and London: Johns Hopkins University Press, 1978). While Linz and Stepan are concerned with the reverse situation—the conditions leading to the breakdown of democratic regimes—the contents of their study suggest a number of the factors related to the breakdown of authoritarian regimes. This is especially true of vol. 1 of this study, Juan Linz's *Crisis, Breakdown, and Reequilibration*.

Part 6
Conclusion:
The Continuing Struggle for Democracy in Latin America

14
Latin American Democracy: The Historic Model and the New Openings

Howard J. Wiarda

That democracy is in trouble in Latin America hardly needs repeating here. The rash of military coups, the widespread violations of human rights, and the resurgence of authoritarian regimes are familiar themes in both popular and more academically oriented accounts. Although some writers feel that the cycle may be about to repeat itself again, foreseeing a general military return to the barracks soon and a reassertion of civilian government, and though in Brazil, Ecuador, and even Chile the military has made some efforts to bend to popular demands, or to make plans for the restoration of civilian rule, other observers remain sketpical of both the cyclical theory and the promises and pronouncements of the military rulers. Since the causes are deep-rooted rather than surface, modern military (or civil-military) authoritarianism may be a lasting phenomenon.

The authors of this volume have provided a number of explanations to help account for the failures of democracy and the authoritarian resurgence. These include the historic absence of strong democratic institutions and practices in the Latin American tradition as well as the more recent (since the 1930s) transformation from the *inclusionary* politics of the earlier populists, both civilian and military, to the more *exclusionary* politics of the modern authoritarians, again both civilian and military. The reasons include also the weakness and lack of organization of the peasant and labor sectors, the strongly corporate interests of the army or the economic and bureaucratic elites, the incapacity of the political parties to develop as well-organized and legitimated institutions, and elections that are at best tentative rather then definitive. Our contributors have pointed to the lack of incorporation into the policy-making process of those groups, such as women or rural laborers, that government programs were designed to benefit; to the pervasive presence of elitist and paternalistic attitudes throughout Latin America; to the changed international economic context in which declining terms of trade and spiraling prices for oil and manufactured goods have helped undermine even the best intentioned of Latin American democratic regimes; to the machinations and interventions of the U.S. government as well as the mistakes and failures of the Alliance for Progress; and to the incompetence and lack of political skills on the part of many of Latin America's own democratic-Left leaders.

Modern authoritarianism has multiple causes and also varieties in Latin America. Cultural and historic factors are undoubtedly important, but so too are explanations linking authoritarianism to the reaction against heightened mass mobilization and the perceived threats of populist or leftist movements in such countries as Argentina, Brazil, and Chile; to the systemic stresses generated by modernization and an explosion of demands in countries lacking the institutional structures to handle these new pressures; and to the strategies of modernizing civil-military elites (for example, the state capitalism of Brazil, which called on the lower classes to shoulder the costs) for accelerating development. It should be noted also that Latin American authoritarianism may take a fairly well-institutionalized form as in Argentina or Brazil, as well as a noninstitutionalized familial or caudillistic form as in Nicaragua or Paraguay.

But democracy is in trouble in Latin America, we have said, not just because military-authoritarian regimes have taken power in two-thirds of the nations of the area, but also because the recent literature and interpretations of Latin America have led us to be skeptical of democracy's very viability there. These interpretations too have been strongly present in this collection. The continuing existence of elitist, paternalistic and oligarchic forms even in the most ostensibly democratic institutions, the seeming preference for technocratic and administrative regimes rather than genuinely pluralist and participatory ones, and the powerful statist and corporatist influences that often militate against democratic rule have given rise to explanations of Latin American politics and behavior strongly at variance with our democratic preferences. The argument that such terms as "democracy," "representation," "participation," "pluralism," and the like may mean something different in the Latin American context may accurately reflect political and social realities; but for those who believe democracy is one and universal, or approximately so, such a redefining of the basic terms leaves us vaguely uncomfortable and suspicious that these concepts provide new rationalizations for Latin American authoritarianism.

In the sections that follow an effort will be made to sort out these conflicting models and interpretations of Latin American "democracy," to explore some of the newer currents present, and to assess democracy's present and future prospects throughout the area.

The Democratic Bias in Latin American Studies

The democratic bias in U.S.-based Latin American studies goes back a long way, reflecting our history, our sense of political superiority, and our belief that democracy U.S.-style is both the best form of government *and* exportable to other lands. The long history of this perspective need not concern us here; instead, attention will be focused on three recent and prominent schools of thought that have applied the democratic focus to Latin America. These might be termed the "pathology of democracy" school, the "developmentalist" school, and the "Andersonian" school.

The "Pathology of Democracy" School

The "pathology of democracy" school was prominent in Latin American studies in the early years, the 1930s, 1940s, and 1950s. Although often viewed as dated and old-fashioned, the vestiges of this approach remain strong in some quarters even today. Because he used the term and was the principal author of that series of studies purporting to measure the "progress" of Latin American "democracy," the "pathology of democracy" school is most closely identified with the name of Russell H. Fitzgibbon, an unfortunate association in many ways because Fitzgibbon was a sophisticated political scientist whose writings on Latin America still have much relevance for us and because he was but one of a whole generation of scholars—Harold Davis, William Stokes, Alexander Edelman, Rosendo Gomez, Asher Christenson, Mary Wilhelmine Williams, Austin MacDonald, J. Lloyd Mechan, Miguel Jorrín, and William Pierson—whose writings stressed the same or similar themes.

The "pathology of democracy" school measured Latin America almost exclusively from the point of view of the United States. Students of William Stokes, for example, remember him fulminating against the fact that Latin Americans were Catholic, had too many babies, and failed to comprehend the capitalist ethic. Fitzgibbon's indices of democracy were also constructed with a model of the U.S. political system clearly in mind: separate and coequal courts and congress, strong local government, civilian dominance of the military, strong political parties, etc.[1] Mecham's monumental *Church and State in Latin America* similarly stressed the need, in a predominantly Catholic political culture, for the strict separation of church and state as in the U.S. constitution.²

Like their colleagues studying other areas of comparative politics at the time, the "pathology" analysts were strongly formal-legal and institutional in their approach. They criticized the large gap between Latin American constitutional theory and actual political practice. Yet, they seldom took account of the informal and dynamic aspects of Latin American politics that tended to diminish these gaps, and make the Latin American political systems, on their own terms, more rational, predictable, even *systemic*. In viewing Latin America through U.S. lenses, furthermore, they were parochial and ethnocentric. It could even be said that in their blanket condemnations of strong executives, military coups, authoritarian rule, etc. they did a disservice to Latin American studies by blinding us to the way Latin American institutions actually do function.

The "Developmentalist" School

The "developmentalist" school has similarly been so pilloried in recent years that, were it not for the fact that many scholars still accept many or all of its assumptions, it should be allowed to repose along with the "pathology" school. The "developmentalist" school emerged in the early 1960s among a new generation of scholars and was closely related to the assumptions of the Kennedy years and the Alliance for Progress. Its chief advocates in the social sciences included Gabriel A. Almond, S. M. Lipset, W. W. Rostow, and Karl W. Deutsch; in Latin American studies, if one wishes to pick on someone, the main advocates of this approach were George Blanksten, Robert Scott, and Martin Needler.³

The "developmentalists" were somewhat more subtle and "with-it" than the "pathologists," but probably no less biased and ethnocentric. They focused on the dynamics of change, function, and process rather than on formal-legal institutions. But their functional categories bore a close resemblance to the functions performed in the U.S. system, and the end product of the developmental process—secular, pluralist, democratic, participatory, etc.—was also based on the U.S. model. The assumption of a unilinear and universal path to "development" drew heavily on the experience of a small and select group of already developed countries of Northwest Europe and was denigrating to nations of other areas. It saw little of worth in their cultures and politics except "traditionalism" and "problems to be overcome."

The "developmentalist" school was closely tied in with the U.S. conception of democracy—and our efforts to implant it abroad. We have already remarked on how Gabriel Almond, the foremost early advocate of this position, was caught up in what he himself termed "the Peace

Corps mood of the time," the effort to *bring* development to the "less developed" world.[4] But "development" was conceived in almost exclusively U.S., or Western European, terms: political parties, an informed electorate, pluralist social and political groups, an apolitical military dedicated to "civic action," "nonpolitical" trade unions, organized farmers' groups, a capitalist class with a sense of "social responsibility," and a large middle class adhering to all the presumed middle-class virtues—honesty, responsibility, moderation, anticommunism, patriotism, middle-of-the-road politics, and nonexorbitant demands. Many young Latin American scholars took up the call and went in search of these forms of "developmental indicators." It is small wonder that few of them found what they were looking for, since the criteria used had little to do with Latin American social and political realities. Small wonder also that many of these scholars, "the best and the brightest," became "Dr. Yes" spokesmen for the U.S. aid program, since during this period the assumptions of developmentalist theory often undergirded both scholarship and foreign assistance.

The "Andersonian" School

The influential formulations of Charles W. Anderson are, to this editor's mind, the most interesting of the three "schools" here represented.[5] For Anderson began by explicitly rejecting the North American biases of the earlier writers and taking Latin America on its own terms. He denied the popular view of Latin American politics as "unsystematic," arguing instead that it was we, its interpreters, who failed to understand what the "system" was. In his analysis of Latin America's rival "power contenders" jockeying for power, the tentative nature of elections, the cooptation and repression tactics of the ruling elites, the need for new power contenders to demonstrate both a "power capability" and a willingness to abide by the "rules of the game," and the accommodative tradition of Latin American politics and the corresponding absence of profound social revolutions in all but a few countries, Anderson captured much of the essence of Latin American politics and its dynamics of change. Moreover, Anderson took pains to come to grips with Latin American politics through its own political processes and institutions rather than on the basis of some foreign and imported model.

Anderson's work was such a breakthrough, so influential, and so close to my own thinking on the subject that it is difficult to critique it with enthusiasm. Nevertheless there are biases, misplaced assumptions, and oversights in the Anderson scheme that deserve analysis. Further, and closer to our purposes here, the Anderson system was not incompatible with a democratic-developmentalist perspective of Latin America, nor did it presume any incompatibility between Latin American and U.S. interests. Because the Anderson scheme, corrected, can serve as the basis for our later resurrection of a reformulated democratic model(s) for Latin American development, it is worthwhile to make explicit our differences with the Anderson analysis as a prelude to that resurrection.[6]

1. Not included in the Anderson scheme is any discussion of the United States or any other outside "power contender" as an important force in *internal* Latin American politics. This is a major omission, as is the lack of treatment of Latin America's dependency relationship vis-à-vis external political and economic influences.

2. Though masterful in his treatment of the generally nonrevolutionary and accommodative politics of the area, Anderson ignores the degree to which some of the new groups have organized around values different than those previously accepted as legitimate, have aspirations other than that of being coopted, and no longer wish to accept the rules of the old game. One wonders, for example, whether or to what degree the Andersonian model will still apply when the present generation of university-educated activists, who tend to be socialist almost to a person, come to power.

3. As Anderson sees it, the Latin American political process is generally one of nonrevolutionary rule from the top. Not discussed is the possibility that revolutionary change may be accelerating or that revolution may also be initiated from above, through the capture of the pinnacles of the hierarchy by leftist and nationalist elements instead of the usual rightist ones. Post-1968 Peru is perhaps the best example.

4. There is a bias in favor of a consensus and pluralist model in the Anderson scheme that is not altogether different from the North American liberal model and with which it may be quite compatible. Implied in Anderson's formulation is the apparent assumption that both already established and aspiring power contenders hold equally the values and assumptions of the system, which are elitist and hierarchical. However in an elitist system the elitist values are rarely held equally by all elements; rather, what one usually finds is that while the system is thoroughly elitist at the top, it may be much more liberal-Lockean toward the bottom, though for pragmatic and tactical reasons the latter may echo the elitist assumptions. Further, one gains a picture from the Anderson scheme of new "power contenders" gradually but generally harmoniously taking their place along with the old ones in a more-or-less happy, steady progression. That image clearly is at variance with the wrenching and frequently violent character of the Latin American political process. In short, one wishes Anderson had employed a conflict

model along with his consensus framework to explain those aspects of the political process his model glosses over or incompletely explains.

5. The Anderson—and Latin American—scheme of accommodating new power contenders while the old ones are rarely discarded is based on a steadily expanding economic pie. For new pieces to be doled out to new groups while the old ones also continue to receive their share requires an even bigger pie from which to cut the more numerous pieces. Writing in the early-to-mid-1960s Anderson's optimism was perhaps justified, but by the mid-1970s, with spiraling oil prices, declining terms of trade, reduced foreign aid, balance of payments deficits, ruinous foreign loans, long-term stagflation, and enforced austerity, the pie in most Latin American countries was no longer expanding but stagnant or, in some cases, even contracting. A stable or shrinking pie means no new pieces to hand out, increased competition for the few pieces available, and an end to the happy, steady progression and accommodation of which Anderson wrote. And, of course, in such a zero-sum game as the system of Latin American political economy has increasingly become, the conflict model may even assume greater importance than the earlier consensus model.[7]

6. With the addition of ever greater numbers of new power contenders into the political arena (army, church, oligarchy, merchants, industrialists, middle class, labor, peasants, students, women, etc.), there comes a point, again especially in a period of economic downturn, when increased fragmentation and immobility set in. No group can command a majority, yet all groups are strong and organized enough to constitute a veto power over effective policy making. This would seem to be the end point of the Anderson "power contenders" scheme, when all legitimate claimants have been recognized and no one of them can any longer wholly dominate "the system." Argentina and Chile, and perhaps Mexico and Uruguay, constitute cases in point. But if the end product of the Anderson model is a certain national stagnation and *immobilisme*, new interests and groups may arise who see the need to break out of the immobility, transcend the competing and more-or-less equally balanced but therefore stalemated "power contenders" syndrome, and take the country in new perhaps revolutionary directions. Peru is perhaps again a case in point. Hence, the ultimate possibility that may arise from the Anderson rival "power contenders" scheme is that a new elite may emerge that sees the need to overcome and destroy classic "*criollo* politics," or the Anderson model, entirely. That also was not contemplated in his formulation of the "power contenders" scheme.

The Anderson model, thus, while an exceedingly large step away from the earlier biased and ethnocentric views of Latin American politics, was not entirely without its own biases and even a certain (North American?) favoritism toward consensual, nonconflict pluralist politics. Because he is an undogmatic and open political scientist not closed to nuances and changed circumstances, Anderson would doubtless accept and agree with many of these qualifications and modifications of his theory. The task now becomes to see if the Anderson model can be altered and reformulated taking into account both the reservations we have introduced and also the new currents and interpretations in Latin American politics, and whether out of such a reconciliation can come a new understanding of and commitment to democracy in the area. Is the struggle for democracy in Latin America a continuing struggle or is it passé, and how and why?

Some New Currents in Latin America

The Anderson framework, which takes Latin America on its own terms and not from the point of view of the supposedly "superior" political system of the north, provides perhaps the best and most suitable foundation on which to build a theory and set of measures of Latin American democratic development.[8] The task, it would seem, is twofold: (1) to incorporate into the Andersonian scheme the qualifiers, new realities, and addenda introduced above, and (2) to relate that specifically to the criteria and definition of Latin American democracy developed in the preceding chapters, especially the last two sections of Chapter 12, "The Struggle for Democracy and Human Rights."

What are these new realities? Impressionistically, without developing all the arguments or presenting all the data here, they would include:[9]

1. The swing to the Left of an entire younger generation throughout Latin America. Socialism and nationalism have become de rigueur, and it is unlikely that these sentiments will be entirely assuaged with age or the incorporation of this rising generation into the government bureaucracy.
2. The organization of trade unions, peasant leagues, and other associations on the basis of principles other than traditional values or those previously considered the only right or legitimate ones.
3. Massive migration to the cities, creating a potentially "dangerous" (in a political sense) "lumpen proletariat" of immense size.
4. Broad social mobilization implying changing societal, political, and organizational structures.
5. Crises and fragmentation within the traditional ruling groups,

including the potential for "revolution from above" launched by leftist factions within the military or by a civil-military alliance.
6. The widespread acceptance among various groups for a reorganization of wealth, power, and distributive justice.
7. The similarly widespread acceptance among virtually all opinion-leaders (journalists, intellectuals, students, young bureaucrats and even clerics) of Marxian class analysis as providing *the* cognitive map for analyzing both present and future.
8. The insistence that whatever the ultimate structural alterations, they must be indigenous and national. The era of aping foreign institutions and models is ending. This implies a search for viable institutions and motors of change derived from national cultural and historic traditions and a rejection of North American models. It also implies a rejection of the social-science models similarly derived from the outside and based upon the experiences of the already developed nations. Dependency, colonialism, and imperialism are rejected in whatever form.
9. A growing impatience with liberalism and the older forms of constitutional democracy. The old generation of constitutional lawyers who still hold to these beliefs is fading.
10. A rejection also of the immobility, fragmentation, and stalemated society implied in the more advanced versions of Anderson's competitive "power contenders" model, and a renewed effort to resolve national problems by breaking out of or transcending *"criollo* politics."
11. The decline of the United States as a model society to emulate. U.S. political and social institutions (cities, race relations, presidency, armed forces, or whatever) no longer command the awe and respect they once did.
12. The decline also of U.S. economic interests and influence in the area. Foreign aid is way down and North American businessmen are no longer as competitive in securing contracts. This not only deprives the United States of various levers by which to manipulate Latin America but it also implies a lack of funds to support the expanding economic pie that is so essential for the maintenance of the Latin American (à la Anderson) systems.
13. The long-range decline in Latin America's terms of trade has also produced increased economic stagnation, with the profound social and political effects that implies. Although we may be entering in the northern nations a period of commodity and raw materials scarcities that may partially reverse this trend, thus far the beneficial effects on the majority of the Latin American economies has not been noticeably discernible.

14. The efforts on the part of many Latin American nations to break out or evolve from their tight dependency relation vis-à-vis the United States to a situation of much more diversified trade, commerce, cultural exchange, military missions, etc. involving other nations and blocs, including the socialist world.
15. The growing trend toward neutrality and nonalignment in foreign affairs, vigorous defense of nonintervention, new alliances with other Third World nations, etc.
16. The trend toward increasing nationalizations of U.S. concerns without fear of retaliation. Related to this is the increased lack of dependence on the advice of U.S. ambassadors, AID officials, or mission chiefs.
17. The gradual replacement throughout Latin America of a "philosophy of order" by a "philosophy of change." In some cases, such as Brazil, the emphasis has been on "order and change," but it is change nonetheless. Change and the acceptance of it have become normal rather than exceptional.
18. Finally, what impresses is the pragmatism of approach and the eclecticism of the models used for achieving development, the new combinations. Throughout Latin America the old ideological wars of the 1930s have been in large part brushed aside. As part of the new pragmatism, change-oriented elements are willing to use either a civilian or a military route to power, and most likely some combination of them. State capitalist forms may be combined with aspects of state socialism. The argument over the laissez-faire state and economy is over (if it ever existed); there is now a widespread acceptance of an organic state system as the key driving force for change. And under such organic-statist auspices, change may take a variety of directions.

It is my assertion that these new currents and "new forces" have now emerged as dominant in various countries of Latin America, or that they will shortly. Moreover, the changes outlined are not just surface and ephemeral changes but reach down deeply into society, affect all areas of life, reflect broad historical transformations, and therefore are not easily amenable to reversal, by North American intervention or otherwise. But if such changes are indeed taking place, they call into question at numerous places our traditional definitions of democracy and even the 1960s Andersonian model of the Latin American political *systems* and development processes. If democracy and the democratic ethos are to survive at all in Latin America, they therefore require a considerable overhaul and redefinition.

Latin American Democracy: Toward a Reformulation

Earlier in this book we had not only critiqued the old biased and ethnocentric definitions, criteria, and measures of democracy in Latin America, but had also offered a new formulation based on indigenous, Latin American institutions and understandings. Although perforce incomplete, our list included the following criteria:[10]

1. Acceptance of strong, personalistic, executive and statist leadership, though such leadership cannot exceed the bounds of acceptable authoritarianism and become totalitarian.
2. Some limited institutional checks and balances; a congress and court system cannot defy a president but they should enjoy some independence.
3. Some, again limited, free speech, free press, freedom of assembly, and so on.
4. Some respect for the rights and autonomy of municipal, provincial, and state entities.
5. Respect for the autonomy, in varying degress, of the various corporate groups (or "power contenders" in Anderson's formulation) that are a part of the national systems: universities, trade unions, and the like.
6. Some, once again limited, pluralism and freedom from arbitrary or capricious authority.
7. Some respect for individual rights and individuality; restraint in the use of force; no indiscriminate torture, terror, or killings.
8. Government must be both "representative" and "participatory," but in the Latin American sense of those terms. It must be in some measure *representative* of the various groups in society, and it must allow for *participation* through a network of associations.
9. Government must be beneficent and paternalistic in providing for the needs of its people. It may be the patron, but that also carries a certain obligation to "take care of" its clientele.
10. Government must provide for both economic development and social justice.
11. A government that violates all these requirements deserves to fall; hence in Latin America the right to rebel against unjust authority is sanctioned.
12. Independence from foreign domination and dependence.

These are clearly broad, sometimes ambiguous, often open-ended criteria, amenable to change and new interpretations. They are meant to be. For it is our argument that democracy in Latin America may be not only quite distinct from the Anglo-American variety but may also take a variety of forms, that there is no one single organizational formula, and that Latin American democracy itself is an evolving, changing concept. The indicators we use to measure it must, hence, reflect this diversity and evolution. The criteria suggested here, therefore, provide a broad outline, a general cognitive map, not a set or pat formula.

Given the unacceptability of the older definitions of democracy and our rejection of a set of criteria based on the U.S. model, and building on the path-breaking formulations of Anderson regarding the political realities of the Latin American systems, on the "new forces" outlined above that oblige us to refashion his model somewhat, and on the new conceptualization of democracy offered here devised from Latin American criteria and expectations rather than imported ones, what can be said about the forms and directions that Latin American democracy may take?

Obviously, by the criteria here used, a wide range of forms may be possible. Further, in terms of the reconceptualization offered, these forms, including some rather authoritarian variants, may be quite unlike what North Americans consider to be democratic. To many, after all, democracy and authoritarianism, or democracy and paternalism, or democracy and military rule, or democracy and corporatism, or democracy and elitism, will be seen as contradictory and mutually exclusive principles. By their lights, a system cannot be democratic if it is simultaneously authoritarian, paternalistic, military-dominated, corporatist, or elitist. That is, to my mind, a plausible position to take, although I find it too narrow and restricted to have validity for Latin America. *By those criteria, not a single regime in all of Latin America could be considered democratic.* But there must be something wrong with a definition that dismisses an entire continent with the "undemocratic" blanket condemnation. Hence the utility of reformulating the definition of democracy to accommodate those regimes in Latin America that, by Latin America's own criteria, may be considered democratic.

To test these propositions, an experiment was attempted by this editor to rank-order the Latin American nations according to the criteria of democracy developed here. For purposes of exploring the degree of comparability between the two indices, the same ordering and scoring scheme used in the Fitzgibbon-Johnson indices of democracy in Latin America, which we have here rejected as being too ethnocentric and based on North American criteria, was employed.[11] The difference is that the criteria of democracy elaborated in Chapter 12 and reviewed above have been substituted for the Fitzgibbon-Johnson criteria.

TABLE 14.1

Measuring Democracy in Latin America

	Argentina	Bolivia	Brazil	Chile	Colombia	Costa Rica	Cuba	Dominican Republic	Ecuador	El Salvador	Guatemala	Honduras	Mexico	Nicaragua	Panama	Paraguay	Peru	Uruguay	Venezuela
Leadership: May be authoritarian but not totalitarian	D	C	C	E	B	A	D	B	C	C	C	C	B	D	C	D	C	D	A
Checks & Balances (Institutional): some effectiveness but not necessarily independent	C	D	C	D	B	B	D	C	C	D	D	C	B	E	D	E	D	D	B
Some free speech, press, assembly	D	D	C	D	B	A	D	B	C	D	D	C	B	D	D	D	D	D	B
Respect for rights of local units	C	D	C	D	C	C	D	D	D	D	D	D	C	D	C	D	C	D	C
Autonomy of various corporate groups	C	C	D	E	B	B	D	B	D	D	C	C	B	E	C	E	C	D	B
Limited pluralism, freedom from arbitrary or capricious authority	D	C	C	E	B	A	C	B	C	D	C	C	B	E	C	D	C	D	B
Individual & human rights, restraint in use of force, no terror or torture	D	C	C	E	B	A	C	B	C	D	C	C	B	E	C	E	B	D	B
Gov't. representative & participatory	D	D	C	E	B	B	B	C	D	D	D	D	B	E	C	E	B	D	B
Gov't. beneficent & paternalistic	D	C	D	E	C	B	A	B	D	C	D	C	C	E	D	E	B	D	B
Econ. development & social justice	D	C	C	E	C	B	B	C	C	D	D	C	C	D	C	D	C	D	A
Right to resist	D	B	D	E	B	B	E	C	C	D	C	C	D	D	C	D	C	D	B
Independence from foreign domination	B	C	B	D	B	C	D	D	C	D	D	D	D	D	C	D	C	C	B

287

TABLE 14.2

Composite Scores and Democratic Rank-Ordering
of Latin American Regimes

	Composite Score	Rank Order
Argentina	29	13
Bolivia	33	8
Brazil	34	7
Chile	16	19
Colombia	45	3
Costa Rica	50	1
Cuba	32	10
Dominican Republic	44	4
Ecuador	32	10
El Salvador	27	15
Guatemala	29	13
Honduras	33	8
Mexico	42	5
Nicaragua	19	18
Panama	32	10
Paraguay	20	17
Peru	37	6
Uruguay	25	16
Venezuela	49	2

Placing (on January 27, 1978) an "A" where it was felt a country was very strong with respect to a particular criterion, an "E" where the country was very weak, and using "B," "C," and "D" as intermediate grades on this continuum, a ranking was obtained for each Latin American country (Haiti is here excluded) on each of the criteria used. Substituting a simple ordinal number ranking for the letter grades (A equals 5, B equals 4, C equals 3, D equals 2, E equals 1) and then totaling up the numbers provides us a gross composite "score" for each country and a rank order. By then assigning labels to the various groupings of states within this rank-order scheme (a score of 40 and above was graded "Democratic," 30-40 was considered "Mixed and Marginal," 20-30 was considered "Authoritarian and Dictatorial," and a score of 20 and below meant that a regime was a genuine "Pariah"), we arrived at an interesting classification. The regimes falling into each of these categories were as follows.

> *Democratic:* Costa Rica, Venezuela, Colombia, Dominican Republic, Mexico.
> *Mixed and Marginal:* Peru, Brazil, Bolivia, Honduras, Cuba, Ecuador, Panama.
> *Authoritarian and Dictatorial:* Argentina, Guatemala, El Salvador, Uruguay, Paraguay.
> *Pariah States:* Nicaragua, Chile.

A few comments are in order. Obviously this scheme needs to be fleshed out by a broad survey of Latin Americanists and hence a wider sampling of diverse opinions; it cannot remain just the rank ordering of a "panel" consisting of a single person.[12] The exercise was considered as an experiment only and hardly social-scientific; it would be interesting, however, if the present test of Latin American democracy could be administered to the same panel of experts used in the Fitzgibbon-Johnson experiments. For, one of the interesting results of this experiment was the degree of correspondence that appeared to exist between its rank-ordering and that of the Fitzgibbon-Johnson measure. Some word should also be said concerning the distinct types of regimes that fall into each category and the possibilities for change within and between them. For each of these classifications, after all, the words "more-or-less" need to be applied; additionally, there are often sharp differences between states that fall at the high or low end of a given category; and a regime may move up or down in the scale by loosening its authoritarian grip or, conversely, violating sufficiently the criteria of Latin American democratic legitimacy offered earlier.

A breakdown of the systems here labeled "Democratic" reveals the following subtypes:

1. The more-or-less liberal and democratic, or social-democratic, regimes of Costa Rica and Venezuela. Though elite and bourgeois-directed and though undemocratic in some aspects, these regimes perhaps most completely fulfill the criteria of democracy here elaborated. They also correspond most closely to the U.S. or European pattern and understanding of democracy, though they often include blends of these with some more

traditional Latin America behavior patterns, (e.g., paternalism, *caudilloism*, democracy from above, etc.).
2. The even more strongly elite-directed, albeit more-or-less democratically elected, regimes of Colombia and the Dominican Republic. Though a host of qualifiers needs to be introduced and though in some arenas these regimes must be characterized as undemocratic, they have not yet crossed that barrier where their own peoples find them entirely unacceptable.
3. The single-party, executive-centered system of Mexico. Obviously authoritarian according to much recent scholarship[13] (not a major or very useful criticism since by the criteria used here probably all the Latin American nations fit Juan Linz's "authoritarian" model[14]), and probably enjoying more democratic legitimacy in the past, when its revolution was still fresh, than it does now, the Mexican regime's composite score still places it rather high in our rank order of Latin American democracies.

Probably the most interesting, and perhaps most controversial, category is our listing of the "Mixed and Marginal" regimes, countries that have both some democratic features as well as some strongly authoritarian or autocratic ones. Here we begin to diverge most sharply from the U.S. criteria of democracy. Few (if any) of the regimes listed in this category have independent congresses and judiciaries, regular competitive elections, multiple political parties, or the other institutional paraphernalia of North American democracy. Although "mixed and marginal," they do rank not entirely badly when measured by Latin American criteria of democracy. Implicit also in this category is the notion that the rigid distinction which North Americans usually draw between "democratic" and "authoritarian" regimes may not be very useful when applied to Latin America, that there are many mixed cases which in that context may be quite viable, and that what is needed is not a rigid artificial dichotomy but rather a sense of the dynamic continuum that is Latin American politics.

All these evaluations and conclusions, of course, require far more elaboration than can be provided here. Still, within the "Mixed and Marginal" category there are some interesting cases that by the criteria put forth above are not altogether undemocratic. The category includes the revolutionary military government of Peru and also the military governments of Bolivia, Honduras, Ecuador, and Panama, which, with varying degrees of enthusiasm and success, have somewhat similarly pursued a number of populist, nationalist, and reformist policies. Brazil is also a mixed case: excessively authoritarian by our criteria in some spheres but obviously open to much change, movement and dynamism in others. Cuba is also an interesting, albeit mixed, case. Apologists for the Cuban revolution will doubtless feel it ranks too low on the democratic scale, while foes of the revolutionary government will surely argue it is ranked too high. By the measures developed here, however, Cuba comes out approximately in the middle, tied for tenth among the nineteen nations ranked. Closer examination reveals that while the Cuban regime, which is in many areas modeled after the system of the USSR, scores rather badly in terms of the political measures of democracy here used, it does rather well in those measures of social and economic justice. If one recalls that in Latin America socioeconomic measures of democracy are often considered as important as political criteria, then Cuba's ranking would seem to be justified.

While democracy in Latin America is thus not flourishing, it is by no means dead. By the criteria we have established, there are more democratic regimes than we had thought, and certainly quite a few more than we would find by using exclusively North American criteria. Moreover the range of regimes that may be considered democratic or mixed is wide, from multiparty states, to one-party states, to essentially no-party states. It may include populist (including military-populist) regimes, state capitalist or state socialist regimes, leftist and revolutionary governments as well as conservative and elected governments, and governments dominated by corporatist, liberal, or syndicalist influences and institutions, as well as many combinations of these. Further, there is much ebb and flow of events that offer hope for new democratic openings: the possibility of a more moderate, albeit still likely military, regime in Chile, the bending of the Ecuadorian junta to popular demands, the freer press and political activity in Brazil than had existed before, and so on. The possibilities and prospects for such new openings are both exciting and hopeful; moreover the likelihood of new combinations of various of these formulas—military or civilian-led syndicalist regimes, for example, new variants of social democracy, etatist regimes directing development but also providing new conceptions of community, participation, and freedom—makes Latin America a very dynamic, innovative laboratory of sociopolitical change and experimentation.

Some will object that through these criteria the definition of democracy has been made so loose and watered down that virtually any regime can call itself democratic. I don't agree; I believe that the criteria can be quite specific and that even more precise and quantifiable measures can be developed to gauge Latin American democracy even more accurately. Some will also object that democracy in the West implies some quite specific institutions and processes to which most Latin American regimes (maybe all!) have so far only aspired.

To this argument I object even more strongly. The thrust of the present case is that definitions of democracy are often culture-bound, that the criteria we have previously used to measure Latin American democracy are biased and ethnocentric, that what we call "the West" is in fact only a small part, largely North American and Northwest European, of that geographic-culture area, that these criteria ignore the Southern European and Latin American traditions, and that in this latter culture area there are definitions of democracy that may be as valid as our own. It is toward the analysis, evaluation, reformulation, and reassessment of democracy in Latin America, based on its own indigenous understandings and political practices rather than the often inappropriate foreign ones, that this discussion is dedicated.

The words of Frank Tannenbaum, articulate Latin Americanist, dedicated social democrat, and lifelong friend of Harry Kantor with whom he shared major views, are worth pondering:[15]

> Contemporary Latin American political difficulties cannot be divorced from their historic past. The Spanish tradition is authoritarian, bureaucratic, and centralized.
>
> Clearly we are talking about a cultural pattern, a set of values that is best absorbed with other things one learns at a mother's knee if they are to be a functional and truly integrated part of the political process. It is doubtful whether a formula derived from either English or American experience can be used for satisfactory analysis of, not to speak of policy making in, Latin America.
>
> One must begin by recognizing that, in spite of appearances, Latin America is not like Europe and in many ways unlike the United States. The question really is, can a pattern of political behavior be transmitted from one culture to another. How effectively can it be done? How long does it take? This, after all, is the question that must be asked if we insist on having (U.S.-style) democratic governments in the area. How many Latin Americans believe in majority rule, in a government under law? How many believe that the law ought to be impartial, equal for all men regardless of family, friends, or special cliques? The answer is that the majority do not. The political phenomenon we are dealing with is not describable in terms of European democratic political theory or United State practice.
>
> The electoral mechanism is not sufficiently flexible for the uninhibited consultation of the new decision-making instrumentalities. But that is not the same thing as saying that these groups do not exist, or that they have no effect upon public policy. Many more interest groups have to be consulted

or satisfied than previously. The decision-making processes have spread downward into thousands of small and large groups. The base upon which the government rests has been broadened. (By these criteria) the political changes that have taken place in Latin America *are in the direction of democracy.*

Notes

1. See Chapter 12.
2. (Chapel Hill: University of North Carolina Press, 1934).
3. The general literature to which we refer is Almond and James Coleman (eds.), *The Politics of the Developing Areas* (Princeton: Princeton University Press, 1960); Lipset, *Political Man* (New York: Doubleday-Anchor, 1963); Rostow, *The Stages of Economic Growth* (Cambridge: Cambridge University Press, 1960); and Deutsch, "Social Mobilization and Political Development," *American Political Science Review,* 55 (September 1961), 493-514. Blanksten contributed the chapter on Latin America for the original Almond and Coleman volume cited above; Scott was included in subsequent volumes in the SSRC series dealing with "Political Culture" and "Political Parties"; Needler pursued a parallel argument in *Political Development in Latin America* (New York: Random, 1968). The values and biases of this literature are examined in Robert A. Packenham, *Liberal America and the Third World: Political Development Ideas in Foreign Aid and Social Science* (Princeton: Princeton University Press, 1976).
4. See Chapter 1.
5. Especially Chapter 4 of his *Politics and Economic Change in Latin America* (Princeton: D. Van Nostrand, 1967); reprinted in, among others, Howard J. Wiarda (ed.), *Politics and Social Change in Latin America* (Amherst: University of Massachusetts Press, 1974).
6. A more extended though earlier discussion, with relevance to a specific case, is Howard J. Wiarda, *Transcending Corporatism? The Portuguese Corporative System and the Revolution of 1974* (Columbia, S. C.: Institute of International Studies, University of South Carolina, 1976), esp. 5-13 and 46-59.
7. See Kalman H. Silvert's still-classic statement in *The Conflict Society: Reaction and Revolution in Latin America* (New York: American Universities Field Staff, 1966).
8. *Supra* n. 5. In a recent survey Anderson's was the most widely accepted of all the studies used in Latin American politics courses; see Henry C. Kenski, "Teaching Latin American Politics at American Universities: A Survey," *Latin American Research Review,* 10 (Spring 1975), 89-104.
9. The list and categories here developed are perforce somewhat arbitrary and impressionistic, though informed by much reading about and travel within the area. While some would doubtless quarrel with some or several of these "impressions," or wish to add categories of their own, other scholars would surely find

much here with which they would agree. An earlier formulation is Howard J. Wiarda, "Can We Learn to Live with a Socialist World? Foreign Policy Implications Stemming from the Portuguese Revolution and Other 'New Forces'." Paper presented at a conference on "Spain and Portugal: The Politics of Economics and Defense," Institute for the Study of Conflict, London, May 29-31, 1975.

10. See Chapter 12 for the full discussion.

11. The scoring system is elaborated in the instructions provided each of the panelists in this quinquennial survey and in the published works reporting the results; see n. 3, Chapter 12. The limitations and flaws in this kind of scoring scheme must also be recognized.

12. Although one person cannot presume to have the detailed knowledge of all the Latin American countries sufficient to speak more than modestly about the validity of this ranking scheme, it might be said the evaluation was informed by a concurrent close reading and editing of chapters on the political systems of all the Latin American countries done by some of the foremost experts in the field; these are collected in Howard J. Wiarda and Harvey F. Kline (eds.), *Latin American Politics and Development* (Boston: Houghton-Mifflin, 1979).

13. Susan Kaufman Purcell, *The Mexican Profit-Sharing Decision: Politics in an Authoritarian Regime* (Berkeley: University of California Press, 1975); Evelyn P. Stevens, *Protest and Response in Mexico* (Cambridge, Mass.: MIT Press, 1974); and José Luis Reyna and Richard S. Weinert (eds.) *Authoritarianism in Mexico* (Philadelphia: Institute for the Study of Human Issues, 1977).

14. Linz "An Authoritarian Regime: Spain." in E. Allardt and Y. Littunen (eds.), *Cleavages, Ideologies and Party Systems* (Helsinki: Academic Bookstore, 1964).

15. *The Future of Democracy in Latin America* (New York: Knopf, 1974). Based on quotations from pp. 68, 73, 85, 117, 207-8.

A Selected Bibliography

The bibliography that follows is not intended as a complete listing of the works on Latin American politics and society. Rather, it is limited to those studies that stress the theme of Latin American democracy, or that suggest alternative approaches and conceptions.

Alexander, Robert, and Charles O. Porter. *The Struggle for Democracy in Latin America* (New York: MacMillan, 1961).
Anderson, Charles W. *Politics and Economic Change in Latin America: The Governing of Restless Nations* (Princeton: Van Nostrand, 1967).
Blachman, Morris, and Ronald Hellman, eds. *Terms of Conflict: Ideology in Latin American Politics* (Philadelphia, Institute for the Study of Human Issues, 1977).
Blasier, Cole, ed. *Constructive Change in Latin America* (Pittsburgh: University of Pittsburgh Press, 1951).
Christensen, Asher N., ed. *The Evolution of Latin American Government* (New York: Holt, Rinehart and Winston, 1951).
Dealy, Glen Caudill. *The Public Man: An Interpretation of Latin America and Other Catholic Countries* (Amherst: University of Massachusetts Press, 1977).
Einaudi, Luigi, ed. *Beyond Cuba: Latin America Takes Charge of Its Future* (New York: Crane, Russak, 1974).
Fitzgibbon, Russell H. "The Pathology of Democracy in Latin America: A Political Scientist's Point of View." *American Political Science Review* 44 (March 1950). Four articles in this *APSR* were devoted to the theme of "the pathology of democracy in Latin America."
―――. "A Statistical Evaluation of Latin American Democracy." *Western Political Quarterly* 9 (September 1956):607-19.

Fitzgibbon, Russell H. and Kenneth F. Johnson. "Measuring Democratic Change in Latin America." *Journal of Politics* 29 (February 1967):129-66.
González Casanova, Pablo. *Democracy in Mexico* (New York: Oxford University Press, 1970).
Hamill, Hugh M., ed. *Dictatorship in Latin America* (New York: Knopf, 1964).
Jane, L. Cecil. *Liberty and Despotism in Spanish America* (New York: Cooper Square, 1966).
Johnson, Kenneth F. "Measuring the Scholarly Image of Latin American Democracy, 1945-1970," *Statistical Abstract of Latin America* 17 (Los Angeles: UCLA Latin American Center, 1976).
———. "Scholarly Images of Latin American Political Democracy in 1975." *Latin American Research Review* 11 (Summer 1976): 127-38.
Kantor, Harry. *The Costa Rican Election of 1953: A Case Study* (Gainesville: University of Florida Press, 1958).
———. *Patterns of Politics and Political Systems of Latin America* (Chicago: Rand McNally, 1969).
———. *The Program and Ideology of the Peruvian Aprista Movement* (Berkeley: University of California Press, 1953).
Malloy, James, ed. *Authoritarianism and Corporatism in Latin America* (Pittsburgh: University of Pittsburgh Press 1977).
Mander, John. *The Unrevolutionary Society: The Power of Latin American Conservatism in a Changing World* (New York: Knopf, 1970).
Martz, John D. and Miguel Jorrín. *Latin American Political Thought and Ideology* (Chapel Hill: University of North Carolina Press, 1970).
Packenham, Robert A. *Liberal America and the Third World: Political Development Ideas in Foreign Aid and Social Science* (Princeton: Princeton University Press, 1976).
Pike, Fredrick and Thomas Stritch, eds. *The New Corporatism: Social and Political Structures in the Iberian World* (Notre Dame: University of Notre Dame Press, 1974).
Schmitt, Karl and David Burks. *Evolution or Chaos: Dynamics of Latin American Government and Politics* (New York: Praeger, 1963).
Silvert, Kalman. *The Conflict Society: Reaction and Revolution in Latin America* (New Orleans: Hauser Press, 1961).
Tannenbaum, Frank. *The Future of Democracy in Latin America* (New York: Knopf, 1974).
Veliz, Claudio. *The Politics of Conformity in Latin America* (New York: Oxford University Press, 1967).

Wiarda, Howard J., ed. *Politics and Social Change in Latin America: The Distinct Tradition* (Amherst: University of Massachusetts Press, 1974).
Wiarda, Howard J. and Harvey F. Kline. *Latin American Politics and Development* (Boston: Houghton-Mifflin, 1979).
Willems, Emilio, *Latin American Culture* (New York: Harper and Row, 1975).
Zea, Leopoldo. *The Latin American Mind* (Norman: University of Oklahoma Press, 1963).

About the Contributors

General Editor

Howard J. Wiarda is professor of political science and chairman of the Program in Latin American Studies at the University of Massachusetts. During 1979-80 he was a Fellow at the Center for International Affairs, Harvard University. He is the author of numerous scholarly articles, and his books include *Dictatorship and Development; The Dominican Republic: Nation in Transition; The Brazilian Catholic Labor Movement; Dictatorship, Development and Disintegration: Politics and Social Change in the Dominican Republic; Corporatism and Development: The Portuguese Experience; Politics and Social Change in Latin America: The Distinct Tradition;* and *Latin American Politics and Development*. His present research focuses on the political theory of Iberia and Latin America, state-society relations in Latin America, and the labor and industrial relations systems of southern Europe.

Coauthors

Lee C. Fennell is professor of political science at the University of the Pacific, where he served as chairman of the department for three years before being appointed dean of institutional research and university registrar in 1978. In the field of Latin American politics, his areas of primary research interest are political culture, political parties and elections, and legislative behavior.

William L. Furlong is associate professor of political science, Utah State University, Logan, Utah. He has published articles on municipal administration, political development, and international affairs in Latin America. He has spent extensive time in Argentina, Peru, and Mexico and is now consulting on a rural development project in Bolivia. He is currently doing research on the Panama Canal treaties.

Lawrence S. Graham is professor of government and associate director of the Institute of Latin American Studies, University of Texas at

Austin. He has worked and conducted research in Brazil (1964-65), Peru (1967-68 as a public administration advisor with the Institute of Public Administration, New York), Mexico (summers of 1966 and 1969), Portugal (1971 and the summers of 1972 and 1975), and Romania (1977-78, under the auspices of the National Academy of Sciences). Among his publications are *Civil Service Reform in Brazil* (1968), *Development Administration in Latin America*, ed. with Clarence E. Thurber (1973), and *Contemporary Portugal*, ed. with Harry M. Makler (1979). His present research interests focus on politics and bureaucracy in Latin America and southern Europe.

Jack W. Hopkins is currently professor of public and environmental affairs at Indiana University, where he is director of public affairs graduate programs and director, International Program. He is the author of *The Government Executive of Peru* and *Latin America in World Affairs*. He has taught at Georgia Institute of Technology, Georgia State College, Emory University, The American University, Texas Tech University, and the Universidad Nacional de Cuyo (Argentina). His present research interests are developmental administration and public administration.

Michael J. Kryzanek is assistant professor of political science at Bridgewater State College. He has written extensively on opposition politics in Latin America, with special emphasis on the political situation in the Dominican Republic. His research has been published in the *Journal of Latin American Studies, Caribbean Studies*, and *Revista/Review Inter-Americana*.

Paul H. Lewis has taught political science at Tulane University, in New Orleans, since 1967. He received his bachelor's degree in 1960 from the University of Florida, where he studied under Harry Kantor, and his doctorate at the University of North Carolina in 1965. He is the author of *The Politics of Exile* (1968), a study of Paraguay's *Febrista* party, and of *The Governments of Argentina, Brazil, and Mexico* (1975).

Anthony P. Maingot was born in Trinidad, West Indies. He received his doctorate from the University of Florida in 1967. He taught at Yale from 1966 to 1972 and was director of the Antilles Research Program there. From 1972 to 1974 he was professor of international relations, University of the West Indies, St. Augustine, Trinidad. He is presently professor of sociology and chairman of the Department of Sociology/Anthropology at Florida International University in Miami, Florida. His recent publications and research interests deal with ideology, ethnic, and class relations in the process of development.

Ronald C. Newton is a professor of history at Simon Fraser University, Burnaby, British Columbia. He has published articles on the politics of the University of Buenos Aires and, in the *Hispanic American Historical Review*, on Spanish American corporatism. His book on immigrant communities in Buenos Aires, *German Buenos Aires, 1900-1933*, was published in 1977 by the University of Texas Press, and he is presently completing a book on the Third Reich, Argentina, and the German-Argentines, 1933-1955.

Neale J. Pearson is an associate professor of political science at Texas Tech University. His major publications include articles on peasant unionism in Guatemala, Brazil, Honduras, and Latin America. He is an annual contributor on Chile and Peru to the *Annual Yearbook* of the *Encyclopedia Americana*.

Iêda Siqueira Wiarda is a post-doctoral research associate in the Political Science Department, University of Massachusetts, and a consultant on population policy to various agencies. She has worked on issues of politics and population policy since 1970 under grants supported by the National Institutes of Health and is presently the recipient of a combined grant from the Ford and Rockefeller Foundations to work on the project, "Women's Participation in Development: Influentials and Groups in the Diffusion of Family Planning in Brazil." She is the author of numerous articles and reviews and a monograph on the Venezuelan Family Planning Program, and is coauthor of the forthcoming *Brazil: Nationalism, Development, and the Politics of Population Policy*.

Index

Abortion. *See* Family planning
Acción Democrática. See Democratic Action Party
Acción Popular (Peru), 186, 266
AD. *See* Democratic Action Party
Adams, John Quincy, 5
Agency for International Development (AID), 12, 16, 114, 124, 178, 179
Agor, Weston H., 152
Agrarian Reform Law (1975) (Honduras), 100
Agrupación de Trabajadores Latino Americanos Sindicalizados (ATLAS), 85
Alba, Victor, 84, 103-104, 196, 219
Alessandri, Jorge, 209-210
Alexander, Robert J., 84-85, 100, 218
Allende, Salvador, 92, 152, 156, 179, 209-211
Alliance for Progress, 5, 6, 167-183, 278
  charter, 170
All-Trinidad Sugar Estates and Factory Workers' Trade Union, 220
Almond, Gabriel A., 11, 13, 59, 278
Alternidad, 133-134
Alvear, Marcelo T. de, 208
American Declaration of the Rights and Duties of Man, 232
American Federation of Labor, 84
American Federation of Labor-Congress of Industrial Organization (AFL-CIO), 86, 99
American Institute for Free Labor Development (AIFLD), 86, 87, 99
American Political Science Association, 63

American Political Science Review, 10
American Voter, The (Cambell), 27
ANACH. *See* National Association of Honduran Peasants
Anderson, Charles W., 31, 54, 148, 151, 161, 195
  Andersonian school of thought, 279-282: qualified, 282-284
APRA. *See* Apristas
Apristas, 9, 71, 74, 80, 92, 100, 102, 130-131, 157, 182, 186, 195, 260, 261, 266
Arbenz Guzman, Jacobo, 98
Araujo Salles, Dom Eugenio de, 82
Argentina, 3, 61
  Alliance for Progress aid, 178
  authoritarian-technocratic regime in, 20, 156, 256
  critical realignment in, 53-54
  democracy in, 206-209
  labor movement in, 79, 82, 83, 84-85, 87, 92, 100
  oligarchy in, 52, 74
  political parties in, 149
  populism in, 72, 75
  relations with U.S., 15
Ariel (Rodó), 173
Armed militia, 92
Astiz, Carlos A., 149
Autarky, 190
Authoritarian-military regimes. *See* Corporate-authoritarian governments; Latin America, military regimes
Avineri, Shlomo, 228
Azules, 44

Baker, Ross K., 156

Balaguer, Joaquin, 130, 178
Baliño, Carlos, 218
Banana Workers of the North Coast Federation of Workers (Honduras), 93
Barracks revolt. *See Cuartelazo*
Barrientos, Rene, 75
Basic Education Movement (MEB), 83
Batista, Fulgencio, 75, 85, 168
Batlle y Ordóñez, José, 73
Batllismo, 73
Beck, Carl, 150-151
Belaúnde Terry, Fernando, 151, 152, 156, 186, 195
BEMFAM. *See* Sociedade Civil Bem-Estar Familiar no Brasil
Benavides, Oscar, 75
Bendix, Reinhard, 11
Betancourt, Rómulo, 71, 90, 157, 185, 195, 267
Black, C. E., 59
Black legend, 5
Blancos, 73
Blanksten, George, 278
Bogotá Conference (1948), 232
Bolívar, Simón, 6, 14
Bolivia
  Alliance for Progress aid, 178, 180
  caudilloism in, 6
  critical realignment in, 54, 60
  political system in, 32, 290
  populism in, 74, 75, 261
  trade unionism in, 90, 92
Bonilla, Frank, 160, 161
Borges da Costa, Letitia, 113
Bosch, Juan, 71, 130, 157, 178
Boulart, João, 179
Brazil, 3, 59
  Alliance for Progress aid, 178
  authoritarian-technocratic regime in, 20, 156, 243, 257-258, 290-291
  Communist Party in, 83
  constitution of, 117-118
  development in, 189
  divorce law in, 108-109
  family planning in, 111, 112-113, 118-119
  oligarchy in, 52, 74
  populism in, 72, 75
  relations with U.S., 15, 17, 179
  trade unionism in, 82, 87, 91, 92: population and, 96-97 (tables); salaries, 95 (table)
Brazilian Labor Party (PTB), 91, 266
Brazilian Socialist Party (PSB), 91
Brazilian War College (*Escola Superior da Guerra*), 258
British Empire Workers and Citizens Home Rule Party, 221
British Labour Party, 220, 225
British Trade Union Congress, International Department of the, 221
Brizola, Leonel, 91
Browder, Earl, 219
Bryan, William Jennings, 8
Burnham, Walter Dean, 29, 30
Busch, Germán, 75
Bustamante, Alexander, 224, 225
Butler, Uriah, 221

Caciques, 189
Caldera, Rafael, 136, 137, 149
Calderon, Rafael, 136
Campesino, 99, 151, 159
Campos, Roberto, 198
Carazo, Rodrigo, 137
Cárdenas, Lázaro, 75, 84, 91
Cardoso, Fernando H., 158
Carter, Jimmy, 8-9, 15
Castro, Fidel, 15, 34, 75, 85, 154, 167, 186
Caudilloism, 9, 10, 11, 43, 44, 50, 52, 55, 61, 71, 99, 171-172, 174, 202, 241
CCT. *See* Costa Rican Labor Confederation
CCV. *See* Peasant Confederation of Venezuela
Censorship. *See* Freedom of the press
Central American Common Market, 99
Central Intelligence Agency (CIA), 17, 63, 196
Central Organization of Workers of the Peruvian Revolution (CTRP), 92
Central Unica de Trabajadores de Chile, 85
Cesare, Aime, 224
CGT. *See Confederación General del Trabajo*; General Confederation of Workers
CGTP. *See* General Confederation of

Index

Workers of Peru
Chile, 3, 61
   Alliance for Progress aid, 178
   authoritarian-technocratic regime in, 20, 59, 156, 201, 259-261
   critical realignment in, 53, 54
   democracy in, 209-211, 291
   family planning in, 110
   oligarchy in, 52, 74
   political parties in, 135, 182, 186
   populism in, 72, 75
   relations with U.S., 15, 17, 179
   revolution in, 61
   socialists in, 84
   trade union movement in, 74, 79, 82, 83, 85, 90, 92
Chilean Labor Confederation (CTCh), 84
Christenson, Asher, 277
Christian Democratic Party (COPEI) (Venezuela), 136, 267, 268
Christian Democrats, 79, 195
   Chilean, 135, 137, 152, 186, 209, 210
Christian Social Action, 99
Church and State in Latin American (Mecham), 277
Cipriani, Andrew, 220-221
Círculos Operários. See Workers Circles
CIT. *See* Inter-American Confederation of Workers
Clarke, William Alexander. *See* Bustamante, Alexander
CLASC. *See* Latin American Confederation of Christian Syndicalists
CLAT. *See* Latin American Central of Workers
Clay, Henry, 5
CNA. *See* National Confederation of Agricultural Workers
CNC. *See* National Peasant Confederation
CNT. *See* National Worker's Confederation
Cochrane, James D., 152
Colombia, 3, 61
   Alliance for Progress aid, 178, 180
   economic and social programs, 180
   oligarchy in, 75
   political parties in, 131, 133-134, 182, 187

   political system in, 261-262, 290
   trade unionism in, 82, 85, 92, 99
Colombian Labor Confederation (CTC), 84
Colorado Party (Uruguay), 73, 135
Comité Chileno de Protección de la Familia, 110
Committee on Comparative politics, 13
Communism, 79, 82, 84-85, 175-177. *See also* Marx, Karl; Trotskyites
Communist Party
   Cuban, 218-220, 259
   French, 224
   Mexican, 132
Compromisos, 36
Confederación Costarricense de Trabajo Rerum Novarum, 85
Confederación General del Trabajo (CGT) (Argentina), 85
Confederación Nacional Obrera (Cuba), 219
Confederación Regional Obrera Mexicana (CROM), 85
Confederation of Peasant Workers (CTC) (Bolivia), 90
Confederations, 79
Conscientização, 83
Conservaties (Colombia), 133, 134
Conservative Unionists (Argentina), 149
CONTAG. *See* National Confederation of Agricultural Workers
Continuismo, 10
Contraceptive methods. *See* Family planning
Cooperatives, 79, 95
COPEI. *See* Christian Democratic Party
Corporate-authoritarian governments, 3, 4, 173, 176, 202, 276, 289
   exclusionary politics of, 275
Corporate group rights. *See Fueros*
Costa e Silva, Arthur da, 261
Costa Rica, 3
   Alliance for Progress aid, 178
   critical realignment in, 53
   political parties in, 136-137, 181-182, 187
   populism in, 75
   trade unionism in, 85, 92, 99
Costa Rican Demographic Association, 111

Costa Rican Labor Confederation (CCT), 84
Credit unions, 99
Criollo aristocracy, 49-50, 55, 283
Cripps, Sir Stafford, 225
Critical elections concept, 27-30, 38, 61-62. *See also* Latin America, coups d'etat in, elections in
Critical realignments, 35, 41, 43-44, 47-55, 56-58 (table), 59
CSLA. *See* Latin American Syndical Confederation
CTAL. *See* Latin American Workers Confederation
CTC. *See* Colombian Labor Confederation; Confederation of Peasant Workers; Cuban Confederation of Workers
CTCh. *See* Chilean Labor Confederation
CTM. *See* Mexican Workers Confederation
CTP. *See* Peruvian labor Confederaton; Peruvian Workers Confederation
CTRP. *See* Central Organization of Workers of the Peruvian Revolution
CTV. *See* Venezuelan Labor Confederation
Cuartelazo, 35
Cuba, 8, 37
  Communist Party in, 218-220, 259
  critical realignment in, 60
  labor unions in, 219
  Negro problem in, 219
  political system in, 32, 291
  populism in, 74, 75
  socialist party in, 218-220
Cuban Confederation of Workers (CTC), 85
Cultural imperialism, 15, 18
Cultural lag, 155
Cultural relativism, 15, 20-21
Cutwright, Phillips, 59
Cyclical theory, 275

Dahl, Robert, 207
Davis, Harold, 277
Dealy, Glen, 19
Dean, Warren, 39, 41
Delgado Chalbaud, Lt. Col., 267
del Pino, José, 103
Democracy, 3-7

assumptions about, 203-205, 231-241
differences between Iberic-Latin and American, 232-241
and elites, 147-161
and family planning, 123-125
Latin American, 241-250, 285-293
Lockean, 5, 11, 19, 29, 173, 233, 280
measurement of, 287 (table), 288-289
"Pathology of Democracy in Latin America," 10, 17, 20, 277-278
political, 19
right of rebellion in, 246-247
social and economic, 19
struggle for, 7-14, 15-16, 18-21, 201, 231-232
and trade unionism, 102-104, 282
U.S. model for, 10, 12, 14, 17, 62, 283
Democratic Action Party (AD) (Venezuela), 71, 90, 136, 137, 157, 160, 187, 195, 266, 267-268
Democratic Labour Party (DLP) (Trinidad), 222
Democratic Left, 79, 82, 185-188, 194
deOnis, Juan, 179
Dependencia, 175, 217-218, 226, 228
Derechos. *See Fueros*; Human rights
Deutsch, Karl, 11, 59, 62, 278
Developmentalist school, 278-279
Development literature, 12, 16
Development models, 13-14, 188-192, 246
Díaz, Gustavo, 91
Divorce, 108-109
Dominican Republic, 8
  Alliance for Progress aid, 178
  caudillos, 52, 61, 295
  divorce in, 109
  electoral statistics, 43-47
  family planning in, 114
  political party in. *See* Dominican Revolutionary Party
  populism in, 74, 75
  relations with U.S., 17
  revolution in, 61
Dominican Revolutionary Party (PRD), 130, 141

Eaton, George, 225
Echeverria Alvarez, Luis, 91
Economic Commission for Latin America, 193
Economic imperialism, 18

Index

Ecuador
  caudilloism in, 61
  critical realignment in, 54
  military rule in, 261
  political system in, 290, 291
  populism in, 75
  relations with U.S., 17
Edelman, Alexander, 277
Education. *See* Honduras; Trade unionism; Venezuela
Elections. *See* Critical elections; Latin America, elections in
Elitism, 3, 10, 19, 37, 43, 44, 52, 53, 74, 122
  accommodation in, 154
  and development, 152-153
  and leadership, 205, 280
  typology of, 151
  See also Democracy, and elites
El Salvador, 15, 75, 98, 99-100
Emerging Republican Majority, The (Phillips), 27
Estado Novo, 263
Estancia. See Hacienda

Family planning, 108, 109-125
Fanon, Frantz, 224
Fatalism, 172-173, 202
Federación Obrera de la Habana (Cuba), 219
Federación Obrera Regional (FORA) (Argentina), 83
Federation of Agrarian Reform Cooperatives (FECORAH) (Honduras), 99
Figueres, José, 71, 157, 195, 266
Finer, S. E., 156
First International. *See* International Workingmen's Association
Fitzgibbon, Russell H., 11, 171, 233-234, 241, 277, 286
FORA. *See* Federación Obrera Regional
Ford, James W., 219
Foster, William Z., 219
Franco, Jean, 6
Freedom of the press, 174, 234
Frei, Eduardo, 152, 179, 186, 195
Freire, Paulo, 83
Frondizi, Arturo, 185, 186
FUC. *See* United Peasant Front
Fueros, 234, 235, 241, 242, 243-244, 248, 249
Fuerzas vivas. See Fueros

Gaitán, Jorge, 75
Galileia Plantation, 91
Geisel, Ernesto, 248
General Confederation of Workers (CGT) (Honduras), 102
General Confederaton of Workers of Peru (CGTP), 92
Generation of '28, 157
German Christian Foundation, 86
Gollancz's Left Book Club, 225
Golpe de estado, 35-36, 39, 90, 102
Gómez, Juan Vicente, 157
Gomez, Rosendo, 277
González, Celeo, 99
Gordon, Lincoln, 177
Goulart, João, 83, 102, 156, 185, 235
Greenstein, Fred I., 212
Grito, 36, 52
Grove, Marmaduke, 74
Grunwald, Joseph, 195
Guatemala, 61, 98
  critical realignment in, 53
  political parties in, 186
  populism in, 74, 75
  relations with U.S., 17
  revolution in, 61
  trade unionism in, 186
Guerrilla struggle, 36, 91
Guyana, 92, 93, 223
Guzmán, Antonio, 130, 141

Hacendados, 52
Hacienda, 93, 246
Haiti, 8, 49, 75, 85, 179
Hand-to-hand struggle. *See Machetismo*
Haya de la Torre, Víctor Raúl, 71, 82, 131, 157, 267
Hegel, Georg W. Friedrich, 5, 6
Herrera, Felipe, 169
Hispanic, 64
History-as-failure, 6, 16
Holt, Pat, 177, 182
Honduras, 75
  caudilloism in, 61
  credit unions in, 99
  critical realignment in, 54
  education in, 98 (table), 99
  land pressure in, 98
  political system in, 290
  relations with U.S., 17

rural population of, 98
trade unionism in, 83, 90, 92, 93, 102
Human rights, 3, 9, 15, 141, 232-250
Huntington, Samuel P., 11

Ibáñez, Carlos, 71, 74
Iberia. *See* Portugal; Spain
Illia, Arturo, 156
Imaz, José Luis de, 148, 152
INA. *See* National Agrarian Institute
Indians. *See* Latin America, Indian subculture in
Inter-American Confederation of Workers (CIT), 84, 85
Inter-American Conference on the Problems of War and Peace (1945), 232
Inter-American Press Association, 174
Inter-American Regional Organization of Workers (ORIT), 80, 84-85, 86, 87, 99, 103
Intereses creados. See Fueros
International Confederation of Free Trade Unions (ICFTU), 84, 85, 86
International Labor Organization, 100
International Petroleum Company, 151
International Planned Parenthood Federation (IPPF), 110, 111, 113, 114, 115
International Solidarity, 86
International Workingmen's Association (IWMA), 83
Intransigent Radical Civic Union (Argentina), 149

Jagan, Cheddi, 223-224
Jamaica, 92, 224-226
Jamaican Labour Party (JLP), 225
James, C.L.R., 222
Jauregui, Arturo, 80
Johnson, John J., 173
Johnson, Kenneth, 171, 179, 286-289
Johnson, Lyndon, 8
Jorrin, Miguel, 277
Joseph, Eugene, 222
Juan Carlos (king of Spain), 248
Julião de Arruda Paula, Francisco, 83, 91
Justo, Agustín Pedro, 75
Juventud Agraria Católica (JAC), 82
Juventud Obrera Católica (JOC), 82
Juventud Universitaria Católica (JUC), 82

Kantor, Harry, 181, 268, 292
Kelshall, John, 222
Kennedy, John F., 5, 6, 15, 169
Key, V. O., 27, 28-29, 61
Kling, Merle, 36-37, 151
Krieger Vasena, Adalberto, 198
Kubitschek, Juscelino, 169

Labor and Socialist International, 220
Labor movements, 79. *See also* Trade unionism
Labor Party (Brazil), 185
LaBrea oil field, 151
Landless Workers Union. *See Movimento dos Agricultores sem Terra*
Landownership, 79, 91-92, 156, 193, 210-211
Landsberger, Henry A., 94, 160
LaPalombara, Joseph, 205
Latifundia. See Landownership
Latin America
  agricultural production in, 193
  authoritarian governments. *See* Corporate-authoritarian governments
  Catholic Church in, 9, 98-99, 159, 238, 244
  Catholic political culture in, 5, 10. *See also* Roman Catholic activists
  civil-military relations in, 237-238
  coups d'etat in, 28, 35-41, 42 (chart), 63, 151. *See also* Critical realignments
  cultural traits of, 170-177, 292-293
  democratic regimes in, 3, 289
  distribution of wealth in, 194, 283
  elections in, 32, 34-35, 235-236
  ethnocentrism about, 6, 8, 13, 14-15, 38
  exports, 53, 193-194, 283
  imports, 3, 284:
    and incidence of coups, 42 (chart)
  independence from Spain and Portugal, 49
  Indian subculture in, 9
  industrial growth, 190-192
  labor codes, 100, 102
  labor movement in, 17. *See also* Trade unionism
  land title systems, 17
  military regimes, 3, 21n1, n2, 6, 19, 142, 186, 255-257, 276

Index

mixed and marginal regimes, 289, 290
pariah regimes, 289
periodicity in, 55-59, 62
political parties in, 127-143, 181, 236
political systems in, 31-32, 33 (chart), 34, 236-237, 238-241, 245-246, 280-282, 284
population, 79: and per capita income, 81 (table)
populism, 71-76, 246, 262-263, 264-266: and *inclusionary* politics, 275
public funds, 237
realities of, 282-284
relations with U.S., 52-53
republics of, 3
revolutionary concept in, 32, 35, 36, 37, 47, 59
voting age population, 44 (table)
women in, 107-125
See also individual countries
Latin American Central of Workers (CLAT), 80, 86, 87
Latin American Confederation of Christian Syndicalists (CLASC), 80, 85, 86, 87
Latin American Studies Association, 9
Latin American Syndical Confederation (CSLA), 83
Latin American Workers Confederation (CTAL), 82, 83-84, 85, 86
Lebret, L. J., 82
Leo XIII, 82
Levingston, Roberto, 256
Levinson, Jerome, 179
Liberación Nacional (Costa Rica), 266
Liberal Party (Colombia), 133, 134, 187
Lieuwen, Edwin, 39, 156
Ligas, 79
Ligas Camponesas (Brazil), 83, 91
Linz, Juan, 290
Lipset, Seymour M., 11, 59, 62, 148, 173, 278
Lleras Camargo, Alberto, 185, 196
Locke, John. *See* Democracy, Lockean
Lombardo Toledano, Vicente, 84
López Mateos, Adolfo, 185
López Portillo, José, 132
Luso-Hispanic tradition, 64, 234

MacDonald, Austin, 277

Machetismo, 35
McLelland, Andrew, 99
MacRae, Duncan, Jr., 27, 29
Maharaj, Stephen, 222
Maldonado, Mario, 99
Malloy, James, 150-151
Manchester Liberalism, 82
Manifest destiny, 5, 8
Manifesto of the Communist Party (1848), 226
Manley, Michael, 226
Manley, Norman, 224, 225
Manpower Citizens Association (MPCA), 93
Maritain, Jacques, 82
Marx, Karl, 5, 228
Marxism, 19, 59, 149, 175, 283
Marxists-Leninists, 186, 196, 221, 222, 223, 224, 259, 263-264
Maspero, Emilio, 80, 86
MASTER. *See Movimento dos Agricultores sem Terra*
Mater et Magistra, 159
MEB. *See* Basic Education Movement
Mechan, J. Lloyd, 277
Meldrum, James A., 27, 29
Melgar Castro, Chief of State; 99-100
Mella, Julio Antonio, 218
Méndez Montenegro, Júlio César, 186
Mendoza, Ofelia, 110
Mexican Workers Confederation (CTM), 84, 103
Mexico, 5, 8, 37, 61
  Alliance for Progress aid, 178
  authoritarian-technocratic regime in, 20, 52
  critical realignment in, 54
  labor movement in, 79, 84, 90, 91, 92, 99
  political parties in, 131-133, 154
  political system, in, 32, 290
  populism in, 75
  relations with U.S., 179
  revolution in, 53, 60
Middle class, 202
  values, 173-174
Mills, C. Wright, 76
Minifundio, 193
Minor, Robert, 219
MNR. *See* National Revolutionary Movement

Modernization, 12, 55, 76. *See also* Development models
Monetarism, 197
Monroe Doctrine, 5
Morales Bermúdez, Francisco, 92, 260, 261
Morse, Richard M., 5
Mounier, Emmanuel, 82
Movimento dos Agricultores sem Terra (MASTER) (Brazil), 91
Movimiento de Organización Venezolana (ORVE), 267
Movimiento Justicialista (Argentina), 262, 263
Multinational firms, 93
Múñoz Marin, Luis, 71
Myth of democratic incapacity, 9

National Action (PAN) (Mexico), 132
National Agrarian Institute (INA) (Honduras), 99, 100
National Confederation of Agricultural Workers (CNA) (Peru), 92, 103
National Confederation of Agricultural Workers (CONTAG) (Brazil), 83
National Front (Colombia), 133, 134, 180, 182
National Liberation Party (Costa Rica), 187
National Movement for the True Independence of Trinago (NAMOTI) (Trinidad), 223
National party (Uruguay), 135
National Peasant Confederation (CNC) (Mexico), 91
National Peasant Union (UNC) (Honduras), 99, 100, 102
National Revolutionary Movement (MNR) (Bolivia), 90
National Worker's Confederation (CNT) (Peru), 92
Needler, Martin, C., 62, 156, 278
Nettleford, Rex, 224, 225
Nicaragua, 8, 64, 75
  authoritarian-technocratic regime in, 20
  trade unionism in, 85, 90
Nixon, Richard, 167
North Atlantic Treaty Organization (NATO), 63

Obregón, Alvaro, 160

O'Conner, Quintin, 222
Odria, Manual, 75
  Odristas, 196
Oil
  Mexican, 84
  Peruvian, 151
  Venezuelan, 3
Oilfield Workers' Trade Union (OWTU) (Trinidad), 221
Oligarchies, 52, 53, 55, 73, 207
Ongania, Juan Carlos, 256
Operation Pan America, 169
Opposition politics. *See* Latin America, political parties in
Organization of American States Charter, 232, 243
ORIT. *See* Inter-American Regional Organization of Workers
ORVE. *See Movimiento de Organización Venezolana*

Pact of Sitges (1958), 133
PAN. *See* National Action
Panama, 8
  Alliance for Progress aid, 178
  political system in, 290
  populism in, 75
  revolution in, 54
  trade unionism in, 85
Pan-American Federation of Labor (1927), 83
Panday, Basdeo, 222, 223
Paraguay, 52, 61, 64, 75, 243
Paraguayan Bar Association, 243
Paridad, 133-134
Pariñas oil field, 151
PARM. *See* Party of the Authentic Mexican Revolution
Parsons, Talcott, 11
Partido Bolchevique Leninista (Cuba), 219
Partido Democrático Nacional (PDN) (Venezuela), 267
Partido Popular (Cuba), 218
Partido Revolucionario (Guatemala), 186
Partido Socialista Cubano, 218
Party of National Liberation (PLN) (Costa Rica), 137
Party of the Authentic Mexican Revolution (PARM), 132

Index

Party of the Institutional Revolution (PRI) (Mexico), 91, 132-133, 154, 182, 185
"Pathology of Democracy in Latin America," 10
 school of thought, 277-278
Paz Estenssor, Victor, 185
PDN. *See Partido Democrático Nacional*
Peace Corps, 6, 99
Peasant Confederation of Venezuela (CCV), 92-93
Peasant League (Brazil). *See Ligas Camponesas*
Peasant union movement. *See Sindicatos*
Pelego, 102, 104
People's National Movement (PNM) (Trinidad), 221
People's National Party (PNP) (Jamaica), 225, 226
People's Progress Party (PPP) (Guyana), 224
People's Promotion Movement (Honduras), 99
People's Radical Civic Union (Argentina), 149
Pérez Jiménez, Marcos, 71, 75, 136, 152, 167, 267
Perón, Juan Domingo, 34, 71, 72, 74, 75, 85, 160, 167, 256, 262, 263
 Peronistas, 84-85, 100, 149, 256
Personalism, 10, 11, 171-172, 175-176, 265. *See also Caudilloism*
Peru, 9, 61
 authoritarian-technocratic regime in, 20, 156, 243
 Communist Party in, 92
 coup d'etat in, 35, 151, 156
 and elites, 149
 oil fields in, 151
 political parties in, 71. *See also* Apristas
 political system in, 32, 35, 290
 populism in, 75
 revolution in, 54, 60
 trade unionism in, 82, 90, 92
 and women, 119-120
Peruvian Labor Confederation (CTP), 84
Peruvian Popular American Revolutionary Party (APRA). *See Apristas*
Peruvian Workers Confederation (CTP), 92
Philippines, 8

Pierre, Lennox, 222
Pierson, William, 277
Pinochet, Augusto, 135, 259
Pius XI, 82
Plan Político (1971), 99
PLN. *See* Party of National Liberation
Pluralism, 12, 20, 150, 239-240
 defined, 244
Political Man (Lipset), 173
Politics of the Developing Areas, The (Almond and Coleman), 11, 13
Popular Socialist Party (PPS) (Mexico), 132
Porfirian system, 74
Portugal, 32, 35, 54, 60, 63-64
Positivism, 189
Postal, Telephone and Telegraph International (PTTI), 86
Powell, John, 90
Power contenders, 280-281. *See also* Elitism
PPS. *See* Popular Socialist Party
PRD. *See* Dominican Revolutionary Party
Prebisch, Raúl, 169, 193, 194
Prestes, Column, 74
PRI. *See* Party of the Institutional Revolution
Pronunciamiento. *See Grito*
PSB. *See* Brazilian Socialist Party
PTB. *See* Brazilian Labor Party
Puerto Rico, 8, 90
Punta de Este Conference (1961), 168
Pye, Lucian, 248

Quadragessimo Anno (1931), 82, 159
Quadros, Janio, 179, 185

Real Majority, The (Scammon and Wattenburg), 27
Republican Democratic Union (URD) (Venezuela), 267, 268
Rerum Novarum (1891), 82, 159
Rerum Novarum (Chile), 84
Revolución, 35
Revolutionary Institutional Party (PRI). *See* Party of the Institutional Revolution
Revolutionary Latin American Confederation of Workers, 85
Roca, Blas, 219

Rodó, José Enrique, 173
Rodrigues Lima, Octavio, 111
Rojas, José, 90
Rojas Pinilla, Gustavo, 71, 75, 134, 167
Rojos, 44
Roman Catholic activists, 82, 85, 92
Romualdi, Serafino, 86, 99
Roosevelt, Theodore, 5, 8, 15
Rostow, W. W., 11, 59, 188, 278
Rural Assistance Service (SAR), 82-83
Russett, Bruce R., 59

Sánchez Cerro, Luis, 75
Santo Domingo, 8
SAR. *See* Rural Assistance Service
Sartori, Giovanni, 203
Schattschneider, E. E., 27, 29
School for Political Education, 196
Scott, Robert E., 155, 278
Segal, Aaron Lee, 114
Servico de Orientacão da Familia (SOF) (Brazil), 112-113, 124
Shils, Edward, 11
Silva Michelena, José A., 161
Silvert, Kalman H., 31, 39
SINAMOS. *See Sistema Nacional de Apoyo a la Mobilización Social*
Sindicatos, 79, 83, 87, 90-92, 93, 94, 95, 97, 102. 103
Sistema Nacional de Apoyo a la Mobilización Social (SINAMOS) (Peru), 260-261
SITRATERCO union, 99
Socialist Party (Chile), 209
Socialists, 79, 82, 84, 208, 218-226
Social Science Research Council's Committee on Comparative Politics, 13
Sociedade Civil Bem-Estar Familiar no Brasil (BEMFAM), 111, 113, 115
Solari, Aldo, 148
Solidarity Fund of the World Confederation of Labor (WCL), 86
Somoza, Anastasio, 75
Spain, 5, 8, 54, 64, 243
Spanish-American War (1898), 8
Stages of Economic Growth, The (Rostow), 188-189
Statute of Democratic Guarantees, 210
Stein, Barbara H., and Stanley J., 41
Stokes, William, 277

Stroessner, Alfredo, 261
Structuralism, 193-198, 202
Sundquist, James L., 29, 30
Syndico-anarchists, 218
Szulc, Tad, 185

Tannenbaum, Frank, 292
Taylor, Philip B. 157, 158
Tejera, Diego Vicente, 218
Tenentes, 74
Terrorism, 36, 247
"Theory of Critical Elections, A" (Key), 27
Third International, 218
Thompson, William R., 156
Toro, David, 75
Torrijos, Omar, 15, 75
Trabajos, 36
Trade unionism, 80, 82-87, 88-89 (table), 93-104, 160
  education programs, 86-87
  and salaries, Brazilian, 95 (table)
  See also Armed militia; *Sindicatos*
Transcendentalism, 172, 176
Trinidad, 220-224
Trinidad Labour Party, 221
Trinidad Workingmen's Association, 220
Trotskyites (Cuba), 219
Trujillo, Rafael, 47, 130, 167, 178, 186

UNC. *See* national Peasant Union
Unidad Popular (Chile), 209
Unión Cívica Radical (UCR) (Argentina), 149, 206, 207, 208
Unión de Trabajadores de Colombia, 85
United Fruit Company, 97, 99
United Labour Force (ULF) (Trinidad), 222, 223
United Nations Fund for Population Activities (UNFPA), 114
United Nations Universal Declaration of Human Rights, 232, 243
United Peasant Front (FUC) (Honduras), 99, 100
United States
  critical elections concept in, 28-30.
  See also Democracy; Latin America, ethnocentrism about; individual countries
Unity Party (Costa Rica), 137
University Reform, 74

URD. *See* Republican Democratic Union
Uruguay, 3, 61
　Alliance for Progress aid, 178
　authoritarian-technocratic regime in, 20, 201
　labor movement in, 79, 85, 92
　political parties in, 135, 182
　populism in, 73, 75
　relations with U.S., 15

Vallier, Ivan, 159
Vance, Cyrus, 141
Vargas, Getulio, 71, 75, 160, 263
Vatican II Council, 82
Velasco Alvarado, Juan, 92, 260
Velásquez, Fidel, 103
Venezuela, 3
　caudillos, 52
　education in, 98 (table)
　and elites, 149, 152
　family planning in, 114
　labor movement in, 79, 90, 92
　peasant leaders activities, 90 (table)
　political parties in, 136-137, 181, 187, 267-268
　populism in, 75, 262
　rural population of, 97-98
Venezuelan Labor Confederation (CTV), 84

Verstehen approach, 15
Videla, Gabriel González, 256
Villa, Pancho, 91
Villeda Morales, Ramón, 185, 196

Weekes, George, 222
Welsh, William, 152
Western thought, 227 (table)
West Indian Independent Party (WIIP) (Trinidad), 221, 222
Wiarda, Howard J., 153, 154-155
Williams, Eric, 221, 222
Williams, Mary Wilhelmine, 277
Wilson, Woodrow, 5, 8, 15
Workers and Farmers Party (WFP) (Trinidad), 222
Workers Circles, 82, 83
World Bank, 114
World Confederation of Labor (WCL), 86
World Federation of Trade Unions (WFTU), 84
World Population Plan, 118

Yrigoyen, Hipólito, 206, 207-209, 211

Zapata, Emiliano, 91